THE
TORONTO
BOOK OF
LOVE

Also by Adam Bunch

The Toronto Book of the Dead

THE
TORONTO
BOOK OF
LOVE

ADAM BUNCH

DUNDURN
PRESS

Publisher: Kwame Scott Fraser | Acquiring editor: Dominic Farrell
Cover designer: Laura Boyle
Cover image: shutterstock.com/mamita

Library and Archives Canada Cataloguing in Publication

Title: The Toronto book of love / Adam Bunch.
Names: Bunch, Adam, 1980- author.
Description: Includes bibliographical references.
Identifiers: Canadiana (print) 20200342878 | Canadiana (ebook) 20200342959 | ISBN
    9781459746671 (softcover) | ISBN 9781459746688 (PDF) | ISBN 9781459746695 (EPUB)
Subjects: LCSH: Love—Ontario—Toronto—History. | LCSH: Interpersonal relations—
    Ontario—Toronto— History. | LCSH: Toronto (Ont.)—History—Anecdotes.
Classification: LCC HQ801 .B86 2021 | DDC 306.7309713/54—dc23

We acknowledge the support of the Canada Council for the Arts and the Ontario Arts Council for our publishing program. We also acknowledge the financial support of the Government of Ontario, through the Ontario Book Publishing Tax Credit and Ontario Creates, and the Government of Canada.

Care has been taken to trace the ownership of copyright material used in this book. The author and the publisher welcome any information enabling them to rectify any references or credits in subsequent editions.

The publisher is not responsible for websites or their content unless they are owned by the publisher.

Printed and bound in Canada.

Dundurn Press
Toronto, Ontario, Canada
dundurn.com, @dundurnpress

For Amy

CONTENTS

INTRODUCTION

In 1908, Toronto was a booming metropolis. More than two hundred thousand people called it home. It was expanding quickly, swallowing up neighbouring villages. The first skyscrapers towered above the downtown core, streetcars rattled through rush hour, and horses were just beginning to give way to cars. Construction was everywhere: new train tracks, telephone wires, sewers and street lamps were being installed. And at the bottom of the harbour, eleven metres beneath the surface of the water, city workers were putting in a water pipe.

But one winter day, not long before Christmas, they came to a sudden halt. They'd found something remarkable down there on the bottom of the lake, just to the east of Hanlan's Point, near the Toronto Islands — something that had sat there, undisturbed, for thousands of years.

In an instant, those construction workers were transported back in time. Eleven thousand years ago, Lake Ontario was much smaller than it is today. The water level was considerably lower, so the shoreline was five kilometres farther south. The area where Toronto now stands was a vast plain of subarctic tundra and spruce forest. The last ice age had just ended, and as the enormous continental glacier that covered the land retreated, great prehistoric beasts moved in. Mammoths and mastodons, ancient caribou, muskox, and bison roamed where lawyers, accountants, and shopkeepers do today. With them came the Paleoamericans, ancestors of today's Indigenous Peoples, nomadic hunters with stoned-tipped spears. Archaeologists believe they were the very first human beings ever to set foot on that land.

And on one particular day, all those thousands of years ago, a family walked across the place where a city of millions would eventually be built. They were heading north from the lake toward what's now downtown Toronto. They were wearing moccasins, and, for at least a few steps, they walked through clay, leaving their footprints behind.

Over the next few thousand years, the lake grew, filling with water until it became the Lake Ontario we know today. And those hundred footprints, preserved in that clay, were hidden from view. That is, at least, until 1908, when those city workers discovered them.

It was easily one of the most spectacular archaeological finds in Toronto's history, quite possibly the earliest evidence of humans ever found in the city. "It looked like a trail," a city inspector told the *Toronto Evening Telegram*. "You could follow one man the whole way. Some footprints were on top of the others, partly obliterating them. There were footprints of all sizes, and a single print of a child's foot."

Many think of history as a dry list of dates and events; too often, that's the way it's presented. But the discovery of those footprints on the bottom of the lake provided a visceral reminder of the truth, an instant connection to people who lived and died thousands of years before the modern city was founded. People who might have lived in a world of mammoths and spears, but who seem to have been a family — who surely loved each other as we do, felt the same feelings we feel today.

Toronto, as it so often is, was in a rush in 1908. The city wanted to build a tunnel, and it didn't want to slow down. So, the workers kept going. They simply poured concrete over the footprints and continued on with their work. After being miraculously preserved for eleven thousand years, the precious evidence of those human lives was gone in an instant.

Toronto has earned its reputation as a city that doesn't always appreciate its past. Throughout the twentieth century, as the city grew into a metropolis filled with millions of people, much of its heritage was lost. Victorian storefronts were brought down to make room for parking lots. Whole neighbourhoods were razed for new developments. Thousands of precious archaeological sites were dug up and destroyed.

As a result, Toronto is a place where it can feel especially difficult to connect with the past. And yet, it still surrounds us. As I wrote in *The Toronto Book of the Dead*, there's no escaping it: the city of today was created by all those who have come before us. We live in their houses. We drive on their roads. We've inherited their traditions and institutions. Toronto — like every city — is a city of the dead.

And while it can sometimes be hard to remember in a city that doesn't have the romance of cobblestone streets and ancient monuments, those ancestors were more than just names on a page. They were, of course, people much like us. Victorian teenagers got jealous, stodgy old politicians felt joy, and the most reserved gentlewoman could feel heartsick with longing or giddy with the rush of a new crush. Settlers fought duels over salacious insults, and fur traders shared tender moments on their wedding nights. Even centuries ago, Wendat hunters felt the excitement of a first kiss. And that ancient nomadic family, walking through soft clay in their moccasins, knew what it was to fall in love.

Love stories are one of the most powerful ways we have to connect with those who have come before us. An anecdote about how our parents met. A grandmother's engagement ring or an old photo from a wedding day. A dusty love letter dug out of an attic or found stashed away in a shoebox hidden at the back of a closet. These treasures have been passed down through generations, along with the stories connected to them, a way of knowing more about who we are and where we came from.

The city has its own heirlooms. Toronto has been the scene of countless romances, and no matter how many old buildings come crashing to the ground, the evidence is all around us. The city's love stories can be found in a forgotten monument, or an old poem, or the name of a west-end street. They are kept inside a lovingly carved box and the glow of a neon sign. You can smell them in the fragrance of a garden that blooms every spring. Through them, the dead can be brought back to life, passions resurrected as their blood flows again in tales of romance, marriage, and scandal.

And in sharing those love stories, we learn more about ourselves and our city. No love story is just a love story. It's a reflection of a time and of a place. Through tales of infatuated rebels, lustful clowns, and heartbroken spies, we can learn more about how our modern metropolis came to be. About the passionate, romantic, scandalous events that made the city the place it is today.

Because Toronto — like every city — is a city of love.

FOUNDING

1
A TORCH IN THE NIGHT

A concrete goliath towers over the University of Toronto. It has stood there on the corner of St. George and Harbord Streets for half a century, a brutalist colossus soaring fourteen storeys into the air. Robarts Library has earned its nickname: Fort Book is a fortress filled with information, its thick grey walls protecting millions of volumes. Venture inside its imposing exterior and you're standing at the heart of the largest academic library system in the country. And just off to one side, through an unassuming revolving door on the southern edge of the building, you'll find a treasure trove: a collection of some of the oldest and rarest books to be found anywhere in the world. It's an awe-inspiring space. A cathedral of paper and concrete. There between the formidable pillars are soaring bookshelves stretching high above your head, five storeys into the air. This is the Thomas Fisher Rare Books Library.

Nowhere in Canada is there a bigger public collection of rare books and manuscripts — hundreds of thousands of them. Here, you can find a copy of Shakespeare's First Folio, an original edition of Isaac Newton's *Principia*, and Charles Darwin's own marked-up proofs. There's a Babylonian tablet from nearly four thousand years ago. Ancient Egyptian papyrus. And five hundred historic valentines, too.

Tucked away in the archives beneath the library, kept safe in its place among some of the most precious books on earth, you'll find an old, brown, hardcover tome. It's hundreds of years old, worn by time. And as you carefully crack it open, you'll be transported to another age. There, among its yellowing pages, you'll find a brief, fleeting glimpse of the romances that once played out in the place where Toronto now stands.

Centuries before the modern metropolis was founded, the northern shores of Lake Ontario were home to the Wendat. (Europeans called them the Huron.) Where there are now parking lots and condo towers, there were once Wendat villages: clusters of longhouses built on the hillsides above rivers and creeks. Vast fields of maize stretched off into the distance, the corn intermingled with beans and squash. The rivers teemed with migrating salmon as travellers came and went in their birchbark canoes. Wendat hunters prowled the immense forests beyond the fields, where bears, wolves, cougars, and moose roamed between the great old oaks and pines. Eagles perched in the treetops. Endless flocks of passenger pigeons, an aerial ballet of flashing colour, filled the sky. Thousands of people could live in one of those villages, living on the land their ancestors had called home for hundreds and thousands of years.

Many of them were young and in love.

The worn pages of that old book in the Thomas Fisher Library give us one account of those love affairs. It was written by a French soldier: Louis-Armand de Lom d'Arce de Lahontan. He was a baron who'd been sent to Canada to wage war against the First Nations but never took to his mission. He witnessed terrible atrocities committed in the name of the French Empire, and could never understand why his country was waging war against the First Nations instead of partnering with them. When he was sent off to command fur-trading posts in the remote reaches of the Great Lakes, he spent years living among the Wendats, developing a deep appreciation for their culture — even if it was coloured by the prejudices of his time. "A solitary Life is most grateful to me," he wrote, "and the manners of the Savages are perfectly agreeable to my Palate."

When Lahontan returned to Europe, he published a series of books about his travels through the Indigenous lands of North America. And three hundred years later, you can find some of his writing in the Thomas Fisher Library, including a book with a particularly catchy title: *New Voyages to North-America: giving a full account of the customs, commerce, religion, and strange opinions of the savages of that country with political remarks upon the courts of Portugal and Denmark and present state of the commerce in those countries, Vol II.*

Lahontan's accounts aren't always entirely reliable — he wanted to sell books and add to his own glory — and while he respected the culture of the First Nations much more than some of his countrymen did, his condescending enthusiasm helped lay the foundation for the "noble savage" stereotype that persists to this day. But his books provide one of the few written sources we have from the era when the longhouses of the Wendat were a common sight on the shores of the Great Lakes — including what happened when young couples fell in love.

On some nights, he wrote, there was a light in the darkness: the flickering yellow and orange of a young man moving between the longhouses, a torch in his hand. When he found the house he was looking for, he would slip inside, and she'd be waiting there for him, in bed. By then, they would have already spent time together, chatting during the day, sharing stories and laughing, but never crossing a fine line. They wouldn't have kissed or cuddled or talked about anything to do with romance or love. Those were topics best left for the hours after dark.

There in the longhouse, he would approach her bedside, his torch still flickering in his hand. His heart must have been beating nervously in his chest as he waited to see what she would do. If she chose to reject him, she would simply keep hiding under her covers until he went away. But if her answer was yes, she would blow out the light of the torch as an invitation to join her in bed.

The Wendat enjoyed freedoms that the French soldier found both astonishing and admirable. Young men and women were allowed to sleep together without any promise of marriage. Having multiple partners was fine. And control was ultimately in the hands of the women; they decided who they wanted to sleep with and when.

"A young woman is allowed to do what she pleases," Lahontan wrote, "let her conduct be what it will, neither father nor mother, brother nor sister can pretend to control her. A young woman, say they, is master of her own body, and by her natural right of liberty is free to do what she pleases."

Young lovers developed relationships over time, gradually getting to know each other before making a decision about their future. A man was often about thirty years old before he decided it was time to get married. And when he did, he would propose to the woman he loved by giving her a gift: a beaver robe or a wampum necklace. If she took it, they would sleep together for a few nights before she made her decision. If she accepted his proposal, the wedding was held in the home of their oldest family member: a great feast with dancing and singing. According to Lahontan, the ceremony took place after most of the groom's guests had left. The couple stood on a mat, holding a long wooden rod between them as the elders spoke and the newlyweds danced and sang. At the end of the ceremony, the stick was broken into pieces: one for each of the witnesses.

Even married couples kept their physical affections private. Public displays were frowned upon. And while finding time to be alone could be difficult in a longhouse filled with people, couples might slip away into the fields or forests for some privacy.

Lahontan seems to have mistaken this reserve for a lack of passion. "They are," he wrote, "altogether strangers to the blind fury we call love. They content themselves with a tender friendship … one may call their love simple goodwill."

But the Wendats' oral history includes tales of heartbreak and passion. And Europeans were amazed by the depth of their mourning when someone they loved died. A widowed husband or wife would barely speak for the first ten days after the funeral, lying on a mat wrapped in furs, their faces pressed to the ground. "They do not warm themselves even in Winter," one missionary explained, "they eat cold food, they do not go to the feasts, they go out only at night for their necessities." The mourning would last a year beyond that as they avoided feasts and gave no greetings their neighbours. Remarrying was out of the question during that year. Many grieving widows blackened their faces and wore dishevelled clothes long after their husbands had died.

But in Wendat villages, unlike the cities of France, death wasn't the only way a marriage could end. Divorces were commonplace. If a woman found herself falling out of love or married to a husband who failed to live up to his commitments, she could simply end their marriage. And he could do the same. "They are very careful in preserving the liberty and freedom of their heart," Lahontan marvelled, "which they look upon as the most valuable treasure upon Earth: from whence I conclude that they are not altogether so savage as we are."

Still, not everyone shared the baron's appreciation for Wendat romance. The first explorers and fur traders to reach the Great Lakes were followed closely by missionaries: the Jesuits in their black robes and the

Récollets in their pointed grey hoods. Priests were horrified by the freedom they found there. Determined to turn Wendats into proper Catholics, they did everything they could to end divorce and stamp out premarital sex. The Jesuits even collected donations from their supporters in France: money they could give to Wendat wives so they wouldn't leave their husbands. The missionaries were thrilled to see converted young women adopting a gloomy air to discourage the attentions of young men. And they wrote glowingly of one man who rushed naked into the woods in the dead of winter, rolling around in the snow to quench his urges. Many, however, refused to give up their romantic freedom in return for the priests' promises of what God would do for them in return.

Battles over love and marriage became an important front in the missionaries' quest to wipe out Wendat culture and assimilate them — the opening salvos in a cultural genocide that would last for centuries. The Wendat suffered terribly as the long arm of European empires reached west into the Great Lakes. The first wave of smallpox is thought to have killed half the population in just six years. And then came the Beaver Wars: bloody battles over the fur trade engulfed the region for the better part of a century, killing thousands more.

By the time Lahontan visited the Wendat in the late 1600s, they'd been driven from the northern shores of Lake Ontario; today, you'll find the Huron-Wendat Nation just outside Quebec City. But Toronto is still filled with reminders of the days when their ancestors lived — and loved — in the place where the city now stands. A burial mound in Scarborough. Gorgeous pottery and countless other artifacts lifted from the earth. The curve of a street that still follows the route of an ancient portage trail. And even a book written by a long-dead French solider kept in the archives beneath a concrete library.

2

SCANDALS OF THE FRENCH EMPIRE

The village stood high above the winding river, perched atop a ridge with a commanding view of the valley below. Dozens of longhouses shone in the September sun, kept safe behind a wooden palisade of tall logs. Great fields of maize stretched off into the distance and along the river's edge, while hunters stalked deer in the forests beyond. This was the village of Teiaiagon, home to hundreds of Seneca people.

The Seneca were one of the five nations of the Haudenosaunee Confederacy (who Europeans called the Iroquois). They had long been living on the southern side of Lake Ontario, but in recent years, as the Wendat were driven north, the Haudenosaunee had spread their reach across the lake. By the 1670s, it was the Seneca who called the forests of Toronto home.

They built at least two villages in the place where the modern city now stands. Ganatsekwyagon was in the east, near the mouth of the Rouge River. Teiaiagon was in the west, near the mouth of a river they called *Niwa'ah Onega'gaih'ih* — little thundering waters. Today, it's known as the Humber River. Each of the villages watched over a branch of one of the most important trade routes in the Great Lakes: the Toronto Carrying Place. From Teiaiagon, the portage trail followed the path of the Humber up toward Lake Simcoe. It had been used by countless generations of First Nations travellers as a shortcut between the lower Great Lakes and the upper Great Lakes.

Now, the French wanted to use it, too.

On that September day in 1681, a small flotilla of canoes appeared on the river. They paddled up from Lake Ontario, thirty men in birchbark boats filled to the brim with supplies. They were French: an expedition led by the notorious explorer René-Robert Cavelier, Sieur de La Salle. They were among the first European visitors to the village, at the beginning of a dangerous voyage through the heart of a continent they barely knew, to places no European eyes had ever seen before. Many of them would never make it home. But by the end of their voyage, they'd have claimed half of North America in the name of France. Soon, Frenchmen like them wouldn't just be passing through the place where Toronto now stands. They'd be living there: building forts, trading furs, laying the very earliest European foundations for the city to come.

But it all started with the first few visitors, many of whom were brought to the Toronto Carrying Place by a trio of ill-fated French relationships: one disturbing marriage, one scandalous separation, one doomed engagement.

It took weeks for the news to travel from Paris all the way across the Atlantic and up the St. Lawrence River to the tiny settlement of Quebec. And when he first heard it, Samuel de Champlain refused to believe it. It was too terrible to be true. And yet it was: the king of France had been brutally murdered, stabbed to death by an assassin when his carriage got stuck in a traffic jam. And with King Henry IV dead, the entire future of Canada suddenly hung in the balance.

It was 1610. Nearly a century had passed since Jacques Cartier became the first French explorer to sail up the St. Lawrence, claiming the Indigenous lands he saw there for France. But it was only in recent years that the French presence in North America had really solidified. That was largely thanks to King Henry, whose support for the colony was so vital he's been called "The Creator of New France." It was largely thanks to Henry's backing that Samuel de Champlain was able to explore farther into the interior of the continent, expand the fur trade, and found a new town: Quebec City was just two years old when the assassin's knife found its mark.

With King Henry's death, New France was in real danger. The dead king's son was too young to shoulder the responsibilities of the Crown, so it was Henry's widow who took over. Marie de' Medici was from one of the most powerful families in Europe, and with her attention focused on France, she didn't care much about Canada. Support for the nascent colony of New France was crumbling quickly. One of Champlain's patrons had already been fired; his own salary was under threat. The explorer had little choice but to rush back home across the ocean. Said to have hit a sleeping whale with his ship along the way, he arrived in Paris seven weeks later determined to save his colony. Champlain spent that winter scheming and schmoozing, painstakingly rebuilding the support he would need to keep New France going.

A key part his plan: a wedding. The explorer was going to get married.

It was a deeply disturbing match. Champlain needed to cement an alliance with an old friend: an influential member of the French court who could provide a generous dowry if Champlain married his daughter. Neither of the men seemed to care that Hélène Boullé was only twelve years old and very much opposed to the idea of marrying the forty-three-year-old explorer. Even by the standards of the time, she was clearly too young for married life. Champlain agreed they wouldn't consummate the marriage right away; they'd wait at least two years for that, when Hélène was fourteen and he was forty-five. But he wasn't about to let an unsettling age difference or the feelings of his preteen bride stand in the way of his dreams for his Canadian colony.

The wedding went ahead, held at a church just across the street from the Louvre. And with the marriage,

Champlain got the dowry he was seeking. With his alliances locked down and his lobbying done, Champlain sailed back to New France before the winter was over. He returned to Quebec with a more secure sense of Canada's future, confident enough to push the French presence even deeper into the continent.

Before he left for France, Champlain had sent one of his men to take part in something of a cultural exchange. He'd brought a Wendat emissary with him on his trip to Paris (Savignon was shocked by the brutality of the city and warned others to stay away), while a young Frenchman named Étienne Brûlé was sent to live among the Wendats. The teenage explorer was enjoying his time with them, already beginning to adapt to their way of life; he would eventually marry a Wendat woman as well as a woman in France. And with the colony's financial future now looking more promising thanks to his horrifying wedding, Champlain asked Brûlé to extend his stay and to explore even more of the continent.

That's how Brûlé ended up writing his name into the history books of Toronto. In 1615, he became the first European to set eyes on Lake Ontario. And while the details of his travels are a bit hazy, most historians have assumed the Wendats took him down the Toronto Carrying Place trail, making him the very first non-Indigenous person ever to set foot on the land where Toronto now stands.

He would eventually be followed by millions more. But that was all in the distant future. The French weren't even regular visitors to the area in the early 1600s. It would take a few more decades for that, and a new governor looking to escape a scandalous marriage.

Louis de Buade, Comte de Frontenac et de Palluau was twenty-eight years old when he fell in love with his neighbour in Paris. Anne de La Grange-Trianon was sixteen and, as one historian put it, "witty, cultured and endowed with an iron determination" as well as "the imperious beauty of a goddess." The palace of Versailles still owns a painting of her, in which she's quite literally portrayed as the goddess Minerva, resplendent in her steel armour, with a shield and a bow at her side.

In some ways, Frontenac was a catch, too. While we don't know what he looked like, the young soldier was the godson of the former king, well-connected at the royal court, and said to be quite a charming fellow.

Anne's father, however, didn't want him anywhere near his daughter. He worried that Frontenac was only after one thing: money. La Grange was going to have plenty of it. She stood to inherit an absolute fortune — enough to bail out her new beau, who'd already managed to burn through his own inheritance thanks to a notoriously lavish lifestyle.

Anne's father was so dead set against the match that he sent her away to a convent, trying to keep the young lovers apart. But it was too late. Frontenac and La Grange had already eloped, secretly getting married just weeks before. He was so enraged by the betrayal that he disowned his daughter, vowing to remarry and have more children just so she would never inherit his fortune. And that's exactly what he did.

Frontenac and La Grange were effectively cut out of the will, but that didn't stop them from living as if they were entitled to all the riches of an aristocratic French lineage. They lived in a posh house in Paris and spent a fortune on all the trappings of court life. Within the first twenty years of their marriage, they managed to rack up hundreds of thousands of livres in debts (millions of dollars in today's money). The Frontenacs might have lived like rich aristocrats, but they were desperately broke. And it wasn't long before their marriage began to fall apart.

La Grange was a woman of adventure. She had no interest in playing the role of a traditional wife. Within a few years, she'd left her husband, getting caught up in the intrigues of a civil war by joining the entourage of a princess who opposed the king. When their side was defeated, they were banished to a gloomy castle as punishment.

Alone in their crumbling chateau, the princess and the women of her entourage all shared a bed at night. La Grange developed a particular fondness for a certain Madame d'Outrelaise, who seems to have won her heart. Anne was horrified when Frontenac paid her a visit. "Rather than looking after her husband," the princess remembered, "she ran and hid, crying and uttering laments because her husband had said he wanted to stay with her that night." La Grange was so distraught, the princess called for a priest to perform an exorcism.

As mortifying as that experience must have been for Frontenac, his romantic troubles were only just beginning. Spurned by La Grange, he fell deeply in love with another woman. But she eventually left him to become the mistress of the king — a situation that left Frontenac in a deeply awkward position.

With his marriage in ruins and his finances in crisis, he desperately needed a fresh start. When the position of governor of New France suddenly opened up, it must have seemed like a miracle. If he got the job, his debts would be deferred. Frontenac lobbied hard, pulling every string he could, even getting La Grange to help. And it worked. He set sail for Canada in 1672, leaving all his troubles behind — including his wife.

Since the days of Champlain and Brûlé, only a few French explorers, missionaries, and fur traders had ventured along the Toronto Carrying Place. The king had little interest in the region; he wanted the new governor to concentrate on reinforcing their existing settlements. But Frontenac had different ideas.

Upon arriving in Quebec, he turned his attention west, toward Lake Ontario and the Toronto Carrying Place. He wanted to secure the trade coming down the portage route for the French, rather than allowing it to continue south toward the English colonies of America. So, he decided to build a fur-trading post on Lake Ontario where it emptied into the St. Lawrence: the place we now call the Thousand Islands.

Thanks to his days at the French court, the governor knew just how powerful spectacle could be. And he pulled out all the stops to convince the Haudenosaunee to allow him to build his fort. He arrived with a fleet of 120 canoes paddled in perfect formation, drums rolling, bands playing, banners flapping in the breeze. He was surrounded by a military honour guard, his Wendat and Anishinaabe allies, and four hundred French soldiers wearing the bright blue uniforms of musketeers. Fort Frontenac was built in record time — less than a week — and would soon attract a small number of settlers who cultivated the surrounding land. For the first time in history, there was a European settlement on the shores of Lake Ontario.

Suddenly, the Toronto Carrying Place was much easier to reach. Great warships built at Fort Frontenac could now sail the lake, while canoes could make the trip to Teiaiagon in a matter of days. French explorers, missionaries, and fur traders became more regular visitors to the place where the city of Toronto would eventually be built.

And that was just the beginning. Frontenac had come to Canada mostly as a way to escape his wife and his debts, but he would prove to be one of the most ambitious governors in the history of New France. He imagined a colony that would stretch all the way across the continent. Great expanses of Indigenous land would be claimed in the name of the French Empire.

But to make his dream a reality, he would need to send an explorer on a mission up the Toronto Carrying Place into the unmapped heart of North America. It was an absurdly dangerous voyage that would take years to complete.

Thankfully, he knew just the man to do it.

* * *

René-Robert Cavelier, Sieur de La Salle wasn't an easy man to like. He was gruff, temperamental, impatient, paranoid, and focused obsessively on his goal; he was an explorer willing to risk not only his own life but the lives of his men in order to push on just a little further. Some of his followers worried he was mad. They mutinied against him more than once: abandoning him in the dead of winter, burning down his forts, trying to kill him outright.

But La Salle and Frontenac hit it off. They shared the same dream: a vast New France stretching across North America. And La Salle had the experience to make it real. Born to a rich family in France, he'd been raised on tales of the Jesuit missionaries and their adventures. He and his men had been exploring the Great Lakes for years, paying occasional visits to Teiaiagon. La Salle had learned a lot from First Nations tutors and guides: how to speak their languages, track animals, make fires, and slather himself with grease to protect against mosquitos. He'd abandoned his sword for a hatchet and his boots for moccasins. And he was no stranger to the Toronto Carrying Place; he'd travelled the length of the portage route during some of his expeditions.

Together, Frontenac and La Salle spent long nights crafting a plan, while all the way on the other side of the ocean, La Grange was hard at work on their behalf. She acted as her husband's ambassador at the court of Versailles, helping to get him the support he needed to back La Salle's adventures. It turned out that Frontenac and La Grange did make good partners — as long as they were a few thousand kilometres apart.

The plan was ambitious. La Salle would attempt his most daring voyage yet: travel up the Toronto Carrying Place, across the upper Great Lakes, and then south to the mouth of the Mississippi River, claiming an enormous chunk of the continent for France in the process. It promised to be a wildly expensive undertaking. Even Frontenac and La Grange couldn't give La Salle all the necessary support. If he was going to pull it off, he would need even more help.

Luckily, Frontenac wasn't the only person with a soft spot for the infamous explorer.

Madeleine de Roybon d'Allonne was born in France to a noble family and, just like La Salle, had left it all behind for the promise of Canada. It's thought she probably crossed the ocean looking for a husband. The rugged outposts of New France were full of men, but there was a desperate lack of women for them to marry. Some have even suggested that d'Allonne may have been one of the famous *Filles du Roi* ("king's daughters"). With so few women in his Canadian colonies, King Louis XIV had paid hundreds of women — many of them poor orphans who had little choice in the matter — to sail across the ocean and become wives for his lonely colonists. They would have children, build families, and strengthen New France.

D'Allonne was one of the few who didn't find a husband in the small but growing eastern settlements like Quebec City and Montreal. Instead, she kept heading west, all the way up the St. Lawrence to Fort Frontenac. La Salle had been put in charge of the new fort and he gave her a strip of land where she built a small farm and even ran her own fur-trading post.

It's not clear when the two adventurers began their romance. But it's easy to imagine how they could fall in love: La Salle, the confident explorer, and d'Allonne, the courageous fur trader. Both were from prosperous French families; both were in their midthirties. Soon, they were engaged to be married.

But the wedding would have to wait. It didn't take long for rumours of their love affair to reach Paris. One of the men funding La Salle's explorations wrote him a worried letter, concerned he might have become distracted by d'Allonne's charms. He needn't have worried. La Salle would never put his fiancée ahead of his adventures. Annoyed, the explorer wrote back, explaining that there was no way he was going to get married before he conquered the Mississippi. He was insulted the man had even asked.

In fact, his new sweetheart had joined the ranks of his investors. D'Allonne agreed to contribute more than two thousand livres to the funding of her fiancé's historic voyage (tens of thousands of dollars in today's money).

And so, as the summer of 1681 came to a close, it was with her help that La Salle and his men were able to load their canoes full of supplies and set off down the lake toward Teiaiagon. She may very well have been there to see them off, saying goodbye to the man she'd promised to marry as he paddled away into the distance. She wouldn't see him again for two years.

At Teiaiagon, La Salle enlisted the aid of the Seneca. They would help his expedition make the punishing journey up the Toronto Carrying Place portage. Each of these canoes was twenty feet long and filled with more than a thousand pounds of supplies. It took fifteen days to haul them up the trail, following the twists and turns of the Humber before finally reaching Lake Simcoe, almost one hundred gruelling kilometres away.

It would be many more months before La Salle finally reached his destination, using the help of First Nations guides to reach his goal: the mouth of the Mississippi. He claimed the land around it for France and named it after his king: Louisiana.

The dream La Salle and Frontenac had shared during those long nights of planning had finally come true. As far as the French were concerned, New France now stretched all the way from the mouth of the St. Lawrence to the mouth of the Mississippi. And with the Toronto Carrying Place now more important to them than ever, the scene was set for the first French forts to be built in the place where the biggest city in Canada would one day stand.

La Salle never did marry Madeleine de Roybon d'Allonne. She spent two years waiting for him, but when he finally returned from his mission the wedding was called off. La Salle had achieved the goal that had been driving him for years, and yet he still didn't feel satisfied. Instead of settling down at Fort Frontenac with his fiancée, he would leave her there as he set off on one last adventure.

According to some sources, La Salle was accused of seduction over the affair. There were people who believed he had tricked d'Allonne into falling in love with him by promising marriage before callously abandoning her when the time came. It was a serious legal charge, but she would defend him to her dying day, dismissing the accusations as untrue.

La Salle did leave her with one final parting gift. He drew up the paperwork to officially confirm her ownership of her land at Fort Frontenac. It made her the first European woman to own land in what's now Ontario. And while she stayed home to farm it and run her fur-trading post, the man she'd once promised to marry sailed off to France to secure funding for yet another expedition. They would never see each other again.

On this last adventure, La Salle's luck would finally run out. He was trying to build a permanent settlement at the mouth of the Mississippi. But sick of being mistreated, his men rose up in mutiny once again. They shot him with a musket, stripped his corpse naked, and left it in the woods to be eaten by wolves. What was left of his settlement was eventually overrun by First Nations warriors; most of the settlers were killed, the rest were taken prisoner.

D'Allonne would meet a similar fate. By the time La Salle set off on his final expedition, Frontenac had been replaced. The new governor was much less interested in exploring the Great Lakes than in waging war against the

First Nations who called them home. Just a few months after La Salle's death, the new governor of New France launched a scorched earth campaign against the Seneca: burning villages and crops, killing all those he could find. Baron Lahontan was one of the soldiers under his command.

In retaliation, Fort Frontenac was overrun by the Haudenosaunee. D'Allonne's farm and trading post were destroyed. She was taken prisoner. She'd spend years in captivity before she was finally released to spend her final years in Montreal, trying to convince colonial officials to give her back her old land. By the time they did, she was too old to travel. She died in 1714, a single woman to the end of her days.

By then, a landmark peace treaty had been signed between France and dozens of First Nations: the Great Peace of Montreal. And with quiet returning to the Great Lakes — at least for a while — the French looked west once again. Nearly half a century after La Salle first set foot at the mouth of the Humber, a new trading post was built there. And it was given a familiar name.

The Haudenosaunee word *Tkaronto* is thought to have originally referred to the fishing weirs of Lake Simcoe: it means "the place where trees stand in the water." Since Lake Simcoe was at the top of the great portage route along the Humber, the French called the whole trail the Toronto Carrying Place. Eventually, the name was used for the area at the southern end, too.

So, that's where the French got the name for their new fort, a name that would eventually be passed down to a city of millions. Today, it serves as a linguistic echo of the days when Seneca villages kept watch over its rivers and when ill-fated romances brought French explorers sailing through its waters.

They called it Fort Toronto.

3
FOUR WEDDINGS
& A FUR TRADER

The dull roar of cannon fire echoed out across the water. It was so loud you could hear it all the way across the lake — on the shores of Humber Bay, where French soldiers listened to the sound with dread. It was clear what it meant: far on the other side of Lake Ontario, the British were attacking Fort Niagara. The French had built a series of forts at the mouth of the Niagara River, beginning with a small trading post erected by La Salle himself. Those forts had stood for the better part of a century, all the way into the middle of the 1700s. But now, the French and the British were at war. The Seven Years' War has been called the first truly global war, and its reach extended all the way to the very edges of the French Empire, bringing bloodshed to the shores of Lake Ontario as the two superpowers fought for control of North America. For nineteen days, the British besieged Niagara. But that wasn't the only

French fort on the lake. They'd solidified their presence at Toronto, too.

The Carrying Place was a vital thoroughfare in the fur trade — and the fur trade was the economic engine driving New France. Beaver fur hats were all the rage in Europe. The animals' pelts could be turned into a thin waterproof felt — perfect for a stylish top hat. Tens of thousands of beaver furs could pass through a trading post in a single year. With a post at the mouth of the Humber, the French could meet the First Nations traders as they travelled down from the upper Great Lakes, catching them before they continued south to the British posts in New York State.

The first blockhouse went up in 1720. It was soon followed by a more impressive fort: the one they called Fort Toronto. For the first time, Europeans lived in the place where the city now stands. It was a big success: the trade at Toronto was so profitable that the French built a second fort a few kilometres to the east. Fort Rouillé, which stood at the edge of Humber Bay, was a small collection of buildings kept safe behind a tall fence of sharpened cedar logs, perched atop the small bluff that ran along the lakeshore. At any given time, about a dozen French soldiers called it home.

But as those British cannons rang out across the lake, it was clear the end had come. As the soldiers of Fort Rouillé listened to the battle raging at Niagara, they knew what they had to do. They were under strict orders. They packed up, burned their fort to the ground, and fled forever, retreating back to Quebec.

Fort Rouillé would prove to be the last of the French forts at Toronto. Later that same month, the siege of Quebec City began, ending with the famous Battle of the Plains of Abraham. Within weeks, New France had fallen. It was now the British who would claim dominion over the northern shores of Lake Ontario.

All that was left behind were the scorched remains of Fort Rouillé: a few piles of charred timber, cracked flagstones, and a crumbling brick chimney surrounded by a half-burnt fence. Those ruins would lie there for more than a century — until the 1880s — before they were finally cleared to make way for the grounds of the Canadian National Exhibition. Today, an impressive obelisk marks the exact spot where the fort once stood; it was one of the first monuments ever erected in Toronto. Embedded in the ground is a concrete outline of the old fort's walls. It's a final reminder of the days when the French Empire reached all the way from the Palace of Versailles to the palatial forests of Toronto.

But those fleeing soldiers wouldn't be the last French fur traders to set foot on the shores of Humber Bay.

Jean Baptiste Rousseau's first wedding was held on a Friday in the middle of July 1780. He'd just turned twenty-one when he married Marie Martineau in Old Montreal. But the newlyweds wouldn't stay in the big city for long. They headed west to start their married life together on the frontier, travelling far up the St. Lawrence to the spot where the great river began. A new settlement called Cataraqui was being laid out around the old Fort Frontenac. One day, it would grow into the city of Kingston.

But the young Rousseau wasn't interested in a quiet domestic life. He was raised to be an adventurer. The Rousseaus had been one of the very first French families to come to Canada, arriving in the early 1600s among the early settlers of New France. His father had been one of the legendary *coureurs de bois* — runners of the woods — travelling far into the forests of the interior to trade with the First Nations.

After the colony fell to the British, Jean Bonaventure Rousseau had been awarded the licence to trade at Toronto. He swore allegiance to the British Crown, promised to build peaceful trade relationships with the local First Nations, and headed to Toronto with a canoe full of goods to trade: gunpowder, weapons, ammunition, and alcohol. He built a small house at the mouth of the Humber River, living there for much of the summers, taking over the trade that had once belonged to Fort Rouillé. His young son almost certainly joined him there sometimes, spending formative summers roaming the forests of Lake Ontario and learning the local Indigenous languages. When he grew old enough, he would follow in his father's footsteps, becoming a *coureur de bois,* taking over the trade at Toronto, and acting as a translator between the British and the First Nations.

As a result, Jean Baptiste Rousseau wasn't a very attentive husband. During his first few years of marriage, he spent many long months away from home — and away from Marie. It took a toll on their relationship. With Jean away, Marie's eye began to wander. Within a few years of that joyous wedding day in Old Montreal, she'd fallen in love with another man. The Rousseaus' marriage came to an end in the summer of 1786.

It was a bit of an unusual breakup. The Rousseaus were Catholic, so they couldn't get an official divorce. And with few priests and government officials on the frontier, marriages and divorces were frequently little more than a promise between two people anyway. Instead, they came to a written agreement, giving us a brief glimpse into the sad end of their marriage. "I Marie Martineau," she swore, "having had frequent difficulties with my husband, Jean Baptiste Rousseau, and seeing that we can no longer live together in harmony, have agreed … to mutual and reciprocal separation and to no longer depend upon the other … and in consequence declare him entirely free and independent of me."

For his part, Rousseau wrote a new will, asking his heir to take care of Marie. "Although I ignore even the existence of my wife … I beg him to do his utmost to lead her back to virtue and to [give her] from my wealth an annual pension income for life as a proof that I forgive her, and … as I on my side, have need of being pardoned for the wrongs I've done her."

One of those wrongs may very well have been his own wandering eye. It wouldn't be long at all before the fur trader got married for a second time.

* * *

Margaret Clyne was born in the very same year Fort Rouillé was burned to the ground. She was the daughter of a settler family living in New York or Pennsylvania. With the Seven Years' War drawing to a close, Americans were anxious to push even further west into First Nations lands. Conflict between settlers and Indigenous nations was common. And Margaret's family was living in the homeland of the Haudenosaunee.

She was just an infant when their home was attacked by First Nations warriors. Her father was killed, beaten to death with the butts of their muskets. Her older brother had his skull crushed against a tree. But baby Margaret was spared. She was found in the arms of her older sister. The two young girls were both taken prisoner. And soon, they would be adopted by one of the most famous leaders of the Kanien'keha:ka (one of the Haudenosaunee nations that Europeans called the Mohawk).

Chief Joseph Brant, Thayendanegea, had fought with the British during the Seven Years' War and took up arms with them again during the American Revolution. Driven from his homeland at the end of that war, Brant led many of the Haudenosaunee north to settle on the British side of the border — in Canada. Now known as the Six Nations — having added the Tuscarora to their confederacy — the Haudenosaunee were awarded a tract of land around the Grand River. They're still there to this day. The nearby city of Brantford is named in the chief's honour.

Margaret Clyne might have been born into a settler family, but she was raised as Kanien'keha:ka. She was in her midtwenties by the time Brant led the Haudenosaunee north to Canada — and she went with him. It was there that she would meet Jean Baptiste Rousseau.

They probably met in Cataraqui, thanks to a mutual connection. Joseph Brant's sister Molly lived there, too. She had once been married to an important British official: Sir William Johnson. As the superintendent of Indian affairs, he had been responsible for building alliances with the First Nations. And while he was no stranger to violence — he was there during the attack on Fort Niagara, leading hundreds of Haudenosaunee warriors during the siege — he also seems to have recognized the power of romance as a tool of diplomacy.

Romantic relationships played an important role in the fur trade. Many *coureurs de bois* married Indigenous women, gaining life-saving knowledge and skills from their wives and their wives' families while also cementing a bond between cultures; they built alliances as well as families. (In the Northwest, some of the descendants of those families would even create their own new nation: the Métis.) Some religious leaders and colonial officials in distant cities like Quebec City and Montreal were deeply worried about the effect Indigenous culture might be having on their fur traders. But many of the men themselves enjoyed the freedoms they found on the frontier. They felt at home in a world where priests were few and far between and where, despite the best efforts of the missionaries, strict Christian morals had yet to take hold.

Sir William Johnson seems to have been one of those men. No one's entirely sure just how many women Johnson slept with. People liked to say he fathered seven hundred illegitimate children, some with settlers and some with Kanien'keha:ka women. At least two of those love affairs were serious, long-term relationships. The last of these was with Molly Brant, Koñwatsi'tsiaiéñni. He fell in love with her near the end of the Seven Years' War, transfixed by her dark eyes and her long braids, amazed by the way she could leap onto the back of a charging horse. The two spent the last twenty years of his life together. They're thought to have been married in a Kanien'keha:ka ceremony — a union that the Church of England refused to recognize — held inside a longhouse. They had eight children together.

Johnson died just before the American Revolution, but his widow would play an important role in that war. As a Kanien'keha:ka leader and a staunch Loyalist, Molly Brant coordinated Haudenosaunee support for the British, providing weapons, ammunition, and intelligence. When the war ended, she headed north, spending the rest of her days living in Cataraqui — the same tiny town where Jean Baptiste Rousseau found his marriage coming to an end.

The young fur trader seems to have met Margaret Clyne when she came to visit her famous aunt, travelling the entire length of Lake Ontario by herself in a canoe, spending her nights sleeping on the beach during the long journey. Rousseau was an adventurous young man and could court her in her own language. Clyne was an adventurous young woman who wouldn't expect him to follow the conservative, European way of doing things. It didn't take long for them to fall in love.

The fur trader's second wedding day came in 1786. He and Margaret likely got married in a Kanien'keha:ka ceremony before moving into his father's house at Toronto, living on the east bank of the Humber just a few hundred metres from the mouth of the river. A cherry orchard bloomed behind their home, and the Toronto Carrying Place trail ran right past them as it climbed up a ridge — where Riverside Drive is now — on its long and winding way toward Lake Simcoe. The ruins of Teiaiagon were just a short walk away.

By then, it was the Mississaugas — one of the Anishinaabe nations — who lived in the area around Toronto. In the century since La Salle, the Seneca had been pushed back south across the lake. According to Anishinaabe oral tradition, the Mississaugas began to move south from the lands north of Lake Huron in the late 1600s. A series of battles was fought between the Haudenosaunee Confederacy and their own Three Fires Confederacy before a treaty finally brought peace to the warring nations.

By the time the Rousseaus arrived, the Mississaugas could be found throughout much of what is now southern Ontario. They built their own village just across the river from the ruins of Teiaiagon — and may even have used the site of the old Seneca village itself. While their winters would have been spent hunting in the forests to the north, they spent their summers tending to the great fields of maize they grew near the mouth of the Humber.

The Rousseaus must have carried on a thriving trade with the Mississaugas, playing a crucial role in the area. Their little house on the Humber was a cross-road between nations. A French fur trader and his Haudenosaunee wife were living in the land of the Mississaugas, trading under a licence from the British. And when Margaret gave birth to a child in that house, it wasn't just the first baby of European descent known to have been born at Toronto, it was also both French and British, Indigenous and settler, American and Canadian — a hint of the multicultural city to come.

But that moment was a brief one. Just a few years after Jean Baptiste Rousseau married Margaret Clyne, Toronto was going to change forever.

The British were coming. It began with explorers who passed through on their way deep into the interior of the continent, just like generations of French explorers had done before them. They were eventually followed by surveyors taking careful measurements, drawing up maps, preparing for permanent settlements. It took a few decades after the fall of Quebec, but as the 1700s came to a close, the British Empire was turning its gaze westward, planning to turn the shores of Lake Ontario into a land of cities and farms.

Among the first to arrive was the surveyor Augustus Jones. He, too, was a man of adventure, built for life on the frontier. He spent his summers in canoes and winters on snowshoes. He'd survived multiple cases of malaria and a broken collar bone, cracked when he was thrown off his horse. And he, too, used

love to build bonds with the First Nations. Not only
could he speak the languages of the Kanien'keha:ka
and the Mississaugas, he would marry into both cultures, too: Sarah Tekarihogen (Tekerehogen) was the
daughter of a Kanien'keha:ka chief, while Sarah Henry
(Tuhbenahneequay) was the daughter of a Mississauga
chief. Jones had children with them both, and supported both families at the same time, leading a polygamous
lifestyle far from the colonial centres of power half a
world away.

But Jones's arrival also heralded the end of that freedom. As far as the British were concerned, they'd just
bought Toronto. After the British conquered New France,
King George III issued a decree. The Royal Proclamation
of 1763 would prove to be one of the most important
documents in Canadian history, reaffirmed in the modern Canadian Constitution. It declared that all the land
to the west belonged to the Indigenous people who lived
on it — and that only the government was allowed to
buy it from them, through international treaties. It established a nation-to-nation relationship between the
British Crown and Indigenous peoples.

The Toronto Purchase was the treaty that covered
the land on which the modern city stands today. But it
was a contentious agreement right from the very beginning. While the signed document was what mattered to
the British, for the Mississaugas, the oral promises were
much more important. None of them could read the
document — it was written in English — but they sent
hundreds of people to witness the proceedings. Both

sides came away with very different impressions of what had been agreed.

Years later, the British realized that even the written document was worthless. It was just a blank deed that didn't describe the land in question, and the chiefs' names had been signed on separate pieces of paper and attached to the treaty after the fact. Even by their own dubious colonial standards, the British clearly had no legal right to the land. They would keep that fact a secret for the next decade, however, before getting the Mississaugas to sign a second treaty. Once again, though, they failed to clearly explain the terms — or that the second agreement covered even more land than the first. It would be 2010 before the dispute was finally settled; the Mississaugas of the New Credit First Nation were paid $145 million — the 1700s value of the land in modern currency.

But the British didn't let any of those complications slow them down. Augustus Jones would soon be followed by a wave of settlers intent on turning the shores of Lake Ontario into a bastion of British culture and values. And when they arrived, laws and customs concerning love and marriage would be tightened, reflecting the views that ruled in the capitals of Europe. Common law arrangements and polygamous lifestyles would soon be socially unacceptable.

And so, Jean Baptiste Rousseau's third wedding day would follow that new wave of settlement. As British laws were introduced to Toronto, the validity of the Rousseaus' marriage would be thrown into question. They were remarried by an Anglican priest a couple of

years after the city was founded, with a Protestant ceremony held at Joseph Brant's house, complete with all the
appropriate paperwork.

And just in case that wasn't enough, they would be
reremarried by that same priest a decade later. Rousseau's
first marriage to Marie Martineau had never officially
ended as far as the Church and State were concerned. So,
when Martineau passed away in the early 1800s, the fur
trader and his second wife held yet another ceremony,
just to make absolutely sure they were truly, officially,
and legally married.

On a summer night in 1793, a British warship sailed
through the darkness toward Toronto. It cut through
the black water, heading to a spot just to the east of the
Humber, where a big, natural harbour was created by a
low sandbar. It was there, just outside the bay, that HMS
Mississauga dropped anchor, waiting for morning.

The new British lieutenant-governor and his family
were on board. They'd sailed overnight from Niagara,
come to build a new capital for their new province. They
would need Jean Baptiste Rousseau's help to do it.

In the days to come, the fur trader would prove to
be indispensable, a trusted liaison between the British
and the First Nations, respected by all. The lieutenant-
governor would eventually request his services as his
personal interpreter. And when the fraudulent Toronto
Purchase was renegotiated, it was the fur trader who
would translate for both sides. The Rousseaus would

spend the rest of their lives helping to build the new colony, settling in the nearby town of Ancaster. They would run a general store, a blacksmith shop, an inn, and two mills; Jean would even become a tax collector. The local Anglican church was built on land they donated. In the end, the French fur trader would give his life for the British colony, struck down by a fatal illness while serving in the War of 1812.

But that was all in the future. For now, Rousseau had one simple task. As the July sun rose above Toronto, he headed out to meet the *Mississauga*. They'd been waiting for him to guide them through the dangerous shoals at the mouth of the bay. There, on the banks of Lake Ontario, they planned to build a muddy little frontier town that would eventually become a towering metropolis of concrete and glass.

The Simcoes had arrived.

4

THE FIRES OF ELIZABETH SIMCOE

The sandbar stretched out into the lake, a long peninsula protecting a beautiful bay filled with water as clear as crystal. It was a peaceful place, where huge flocks of ducks and geese floated on rippling waves and loons called out in the distance. On the far side of the bay, a great forest rose up from the shoreline, with oaks and pines looming over the slight bluff that ran along the edge of the lake. There were bears, wolves, and cougars among those trees. At the back of the bay, a sprawling marsh was filled with long reeds and red-winged blackbirds whose full-throated trills pierced the air.

Standing out there on the sandbar, Elizabeth Simcoe could look across the water and see the beginnings of the metropolis to come. This is the place her husband had chosen to build his new city. The Simcoes had arrived just three months earlier, the new lieutenant-governor and his wife sailing into the bay with Rousseau's help before coming ashore. They brought much of their family with them: three small children, a brave white cat with grey spots, and a big Newfoundland dog called Jack Sharp. By then, Simcoe's men had already arrived: his soldiers pitched a few white tents near the mouth of a creek they'd call the Garrison, on a spot dwarfed by the leafy giants of the ancient forest. That's where they'd begun the hard work of bringing those giants down, clearing the bush to make way for the construction of a military base. Fort York would defend the entrance to the bay, a stronghold ready for the day when the Americans invaded — John Graves Simcoe knew that war with the United States was inevitable. It was only a matter of time.

Eventually, the town would be built a few kilometres to the east, near the back of the bay, so that an invading army would have to sail past the guns of Fort York to attack it. A grove of fine oak trees would come crashing to the ground to make way for the first ten blocks of the new town. But for now, the Simcoes were living relatively rough. They owned a pair of tents that folded out to become a little canvas house — they even had wallpaper and wooden floors. This was far from the life of luxury Elizabeth Simcoe was used to. Back home in England, they lived on a beautiful country estate with an army of servants. But she was embracing life on the frontier. She liked the adventure. She enjoyed exploring the forests of Toronto, riding her horse out to the Humber River where the Rousseaus lived, rowing up the Don Valley or out by the Scarborough Bluffs, hiking through the woods to visit the ruins of Fort Rouillé, clambering over fallen trees and getting drenched in the rain. She had a freedom at Toronto she would never have back home in England.

On that particular November evening, the Simcoes had taken a canoe out across the bay to have dinner in a meadow on the sandbar. The peninsula had quickly become one of Elizabeth Simcoe's most beloved places in the world — "my favourite sands," as she put it in her diary. It had long been considered a place of healing by the local First Nations, and the lieutenant-governor's wife found the crisp, clean air invigorating. She'd been a regular visitor ever since she'd arrived, venturing out across the long, low strip of land dotted with meadows and ponds where the ground was draped in flowers of purple and white. She rode her horse among the fir trees and the poplars wrapped in vines. The French had called it *le presqu'ile de Toronto* — the almost island of Toronto. And indeed, a few decades later, a series of great storms would batter away at the peninsula; the crashing waves washed the sand away until the connection to the mainland was severed. The sandbar became the Toronto Islands.

There may have been nowhere in the world Elizabeth Simcoe felt more free than out there on her almost island, thousands of kilometres from the drawing rooms of England, with their strict rules of etiquette and decorum. She was a proper English gentlewoman, but out here on the frontier, she could do things she would never feel comfortable doing back home. And so, after their dinner in the meadow that November night, Elizabeth Simcoe set a fire just to watch it burn.

She'd become something of a pyromaniac since she'd arrived in the colonies. Having marvelled at the thick smoke that hung like fog among the trees during a forest fire in Quebec, she'd become fascinated; her diary is filled with flames. She marvelled at everything from the static in her silk gowns to a house fire that spread through Quebec to the rumours of a volcano somewhere outside that city. And once she reached the frontier, she began to set her own fires. She found them beautiful: the bright flames and billowing smoke.

That night on the peninsula, she set fire to some long grasses. She watched as they quickly burned, the flames and smoke racing fast along the ground. She wrote about it in her diary: "It had a pleasurable effect."

And that wasn't the only freedom Elizabeth Simcoe was indulging out there on her secluded sandbar. She was also spending a suspicious amount of time alone with a dashing young man who was not her husband.

Elizabeth Simcoe had been married for more than a decade, having met her husband when she was a teenager. John Graves Simcoe was a daring young officer recently returned from the battlefields of the American Revolution. The British might have lost the war, but Simcoe had made quite a name for himself fighting against the revolutionaries. He'd never lost a battle, he'd survived a rebel prison, and had been wounded three times. With the war ending, he'd gone home to England to recover and heal — not just from his injuries, but from a broken heart, as well.

Just a few winters earlier, Simcoe had found himself living outside New York City. The area was controlled by the British, but there were still plenty of American rebels about. So, Simcoe spent his days on patrol with his men, leading his Queen's Rangers on guerrilla-style raids, their green uniforms blending in with the forests, a white crescent moon on their hats in honour of Diana, goddess of the hunt. His daring deeds made him a hero to the British, while many Americans came to see him as a particularly vicious foe, accusing him of massacres and remembering him more than two hundred years later as a psychopathic villain in an ahistorical Netflix show.

But on some nights, things were much more peaceful. Simcoe was billeted with an American family who lived in Oyster Bay, a small community on Long Island. And it was there during those cozy winter nights that he fell in love.

Sally Sarah Townsend was eighteen years old. Simcoe was twenty-seven, a brave young officer looking for a wife. They say his fellow soldiers were deeply jealous of the flirtatious hours he got to spend with her. "She was the toast of these young men," as one historian would later put it, "and Simcoe was regarded as a most fortunate being in basking in the daily sunshine of her charms." By the time the fourteenth of February came around, Simcoe was thoroughly smitten.

To prove the depth of his feelings, he turned to a relatively new English tradition. People had been sending Valentine's Day cards for centuries, but it was in the 1700s that they really evolved into the popular romantic tradition we know today. As a lover of poetry, Simcoe seems to have fully embraced the practice. And to celebrate St. Valentine's Day in 1779, Simcoe penned an ode to Sally Sarah Townsend.

The poem began simply enough:

> Fairest Maid where all is fair
> Beauty's pride and Nature's care;
> To you my heart I must resign
> O choose me for your Valentine!

But it quickly evolved into something much more ambitious. Thirteen stanzas and three hundred words long, Simcoe's poem ended with a prayer to the God of Love asking whether his life would ever be more than just endless war:

> "Fond Youth," the God of Love replies,
> "Your answer take from Sarah's eyes."

Along with the poem, Simcoe also attached a sketch: two hearts inscribed with their initials and joined together by Cupid's arrow. Today, it's considered to be the very first Valentine in North American history.

But no matter how strong Simcoe's feelings were, how flattering his poetry or romantic his art, the two could never be together. He'd fallen in love with the wrong woman. Sally Townsend was a rebel spy.

With the British in control of New York, the American general George Washington was desperate for information from inside the occupied city. So, he established a spy ring to feed him secrets from the area. The Culper Ring was a huge success. It tipped Washington off to surprise attacks, a British counterfeiting scheme, and maybe even a plot on the general's own life. It's been called "the spy ring that saved America."

Sally's brother Robert was one of three men enlisted to run the scheme, and while the details are far from clear, many historians believe he brought his sister on board as an informant. It's thought that she may have been spying on Simcoe the entire time he was wooing her, her flirtations nothing more than a rebel ruse. As the daughter of a revolutionary family, she certainly had plenty of reason to hate the British officer who was making himself at home in her house. And it can't have helped that he chopped down her family's beloved apple orchard, using the wood to reinforce a nearby fort.

As you might expect, Townsend rejected Simcoe's plea to take him as her Valentine. The last surviving physical trace of their relationship is a pane of glass from her bedroom window, still preserved at her old house in Oyster Bay (now open to the public as the Raynham Hall Museum). There's a wistful message scratched into its surface — a few longing words of love thought to have been inscribed by the besotted Simcoe: to "the adorable Miss Sally Sarah Townsend."

He wouldn't have to live with the rejection for long; Simcoe's days of living with the Townsends were numbered. Later that same year, he was captured in a rebel ambush and locked up inside a dank prison cell, where his health began to fail him. It was six months before he was finally released in a prisoner exchange so he could head home to England and recover. He sailed back across the ocean, armed with a fresh distrust of Americans and the democratic ideals they fought for, heading to his godfather's quiet house in the countryside so he could lick his wounds and plan his future.

It was there, at Hembury Fort House, that John Graves Simcoe met his future wife.

It was the old admiral Samuel Graves who brought them together. He'd been war buddies with Simcoe's dad — both were captains of ships sailing the St. Lawrence during the Seven Years' War. Simcoe's father had died there, catching a fatal case of pneumonia just a few months before the Battle of the Plains of Abraham. But Graves survived to become an admiral, in charge of the whole British fleet in North America during the early days of the American Revolution. It didn't go very well; he was instructed to maintain control of the entire east coast of the United States with only about two dozen ships, an order that has gone down in history as one of the most impossible tasks ever asked of a naval officer. Admiral Graves was doomed to fail. When he was finally replaced, he headed back home to his wife and their country estate in Devon, where he would live out the rest of his days in relative peace and quiet.

The old admiral and his wife didn't have any children of their own, but they did have a niece: Elizabeth Posthuma Gwillim.

Elizabeth had been an orphan for essentially her entire life. Her father had died during the Seven Years' War, before she was born, having served as aide-de-camp to the famous General James Wolfe on the Plains of Abraham. Her mother had died just hours after giving birth. And so, Elizabeth spent her childhood living with relatives, much of it with her uncle, Admiral Graves. She became the daughter he never had.

Hembury Fort House stood in the Blackdown Hills of Devon, one of England's official Areas of Outstanding Natural Beauty. "Elizabeth fell in love with the beautiful Devon landscape," her biographer, Mary Beacock Fryer, writes, "which she grew to regard as her spiritual home." It was a land of rolling green hillsides and fields, where ancient trees lined sunken roads. It's a land of magic and of myth, filled with tales of faeries and pixies, of warrior ghosts and witchcraft. She went for long walks and horseback rides through the hills, sketching the countryside and collecting plants. Back at home, she turned those sketches into watercolours and stayed up late reading or chatting with her best friend.

She was nineteen years old when young John Graves Simcoe arrived, a gallant warrior in his late twenties, a wounded hero with political ambitions. He made a striking impression. There's a chance the two might have already met; they were born, by complete coincidence, just a few kilometres from each other. But even if they had,

Elizabeth would now make her own new impression. She was pretty and slight, just about five feet tall. She could paint and draw and do needlework, was well read and spoke three languages.

As soon as his wounds healed, John began to join Elizabeth on her rambles through the countryside, up and down those big green hills. He, too, fell in love with the place, fascinated by its history: stories of Druids and smugglers, Bronze Age burial mounds and Stone Age earthworks. Together, they would venture up to the top of the nearest hill: an Iron Age hill fort that had once been used by the Roman army. They would make sketches of the picturesque landscape, recreating them as full paintings when they returned home. And while at first they were accompanied by the admiral's wife — she was skeptical of the young relationship — soon, she let them go out on their own. They would stride down the old sunken roads, with Elizabeth having to run every few steps to keep up with her tall soldier.

"From walks the couple graduated to long rides each morning before breakfast," Fryer writes in her biography. "To Mrs. Graves' chagrin, she found herself looking on, helpless, as the two were obviously falling in love. Admiral Graves was delighted with the train of events, and sought to give the couple every encouragement."

It worked. Just a few months after Simcoe arrived in the Blackdown Hills, the two were engaged. It was the summer of 1782. That December, they made the short trip down the hill from Hembury Fort House to a nearby church. There, they were married in front of their friends and surviving family members. With Elizabeth's inheritance, they bought a beautiful estate of their own, just across the fields from Hembury, where they began their family.

It was almost a decade later that John Graves Simcoe was called back to North America. In the wake of the American Revolution, tens of thousands of refugees fled the United States. Many Americans who'd stayed loyal to the British during the war were forced from their homes by the revolutionaries, their lives threatened, their property burned to the ground. A wave of these Loyalists fled north to the Canadian colonies, where the British still ruled. And while the settlements of Quebec and the East Coast were already well established, the British saw the land to the west as an untamed wilderness. Dismissing the fact that many First Nations already lived around the Great Lakes (as they had for thousands of years), the British decided that the area would make a perfect new home for the refugees. And so, the province of Upper Canada was created in what's now southern Ontario.

For a while, the British were considering William Johnson's son to run the new province. John Johnson had taken over his father's job as the superintendent of Indian affairs — and as Molly Brant's stepson, he had a strong relationship with the First Nations. But in the end, the colonial rulers chose someone else: a vehement defender of all things British whose heart had once been broken by one of those dastardly American rebels. They chose John Graves Simcoe.

In 1791 he set sail for Canada. His mission was clear: to build a prosperous new colony that was British to its core and prepared for the day when war with the Americans would break out once again.

But he didn't go alone. Elizabeth Simcoe joined him on the long journey across the Atlantic. It must have been an exciting and romantic time, spending a winter in Quebec, taking in the views from the city's impressive stone walls: the lower town spread out below them on the banks of the vast St. Lawrence River, with the blue hills of Maine in the distance. It was a "grand scene," she wrote in her diary, "with which we were so delighted that we came to view it again in the Evening & did not return home till it was dark or rather starlight." She would give birth to their seventh child nine months after that romantic stroll, almost to the day.

She was pregnant during the harrowing trek up the St. Lawrence to reach their new colony, but as soon as they arrived in Upper Canada, she would get to work. She had an important role to play. While the lieutenant-governor prepared for war and planned his province, Elizabeth would be tasked with bringing the genteel culture of English drawing rooms to the dark forests and deep waters of the Canadian frontier. Together, they would build a British utopia.

As their ship dropped anchor at the entrance to Toronto Bay on that July day in 1793, John Graves Simcoe had a clear plan in mind. He would build a new capital here; protected by the sandbar, it was much safer than the old capital at Niagara, where an American fort sat just across the river. The newly reconstituted Queen's Rangers were already hard at work clearing trees to make way for the settlement. When it was done, it would be a glorious tribute to the British Empire: a city so undeniably amazing that the Americans he'd fought during the revolution couldn't help but realize how terrible the United States was by comparison. They would voluntarily give up their silly notions of independence and beg to be let back into the Empire.

"I would die by more than Indian torture to restore my King and his family to their just inheritance," Simcoe wrote before he left for Canada. "This colony … should in its very foundations provide for … every embellishment that hereafter may decorate and attract notice, and may point it out to the neighbouring States as a superior, more happy, and more polished form of Government. I would not in its infancy have a hut, nor in its maturity, a palace built without this design."

Indeed, Simcoe set to work making his new settlement as British as possible in every detail. Many of the first few streets in his new town would be named in honour of British royalty: George, Frederick, and Adelaide among them. Yonge Street would be christened in tribute to one British minister of war; Dundas to another. The river known to the Anishinaabe as Wonscotanach would be renamed after an English river: the Don. The *Niwa'ah Onega'gaih'ih* was already being called St. John's River by the time the Simcoes arrived — a reference to Jean Baptiste Rousseau. But it would now be known as the Humber in honour of a river in Yorkshire. And it was Elizabeth herself who named the towering cliffs to the east of the town. They reminded her of some cliffs in Yorkshire, so she gave them the same as that place: Scarborough.

Even the word *Toronto* would be replaced. When Simcoe learned that King George's son — the Duke of York — had won an important victory over the French, Simcoe announced that he would name his new town in tribute to the prince. The honour was a bit premature; the duke's campaign against the French fizzled, and he would soon be caught up in a notorious sex scandal. His former mistress claimed she'd taken bribes in return for using her influence with him. But Simcoe couldn't have known that any of that was coming. To celebrate his town's new name, he ordered a Royal Salute: all the cannons on the shore, all the guns on all the ships in the harbour, all the muskets of his soldiers were fired in honour of a man who would soon be at the centre of what's been called "the greatest scandal in the history of the British Parliament."

Toronto would now be known as York.

This new city would also have a strict class system, much like England's, with power kept in the hands of those at the very top. As far as Simcoe was concerned, democracy was dangerous. During the American Revolution, he'd personally witnessed horrors committed in its name, and now the idea had spread to France, where an even bloodier revolution was underway. So, he would restrict what he once called "tyrannical democracy" in favour of a powerful, British-Canadian elite.

There would be limits on personal freedom, too. Love would be strictly regulated. Marriage would play a vital role in Upper Canada, creating a strong foundation for the colony, but only if it were properly controlled. Settlers on the frontier had enjoyed too much freedom. To be a respectable British province, Simcoe wanted respectable British marriages. That meant not only a crackdown on less traditional forms of love, but also a strict definition of what constituted a "proper" marriage.

For Simcoe, that meant one thing: an Anglican marriage. In Upper Canada, there would be an official state church: the Church of England. The only valid marriages were those performed by Anglican ministers. It was one of the founding laws of the province, adopted on the very first day Simcoe's new Parliament met.

But that limited definition of marriage caused major problems. Upper Canada was already a much more multicultural place than Simcoe wanted it to be. The majority of the settlers weren't Anglican at all. And with only a handful of priests on the frontier, it was hard to get an Anglican wedding even if you wanted one. In one fell stroke, countless marriages had been called into question.

Simcoe had a tremendous amount of control over his new province. There was an elected Legislative Assembly, but it had little power. It could be overruled by the un-elected Legislative Council and by the lieutenant-governor himself. Still, Simcoe couldn't just create whatever laws he wanted; he did need the assembly's support. And even some of his own allies worried their marriages were suddenly invalid. The very first new bill introduced in

Parliament sought to expand the definition of marriage. Simcoe would eventually be forced into compromise. The law was changed to allow exceptions for just a handful of other Christian denominations. But that really just caused even more confusion. The fight would carry on well into the 1800s.

In Upper Canada, for decades to come, it would be unclear who really was married — and who wasn't.

Elizabeth Simcoe had her part to play. There, in her little canvas house on the shores of Toronto Bay, she was helping to recreate the culture of English drawing rooms. As the lieutenant-governor's wife, she was at the centre of social life in the province. Everyone was looking to her to set the example. Even in Canada, she did all she could to keep her hair perfectly coiffed and to dress in the latest fashions. She'd brought servants with her from Europe, including a French chef and a nurse for her children. She'd even brought a spinning wheel with her — hauling it all the way to the frontier even though she never used it, just because it was a gift from the queen.

At York, as spring arrived and the first few government officials began to follow the Simcoes across the lake, Elizabeth hosted dances, dinners, and card games — staples of respectable English culture. At Niagara, she'd even hosted royalty — Prince Edward, father of Queen Victoria, had paid them a visit on the frontier. A "lady of manners" is how one acquaintance described her. "Her conduct is perfectly exemplary, and admirably conformed to that correct model, which ought to be placed before a people."

But she was also enjoying the new freedoms she found out there on the frontier: exploring the wilderness, eating raccoon meat, painting her watercolours on birchbark, and setting her fires.

Thomas Talbot was her husband's private secretary. He was twenty-two years old, a dashing adventurer from one of Ireland's most storied noble families. He'd joined the army at the age of eleven, served as aide-de-camp to the governor of Ireland, and become close friends with the Duke of Wellington — the general who would defeat Napoleon. It was Talbot's military career that had brought him to Canada; he'd served in Quebec City and Montreal before heading out to the frontier with the Simcoes.

At York, Elizabeth spent a lot of time alone with the handsome young Talbot. He was much younger and more vigorous than her husband. Simcoe was not a healthy man — he'd missed Prince Edward's visit, bedridden the entire time, and would eventually die of a severe asthma attack. Talbot was clearly in the prime of his life. When the three of them walked across the frozen bay (on the same day she set her first fire), it was Talbot who took her by the arm, while the lieutenant-governor trailed behind, treading carefully with the help of a cane. She had plenty of adventures with her husband's secretary when her husband wasn't around. They dined together; he frequently drove her home from events in a carriage or a sleigh. They were together when she saw her first bald eagle, soaring through the skies at Niagara. She watched, amused, as Talbot tried to paddle a canoe for the first time. And when she'd been upset by the sight of some passenger pigeons flapping and squawking, trapped in a cage, it was Talbot who paid to have them released. When he met with local Indigenous leaders, he brought gifts back for her: a berry cake and a fawn skin she made into a long shawl. Reading her diary entries, it's easy to imagine a romance budding between the two. Out there on the peninsula, away from the eyes of her husband and the soldiers building Fort York, she and Talbot raced their horses across the sand, hooves thundering on the beaches, the cool autumn air rushing against her face.

But in the end, that's not the life Elizabeth Simcoe chose. Her adventures in Canada were brief. She returned home to England with her husband after just a few years; his health was suffering from their rustic lifestyle. They would never return.

Thomas Talbot would remain a bachelor for the rest of his days, living on the shores of Lake Erie. He built an empire there, entrusted with a huge swath of land, which he distributed to new settlers. Eventually, it would stretch more than a half a million acres, home to fifty thousand people. You'll still find his name written across that part of Ontario to this day: the city of St. Thomas was named after him, and London has Colonel Talbot Road.

But he kept one big chunk of land for himself: a generous patch of wilderness surrounding his home. He'd built a log house on top of a bluff overlooking the lake.

He grew old there, a rich and powerful man living the simple life of a recluse. He raised sheep, cattle, and geese; grew a fruit orchard and a rose garden; and hired one servant with a wife and child. Every year, he would attend a single ball, always taking the first dance with the most beautiful young woman there. But beyond that, he was rarely seen in public.

Decades after the Simcoes left, when Talbot was in his late sixties, a famous writer came to pay him a visit. Anna Jameson was an ardent feminist who had briefly come to Toronto to get a separation from her husband, the attorney general. She leaped at the opportunity to explore the province, and her tour of Upper Canada included a visit with Talbot on his wild estate. While she was a bit scared to meet him, having heard stories of a curmudgeonly hermit who hated women, what she found instead was a welcoming old man who still remembered the charms of courtly life. "In spite of his rustic dress," Jameson wrote in her account of her travels, "his good-humored, jovial, weather-beaten face, and the primitive simplicity, not to say rudeness, of his dwelling, he has in his features, air, and deportment, that *something* which stamps him gentleman ... which thirty-four years of solitude has not effaced."

She stayed with him there in his log house for nearly a week, keeping him company, listening to him talk about his life. She found that tears sometimes came to her eyes as he did. He was happy but lonely. No one knew for sure what had driven him to lead such a reclusive life. But some, Jameson wrote, whispered "that early in life he had met with a disappointment in love, which had turned his brain." He spent the rest of his life there in that log cabin high above Lake Erie, many long years after he and Elizabeth had raced their horses along the shores of Toronto Bay, picnicked in the meadows of the peninsula, and watched her fires burn. Thomas Talbot seems to have died as he lived: a hermit with a broken heart.

As for Elizabeth Simcoe, she would spend the rest of her life in Devon, watching over her country estate. She would never again experience anything like the freedom of those fleeting days on her beloved peninsula. She would outlive her husband by nearly forty years, a widow becoming ever more conservative as she grew older. John Graves Simcoe was laid to rest beneath the chapel they'd built together in those green hills — a spot that many years later would officially be declared Canadian territory: a small patch of Ontario in the middle of the English countryside. And when Elizabeth Simcoe finally died at the age of eighty-seven, she, too, was buried there, beneath that little church, thousands of kilometres from Canada, right next to the man she'd married.

5
THE NEW YEAR'S DUEL

It was the third day of the year 1800. The dawn of a new century. But John White wouldn't live to see much of it. On that cold January morning, he found himself standing in the middle of a field with a pistol in his hand. The last few months had not been kind to him. In 1799 his wife had left him — again. He'd been passed over for a big promotion. The new lieutenant-governor didn't seem to like him at all. And in the last few weeks, what was left of his life had been torn apart. All through Christmas and New Year's, the tiny town of York had been seized by a sordid sex scandal. White — the attorney general of the new province — was at the centre of it all.

So now, he was standing in a wintry field about to fight a duel. York was six years old, a remote frontier outpost still carving a place for itself out of the Canadian forest. Only a few hundred people called the new capital home and only about a dozen houses had been built along the first few streets. A ten-block grid had been laid out: from the shoreline up to Adelaide, from George

Street over to Berkeley. At the very eastern edge of town, far at the back of the bay, was the town's most recognizable landmark: a pair of modest brick Parliament buildings. Today, the spot where they stood is at the foot of Parliament Street, next to the Distillery District, but back then it was not far from the vast marsh that stood at the mouth of the Don River. It was there behind those Parliament buildings that John White and John Small were standing a few metres apart. Two of the most powerful men in Upper Canada were ready to kill each other in the name of honour.

The Whites had been one of the most influential families in the colony right from the very beginning. John was a lawyer back home in Britain, with a reputation for "considerable practice, great respectability and character without reproach." And so, when Upper Canada was created, he was picked as part of the team of government officials to be sent across the ocean to get the colony going. As the first attorney general of the new province, he'd be Upper Canada's top lawyer.

He arrived in York just as the tiny town officially took on its role as the province's new capital. There, he was tasked with the job of bringing British justice to the distant Canadian frontier. What Elizabeth Simcoe had begun to do for social life in the new colony, White would do for the legal system.

It wasn't an easy task, but at first things seem to have gone pretty well. He was respected and powerful, with a handsome salary of £300 to go along with his important new job. He played an active role in the founding of the

Law Society of Upper Canada — an organization that still exists today as the Law Society of Ontario — and served as its first president and treasurer. He even ran for office, getting elected to the Legislative Assembly in no small part thanks to the active support of Simcoe himself. Once in power, White played a leading role there, too, shepherding important legislation through Parliament.

Even better, there were signs that after years of trouble, his family life might finally be improving, too. John and Marrianne had been married back home in England while he was still just a young law student, not long before he got called to the bar. But by the time he left for his new job in Upper Canada, the marriage was on rocky terrain. When John set sail for North America, Marianne and their children stayed behind.

Now, finally, they were all back together. With John settled in York, Marrianne and the children joined him there, ready to give it another go.

And then along came 1799 — a terrible year for the Whites.

When John came to Canada, he was in considerable debt. And things only got worse upon his arrival. His generous salary failed to keep up with his even more generous spending. He was constantly looking for new ways to make money on the side, squabbling with other officials in the capital as they scrambled to collect fees on government business and receive the best grants of land.

It all took a toll. By the end of the century, White's health was failing him. He was growing depressed. He'd alienated himself from the other colonists and nearly lost hope, disillusioned with Canada and his life there. His letters were full of complaints about everything from his fellow settlers to his money troubles, to his wife. In one letter to his brother-in-law, he complained that he felt "banished, solitary, hopeless, planted in the desert … disappointed — and without prospect."

"The attorney general is … not very robust," a friend worried. "His spirits seem to have left him. I fear he is not happy."

And that wasn't even the worst of it. John White was about to spark one of the most salacious scandals Upper Canada had ever seen. He would spread a rumour so sensational it would kill him.

It all started at a Christmas party. In a town as small as York, it was impossible to keep people's paths from crossing. And so, not only was John's wife, Marrianne, at the ball, so was his former mistress: Elizabeth Small, the wife of another important government official. In the midst of all the holiday revelry, Elizabeth Small snubbed Marrianne White, ignoring her when she tried to say hello.

This, apparently, outraged John White, who raced to his wife's defence. The next day, he showed up at the Smalls' house demanding an explanation. When he didn't get one, he confided his terrible secret to a close friend: he and Elizabeth Small had had an affair. He claimed he had broken it off "from fear of injury to his health from the variety and frequency of her Amours with others." It was a shocking insult. Not only was John

White claiming that he'd slept with Elizabeth Small, but that he'd dumped her because she was sleeping with so many other men that he was in danger of contracting a sexually transmitted disease.

The accusation was made all the more believable by the fact that his affair with Small wasn't White's only infidelity. He's believed to have had a secret second family: two children with a mistress by the name of Susanna Page. It wasn't even that rare an occurrence in the capital; York's first priest reported there were at least six "kept mistresses" in town.

White wasn't done with his insults. He kept piling them on, claiming that the Smalls weren't legally married; that Elizabeth had been the mistress of a famous duke back home in England, who, when he got tired of her, had paid John Small to take her off his hands and sail her away to Canada.

The accusations were enough to destroy Elizabeth Small's reputation. White's friend promised to keep all this scathing gossip a secret — with permission to tell only one other person — but that, of course, is not what happened. Over the course of the holidays, the rumour spread like wildfire through the insular town. It didn't take long for word to reach Elizabeth Small's husband. Determined to defend his wife's honour from such terrible insults, John Small challenged John White to a duel.

They met at dawn on the third day of the new year, took up their positions a few metres apart, and then fired their weapons. John Small escaped unscathed. But his shot hit the attorney general with full force. The ball struck White on his right side, tore through his ribs, and carved its way through his flesh all the way to the other side, where it lodged in his spine.

Toronto's first duel was over. John Small had won.

White didn't die quickly. With Marrianne gone back to England, he was taken to the home of his close friends, the Russells. Peter Russell was another one of the most powerful men in the province. Simcoe had chosen the former gambling addict to run the finances of Upper Canada, and when the Simcoes headed home to England, Russell had been appointed as the interim lieutenant-governor. He was one of the few slaveholders in town; he and his sister Elizabeth enslaved Peggy Pompadour and her three children, Jupiter, Amy, and Milly, and kept her husband as a paid servant. They all lived together at Russell Abbey, a small, stately home with a view over the lake, not far from the field where White had fallen.

The attorney general was in agony. The ball had struck a bundle of nerves, leaving him in severe pain, his body rocked by spasms. To Russell it looked like "the most excruciating torture." White was still conscious and able to speak, but there was nothing to be done; it was clear the attorney general didn't have long to live. For the rest of that day, all through the night, and into the morning, his life ebbed away. "Knowing his dissolution to be inevitable," Russell later wrote, "he submitted to his fate with a most pious and Christian resignation to the divine will and forgiveness of all his enemies."

The end came on the evening of the following day. John White finally slipped into unconsciousness thirty-six hours after he was hit by the fatal shot. Within an hour of that, he was dead.

The newspapers would remember him as a good man, despite the sex scandal that had claimed his life. The *Upper Canada Gazette* recalled "the lively sense of his virtues," while the *Constellation* eulogized him as "a professional gentleman, a sincere friend, an honest and upright man, a friend of the poor who had often refused to take fees for the duties he discharged and for advice he had given. He was a man highly esteemed. This is the man whom we have lost!"

The story of John White had come to a bloody end. But for Elizabeth Small, the suffering was just beginning.

John Small and both of the seconds were arrested for their role in the fatal duel. Small was charged with murder. He would be tried by the very same judicial system White had helped to establish.

White had always complained that juries in Upper Canada were too lenient, lamenting the fact that no one accused of murder in the province had ever been convicted of the crime, no matter how clear the evidence against them. Some who would have been hanged in England found themselves walking free on the frontier. And this time would be no different.

Officially, duels were illegal. But they were also a respected tradition stretching back all the way to the days of medieval chivalry. Duels were a relatively common occurrence in Upper Canada's early years, seen as an honourable way to settle passionate disputes, including affairs of the heart. Men who fought duels fairly tended to get acquitted despite the law. Including John Small. The jury accepted the idea that no one had actually seen Small fire his gun. They may have been swayed by the fact that the sheriff clearly approved — he served as Small's second during the duel. And so, John White's killer was found not guilty.

The judge in the case was appalled. He openly disagreed with the verdict, but there was nothing he could do. Small walked free.

It was his wife who would suffer the consequences. Where the justice system failed, gossip would step in. We can't ever know for sure if Elizabeth Small really did sleep with John White, or if it was just a vicious rumour he concocted as revenge. But either way, she paid the price. She was ostracized for her role in the scandal, banished from respectable society. She was publicly spurned and left off the guest lists for all the most important social functions. Any event she was invited to was boycotted by the other leading ladies of York. In the wake of the New Year's duel, Elizabeth Small was a social pariah. No one would even shake her hand.

And so, the Smalls were left to live a lonely life in a little wood cabin on the edge of town, not far from the scene of the fatal duel. In a town as small and petty as York, scandals and rumours could ruin lives.

Sometimes, they could even end them.

6

A DANGEROUS CHARIVARI

Darkness had descended. It was an October evening in 1802. The people of York were settling down for the night. But not everything was still. A crowd of young men was creeping through the heart of the town. They wore disguises to conceal their identities — some in a crude parody of First Nations clothing — and carried with them an unlikely assortment of objects; they almost certainly had everything from pots and pans to horns and rifles. They were planning on making a racket.

Eugenia Willcocks had gotten married that day. She and Augustin Boiton de Fougères were an unlikely match: he was a French aristocrat; she was an Irish immigrant, the daughter of the former mayor of Cork. It was the kind of unusual international romance that foreshadowed Toronto's future as a multicultural metropolis. But as the newlyweds spent their first night of matrimony together at her father's home, those days were still far away. For now, York was still a sleepy British town on the quiet shores of Lake Ontario.

Or, at least, those shores were usually quiet. Once the crowd of young men reached the Willcocks house, it began. A terrible, cacophonous racket. Pots and pans and god knows what else banging and clattering and clanging together as loud as could be. Horns blowing. Guns firing off in the night. Yelling and whooping and every other noise those young men could think to make. The charivari had begun.

The raucous tradition of charivaris was established long before that loud evening in 1802. It can be traced back to Europe, and to the French settlers who brought the practice with them to New France. As settlers moved west into Upper Canada, the tradition spread with them. Charivaris generally happened on nights when an unusual or controversial marriage had taken place, like when an old man married a young woman, or two cultures mixed. It was a way of smoothing over the collective unease. A boisterous crowd would serenade the newlyweds with a hideous racket, interrupting the marital bliss of the wedding night to demand the happy couple emerge and buy them off with alcohol before they would agree to leave them in peace. Sometimes, the rabble-rousers might even get up onto the roof, blocking the chimney to smoke the newlyweds out.

The marriage of Eugenia Willcocks and Augustin Boiton de Fougères was certainly a remarkable one. Fougères was one of a few Upper Canadians who'd been born and raised in France. When the bloody terror of the French Revolution broke out, he'd taken up arms against the revolutionaries, joining an army that hoped to crush them and return the monarchy to the throne. It failed miserably, ending in a terrible massacre, and he was forced to flee. He headed to Upper Canada with a group of French aristocrat refugees. They settled along Yonge Street, well to the north of York — where the suburbs of Markham and Vaughan are today.

Now, the francophone Fougères had married into one of the province's leading anglophone families. Eugenia was the daughter of William Willcocks. A former mayor and sheriff of Cork, he'd left Ireland behind to lead a group of settlers to Upper Canada. Things had gotten off to a very rough start: his first batch of settlers deserted him along the way; his second was captured at sea by the French navy. But after finally making it to York, he'd become one of the leading figures in the new town, serving as a judge and the first postmaster.

With things finally going well, Willcocks wrote to his family back home in Ireland, letting them know it was now safe to join him. Eugenia made the journey with her mother and two sisters, abandoning the life they'd known back home for a new one on the Canadian frontier.

The young Willcocks women were quick to find love in their new home. Eugenia's sister Phoebe would marry William Warren Baldwin — a doctor and architect who was destined to become one of the most influential politicians in Canada. And it wasn't long before Eugenia met the adventurous French aristocrat Fougères. Soon, they were engaged to be married.

But not everyone in town seems to have felt entirely comfortable with the match. The French and English had long been mortal enemies, warring on and off for centuries. A French aristocrat marrying into a prominent anglophone family must have been disturbing to some people. And that's exactly what a charivari was for: a hazing ritual to help the community accept a match that might otherwise cause discord.

Still, charivaris didn't always go to plan. They could easily get out of hand. If the couple refused to come out and face the drunken mob, things could escalate. Some Upper Canadian charivaris ended with the couple being dragged out of their house, sometimes even tarred and feathered or tied to a rail and paraded around town. At least one bride was raped. On occasion, the charivaris could even end in death. Some terrified families fired their rifles into the unruly crowds. One young man was accidentally shot and killed by his fellow revellers. A Black man in St. Catharines was once brutally murdered during a charivari — even though his attackers were perfectly aware he wasn't the groom they were after.

On that autumn night in York, with the charivari raging outside his front door, William Willcocks must have felt like his daughter and her new husband were in danger. He went to get his rifle. So did his son and his future son-in-law, William Warren Baldwin. Together, the three armed men burst from the home to confront the crowd. They threatened to open fire if everyone didn't leave immediately.

Some did run off. Others were still there when the authorities were called and the constables arrived. One man was arrested. But by about ten o'clock, the trouble-makers had dispersed. All was quiet once again.

For a while.

The mob wouldn't be so easily dissuaded. The following night, they were back — despite the rain. And then again, the night after that. "Such a noise with drums, Kettles, Cowbells and Horns was never before heard at York," one witness wrote in his diary. "They keep'd it up till Past Midnight, round the town." When Willcocks and the newlyweds failed to appear, the celebratory horde began to harass neighbours, dragging people out of bed to demand liquor, dancing into the wee hours of the morning.

It wasn't until the fourth night that things came screeching to a halt. When the merrymakers messed with the Willcockses' haystacks, it was the final straw. The furious esquire threatened vengeance unless they abandoned their carousing and went home for good. And with that, it seems, the long charivari finally ended. Calm returned to York.

Sadly, the new marriage wouldn't last long. Just two years after her riotous wedding night, Eugenia Willcocks fell ill and died. The newly widowed Fougères would leave York and eventually disappear back home to Europe. Many of his fellow French refugees did the same. Aristocrats accustomed to the salons of Paris found it hard to carve out a life for themselves in the Canadian bush. And with Napoleon crowning himself emperor of France, the bloody days of the revolution were over; royalist heads were now safe from the guillotine. The French colony in Upper Canada was abandoned.

But the charivaris continued. They were held across Canada for decades to come — in some places, they're said to still happen. In others, the tradition began to evolve, transformed into a means of political protest. Soon, charivaris in France were being used as a noisy form of dissent against the monarchy and corrupt government officials. A century later, they would spread to Africa, used by Algerian freedom fighters in their "nights of the pots." In Latin America, the tradition became known as the *cacerolazo*, as citizens took to their balconies to loudly denounce dictators. When the students of Montreal marched in the streets in 2012, they brought their pots and pans with them. The protests became known as the "*casseroles.*"

And in 2020, as a deadly new virus swept across the globe, forcing billions of people to shelter in their homes, the old tradition took on new life yet again. While in some countries the banging of pots and pans provided a safe way to protest their government's response to COVID-19, in others the racket took on a new meaning: a loud show of support for the health care workers who were risking their lives to save others. That's what it meant in Toronto. In neighbourhoods across the city, people emerged from their homes for a few brief moments in the evening. They came out onto their balconies, or their porches, or brought their children out onto their lawns, pots and pans in hand. And then they began to bang away in a clattering, cacophonous riot: a sign of solidarity and of hope.

7

SHIPWRECKS & DISGRACE

The women of York were shocked. They'd come to the ball expecting a pleasant evening with the lieutenant-governor and his wife, one of the many dances and dinners that provided a public stage for the town's elites — a place to see and be seen. But as it turned out, this was no ordinary occasion. For a year now, a social war had been raging in the ballrooms of York. Nearly a decade after the New Year's duel, Elizabeth Small was trying to re-enter society. She was sick of being ostracized from all formal occasions, tainted by her association with the fatal duel and John White's accusations of infidelity. She and her husband had spent years banished to their lonely cabin on the edge of town. But when a new lieutenant-governor was appointed, she saw her opening. She convinced her contacts back in England to speak with Francis Gore on her behalf before he set sail for Canada. And Lieutenant-Governor Gore, determined to bring York together as a community by healing the divisions sown by scandal and gossip, listened. Suddenly, after years of social exile,

Elizabeth Small was back on the scene. She'd spent the last twelve months re-establishing herself. She was there at the ball that night, enjoying her restored reputation.

But the lieutenant-governor's wife was nowhere to be found. Annabella Gore declined to attend. Her message was silent but clear: she'd taken sides against Small. It was a seismic shift in society; all the rules instantly reverted. It was once more absolutely unacceptable to be seen in public with Elizabeth Small. There in the ballroom, the women of York suddenly realized they'd been caught on the wrong side of the front lines. They scrambled to call for their sleighs, rushing to flee the event as quickly as possible, carrioles fleeing into the night.

And just like that, Elizabeth Small was ostracized once again. Francis Gore had lost his battle to restore her reputation. Anne Murray Powell had taken on the lieutenant-governor — and won.

Powell was the grande dame of York society. In the early years of the 1800s, she ruled over the town's social scene. Praised for her good manners and conservatism, she had the power to make or break someone's reputation. And she wasn't afraid to use it. York might have been a tiny outpost on the very edge of the Empire, but in Anne Murray Powell's town, strict rules of decorum were to be vigorously enforced. Adultery was enough to get you driven out of respectable society altogether.

As Toronto historian and librarian Edith Firth once put it, "Mrs. Powell's power was very real." When she first arrived in York in 1798, there were still only a few hundred people living in the new capital. And in such a small and isolated community, bickering and feuds were commonplace. "Their many parties, dinners, and balls were not mere diversions but battlegrounds upon which fights over social position were won and lost," Powell's biographer, Katherine McKenna, explains. Lives could be changed with a line of whispered gossip or a carefully executed snub. And her stubborn adherence to social norms made Anne Murray Powell a master of those social battles. As the town grew, so did her power.

When Elizabeth Small tried to re-enter polite society, Powell put her foot down. The idea that a woman who'd been publicly accused of adultery would try to regain her reputation was unacceptable. When Gore made it clear that Small had his support, Powell still refused to attend any event Small was attending. She kept it up for a full year, willing to miss out rather than compromise her principles. She didn't even back down when the lieutenant-governor openly snubbed her. And when Powell finally had a chance to fully explain her reasoning to the lieutenant-governor's wife, Annabella Gore agreed and followed her lead by refusing to attend that year's edition of the Queen Charlotte's Ball. In the face of his wife's dissension, the lieutenant-governor was powerless. Powell had won.

"Anne and other wives of the men who dominated political life clearly exerted a great deal of influence on public events," McKenna writes. "Their behavior to each other and to men could result in devastating consequences — fatal duels, social ostracism, and political downfall.... A man whose wife lost in the social stakes would suffer a serious blow to his advancement."

The reverse was true, too. Wives and husbands could make formidable teams. And there were few more formidable than the Powells. With his wife's help, William Powell would work his way to the very top of the legal profession in Upper Canada: as chief justice, he was the highest-ranking judge in the entire province. He became a trusted advisor to more than one lieutenant-governor, and wielded enormous influence. The Powells were, without a doubt, one of the most respected couples in town.

That success came with social responsibilities. When York's first church was built — the small wooden ancestor of today's towering St. James Cathedral — the Powells held the very best pew. They expanded their small log cabin on Front Street (where the Royal York Hotel now stands) into a stately home overlooking the lake. Their country estate, Caer Howell, was impressive enough to be turned into a hotel after they died. And as leaders in the community, they were expected to entertain on a regular basis. They hosted lavish dinners at least twice a week, with as many as sixteen guests sitting down at their dining-room table. Once, a shelf in their cellar gave way with a crack that shook the whole house, buckling under the weight of more than a hundred bottles of brandy.

The Powells paid a small fortune to keep themselves stocked with all the best food and wearing the most fashionable clothes. They had an example to set and they dedicated themselves to that task wholeheartedly, holding themselves to the highest possible standard — and everyone else, too. But behind the veneer of etiquette and decorum, York's most respectable couple was hiding a remarkable secret.

They'd begun their own marriage in a most scandalous fashion.

Anne Murray Powell's obsession with propriety could be traced back all the way to her teenage years. She was sixteen when she left England for America, sent to live with family in Boston. There, her aunt put her to work serving customers in the family's hat shop. It was meant to give her independence and worldly experience, but young Anne was mortified. She was from a new generation who felt that any respectable woman's place was in the home — a view, just beginning to take hold, that would last for nearly two centuries. A job was far beneath her. She was devastated by what it was doing to her social standing: "a state of degradation," she called it. She would later remember it as the most unhappy time of her life. She would spend the rest of her days trying to make up for it, steadfastly enforcing the social rules that proved she was a woman of class and sophistication.

She didn't think much of Billy Powell at first. She was still a teenager when they met. He was simply the older brother of her best friend. And she wasn't thrilled by the idea of marrying *anyone*. It wasn't until William's mother died of smallpox that they really became close — as Anne comforted him in his grief, they fell deeply in love. The thought of being away from each other was too much to bear. So, Anne made a promise: if they were ever going to be torn apart, they would get married first. They got secretly engaged, hiding it from their parents, who thought they were far too young to marry.

And then came the American Revolution. Tensions in Boston had been rising for years. When open rebellion broke out, the first battles were fought in the countryside surrounding the city. It was soon under siege by rebel forces.

It was a hard time. William took up arms to support the British and helped organize a "Declaration of Loyal Citizens." But even his own uncle was an avowed rebel. It didn't take long for it become clear that Boston was a dangerous place for someone as loyal to the British as William Powell. He would need to flee the city for his own safety.

William asked Anne to marry him right there and then — to run away with him. She said yes. But their parents were still a problem. William didn't even bother asking his father; he knew he wouldn't agree. And all they could get from Anne's aunt was a promise not to actively stand in their way, while pretending they'd never mentioned it.

That was enough for the young lovers. In 1775, they eloped, getting married in Boston and then escaping the city by sea. She was twenty. He was nineteen.

William's family was outraged when they found out: his uncle tried to separate them; his father disowned him entirely. Even Anne's aunt suffered for her passive support as gossip flew around Boston. "Anne and William had begun their married life with the feeling that they had a great deal to live down," McKenna writes, "and much to prove concerning their 'respectability.'" Both of them would spend their lives trying to show the world they were upstanding citizens. No matter how bad things would get from then on, Anne Murray Powell always had her manners: "An inflexible coat of armour shielding her from the world," as McKenna describes it.

Unwelcome in the United States and shunned by William's family in England, the newlyweds eventually headed out to the Canadian frontier to make their life together. They arrived in Upper Canada before the province had even officially been created. They'd been living there a while by the time the Simcoes arrived. When they did, Anne and Elizabeth became friends. "She is a very sensible pleasant woman," Simcoe wrote in her diary. "[Her] company is very pleasant to me."

Still, even while they hobnobbed with the new rulers of the province, the Powells would always be haunted by their American roots. British-born settlers tended to look down on anyone who'd lived south of the border. Anne was always self-conscious about the American habits and customs she'd picked up during her time in Boston. And William's professional rivals were quick to use his past against him. They repeatedly accused him of treason, going as far as to forge a treacherous letter they claimed he'd written to the American secretary of war. The Powells responded to their American insecurities by becoming as demonstrably British as they possibly could.

Once the Simcoes returned to England, it was Anne Murray Powell who took on the responsibility of making York as British and aristocratic a place as possible. She spent many long years trying to build a bastion of respectability and grace among the old trees and muddy streets of the isolated frontier town. While William was the arbiter of the law, Anne became the arbiter of social conventions. And while their uncompromising natures made them plenty of enemies, it also earned them plenty of respect. They found themselves at the very top of society — only the lieutenant-governor and his wife were above them in the provincial hierarchy.

The Powells found themselves leaders of a powerful group that became known as "The Family Compact." This insular clique of staunchly conservative Tories was deeply Protestant and fiercely British. Many of them were veterans of the American Revolution and they shared both John Graves Simcoe's visceral distrust of democracy and his vision for Upper Canada: a British monoculture with one official language, one official religion, and themselves as the ruling class. As the historian Gerald M. Craig once put it, they "sometimes seemed to be more British than the King." The Family Compact did everything they could to keep power in their own hands: all the best government jobs, appointments, and free land. They dominated the government, filling the unelected posts in the Legislative Council and the

Executive Council. They had a veto over new laws and the lieutenant-governor's ear.

The families who made up the Family Compact planned to pass their power and privilege down to their children, arranging professional opportunities and suitable marriages for their sons and daughters. The Powells were no different. But as their family grew, so did their disappointments. Raised by such strict parents, some of the Powell kids began to rebel. Anne Murray Powell's family could never live up to her stringent expectations. And in the end, they would bring her down with them.

John was a troublemaker at school. Eliza would die a spinster. William eloped with a woman his parents disapproved of, and then drowned in the Niagara River. But the real disgrace started with Jeremiah. The Powells had always hoped to secure a respectable profession for their favourite son, but Jeremiah had other ideas. He seems to have had a lust for adventure. Despite his parents' impassioned pleas, he was so determined to make something more of himself that not only did he leave Upper Canada, he headed all the way south to Haiti.

It was a dangerous time in Port-au-Prince. The Haitian Revolution had just ended. The country had long been ruled by the French as a slave colony they called Saint-Domingue. The leaders of the French Revolution had abolished slavery, but it was French royalists who still controlled Haiti — and they had no intention of freeing the half-million people they enslaved.

When those people launched a revolution — the biggest uprising against slavery since Spartacus led his revolt against the Romans — the French royalists asked for help. Thousands of British troops were sent to the island, hoping to crush the uprising, restore slavery, and secure the island's sugar riches for themselves. None other than John Graves Simcoe was sent to the island to lead the British into battle. But he was an avowed abolitionist who believed slavery was evil. He lasted only a few months before he seems to have gotten sick of fighting for a cause he didn't believe in and headed home for England, nearly getting arrested for desertion.

The Haitian Revolution raged for thirteen years and claimed hundreds of thousands of lives. But in the end, it was successful. Haiti had become a free, independent country, and was just beginning to establish itself. In 1804, a constitution was still being drafted and the bloodshed wasn't over yet. The very same year that Jeremiah Powell arrived, Haiti's new leader, Emperor Dessalines, had ordered the massacre of all the French settlers still living on the island. Thousands were killed.

At first, though, Jeremiah was welcomed by the emperor. Despite his British roots, he was given a guarantee of safety while he established an import business, selling weapons and other goods directly to Dessalines himself. Everything went smoothly for a while. Right up until the unforgiving emperor discovered that Jeremiah Powell had accidentally sold him some gold trinkets that weren't actually gold at all. Things went south from there in a hurry.

Jeremiah, however, was in luck. Just as it seemed as if his life was in danger, a ship turned up. On board was a man named Francisco de Miranda, a revolutionary South American leader who was on his way to Venezuela, where he planned to liberate the country from Spanish rule. Jeremiah Powell, more than eager to leave Haiti behind, suddenly decided he believed quite strongly in the idea of Venezuelan independence. He joined Miranda and sailed for South America.

The revolution would not go well. The Spanish had been warned; they were waiting for them when they arrived. As they tried to land their ships, they came under attack. Miranda fled, his forces defeated, and those who were left behind were rounded up and arrested — Jeremiah Powell among them. Ten of the men were hanged the very next day, their bodies torn in quarters, their severed heads stuck on poles for public display. Jeremiah was one of the lucky ones: he was convicted of piracy and sentenced to ten years in a South American labour camp.

When the news eventually reached York, the Powells were mortified. It must have been both frightening and deeply humiliating for Anne Murray Powell. She was a woman who had no patience for scandal, but now a member of her own family had been disgraced, thrown into jail as a pirate. William pulled every string he could on his son's behalf. He spent months — and hundreds of pounds — travelling across Upper Canada, the United States, and England looking for leads. He even somehow managed to get Dr. Edward Jenner, inventor of vaccines, to write a letter to the king of Spain on his behalf.

Eventually, it worked. Jeremiah was given a royal pardon and released from prison. Anne Murray Powell was utterly relieved. "While his life was in danger," she wrote, "the scene before me seem'd closed forever. All was cheerless. His safety brightens the prospect, & ... bids me to look forward to years of serenity."

But that wasn't to be. Jeremiah came home to York only briefly before heading back to South America, anxious to start yet another new adventure. This time, as he was sailing across the Atlantic on business, his ship disappeared, lost at sea. Some think it must have been caught in a terrible storm, driven beneath the waves. Others have suggested that the ship was seized by pirates off the Spanish coast, and Jeremiah killed. Either way, the Powells' favourite son was dead.

It was just the beginning. The next scandal would be even bigger. So big, in fact, that it would drive Anne Murray Powell out of society altogether. The death of her beloved son wasn't the last time she'd lose a child at sea.

The Belle of York was in love. The young Anne Powell was named after her impressive mother, and was growing into one of the most beautiful and promising women in the capital. As a teenager, she was already charming and caring, with a striking fashion sense, a delight at dinners and balls.

Plenty of men would have been happy to have her hand in marriage. But the young Anne rejected her first serious suitor after a long courtship. Her next potential husband was Laurent Quetton St. George, a royalist refugee from France. He'd fought alongside Augustin Boiton de Fougères against the revolutionaries of Paris before they both fled to Upper Canada. But Anne Murray Powell refused to let her daughter marry "that animal" — not only was he French, he was extravagant. Unforgivable.

It wasn't until Anne was in her late twenties that she finally, truly fell in love.

John Beverley Robinson was one of the most promising young lawyers in Upper Canada. His father had served under John Graves Simcoe during the American Revolution; the family had come to Upper Canada with the first wave of settlers when Robinson was still a young boy. He was clearly destined for great things; he'd already become the acting attorney general at the tender age of twenty-one. In time, he would be elected to the Legislative Assembly and even be named as the chief justice, just like William Powell before him. In fact, the old judge had taken him under his wing as his protégé. One day, Robinson would rise to the very top of the Family Compact. He would eventually be knighted for his service and given a noble title: Sir John Beverley Robinson, 1st Baronet, of Toronto.

That was all still many years away, but his promise was obvious. Anne was more than smitten. She spent a lot of time with the young lawyer, falling deeply and hopelessly in love with him. It seemed to everyone as if the young lovers were destined to get married. To Anne Powell most of all. When Robinson travelled to England to further his legal education, she followed him there. They toured around London together as Robinson showed her the sights of the great imperial capital.

But Anne's heart was about to be broken. Robinson had fallen in love with another woman since arriving in London. He was already engaged. And his new sweetheart wasn't impressed by all the time he was spending with Anne. His fiancée demanded that he stop seeing the young Miss Powell. He agreed.

Reverend John Strachan, the Anglican minister who would go on to become the first Bishop of Toronto, was deeply worried by the news. He had once been Robinson's teacher. They would lead the Family Compact together for many years to come. He, like everyone else in York, had expected the young lawyer to marry Anne Powell. Breaking an engagement was very serious business. You could be sued for breach of promise. The priest sent Robinson a letter that aimed to get to the bottom of things. "One thing is certain," he wrote, "by every account the young [lady] was distracted after you … [her behaviour seems to] indicate some sort of expectation which to me requires some explanation to fully comprehend."

But it was too late. When they returned to York, Robinson began his new life with his new wife, Emma, while Anne Powell was left nursing a broken heart. And while she did try to find a new purpose for her life, exploring the possibility of becoming a teacher, that dream was quickly snuffed out by her mother. She didn't think her daughter's professional ambitions were appropriate for a woman from a respectable family.

It didn't take long for signs of trouble to appear. Anne was a changed woman — it now seems clear she was suffering from some kind of mental illness. Where she'd once been sweet and charming, she was now jealous, even tyrannical. She developed a terrible temper. And her love for John Beverley Robinson grew into a terrible obsession. She sent him troubling messages that one of their friends described as "some of the D——dest letters you ever saw." Emma Robinson burned many of them before her husband even had a chance to read them, refusing to let Anne into their house. One story, told many years later, even claimed that the Robinsons came home one night to find her there, uninvited, caressing their infant child.

When the Robinsons headed out on another trip to England, Anne Powell was determined to follow them. It would be a chance not only to be with her old sweetheart, but to break free from her parents' control. Everyone tried to talk her out of it: her mother, her brother, Reverend Strachan, even Robinson himself. But there was no stopping her. The best Anne Murray Powell could do was to delay her long enough to give the young lawyer a forty-eight-hour head start.

Even then, Anne wouldn't wait. She escaped from her mother's custody, running away from home without any money or luggage, racing out of town on a sleigh. She quickly caught up with the Robinsons and followed them all the way to New York City, where their ship to England was waiting for them. The young lawyer did everything he could to keep her from following any farther, convincing the ship's captain she shouldn't be allowed on board. And yet, still, she wouldn't leave them alone. She caught the very next ship she could find.

In the end, it took a storm to stop her. As her ship sailed past the southern coast of Ireland, it was caught in a terrible tempest. All afternoon and into the night, the gale kept pounding away at the vessel, until it was swamped under an onslaught of crashing waves. Six crew members were swept overboard, along with a passenger, the lifeboats, the masts, and everything else on deck. The ship was plunged into darkness. Below decks, the water was now knee deep. Cabins had been destroyed; pieces of wrecked furniture floated by. Many of those on board had been severely wounded. Some crew members gave up at that point, choosing to spend their final hours getting drunk rather than fighting to save their doomed ship.

Anne Powell wasn't going to give up that easily. The captain and some of the crew lashed themselves to the pumps to keep from being washed overboard while working desperately to keep the dying ship from filling with water. Powell joined them; the Belle of York began pumping away as fast as she could, doing everything in her power to save her own life and those of everyone on board.

All night, they worked, and into the wee hours of the morning. But they were drifting ever closer to the jagged rocks of the Irish coast. It was nearly three in the morning when the captain called everyone together, telling them what he'd known for hours: there was no escaping their fate. Soon, their ship would smash into those rocks and be torn apart. Some women couldn't help but scream in terror at the news; the rest watched in silent horror as the great cliffs of Ireland drew ever closer in the chaotic black night. "Our situation at that moment," one of the few survivors would later write, "is indescribable, and I can scarcely dwell upon, much less attempt to detail, its horrors."

Minutes later, the ship struck the rocks with the crack and snap of splintering wood. A shallow reef tore away the bottom of the boat. As the bow pitched downwards, more than a dozen dead bodies were thrown together at the front of the ship. And yet still, Anne Powell fought on, clinging to the wreckage, stubbornly holding on to what was left of the ship until it finally split in half, pitching her into the dark waves as they broke against the rocks. She had, as one witness described it, fought to the very last moment "with almost supernatural energy." Her body would later wash up on shore, identified only by a pin she wore. She was buried there in the Irish soil, laid to rest in the small graveyard of an old church near the cliffs where she had died.

Anne Murray Powell had been warring with her daughter for years. As they clashed over Anne's behaviour and her plans for her future, the grande dame of York found herself running out of patience. Her daughter was putting her family's reputation at risk. Powell worried the young woman had gone insane. And when Anne made her mad dash after John Beverley Robinson, it was the final straw. Her mother openly took the other side in the affair. It wasn't Anne she felt sorry for. "Dear little woman," she said of Emma Robinson, "my heart bleeds for her."

William agreed. He was in England at the time, sending a series of angry letters back home to his wife. He called his troubled daughter a "freak," a "fiend," a "miserable wretch," a "witch," a "monster in human disguise," a "Plague," and a "baneful Comet." He could barely stand to think of her. "Vanity, folly & malice are so blended in her Composition that I can only expect mortification when I hear of her." He worried that if he ever saw her again, he wouldn't be able to hold himself back. "My indignation is so uncontrollable, that I should fear some bit of violence might result."

The Powells talked about having Anne thrown into a lunatic asylum, into debtor's prison, or into a convent. But wherever she ended up, they were going to make one thing clear: her behaviour was so unacceptable, so harmful to their good name, that they would be forced to disown her forever. "If she returns," Anne Murray Powell wrote, "legal measures must be taken to ensure her separation from a family she has rendered miserable, by subjecting them to the feeling of disgrace."

It was then, at the height of their anger, that they received the terrible news. Their daughter was dead.

William was stunned. "It is not possible to describe to you my best friend," he wrote home to his wife, "the internal Effect of this Intelligence. Horror was at first the principal, Sorrow and regret succeeded and quite overpowered me for a time, when a thousand various Emotions succeeded." He wandered the streets of London in a daze — there, in a bizarre coincidence, he stumbled into John Beverley Robinson. His protégé pretended not to see him.

Anne Murray Powell was equally shocked. "It is impossible to say what I have felt and what I continue to feel," she wrote. "The recollection of her early promise, and the conviction of what she could and might have been to her Parents and her family, overpowers all resentful feelings.... I can think of nothing else, she is ever before my eyes.... I will not, I dare not doubt the felicity she now enjoys, and I seek consolation in the hope, that after all the afflictions of this miserable world we shall meet where sorrow never enters."

The shipwreck of the *Albion* marked the end of the reign of Anne Murray Powell. Her days ruling over the society of York were over. She had spent her entire life, ever since those humiliating days in the hat shop and her scandalous wedding, building a reputation as one of the most respectable women in Upper Canada. But now, her own family had failed her. One son had eloped and died. Another had been charged with piracy and then killed by pirates himself. And now her daughter, once so promising, had been drowned at sea in a desperate bid to follow the object of her obsession. The disgrace was simply too much. The Powell name was in tatters. Their credibility had been ruined.

Once, many years earlier, Anne Murray Powell had driven Elizabeth Small out of society for a lack of propriety. Now, she would apply the same standard to herself. The old grande dame of York withdrew from public life. She would accept an occasional invitation from the lieutenant-governor, or lend her name to a charitable cause, but never again would she preside over the extravagant balls and the elaborate dinners where she had once ruled supreme.

8

THE INSPECTOR GENERAL OF PRIVATE ACCOUNTS

His name is written across the neighbourhood where his forest once stood. Alexander Street and Wood Street remember him. And there at the corner where Alexander meets Church, you'll find a statue erected in his honour. He looks dashing and debonair. In one hand, he holds a top hat and gloves; in the other, an elegant cane. His long coat billows in the wind. He almost seems to smile. Today, he's celebrated as a social pioneer, commemorated and celebrated. But in 1810, Alexander Wood was driven from the town of York, banished into exile. And more than two hundred years later, the true details of his life remain shrouded in mystery.

Wood arrived in Canada during the very same year York was founded, leaving Scotland to settle in Kingston for a while before making his way to the tiny new capital. When he arrived at the end of the 1700s, there were only a few hundred people living in town; York was still little more than a collection of modest wooden buildings nestled between the forest and the lake. Wood quickly established himself as one of the most successful merchants in the humble capital, serving an elite clientele. He imported all the best goods from London and Glasgow, bringing a small slice of British sophistication to the frontier. His customers included the most powerful people in town, including the lieutenant-governor himself.

In fact, some of them were more than just customers. Wood's best friends included York's most influential figures. He was particularly close with the Powells, spending much of his time visiting them at their home. He was good friends with Reverend John Strachan, too. "Our sentiments agree almost upon everything," the priest enthused. Soon, Wood was appointed as a magistrate, helping to uphold and enforce the law. Some sources suggest he was also hired as inspector general of public accounts, taking on an important role in the colony's finances. He was a respected leader and entrepreneur with a bright and promising future.

And then it all came crashing down.

The details are hazy, and the truth unclear. But it all started in 1810, when Wood claimed he was approached by a woman named Miss Bailey. According to his account, Miss Bailey told him she'd been raped. Since Wood was a magistrate, she hoped he would be able to bring her attacker to justice. There was one vital clue: during the assault, Miss Bailey had scratched her assailant on his genitals with a pair of scissors. If Wood could find the man with wounded privates, he would find the rapist.

And so, he approached a series of men, explaining they were suspected of the rape, and asking them to unveil their naked groin so he could check and see whether they bore the scratch that would solve the case. One by one, the men agreed. But none of them was scratched and none of them appreciated Wood's intimate examination.

The story spread quickly through the small town. Wood's investigation became a scandal. He found himself the object of ridicule — even fear. His business dried up; customers refused to come anywhere near his shop. A new nickname was hurled at him as he walked in the street; they called him the "Inspector General of *Private* Accounts."

"I have laid myself open to ridicule & malevolence, which I know not how to meet;" Wood complained to Judge Powell, "that the thing will be made the subject of mirth and a handle to my enemies for a sneer I have every reason to expect."

But it was more serious than just a bit of public ridicule. Many believed that by forcing the men to undress, Wood had seriously abused his position as a magistrate. An official inquiry into the affair seemed inevitable.

But Alexander Wood had powerful friends. Even though he was horrified by what Wood had done, Judge Powell stepped in and quashed the investigation, letting him go free as long as he promised to leave York and return home to Scotland. That autumn, the merchant packed up his things, left a clerk in charge of his shop, and set sail back across the Atlantic.

His exile didn't last forever. Wood was able to return after a couple of years — and with the town distracted by the horrors of the War of 1812, it seemed for a while as if he would be able to slip under the radar just enough to carry on his life in Canada, returning to his store and his position as a magistrate. He even renewed his friendship with John Strachan, dining at the priest's home every week.

Not everyone forgot, though. The Powells never forgave him. Many years later, when Wood was appointed to a panel assessing war claims, Powell refused to swear him in. The old scandal was stirred up once more. This time it ended up in court, where all the sordid details were rehashed for the official record. Wood won, but Powell refused to pay the damages — and the story would follow the merchant for the rest of his life. He would remain a bachelor to the end of his days, raising more than a few eyebrows in a province where homosexuality was not only illegal, but punishable by death according to the letter of the law. Even two centuries later, his notorious scandal is depicted on a plaque attached to the plinth of his statue. He kneels down to examine the exposed crotch of a man with his pants down around his knees, the bare bum polished by the passersby who rub it for luck.

The statue stands on what was once Wood's own land. Upon returning to York, he bought a patch of countryside beyond the town limits. It was a big swath of old forest, which stood northeast of Yonge and Carlton Streets. Some say the townspeople adopted a derisive nickname for that forest — Molly Wood's Bush — since *molly* was a homophobic epithet. In time, Wood's woods were swallowed up by the city. The grand old trees came crashing down, replaced by homes and stores, restaurants and bars. Today, more than two hundred years after the scandal, Wood's old land has become home to the heart of Toronto's LGBTQ+ community. The Church Street Village now stands where those old trees once did.

Wood has become something of a historical gay icon, adopted as a seminal queer figure in the city. But the truth of his life remains a mystery. It's hard to know what really happened back in 1810, whether Wood made an innocent but terrible mistake, abused his position, or concocted an ill-conceived cover story for consensual sexual relationships with men who were quick to distance themselves once the story went public. In a town where being honest about your sexuality risked not only social ostracization, but exile and even death, it's impossible to know the truth.

We'll almost certainly never know for sure whether Alexander Wood was actually gay. We're not even completely sure what he looked like. The bronze statue that stands at the corner of Alexander and Church is based on the only image of him we think we have: a simple portrait that might not even be him at all. As Ed Jackson points out in the book *Any Other Way: How Toronto Got Queer*, the scandalous magistrate is, in many ways, an invention.

The story of Alexander Wood is far from the last time in the city's history that someone's sexuality would be shrouded in mystery. Thanks to the prejudices that ruled in the town of York back in the early 1800s — and in the city of Toronto for far too long after that — we know very little about queer pioneers in the city's founding days. They were there, of course, but forced to live and love in secret. Wood has become a necessary legend, a quasi-mythical figure who stands in for all those we will never know. A confident, sophisticated gay man, top hat and cane at the ready, his coat billowing in the breeze, immortalized in bronze.

THE WAR OF 1812

9
THE MYTH OF THE
STIRRUP CUP

There's an old story about the willow trees of Trinity Bellwoods Park. Some say an aged grove of willows used to stand in that place, planted more than two hundred years ago. Back when they were young and new, they stood in a forest far outside the growing town. The willows were surrounded by big old oaks and pines, maples, beech, and ash. They watched over the Garrison Creek as it splashed by on its way down toward the lake. It was a remote place. To reach it, you'd have to make the trek up from Fort York along a rough dirt trail, or the long journey from town along the new Dundas Road. In the early 1800s, Trinity Bellwoods was still the domain of wolves and deer.

There was a little cottage nearby, a modest frame house surrounded by the deep forest. This is where the Shaw family lived. They called their home Oak Hill. It was there, in that little house, that Isaac and Sophia are said to have met for the first time and fallen in love.

According to the stories, during some of those romantic visits, the young couple would slip away for a while,
disappearing to make love under the grove of willow
trees her father had planted. Those trees were said to
have stood there for at least a century to come — and
their descendants might still grow there to this day, a
reminder of a tragic love affair and the doomed soldier
who would become a Canadian hero.

Sophia Shaw was just a toddler when she arrived at
York, the daughter of an officer in the Queen's Rangers.
Aeneas Shaw had fought under Simcoe during the
American Revolution and fled north to New Brunswick
after the war; all his property had been seized by the
rebels. When he heard Simcoe was being put in charge
of Upper Canada and getting the Queen's Rangers back
together, Shaw was determined to be a part of it. He led
a dozen men on a dangerous expedition to meet up with
their old commander in Montreal, walking there from
the Maritimes in the dead of winter, trekking hundreds
of kilometres on snowshoes to join him.

Shaw and his family eventually moved to Niagara,
where he was picked as a member of Simcoe's Executive
Council. It was there that Sophia was born. She was
only a year old when her father was sent across the lake
to Toronto. He commanded the first group of Queen's
Rangers to begin clearing the forest and building Fort
York, preparing to defend the tiny new capital from an
American invasion before it had even been founded.

Aeneas and his wife, Ann, soon brought their
whole family across the lake with them. They built a

small log cabin near Fort York — which they jokingly called Lambeth Palace in tribute to the archbishop of Canterbury's truly palatial residence in England — and another on their country estate further up the creek. That one became their main residence. But a log cabin was far from enough room for such a big family — by 1798, the Shaws had seven sons and six daughters — so they built their little frame house nearby. They called it Oak Hill, after their old home in Scotland. That's where they say Sophia Shaw met Major-General Isaac Brock for the first time.

Brock was a British officer, frustrated that he'd been sent to the colonies instead of to fight in the wars that had been raging across Europe ever since the French Revolution. He'd been in Canada for nearly a decade now, readying defences in preparation for an invasion by the Americans. During his time at York, he was a frequent visitor to Oak Hill, consulting with Major-General Shaw as war with the United States drew ever closer.

It was during one of those visits that he must have met Sophia. We only have a single glimpse of what Brock looked like: one portrait painted during his lifetime, endlessly copied and recopied in the centuries since. But we know he was tall, good-looking, and brave. Sophia was gentle and kind, loved by all who knew her. She was still a teenager back then, and Brock in his early forties. But according to the legends, the two fell deeply in love.

They longed to be together. But Isaac Brock was far from a rich man; in fact, he was sending much of his relatively modest salary to his brother, insisting on paying

him back for buying Brock's military commission —
rank was often purchased back then. Until Brock paid
his debt and established himself on a secure financial
footing, he was sure he couldn't offer his new bride the
life she deserved. Rather than getting married right away,
the couple got secretly engaged. Or so the story goes.

That's when tragedy struck. In 1812, all their worst
fears were realized. In recent years, tensions between the
British and the Americans had been reaching a boiling
point. As war between the French revolutionaries and
the rest of Europe engulfed the continent, a French general had worked his way up the ranks to seize power and
declare himself emperor of France: Napoleon Bonaparte.
He'd won victory after victory and now controlled nearly all of continental Europe. Britain was the last major
power left standing against him.

The United States was officially neutral and sold
goods to both sides. When Britain tried to ban them
from trading with Napoleon, the Americans were enraged. And when the Royal Navy, desperate for man-
power, began to stop and board American ships looking
for deserters, the Americans got even angrier. The British
weren't even being picky about who they grabbed off
those ships; sometimes they seized anyone who seemed
like they might even be a little bit British, forcing them to
join the Royal Navy and the fight against Napoleon. They
called it "impressment." When American ships resisted,
British ships opened fire. American blood was spilled.

The bitter wounds of the American Revolution had
never fully healed. And now, with the British distracted

by Napoleon and showing ever more disrespect to the young United States, the time to settle old scores had come. The Americans declared war on Britain and made plans to invade the Canadian colonies. The War of 1812 had begun.

Many in the United States assumed it would be a quick and easy victory. Thomas Jefferson was confident enough to declare, "The acquisition of Canada this year, as far as the neighborhood of Quebec, will be a mere matter of marching." And while that quote has been used to poke fun at him ever since, many Canadian settlers assumed the same thing. In the years since the revolution, tens of thousands of Americans had moved north of the border, drawn to Upper Canada by the promise of free land. Surely those Americans would welcome the chance to be brought back under the Stars and Stripes? "We can take Canada without soldiers," the American secretary of war predicted. "We have only to send officers into the provinces, and the people, disaffected towards their own government, will rally round our standard." As the United States planned the invasion, they were confident they would be welcomed as liberators. Upper Canada would soon be theirs.

But not if Isaac Brock had anything to say about it.

He'd spent much of his life preparing for this moment. Over the course of the last decade, his impact had been felt across Upper and Lower Canada: he'd built defensive towers, walls, and batteries; reinforced fortifications; trained local militia; and built alliances with the First Nations. When the Americans invaded, Brock was ready for them.

It all started at Detroit. In July 1812, American general William Hull kicked off the invasion by leading his forces across the river into Upper Canada, looting and burning farms and homes before retreating back across the border into the safety of Fort Detroit.

That's when Brock arrived from York to meet his most important ally. The Shawnee chief Tecumseh had built a confederacy of more than two dozen First Nations from around the Great Lakes. He led thousands of warriors in support of the Canadian colonies in return for the promise of an independent Indigenous nation — a promise that would be broken as soon as the war was won.

At Detroit, Brock and Tecumseh came up with a clever plan to defeat the Americans. Thanks to intercepted messages, they knew Hull's men were unhappy with his leadership and that he was rapidly losing confidence. They also knew he had a racist fear of Indigenous people. He was vulnerable to a bluff. And so, Brock dressed his Canadian militia in the uniforms of professional British soldiers to make Hull think they were a more impressive force than they actually were. Tecumseh, meanwhile, had his warriors march through the woods surrounding the fort, looping back over and over again so they seemed like an immense army. Brock sent the American general a message playing on his racist fears: "Sir; ... it is far from my inclination to join a war of extermination, but you must be aware that the numerous body of Indians who have attached themselves to my troops will be beyond my control the moment the contest commences."

As the assault began, with Brock riding confidently toward the fort at the head of his army, Hull lost his nerve. He surrendered. Brock had won his first battle without losing a single man.

The western frontier was safe for now. But the Americans were planning a four-pronged attack. Next up: Niagara. An American army was already gathering on the other side of the river, getting ready to invade. So, Brock hurried east.

He'd been knighted for his quick thinking and heroism at Detroit, but thanks to the heroism he was about to display at Niagara, he wouldn't live long enough to hear the news.

It was in the wee hours of a windy October morning, long before the sun rose, that the Americans launched their attack. The invading army, thousands strong, rowed across the river as British artillery opened fire and musket balls hissed through the air. Many were killed on the crossing, corpse-filled boats drifted downriver into Lake Ontario, but the Americans eventually secured a foothold on the Canadian side and began their climb up the steep cliffs of the escarpment. The Battle of Queenston Heights had begun.

Many familiar names were there to meet the invaders that fateful day: the old fur trader Jean Baptiste Rousseau; the young lawyer John Beverley Robinson; Joseph Brant's son John. And the battle would cement Isaac Brock's place among them in the history of Upper Canada.

By the time Brock was roused from his slumber at Fort George, several kilometres away, the Americans had fought their way to the top of the cliffs and seized the heights. It was about seven in the morning when he arrived, gathering a few men at the base of the escarpment. The Americans were far above, obscured by the trees. "Take a breath, boys," he told his men, "you will need it in a few moments." Then he dismounted from his horse, drew his sabre, lifted it high into the sky, and led the charge.

Brock rushed up the steep hill through a hail of fire as American riflemen took aim, his men following close behind. His bright red coat must have made an easy target. The musket ball hit him in the chest, just above his heart. You can still see the hole it made in his coat; it's on display at the Canadian War Museum in Ottawa. The general fell to the ground, his lungs filling with blood as one of his men rushed to his side. "Are you much hurt, sir?" Brock couldn't reply, just placed his hand on his chest as his strength faded. His men would win the battle, but he wouldn't live to see it.

There have been many stories told about Brock's final moments. Some say he used his last breath to give one final battle cry: "Push on, brave York volunteers!" Others claim he asked those present to hide his body so the sight of their fallen general wouldn't sap the morale of his men. John Beverley Robinson gave a less elegant account of what he saw: an American cannonball striking down one of the men at the general's side, pitching his corpse awkwardly on top of the dying hero. Others say Brock's horse was killed with him, buried in the same grave high atop the heights, where the fallen hero is now remembered by a massive column that towers above the cliffs he died to defend.

But perhaps the most heartwarming legend of all those that swirl around Brock's death is the legend of Sophia Shaw. Her older sister Isabelle lived not far from Queenston, in the town we now call Niagara-on-the-Lake. Isabelle had married John Powell — son of Anne Murray Powell — and Sophia would sometimes venture across the lake to visit them. They say that just a few days before the battle, Sophia arrived to attend a ball at Fort George with her beloved Isaac. So that's where she was on that bloody day: at her sister's house in town.

According to the story, Brock woke in the wee hours of the morning to the sound of American cannons booming in the distance. As church bells rang out in warning, the general leaped onto his loyal black steed, Alfred, and rushed out of Fort George in the dark, racing through the cold, wet October morning to join the fight. As Alfred's hoofbeats thundered along the town's muddy roads, the citizens came to their windows to see Brock on his way and offer him a prayer.

But according to the story, he didn't head straight to the battlefield. Instead, he made one quick stop, sparing a few moments to pass the Powells' house and say goodbye to his sweetheart. Secretly engaged and deeply in love, he and Sophia said one final farewell before he headed off to battle. She handed him a coffee in a stirrup cup, made for drinking on horseback. He downed the drink, said goodbye, and rode away to his death. In this version of the story, as he lay dying from the musket ball in his chest, one last word escaped his lips: "Sophia."

Niagara-on-the-Lake — called Newark back then — would suffer terribly during the war. The spring after Brock was killed, the Americans seized the town and occupied it for seven months. When they were finally driven out, they set fire to it as they left, razing it nearly to the ground. The Powells' home was burned with it. A new house was built on the same spot, which is still there today. Now it's a bed and breakfast called Brockamour, in tribute to the tragic love story.

They say Sophia stayed loyal to her beloved Isaac even in death. According to some, she enjoyed a long and healthy life, but never married. Her heart still belonged to her fallen soldier. Even years after he died, when she appeared at a garden party held at the lieutenant-governor's residence on King Street, she was seen in full mourning dress, her face covered by a black veil. She lived a long and lonely life, passing away at the age of eighty, buried at the Necropolis Cemetery in Cabbagetown.

Others say she followed her sweetheart to the grave just a few years after he died, and spent her final days locked in a room at the Powells' new home. Passersby could hear her sobs even on the street, until she finally died of a broken heart. Some say that on certain quiet nights, as you walk through the heart of Niagara-on-the-Lake, you can still hear the faint sound of a woman's sobs, the crying ghost of Sophia Shaw.

In the end, whichever version of the story you tell, it's almost certainly a myth. Most historians seem to believe there's no evidence Sir Isaac Brock ever fell in love with Sophia Shaw, was secretly engaged to her, or said a tragic final farewell with a drink from a stirrup cup. But the story has lived on, passed down from one generation to the next, a romantic piece of Canada's founding myth.

Brock was a British soldier who didn't want to be in Canada and who died moments into his first real battle on Canadian soil, but he is still remembered as a national hero. With his quick victory at Detroit and his heroic charge at Niagara, he'd shown that the colonies of British North America wouldn't be so easily conquered. The Americans wouldn't be welcomed as liberators. There were thousands willing to fight, and Brock had given them hope they might even be able to win. By the end of the war, it would be clear that the settlers north of the border weren't the same as those to the south. They were something different. And in the centuries since, as generations of Canadians have told stories about where the idea of their nation began, they've told stories of Sir Isaac Brock — a man of myth and legend as much as flesh and blood.

10
SHOULD I FALL

On the last night of his life, Zebulon Pike sat aboard a warship anchored off the coast of Toronto. The USS *Madison* rolled gently in the waves along with the rest of the American fleet: fourteen ships carrying nearly two thousand soldiers. They waited patiently there in the dark, biding their time in the waters just to the south of the peninsula. In the morning, they would attack York.

The Americans were desperate for a victory. The first few months of the War of 1812 had been a disaster for them, thanks in large part to the victories of Sir Isaac Brock. They'd failed to gain a foothold on Canadian soil before winter set in. Now, as spring arrived and the waterways thawed, they needed a quick win to boost morale. York seemed like a perfect target. It was tiny, isolated, and much less well-defended than the city of Kingston, but it still held symbolic value as the capital. And at the foot of Bay Street, York's shipwrights were hard at work building a sloop of war named after their greatest hero. When it was done, HMS *Sir Isaac Brock* would be one of the most powerful warships ever to sail the Great Lakes. If the Americans could seize it and finish it themselves, they could control Lake Ontario and secure access to the St. Lawrence. If all went according to plan, they could sail downriver and besiege Montreal. Victory at York might eventually lead to victory in the entire war.

And so, on an April day in 1813, the American fleet sailed across Lake Ontario. They were spotted at dusk; a lookout perched atop the Scarborough Bluffs sounded the alarm. That night, York was alive with activity: cannons roared in warning as townspeople braced for the impending invasion — some rushing to evacuate the town, others grabbing their muskets. Every man between the ages of sixteen and sixty was expected to defend the town.

Meanwhile, out there in the darkness, the American fleet waited. And Zebulon Pike sat down to write his last love letter.

Her name was Clarissa Harlowe Brown. He called her Clara and she called him Montgomery. She was his cousin, tall, with dark hair, and so serious that she seemed older than her eighteen years, always wearing black. She was well educated, wrote her diary in French, and would collect an impressive library over the course of her life, filling it with books in three languages.

But there was a problem when the young cousins fell in love. Clara's father opposed the match and refused to give them permission to get married. It wasn't, as you might imagine, because Zebulon was his nephew and the young lovers were related. Instead, it was Pike's profession that Captain Brown didn't like. He was a military man himself, a veteran of the American Revolution, and he knew what kind of sacrifices the wife of a soldier was forced to make. It wasn't the life he wanted for his daughter. He refused to give the couple his blessing.

But that didn't stop them. Zebulon and Clara eloped, sneaking away to Cincinnati where they tied the knot. Her father was furious; he forbade his nephew-turned-son-in-law from ever stepping foot on his property again.

He was right to be worried. The couple's life together was hard. Clara didn't like living in a military fort surrounded by soldiers. And her husband was away for long periods of time. He would become known as one of the great American explorers, sent off to map the West. One of the most famous mountains in the United States is named after him. "Pikes Peak" replaced the ancient Ute name for the mountain where their history says they were created: *Tava*. Today, it's nicknamed "America's Mountain."

Things only got harder for the Pikes when the War of 1812 began. Zebulon was called off to join the fight, spending the war's first summer training troops on Staten Island and then a miserable winter running out of supplies in Plattsburg. He was finally called into action as spring drew near. Promoted to the rank of brigadier general, he led his men on a gruelling winter march north to Lake Ontario, struggling through three feet of snow. One of his men was killed by the cold; several lost limbs to frostbite. A month later, they boarded their ships, bound for York. "If we go into Canada," Pike had written to his brother, "you will hear of my fame or of my death."

As dawn broke above the shores of Lake Ontario, the attack began. The American warships sailed around the peninsula — but stopped short of trying to sneak past Fort York into the bay. Instead, they dropped anchor outside the harbour, not far from where the Exhibition grounds are today. From there, they would launch their invasion.

The leader of the operation was supposed to be an American general called Henry Dearborn. But when the time came, the old general found he was too seasick to lead the attack. So, he stayed behind while his men climbed into small, flat-bottomed boats to be lowered over the sides of the great warships.

As the Americans rowed toward shore, the defenders of York opened fire. Musket balls sizzled through the air. Mississauga and Ojibwe warriors fired from the edge of the forest and were quickly joined by professional British soldiers in their bright red coats. It was there on the shores of Humber Bay that the Battle of York claimed its first lives: dozens lay dead and bleeding as the invaders returned fire, struggling to row ashore and then clamber up the steep banks toward the men hidden among the trees. The great guns of the American warships pounded away at the shore. Fragments of skeletons would be found in that soil for at least a century to come.

Brigadier-General Pike watched from the *Madison* but couldn't just stand by while his men risked their lives. "By God, I can't stay here any longer," he told one of his staff. "Come, jump into the boat." And with that, Pike rowed in to join the battle and take over command of the attack. It would prove to be a fatal decision.

It was hard fighting, but the defenders were badly outnumbered. Bit by bit, Pike and his Americans pushed them back, securing a beachhead. From there, they began to advance onward into the trees as a marching band played "Yankee Doodle Dandy." American sharp-shooters led the way, their green coats blending into the trees. They advanced slowly over the soggy ground and melting snow, using fallen logs as cover as they picked off the defenders one by one.

Hours passed before they finally emerged from the forest at the ruins of Fort Rouillé. There, a defensive battery was waiting for them, armed with artillery. It opened fire, grapeshot hurtling through the air toward them. Pike ordered his buglers to sound the advance and the Americans rushed forward as their ships bombarded the battery.

Before the Americans could reach it, the battery exploded. A British soldier had accidentally dropped a lit fuse into a pile of ammunition cartridges. The blast ripped the battery apart, knocked out one of its guns, and killed ten of its defenders. The rest had no choice but to retreat, scrambling back across the open ground into the relative safety of Fort York.

Zebulon Pike waited. It was now a little after noon. With the warships pounding away at the fort and the defenders all withdrawn from the field, he assumed the battle was coming to an end. He ordered his men to halt within striking distance of the fort and lie down while they waited for a white flag to appear.

Pike had only minutes left to live. He took a seat on a tree stump, spending his final moments questioning a prisoner while he waited for Fort York to surrender.

That's when it happened.

The ground shook and a great roar split the air, so loud it could be heard all the way across the lake in Niagara. There was a flash and a shockwave that raced out from the fort, hurling the American soldiers backwards — some soaring twenty metres through the air. It burst lungs and tore through intestines. A great shower of debris — stone, wood, and metal — was thrown high into the air before it came racing back toward the ground in a deadly hail. It tore through skin and crushed bone. Dozens of American soldiers lay dead. Hundreds were wounded. The great magazine of Fort York, storing tens of thousands of pounds of gunpowder, cannonballs, and musket rounds, had exploded. The blast was one of the biggest in the entire history of North America.

The British general had ordered the destruction of the grand magazine as his soldiers abandoned the fort, not wanting the ammunition and supplies to fall into American hands. The explosion must have been bigger than even he imagined it would be. Some of his own men were killed in the blast. But the full force was directed toward the attacking Americans.

Zebulon Pike was right in its path. As the smoke cleared, he was found lying on the ground, crushed by a boulder with his ribs caved in. There are a few different versions of what happened then. Some say he was carried back to his ship to die, some that he spent his final moments with his head resting on a bloody Union Jack. Others suggested that he used his final breath to urge his men to victory: "Push on, my brave fellows, and avenge your general!"

The Americans were furious. They'd won the battle. Fort York lay in ruins; the Stars and Stripes now flew above the wreckage. But the British soldiers were retreating to Kingston instead of staying behind to be taken prisoner. A column of black smoke was rising from the horizon as HMS *Sir Isaac Brock* was burned rather than being allowed to fall into their hands. And their beloved brigadier-general had been killed. As far as the invaders were concerned, the explosion of the magazine had been a war crime.

And so now they would sack York. The two sides had reached an agreement for the surrender of the town: the Americans could ransack as much public property as they wanted, but private property was to be protected. That was something Pike had already told his men before the attack began. "The poor Canadians have been forced into this war," he wrote in his orders, "and their property should be held sacred." Those who disobeyed, they were told, would be shot.

But now, there was no holding them back. General Dearborn dragged his feet when it came time to sign the articles of capitulation, allowing his soldiers to run riot through the town. For nearly a week, they looted and pillaged homes and public buildings alike. They burned the Parliament buildings and the lieutenant-governor's residence to the ground.

With the British soldiers having abandoned the town to its fate, it was up to York's own residents to save it. Some local leaders, like William Powell and Reverend Strachan, stayed behind, risking their own lives to protect what they could. Strachan, in particular, would be remembered as a hero for his actions that week. He badgered General Dearborn into signing the surrender, tended to wounded soldiers, and nearly got shot when he confronted some of the marauding looters himself. They say that when the Americans returned a few months later, Strachan gave them such a talking to that they agreed to return the library books they'd stolen the first time. The stories helped to cement his position as a leader of the Family Compact.

After six days of destruction, the American fleet finally sailed out of Toronto Bay, leaving the battered capital in peace. The ships were weighed down with treasure as they left. The invading soldiers had stolen everything they could get their hands on: money, silver, furniture, food, booze, tobacco, even the town's fire engine and the horse that went with it. But there was more than just booty on board. One of those ships was carrying Zebulon Pike's last love letter.

The night before the battle, once he'd finished writing, Zebulon Pike had handed his letter to his aide. "Should I fall and you survive," he told him, "hand this yourself to Mrs. Pike." And so, Clara was given the heartbreaking message she'd long been dreading, the one her father must have worried about all those years ago when he tried to save her from the life of an army wife:

> My Dear Clara, — we are now standing on and off the harbor of York, which we will attack at daylight in the morning: I shall dedicate these last moments to you, my love, and to-morrow throw all other ideas but my country to the winds.... I have no new injunction, no new charge to give you, nor no new idea to communicate; yet we love to commune with those we love, more especially when we conceive it may be the last time in this world. Should I fall, defend my memory, and only believe, had I lived, I would have aspired to deeds worthy of your husband. — Remember me, with a father's love — a father's care, to our dear daughter; and believe me to be, with the warmest sentiments of love and friendship,
>
> Your MONTGOMERY.

11
FITZGIBBON'S LEAVE

The siege was beginning. Thousands of British and Canadian soldiers were gathered outside Fort Erie ready to attack. It was the summer of 1814 — two years since the Americans had first invaded. The war had taken a brutal toll on York and the rest of Upper Canada. But every time the Americans attempted to invade Canada, they'd been pushed back — and with Napoleon now defeated in Europe, the British could send even more troops to defend their Canadian colonies.

A few weeks earlier, the Americans had launched yet another invasion across the Niagara River into Upper Canada, but they'd failed to make much progress. They'd been forced to retreat to Fort Erie, a British fort they'd seized; the last on the Canadian side of the river. The British and Canadians had come to push them back across the river, back across the border into Buffalo, back out of Canada and into the United States. Maybe, this time, for good.

But it wouldn't be easy. There were more than two thousand Americans inside the fort. They'd spent the last week hard at work improving its defences. They'd expanded the earthworks. Mounted cannons. Dug a ditch and lined it with sharpened sticks. They'd cut down all the surrounding trees so there would be nowhere for the attackers to hide. It was clear that the Siege of Fort Erie would be a bloody battle.

In fact, the blood had already begun to flow. The British had launched a raid across the river, trying to cut off the Americans' supplies before the real battle got underway. But it ended in disaster: nearly a dozen men were killed. Two more were lost during a much more successful mission to seize the American ships bombarding them from the river. And now, the British commander was finally on the brink of mounting a full-scale assault on the fort. The cannons were ready to open fire, to pound away at the thick stone walls ahead of the attack. More men were surely about to die.

That's when Captain James FitzGibbon asked if he could take some time off.

It was a wildly unexpected request. Captain FitzGibbon was no coward, far from it; he would go down in history as one of the great heroes of the war. He'd signed up with the army as a fifteen-year-old in Ireland, and he'd fought his first battle while he was still just a teenager. By the early 1800s, he'd found himself in Canada serving under Isaac Brock. Impressed by the young soldier, Brock had promoted him, making him an officer even though at the time it was usually necessary for a soldier to buy his way into those ranks. The decision paid off. When the Americans invaded, FitzGibbon quickly proved his worth: making a dangerous run down the rapids of the St. Lawrence, commanding troops at the Battle of Stoney Creek, leading a small group of soldiers on daring guerrilla raids. They called the unit he led "The Bloody Boys." They called him "The Green Tiger."

A year before the Siege of Fort Erie, FitzGibbon had cemented his place in Canadian history — thanks to a woman in Niagara. When American soldiers forced her to put them up in her home, it backfired spectacularly. Laura Secord was no fan of the invaders; she was still nursing her husband back to health after he'd been wounded at the Battle of Queenston Heights. When she overhead their plans to attack, she set off alone through the countryside, walking for thirty kilometres to find the British and warn them. It was Captain FitzGibbon she found. Thanks to her help, and the contribution of a few hundred Haudenosaunee warriors, FitzGibbon and the British won the Battle of Stoney Creek.

The victory helped turn FitzGibbon into a popular hero. No one doubted his bravery. But the war was growing ever more bitter. The Battle of York had sparked a new, more brutal phase of the conflict — a spiralling cycle of revenge. The War of 1812 had already claimed thousands of lives. FitzGibbon had seen dozens, even hundreds, of men fall around him. Brock had been killed. So had Tecumseh, his corpse torn apart by American soldiers in search of morbid souvenirs. There was no reason for FitzGibbon to believe he would be spared. With the Siege of Fort Erie about to begin, he was understandably worried that he would die there on the banks of the Niagara

River. And while he was perfectly willing to lay down his life for Canada, he now had more to worry about than just himself. James FitzGibbon had fallen in love.

Mary Haley was the daughter of a retired soldier, a Loyalist veteran of the American Revolution who now ran an inn in Kingston. No one's entirely sure how she met the young FitzGibbon, but it seems to have happened during his early days in Canada, when he was stationed at Quebec City serving under Brock. They say that Mary won his heart during those two long years of war by knitting him an endless supply of socks — having heard that provisions were so low on the Niagara front that some soldiers were forced to go barefoot. By the time FitzGibbon found himself outside the walls of Fort Erie, the couple was engaged. The only reason they weren't already married was that FitzGibbon was worried about money, and was putting off the ceremony until he was financially secure.

But now, with death looming, FitzGibbon realized he might have waited too long. He came up with a plan. He approached his colonel and made his extraordinary request: he wanted three days leave, just as the siege was about to begin. He didn't give any reason. He simply promised it was deeply important to him and that he would be back before the real battle began.

It was a spectacularly bold move. Most soldiers would have been denied. But there was no questioning the loyalty of the Green Tiger, no reason to worry he would run away and never return. The colonel granted his request.

The race was on.

FitzGibbon mounted his horse and rode like the wind. The journey took him hundreds of kilometres over rough roads — little more than dirt paths carved through deep forests — all the way around the Niagara Peninsula and then east toward Kingston. He sent word ahead to his fiancée; he asked her to meet him partway, outside the church in Adolphustown, near Prince Edward County.

It was there that the ceremony was performed. As soon as it was over, the soldier said goodbye to his new wife — right there on the steps of the church — got back up on his horse, and rode away, rushing back to the battle at Fort Erie.

Now, if he died, Mary wouldn't be left empty-handed. As his fiancée, she would have gotten nothing. But as the wife of a captain, she was promised a pension if he died. If he was destined to take his last breath on that battlefield, FitzGibbon's final act would be to take care of the woman he loved.

The siege was indeed bloody. The bombardment by the British cannons failed to make much of a dent in the fort's big stone walls. And when the soldiers launched their initial assaults, marching forward through rain and darkness, they were cut to pieces. Officers were struck down by muskets. Soldiers were torn apart by cannonballs. Some panicked and fled. Others drowned in the river, swept away by the swift current as they tried to swim around the American defences. Even worse, in an echo of what had happened at Fort York a year earlier, a large supply of ammunition exploded, leaving hundreds of men dead or wounded, corpses burned black by the fiery blast. The attack was an utter disappointment. They'd failed to take the fort, and while there were only a few dozen casualties on the American side, nearly a thousand British and Canadian soldiers were dead or wounded. The surgeon was forced to work for three straight days and nights without rest, desperately stitching men back together. They say that at roll call the morning after the assault, soldiers openly wept at the number who were missing.

But all was not lost. The Americans were still trapped inside the fort. When they tried to fight their way out a few weeks later, they failed to break through. By the time the British withdrew — leaving the Americans with their small, useless foothold on the Canadian side of the border — winter was approaching. Yet another summer had passed without the Americans making any real headway in their invasion of Canada. Their grand plan — a sweeping march through Niagara, across the Burlington Heights, and on into the capital of York — had never gotten off the ground.

In fact, things had gone so badly that the United States was now in danger of being wiped out completely. The British attacked them head on, in the heart of their own country. At the same time FitzGibbon was fighting at the Siege of Fort Erie, the British attacked and occupied the American capital. British troops marched through the streets of Washington, DC, setting fire to the White House and the Capitol Building — in part, as revenge for the burning of York. It was only a great thunderstorm and a powerful tornado that finally drove them out of the city.

Before the winter fully set in, the Americans abandoned Fort Erie. And Canada with it. They retreated back across the border, blowing up the fort behind them as they left so the British couldn't reclaim it. For three straight summers, they'd tried to conquer Canada. And for three straight summers, they'd failed. They would never try again. Just a few weeks later, on Christmas Eve, 1814, a peace treaty was signed. The War of 1812 was over.

We'll never be able to fully understand the extent of the toll it took. The psychological trauma that would last for decades to come, the relationships strained and broken. Countless marriages and families had been torn apart. Tens of thousands of people had been killed. But James FitzGibbon wasn't one of them. He was still alive.

With the war finally over, the captain and his wife began their life together. They moved to the capital, living inside Fort York itself. Mary would never be much of a socialite, but James became one of York's leading citizens. The reputation he had built for himself during the war was only the beginning. FitzGibbon would spend the next three decades defending his city from violence, often acting as a peacekeeper between the warring factions that threatened to tear Toronto apart.

The American threat that had loomed over Upper Canada ever since the province was founded would eventually fade away. But blood would still be spilled in Toronto's streets. Widows would be made; families struck down by grief. Next time, it wouldn't be a foreign enemy threating the peace of the city, it would neighbour fighting neighbour. With the American invaders defeated, a new battle approached: a violent clash over the future of Canada and what kind of a country it should be.

The next time James FitzGibbon took up arms against an enemy, he'd be facing a very different threat. A quarter of a century after the Siege of Fort Erie, FitzGibbon would find himself on the front lines yet again. This time, he'd be fighting to defend Toronto from its own citizens.

Rebellion was brewing.

DEMOCRACY

12

THE REBEL ISABEL

Isabel Baxter can't have had any idea what she was in for. She was still only a teenager when her ship docked at Quebec City, dwarfed by the soaring cliff that rose high above the great river below. She had come to make a new life in Canada — with a new husband. He was out there somewhere on shore, waiting for her to disembark. She hadn't seen William in years — not since they were both children attending the same one-room schoolhouse back in Scotland. She couldn't even remember what he looked like. But this stranger was the man she was about to marry.

It wasn't her idea. Or even his. It was his mother who made the match. Arranged marriages were a common practice back then, when Canadian women were in short supply and men were hard to find in Scotland. The old woman must have hoped that Isabel — a solid and reliable girl — would have a positive influence on her son. William had spent his Scottish youth drinking and gambling, even fathered an illegitimate child. But now his mother was following him to Canada where she could keep an eye on him. She brought that illegitimate son with her, and Isabel to be William's bride. Hopefully, a family would ensure he never returned to his wild ways.

It didn't work. The couple would be married in Montreal just three weeks later, then they would all head west to begin their new life. And while William never did go back to drinking and gambling, he would find a new passion out there in Upper Canada: politics. And politics would prove to be an even more dangerous vice.

Isabel didn't know it as she stepped off that ship in Quebec City, but the man she was about to marry was destined to become one of the most notorious figures in the history of Toronto. His radical views would soon make him the city's most wanted man. He would be forced to flee into exile with a price on his head. He was willing to risk everything for his beliefs. Including his life. And his family.

Isabel Baxter was about to marry William Lyon Mackenzie.

It was four years later that Isabel Baxter Mackenzie came home to find that her house had been trashed. It was a modest wooden home, tucked away behind a little fence, with a small garden; it stood on what's now called Front Street — just down the road from the St. Lawrence Market. It was surrounded by the bustle of the town, with a view of the lake and the busy wharf right across the street. The Mackenzies lived upstairs, and in the back, but the ground floor was mostly dedicated to a newspaper office. William Lyon Mackenzie's *Colonial Advocate* had become one of the most urgent voices for change in Upper Canada. There, in their front room, a big printing press churned out his radical ideas in paper and ink.

In Upper Canada, the Family Compact still ruled supreme. And their fear of democracy had only grown stronger. The War of 1812 had shown them all the upheaval and bloodshed it could cause. To them, democracy felt not only like a threat to their power, but to their lives. So, they used their power to crack down on anyone who opposed them. Those who dared to argue in favour of democratic reform were liable to find themselves under attack: denounced, imprisoned, exiled, beaten bloody in the streets, sometimes even tarred and feathered. And William Lyon Mackenzie was the Family Compact's number one target.

Upper Canada had never been as monolithic and British as those in power would have liked. And as the Family Compact's abuses piled up, more and more settlers came to believe that real democracy was necessary. The Reform Party was born, opposing the Tories and arguing for democratic change; for the right of Canadians to have more power over their own affairs.

Mackenzie was the most notoriously radical of all Reform leaders. He used the *Colonial Advocate* to denounce the Family Compact at every turn. He called them parasites, demons, jackals, and fungus. As he later put it, "The family compact surround the

Lieutenant-Governor, and mould him like wax, to their will; they fill every office with their relatives, dependents and partisans.... The whole of the revenues of Upper Canada are in reality at their mercy."

Mackenzie was determined to get his word out. In fact, he was giving away more free copies of his newspaper than he was selling, sending them to influential citizens in the hope he could sway their opinion. He was running up a mountain of debt doing it. By the end of 1825, just three years into the Mackenzies' marriage, he was in real trouble, forced to shut down publication for six months and flee York in order to avoid his creditors.

That's when the Family Compact struck.

On a June day in 1826, a mob of angry young men marched down to Front Street, to the Mackenzies' home. They burst into the house and began to trash the newspaper office. Isabel wasn't home when they did, but William's mother and son both were — they hid in fear while the mob broke the printing press and seized the type, scattering the metal letters everywhere: on the floor and in the garden — some of them were even hurled into the lake. The event would become known as the Types Riot. It was a brazen attack, carried out in broad daylight. Some of York's most prominent citizens watched it happen, looking on with approval; two of them were magistrates, responsible for upholding the law.

As Isabel Baxter Mackenzie surveyed the damage after the riot, she must have realized what a dangerous life she'd married into. But she agreed with her husband. She may not have chosen him, but she believed in his cause. By all accounts, she was a well-read woman, with a strong knowledge of political history; she could see what was happening in Upper Canada perfectly well. And while she may have been calmer and more stable than her impulsive husband, she still held strong views. "The spirit of independence fired her imagination," as historian Charlotte Gray puts it, "and the blood of dispossessed Scots ran just as strongly through her veins as through his. She believed utterly in the Reform campaign; she shared Mackenzie's outrage at the corruption and lethargy of the Family Compact rulers."

The Types Riot was only the beginning. The Mackenzies' marriage would be engulfed by political violence for decades to come. Mackenzie sued the rioters and won. The money was enough to restart the newspaper and even enter politics himself. Within months, he'd won a seat in the Legislative Assembly. Now, he had a bigger voice than ever before. He kept up his propaganda campaign against the Tories of the Family Compact, calling them names, interrupting their meetings, demanding change, and generally being a thorn in their side.

The Family Compact fought back. That winter, the Tories in the assembly voted to kick Mackenzie out of office. His supporters stormed Parliament and in the by-election that followed, Mackenzie was re-elected in a landslide. Only one person in his riding voted against him. A victory parade of more than 130 horse-drawn sleighs marched down snowy Yonge Street to the sound of bagpipes, bringing their democratically elected representative back to office.

Five days later, the Tories kicked him out again. There was another by-election. And another landslide victory for the famous Reformer. It happened over and over again, as the Family Compact got angrier and angrier. During a visit to Hamilton, Mackenzie was beaten by thugs and left bloodied in the street. In York, he was pelted with garbage and burned in effigy. That day, Mackenzie was only rescued from the mob thanks to the peacekeeping James FitzGibbon — the old hero of the War of 1812 had broken up more than one street fight in recent years. When Mackenzie's new office on Church Street was attacked, his apprentice could only keep the mob at bay by firing a pistol out the window; some people like to say he used type from the printing press as ammunition.

For a while, Mackenzie went into hiding. He feared for his life. But his support kept growing. He would soon find himself in a more powerful position than ever before.

As Reformers and Tories battled in the streets of York, a pandemic was raging across the globe. Cholera would kill tens of thousands of people when it reached the Canadian colonies in the summer of 1832. The streets of York were filled with death carts. Thousands fled the town, while hundreds died sudden and horrifying deaths. In the wake of the outbreak, even the Family Compact agreed that in order to be ready for the next wave, the growing town needed its own municipal power: a democratically elected government with the authority to make and enforce its own bylaws.

And so, in 1834, the Town of York officially became the City of Toronto. William Lyon Mackenzie was elected as the city's first mayor. He spent much of his year in power battling a second outbreak of the deadly disease. Under his watch, the first wooden sidewalks were built; garbage collection was introduced; there were new regulations around the disposal of waste and corpses; and pigs were no longer allowed to run free in the streets. Mackenzie operated some of the ambulances and death carts himself. He caught the disease and was lucky to survive.

But when his year as mayor was done, Mackenzie returned to provincial politics. And there, he discovered he still couldn't get anything done. It didn't matter how much popular support he could muster, the system hadn't really changed. The Family Compact had the power and they made it abundantly clear they had no appetite for reform — or for William Lyon Mackenzie. Even if that's what the people of Upper Canada wanted.

The Mackenzies had spent years fighting for democracy, risking their safety, sacrificing their time and money, dedicating their entire family life to supporting that one goal. But their patience was wearing thin. Soon, it would run out entirely.

There were men at the door. The Mackenzies were living on York Street now, in a red brick house just south of Osgoode Hall. It had plenty of space for their growing family, even a garden out back filled with raspberries, gooseberries, grapes, and currants. They had a stable for the horses, too, with enough room for a cow. The Mackenzies would live in at least twenty houses during their four decades of marriage, but this was the home Isabel and William would always remember as their favourite. And now, it was in danger.

The rebellion had begun.

Mackenzie had always believed he could find a peaceful solution to the problems that plagued Upper Canada. He had faith in the British system. Together, in 1832, the Mackenzies had even travelled all the way to England to make the case. William was sure that if only the colonial rulers in London knew what was happening in Canada, they would be outraged enough to fix things.

Ten years after she first arrived at Quebec City, Isabel Baxter Mackenzie found herself sailing across the Atlantic once more — this time, in the other direction. She was in her late twenties and pregnant yet again; she would give birth to her seventh child that fall, thousands of kilometres from home and the rest of their children. In England, the couple lived in cramped quarters, with little income and plenty of mounting debt. But they were just a couple of kilometres from Westminster — a short walk away from the heart of power in the Empire.

Mackenzie began to have meetings at the Colonial Office, presenting the mountain of evidence he'd collected. For a while, it really did seem as if the British were taking his concerns seriously. He was invited to share his thoughts in the major newspapers. He published a book. He even met with the prime minister. When he produced petitions signed by tens of thousands of Upper Canadians, the documents were presented to the House of Commons with the support of the government. When they asked him to submit a written copy of all of his grievances, he responded by staying up for six straight days and nights, writing furiously, switching from one hand to the other when the first cramped up.

It looked like they were winning. The colonial secretary — the man who oversaw the entire British Empire — sent a stern letter to the Family Compact demanding changes. And when they refused, he fired two of Mackenzie's greatest enemies. It must have been an incredibly joyous time for the couple. After years of anguish and frustration, it looked like they were finally winning the battle for reform. And just three weeks after the colonial secretary sent his letter, Isabel gave birth to a baby boy — their first after six straight girls.

But then it all quite suddenly fell apart. The British government began to change course. The colonial secretary was replaced by a man who took the Family Compact's side, rehiring the officials who'd just been fired. The Mackenzies' victory suddenly evaporated. William and Isabel sailed back to Canada, defeated. A few months later, baby Joseph died. Darkness had descended once again.

But the colonial authorities were far from the only people they'd met in England. They'd also spent plenty of time getting to know the radicals and reformers behind the democracy movement in England — they'd even named their baby after one of them. Those English reformers were even more radical than Mackenzie. They told him the Canadian colonies should be independent from Britain. And they made it clear that if his attempts to achieve peaceful reform failed, they thought he should simply overthrow the government.

After four more years of abuse at the hands of the Family Compact, those ideas began to make a lot of sense to him. Mackenzie spent the summer of 1837 travelling through the province, gathering support for an armed revolution. "Mark my words, Canadians!" he wrote. "The struggle has begun — It will end in freedom. We are determined never to rest until independence is ours…. Up then brave Canadians! Get ready your rifles and make short work of it…. Woe to those who oppose us."

His rebellion began on a Tuesday morning in December. Mackenzie led a motley rebel army of five hundred men down Yonge Street to seize the city, overthrow the government, and declare an independent Republic of Canada.

The loyal Tories rushed to defend the city. They'd been tipped off; some had seen the rebels gathering north of the city. And while the lieutenant-governor was slow to take the threat seriously, James FitzGibbon wasn't. As he leapt into action, preparing for the defence of Toronto, soldiers were sent to the Mackenzies' house on York Street. Isabel was there to meet them.

They claimed they were there on orders to protect the family. But they began to trample through the house, sticking their swords through mattresses and under the beds, looking for hiding rebels. They rifled through cupboards and drawers, hunting for William's letters and plans. All the while, Isabel must have been watching nervously. She knew her husband's files were hanging from the ceiling of their bedroom. The soldiers repeatedly passed right under them; according to some versions of the story, plumes on their helmets even brushed against the papers.

Finally, she was able to find an excuse believable enough to get the men out of the house for a few minutes — just long enough for her daughters to grab the files and feed them into four wood stoves, burning the evidence.

The men were supposed to keep the family under watch, but when Mackenzie's mother — then in her late eighties — marched downstairs and berated them for harassing women and children, the soldiers retreated. And for the moment, Isabel could only wait and hope her husband would return in one piece.

He didn't. Word eventually reached the house on York Street: the rebellion was over; it had been crushed. But William still hadn't come home. Isabel had no idea what had happened to her husband. She hadn't heard from him in weeks, since well before the uprising began. But there was hope. Rumours of his daring escape ran wild as the lieutenant-governor put a price of a thousand pounds on his head. Some said Mackenzie had hid out in a cave on the Niagara Escarpment. Or in a haystack. Or a pigpen. A local farmer had saved him by giving him

a horse to ride. "The horse was true as steel, sure foot-
ed, spirited," the rebel leader would later remember. He
rode fast through the December cold, slipping across the
Niagara River into the United States. He was safe.

When Isabel Baxter Mackenzie finally heard the
good news, she rushed to her husband's side.

Navy Island is in the middle of the Niagara River, not
far above Niagara Falls, just barely on the Canadian side
of the border. It was there, living in a pair of wooden
huts, that the Mackenzies regrouped after William's
failed revolution. They weren't ready to give up quite yet.
They were joined by what was left of his supporters. He
declared the island to be the independent Republic of
Canada. From there, he planned to continue the fight.
As far as he was concerned, the rebellion wasn't over yet.

Isabel had left the children behind in Toronto, catching a stagecoach to Buffalo — briefly frightened when
she overheard a rumour that her husband was dead —
hanged or drowned. Soon, she reached the river and
boarded an American steamship that the rebels were
using to ferry supplies to their island: the SS *Caroline*. It
was on Christmas Day that she finally reached her destination, reunited with her husband at last.

The danger, however, was far from over. Just a few
nights later, the Upper Canadian authorities launched
a raid across the river. But instead of attacking the
rebels on the island, they crossed all the way over to
the American side of the border. Their target was the

Caroline. They seized the ship, towed it out into the middle of the river, set it on fire, and left it to drift over Niagara Falls. They'd cut off the rebels' supply line. But things hadn't gone entirely smoothly. As they fought to take control of the ship, they shot and killed an American watchkeeper, Amos Durfee. It sparked an international crisis, with many outraged Americans calling for war. Durfee's body was eventually strung up in front of a tavern in Buffalo as a way to recruit even more men to Mackenzie's cause.

Isabel helped William prepare for war. There were about two hundred men on Navy Island, but Isabel was the only woman who spent any real time there. She got busy with her needle and thread, turning her petticoats into cartridge bags to be used in the battles to come. They say her mere presence on the island inspired all the men she came in contact with, as she camped out there in the middle of the river, sewing hour after hour in the name of democracy and revolution while their enemies bombarded the island. At one point, while she was cooking dinner, an artillery shell crashed through the roof of their shack and landed in a barrel of beans, sending animal feed flying through the air.

Luckily, she'd escaped unharmed. But it was rough life. It took a toll. It wasn't long before she fell ill and was too sick to continue. Mackenzie helped his wife back to Buffalo so she could recover. When he did, he was arrested by the American authorities — his adventures on Navy Island had violated the country's neutrality laws. The arrest barely slowed him down; he was only briefly in custody, released thanks to the bystanders who immediately stepped forward to bail him out.

Still, things on Navy Island weren't going well. As time passed, the rebels' numbers were dwindling. Mackenzie's promises of land and silver must have been hard to believe. He seemed to be spending more time designing his republic's flag than in planning his coming war. When he and the rest of the leadership fell out, Mackenzie finally realized his cause was lost. As the rebels abandoned Navy Island, Mackenzie abandoned his rebellion.

The fight would carry on for another year without him. The Patriots, as they called themselves, launched a series of border raids and fought more than a dozen minor battles along the St. Lawrence and Detroit Rivers. More than a hundred men died in the Patriot War before the uprising was finally, fully, and completely crushed. William Lyon Mackenzie's dream of a Canadian revolution was over.

You can still visit the Mackenzies' last home in Toronto. It's operated as a museum now. Mackenzie House is an elegant building, with yellow brick and black shutters. It stands on Bond Street, in the heart of downtown, just around the corner from Yonge-Dundas Square. Inside, you'll still find some of the couple's own belongings, including their copy of the "Wanted" poster that called for Mackenzie's capture; they proudly framed it and hung it on their wall. Walking through their home, you can still get a hint of what it must have felt like when they were living there a century and a half ago. This is where the rebel mayor and his rebel wife spent their final years together.

After the failed rebellion, they would spend a decade living in exile, most of it in Rochester and New York City. Those were terrible years. All of Mackenzie's attempts to launch a new newspaper failed. At times, the family could barely afford to eat. At least one landlord threatened to throw them out for failing to pay the rent; others refused to take them in. Mackenzie fell into a deep depression. There were illnesses in the family. A fire swept through their home. One of their daughters suffered a mental breakdown and had to be institutionalized. A second died. So did William's mother, who'd played such an important role in their lives ever since she'd brought Isabel to Canada all those years ago. Her son couldn't even attend her funeral; he could only watch the procession from a distance, through the barred window of his prison cell. He'd finally been convicted of breaking U.S. neutrality laws. He barely made it out of the prison alive: one morning, an assassin's bullet was fired into his cell.

But Isabel stuck with him through all those hard times, just as she always had. And there would, eventually, be a glimmer of hope. News from up north. Years after the rebellion, the political tide would finally turn. Democracy *would* come to Canada.

Eventually, the old rebels of 1837 would be pardoned. The Mackenzies would finally be welcomed home. Not everyone was glad they were back. William's first tentative visit sparked riots. But they had supporters, too. William couldn't resist getting back into politics and he was re-elected, giving passionate speeches in the legislature, pushing for even more reform, a thorn in the side of the powerful once again.

The Mackenzies would never be rich. But many in Toronto remembered their years of struggle, the sacrifices they'd made in the name of Canadian democracy. Their friends and supporters pooled their money together and bought them a nice new home, right downtown: Mackenzie House.

Isabel Baxter Mackenzie might not have chosen her husband, but she did choose her cause — a rebel in her own right. She'd stood with William from the very beginning, and she would stand with him to the end. After years of riots and rebellion, the Mackenzies finally had somewhere to grow old together in peace.

And that's just what they did.

13
NO PITY FOR THE BLACKSMITH

He was so close. For two days and two nights, he and his companions had been rowing across Lake Erie, freezing in the winter winds, fighting the rough waves, drenched by the icy water that threatened to swamp the small boat. They'd barely eaten, hadn't slept, but were now finally within striking distance of the southern shore. If they made it, they'd have reached the United States. Freedom.

But now the wind was blowing in the wrong direction. A great gale was gathering, the waves were growing bigger, and the boat was being pushed back, away from the shore, away from safety, out toward the middle of the lake. For hours they fought the wind and the waves with everything they had, desperately trying to keep from being blown backwards. But it was all in vain. Finally, they gave up and let their boat float back toward Canada. Toward danger.

They came ashore near the mouth of the Grand River. A farmer was waiting for them there. He'd been watching them for a while; he assumed they were smugglers bringing salt across the border illegally. He gathered a few neighbours and seized the men when they landed, carrying their prisoners off to a nearby town to be handed over to the authorities.

It would be a while before they realized who they had in their custody. The man who tried to row across Lake Erie was one of the most wanted men in the province. They'd captured Samuel Lount, the rebel blacksmith.

It had been twenty years since Samuel and his wife, Elizabeth, had settled in Upper Canada. They ended up living in Holland Landing, near Lake Simcoe, where they earned the respect of the community. Lount was a soft-spoken blacksmith, who lent his skills to many other projects: he owned a tavern for a while, farmed, surveyed with his brother, and helped build the first steamship on Lake Simcoe. He was a kind and generous man, known to give free axes to new settlers who arrived without their own. He was so popular he was eventually drafted into politics, running and winning a seat for the Reform Party, becoming close friends with William Lyon Mackenzie.

But his political career would be short lived. Lount was a victim of a corrupt election; he lost his seat — and with it, his faith in the system. When Mackenzie began to talk of revolution, Lount listened. The rebel mayor convinced him they could launch a bloodless coup. Not a single drop of blood would have to be spilled.

Lount was in. As Mackenzie travelled the province drumming up support for the rebellion, Lount's smithy rang with the sound of revolution: hammers forging pikes in preparation. By the time the day came to meet the rest of the rebels at Montgomery's Tavern — on Yonge Street near Eglinton Avenue, well north of Toronto back then — Lount had gathered ninety men to the cause. They were among the first to arrive.

It quickly became clear that Mackenzie's revolution would not, in fact, be bloodless. When a Tory from Richmond Hill tried to gallop straight through the rebel barricades on Yonge Street, riding south to warn the lieutenant-governor, he was shot. And while he lay slowly dying inside the tavern, the rebels suffered a loss, too. They captured a prisoner while on patrol: the Tory judge John Powell, grandson of Anne Murray Powell and son of the Powells whose old Niagara home was haunted by the ghost of Sophia Shaw. When he was politely asked whether he was carrying a pistol, Powell lied. As soon as he got his chance, he shot his captor dead and escaped, fleeing south to the city to raise the alarm. A few weeks later, he would be elected mayor of Toronto, hailed as a hero for shooting that man in the back.

The rebellion hadn't even started yet and already two men were dead. Lount was beginning to have doubts.

Meanwhile, the element of surprise was slipping away. In Toronto, James FitzGibbon was rushing around, organizing the militia, posting guards, preparing the city's defences. And that was bad news for the rebels. When Lount heard the reports of what FitzGibbon was up to, he did everything he could to convince Mackenzie to strike immediately, before the city was fully prepared. At first, the rebel mayor was determined to wait. Many of his supporters hadn't arrived yet; they were still a couple of days away from the date he'd been telling everyone to show up. But in the end, he agreed. They would march south now, with the five hundred men who had gathered so far.

That created another problem: the man who was supposed to be leading their army — an experienced Dutch general named Van Egmond, who'd fought both for and against Napoleon — wasn't there yet. The backup, Captain Anderson, was dead — he was the man who'd been shot in the back by John Powell. When Mackenzie asked Samuel Lount to take command of his army, Lount refused. That left the job to Mackenzie himself.

He proved to be a poor option. Before they'd even left the tavern, it was clear Mackenzie was beginning to buckle under the stress. As one rebel would later remember, "Little Mac conducted himself like a crazy man all the time we were at Montgomery's. He went about storming and screaming like a lunatic, and many of us felt certain he was not in his right senses." When Mackenzie finally mounted his white pony, stuffed into as many jackets as he could possibly wear in an attempt to make himself bulletproof, he didn't seem to be in any hurry. Not long after they'd started to march south, he let his men take a long lunch break; he then paused again to burn down the house of one of his enemies. Lount barely talked him out of burning down a second. They still hadn't reached the city by the time the sun began to set.

The battle finally came at dusk, as the army neared the capital. FitzGibbon had sent a small force of twenty-six men to take up a position on Yonge, hidden behind some bushes near College Street. As the rebel army approached, the government supporters let loose with a volley of musket fire. The battle for Toronto had begun.

It ended almost immediately. A couple of the rebels were wounded in that initial volley, but the rest of the front line — with Lount leading — held true and returned fire. That was enough to scare off the defenders, who broke ranks and fled.

But the rebels didn't last long, either. When they saw Lount and the rest of their front line drop to a knee in order to reload their muskets, they got confused about what they'd seen in the gathering darkness. They assumed they'd all been shot. So, as the defenders fled in one direction, the rebels fled in the other.

Mackenzie's chance to take the city had been lost. As he regrouped with his rebels back at Montgomery's Tavern, hundreds of government supporters were flooding into Toronto from the countryside and neighbouring cities, ready to defend the city and put down the rebellion. Two days after that brief skirmish at Yonge and College, their army would march north to attack the rebels at the Battle of Montgomery's Tavern. It quickly ended the uprising.

Lount was one of the lucky rebels who escaped, fleeing with another one of Mackenzie's men. They spent the next few weeks wandering through the wintry countryside, government agents hot on their heels. They spent two nights sleeping on a forest floor, days hidden in hay-stacks and piles of straw, narrowly avoiding capture as friends, family, and allies risked their own safety to keep them from being discovered. Finally, exhausted and afraid, they decided to make a risky dash for the United States. A French Canadian sympathizer who lived on Lake Erie lent them a small boat and a boy to help. They set it into the water at Long Point: the thin peninsula that reaches out into the lake toward the United States, the tip less than forty kilometres from the shores of Ohio and Pennsylvania. And then they began to row.

In the wake of the rebellion, nearly a thousand Upper Canadians were arrested. The government cracked down hard; anyone who was even suspected of having rebel sympathies was rounded up and thrown into prison. In Lower Canada, where another coordinated rebellion had broken out, a dozen men were executed for treason. Many more rebels in both colonies were exiled without trial. Some were banished across the border into the United States, or to Bermuda. Others were shipped off to the far side of the world, forced to do hard labour in the penal colonies of Australia. The conditions were horrific. Many would die there.

After he was captured on the shores of Lake Erie, Lount was put on trial with another rebel: the farmer Peter Matthews, who'd led a contingent of fifty rebels from Pickering. They both pled guilty to the charge of high treason. Their lawyer thought their best chance was to throw themselves on the mercy of the court. It was a risky decision. Their judge was not exactly impartial.

John Beverley Robinson had done very well for himself since Anne Powell had died in her shipwreck while chasing him to England. He'd fought in the War of 1812 under Isaac Brock; he was there when they took Detroit, and again at the Battle of Queenston Heights. And he continued to build his life as a lawyer, judge, and politician. When nineteen Canadian settlers were accused of treason near the end of the war, charged with the crime of fighting for the Americans, it was Robinson who served as the prosecutor. William Powell presided as one of the judges. Robinson won nearly all of the cases; eight of the men were executed, hanged before having their heads chopped off and stuck on poles for public display. The grisly trials would go down in history as the "Bloody Assize of 1814."

In the years since, Robinson had become even more powerful: he'd not only served as the attorney general, but as a member of the Legislative Assembly and president of the lieutenant-governor's hand-picked Executive Council. He'd even taken over Powell's old job as chief justice. As a leader of the Family Compact, Robinson was a sworn enemy of William Lyon Mackenzie. The rebel mayor had attacked him personally in the pages of the *Colonial Advocate* as "greatly overrated ... a vain, ignorant man." Robinson fired back, calling Mackenzie "a reptile ... What vermin!"

It was no surprise that when Mackenzie launched his rebellion, Robinson was there to take up arms against him as a member of the militia. (Although when it came time for the attack on Montgomery's Tavern, Robinson stayed home, already hard at work writing a history of the rebellion.) Now, as chief justice of Upper Canada, the rebels' lives were in his hands. And he wasn't in a merciful mood.

He sentenced Lount and Matthews to death. The two doomed rebels would spend their final days in irons, waiting for the gallows from inside the most miserable prison cells the Toronto Gaol had to offer.

But Elizabeth Lount wasn't about to let her husband die without a fight. She visited him in his cell. "I found him a shadow, pale and debilitated," she later wrote. "Poor man! Here I beheld him in prison, not that he had burned a city, for he had saved Toronto from flames — not that he had taken the lives of his enemies, for he was opposed to the shedding of blood. But he opposed himself to the oppressors of his countrymen — and for this was doomed to suffer death." They'd been married for more than twenty years. They had seven children together. And so, as her husband awaited his execution, Elizabeth — now in her early forties — began to organize.

She circulated a petition asking the lieutenant-governor to spare the blacksmith's life. Maybe, she hoped, if she could gather enough popular support, the government would be forced to back down and show mercy.

The petition was a dangerous document. With the authorities cracking down on dissent, signing your name meant risking that you might become a target yourself. But even so, thousands upon thousands of Upper Canadians were willing to put down their names, including many who opposed the rebellion. By the time she was ready to present the petition, Elizabeth Lount had collected the signatures of at least eight thousand settlers who believed her husband should be spared.

Still, it wouldn't be an easy sell. There was a new lieutenant-governor in town. Sir George Arthur was not a man with a history of being easily swayed to sympathy. After fighting against Napoleon as a young man, he'd spent the rest of his career ruling over various colonies across the British Empire. In Honduras, he crushed an uprising against slavery — while also alienating white settlers with his "most tyrannical, arbitrary and capricious conduct." As the ruler of Van Diemen's Land — the island penal colony we now know as Tasmania — he oversaw the forced labour of thousands of prisoners. Many were subjected to brutal, even fatal, conditions. And while he was there, he oversaw the Black War — now known by some historians as the Tasmanian War — against Indigenous people in Australia, declaring martial law in order to give settlers free reign to kill as many Aboriginals as they could. Just a few years before he came to Canada, Arthur had ordered a bloody offensive called the Black Line: more than two thousand white settlers and soldiers formed a series of mobile cordons across Tasmania, forcibly driving Indigenous people into a single peninsula where Arthur planned to confine them forever. He promised rewards for the capture of Indigenous people, and paid bounties for their deaths.

Arthur had been knighted for his service and appointed as the new lieutenant-governor of Upper Canada, where he found himself dealing with the aftermath of the rebellion. He was the man Elizabeth Lount would have to persuade.

The day before her husband's execution, she went to meet the new lieutenant-governor, armed with her petition. When she was admitted into the room, he invited her to sit down, but instead she fell onto her knees, begging for her husband's life.

It was a scene she later described, and a heartbreaking conversation she paraphrased. "Do not kneel to me," Arthur said with disdain, "but kneel to your God."

"I'm kneeling in prayer to the Almighty that you will soften your heart," she answered. "My husband does not fear to die — he is prepared for death, but it is his wife and children asking for his life to be spared."

"If he's prepared for death," the lieutenant-governor sneeringly replied, "he might not be so well prepared at another time."

He did admit that the executions had less to do with the crime than with revenge — and the chance to make an example of the two condemned rebels. "Two lives were lost at Montgomery's and two must now suffer." He suggested that if Lount was willing to name names — to hand more of his rebels over to the government so they could be arrested and tried — that his life would be spared. But the rebel blacksmith had already made it perfectly clear: he was more than willing to sacrifice his own life in order to save anyone else from being persecuted for their democratic beliefs.

Elizabeth Lount's desperate pleas fell on deaf ears. The lieutenant-governor refused to be swayed. No matter how many people in Upper Canada called for mercy, the men would die.

The dreadful day finally came on a cool spring morning in 1838, as the rebel prisoners were roused by the ominous sound of hammering. The gallows were being built outside the jail; the sentence would be carried out not only in front of a large public crowd, but also in sight of the other captured rebels, who would watch from the barred windows of their cells. It was grisly and unpopular work — one foreman refused to help — but by eight o'clock, it was done.

They say Sheriff Jarvis broke down in tears when he went to collect the two condemned men from their cells, leading them out to the yard in chains. "We die in a good cause," Lount reassured his fellow prisoners as he passed, "Canada will yet be free."

Outside, a large crowd had gathered to witness the grim spectacle. Militiamen surrounded the gallows, muskets at the ready; the government worried there might be a rescue attempt. But it was not to come. The condemned men simply walked up the eight steps to the gallows and took their places.

Lount turned his head toward the prison's barred windows, a last farewell to his fellow rebels. Then he and Matthews knelt in prayer before turning to the sheriff. "Mr. Jarvis, do your duty. We are prepared to meet death and our Judge." The sheriff placed hoods over their heads, and a noose around each of their throats. All was quiet and tense. Then, the trap door opened and the rope snapped their necks.

Mackenzie, of course, wasn't there to witness the moment for himself, but he still wrote about it in one of his papers. "The spectacle of Lount after the execution was the most shocking sight that can be imagined," the rebel mayor claimed. "He was covered over with his blood, the head being nearly severed from his body, owing to the depth of the fall. More horrible to relate, when he was cut down, two ruffians seized the end of the rope and dragged the mangled corpse along the ground into the jail yard, someone exclaiming 'this is the way every damned rebel deserves to be used.'"

Some even reported that Samuel and Elizabeth's daughter was so deeply traumatized by the sight of her father's corpse being dragged around the yard that she died almost immediately of grief.

Even then, Elizabeth's suffering wasn't over. Lount and Matthews were dead, but the authorities were still afraid of their power, that they would be seen as martyrs for the cause of democracy. The lieutenant-governor worried that a public funeral might become a rallying point for more unrest, so he refused to let the families bury the men. Instead, they were quietly laid to rest in the paupers' cemetery: Potter's Field at the corner of Yonge and Bloor. They were given a simple, flat gravestone with nothing but their names engraved upon it. It would be decades before Mackenzie could ensure they were safety moved to the Toronto Necropolis, where they are still at rest today. Despite Arthur's best efforts, they are indeed remembered as martyrs. The simple stone he gave them has been joined by a fifteen-foot column and an official heritage plaque.

After her husband's death, there was nothing left for Elizabeth in Upper Canada. The government seized the family's property, including their house. Forced from her home, Elizabeth took the children to live in the United States. She would die there, in Michigan, as an old woman many decades later.

But she wouldn't let her husband — and his cause — fade into memory. Two months after Samuel was hanged, Elizabeth Lount published a scathing open letter to John Beverley Robinson, condemning him and the executions.

It came with a warning. "Sir," she promised, "all is not over yet. No government whose only acts are those of violence and cruelty, whose statute book is stained with the blood of innocent sufferers, and whose land is watered by the tears of widows and orphans, can long stand contiguous to a nation abounding in free institutions."

The cause of Canadian freedom, she declared, would live on. The fight would continue. Someday, the Family Compact would lose; democracy would prevail. Her husband, she was sure, had not died in vain. "Canada will do justice to his memory," she told the judge who had sentenced the man she loved to death. "Canadians cannot long remain in bondage. They will be free.... Then will the name of Canadian martyrs be sung by poets and extolled by orators, while those who now give law to the bleeding people of Canada will be loathed or forgotten by the civilized world."

14

A BOX FOR MARY JAMES

It's a small wooden box, just a few inches long and nearly two hundred years old. It was carved by hand and elegantly decorated, despite the circumstances in which it was created: a beautiful artifact chipped and chiselled out of scraps. There wasn't much to work with in prison, just a few pieces of firewood. But there were hundreds more made like it. Today, you'll find them in museums and private collections all over Ontario and Quebec: small wooden boxes carved by the rebels of 1837 — those who were captured and spent months in jail awaiting their fates. Each Rebellion Box is unique, a personalized gift for the family and friends who waited on the outside, hoping and praying the prisoners would someday be set free. And this box, like so many others, bears a sentimental message: a love poem inscribed in ink by the rebel Joseph Gould for the woman he hoped to marry, but worried he would never see again.

Gould was born into a Quaker family in the early 1800s, just a few years after his parents left Pennsylvania to settle in Upper Canada. He grew up in Uxbridge, about fifty kilometres outside York, where many Quakers lived. By his early twenties he had already begun to find success as a farmer and a miller, and he didn't hesitate to enjoy his prosperity. By his own admission, he was getting "a little wild." He liked to attend balls and dances. He liked to flirt with women. He indulged in a series of romances.

Even with all the partying, he'd built a reputation as a hard-working professional. Now that he was twenty-seven, he decided it was time to reign in his excesses and settle down. And he could think of no better type of woman to settle down with than a Quaker woman.

He knew the perfect place to look. Ezekiel James was one of his neighbours, and one of the most respected men in town. His family had been part of the first wave of Quakers to leave Pennsylvania for Canada, settling on Yonge Street when he was a young man. He'd gone on to become one of the first settlers in Uxbridge, living in a log cabin as he cleared his land and established a farm. Before long, he'd done well enough to build himself a stone house and pay for a school to be built. That's where Joseph Gould would get his education. And when Gould was old enough to start building his own life, it was Ezekiel James who gave him the loan that allowed him to start his own farm.

James also happened to have three teenaged daughters. Gould was impressed with all three. "Now those girls," he later said, "were perfect models of what a good Christian girl should be; so innocently pure, unassuming and modest that, after my wild career, I despised myself in their presence, and frequently wished that I could obliterate the history of the last five years of my life."

He found their fashion sense particularly alluring. "They dressed strictly in the old Quaker style — rich, plain, clean and tidy," he remembered. "And to my mind, no dress in the world sets off a young woman so well as the Quaker dress. No trail to sweep the streets, sidewalks and barnyard; no flounces, frills or tuckbacks to catch the dust, rain and snow, and shackle the agility of a girl's movements." Those Quaker dresses weren't just attractive, they were emblematic of a practical lifestyle that he now longed for. "They take less material, less making, less time in washing and ironing, and are warmer, and far more durable, and in every way the most sensible kind of dress." Any woman wearing that kind of clothing seemed like a promising match, someone who would share his temperament and his religious views.

Gould began to spend more and more time with the James family, getting to know the three daughters as they got to know him. In time, it became clear that it was Mary — at nineteen, the oldest of the three — that he was particularly attracted to. And that attraction only grew stronger when he learned that she felt the same way about him, too. He asked her father for his permission to marry Mary; the answer was yes. And Mary was delighted when he proposed.

"I went home," he said, "with a light heart, and bright hopes of the future." If all went to plan, they would be married in just four months.

And then along came Mackenzie's rebellion.

Gould had long been political. As soon as the first post office opened in Uxbridge, he'd subscribed to William Lyon Mackenzie's *Colonial Advocate*. He found himself agreeing with just about everything Mackenzie wrote. He believed strongly in the idea of democratic reform and that the Family Compact had far too much power. He thought the people should have more say over how their government was run. Before long, Gould was an active member of the Reform Party, relied upon to get out the vote during elections.

That was no easy task in the 1830s. Just getting voters to the poll was a major challenge. There was only one place to vote in each riding, and the ridings were huge. Settlements were scattered, with few roads linking them together. The roads that did exist were often nearly impassable, just roughly hewn passages through dense forests. Getting the vote out was a physically demanding job. And the stakes were high: getting stuck in the mud or losing a wheel might mean getting stranded with a wagonful of voters. You could be unable to reach the polling station as the election slipped away.

There was also no election day — it was an election *week* or more. Polls stayed open for at least seven days; they only closed when they went an hour without anyone casting a vote. That meant political parties who got the sense they were losing could keep a poll open indefinitely by having a pool of voters at the ready, sending them in one by one, once every hour. Keeping these voters happy until the time came to vote usually involved plenty of alcohol, as well as having a place for them to sleep if they were forced to wait overnight.

With all those drunk and passionate voters hanging around, taverns and polling places frequently became scenes of violence. "Those open public houses were fertile spots for securing plentiful crops of violence and bloodshed," Gould's biographer, W.H. Higgins, explains. "Broken-heads and black-eyes were ordinary events. And sometimes men were maimed for life, or were killed outright, at those scenes of strife during an election contest."

Things got even worse in 1836. After Mackenzie's failed mission to London, the British made one change. They'd replaced the lieutenant-governor with a new one. Sir Francis Bond Head was supposed to be a reformer; that's why he got the job. But when he arrived in Toronto, it quickly became clear he agreed with the Family Compact. He praised their "industry and intelligence," while calling Mackenzie "an unprincipled, vagrant grievance-monger." And during the election of 1836, he openly took the side of the Tories, campaigning for them in what would prove to be one of the most corrupt and violent elections in Canadian history. Gould was on the front lines as the Reformers lost by a landslide. Even Mackenzie lost his seat, going down to defeat for the first — and only — time. Samuel Lount lost his too. For many, it was the final straw. The very next year, preparations for the rebellion began.

But as Mackenzie drilled farmers for war and blacksmiths forged pikes and spears, Gould was uneasy.

Pacifism is a key tenet of Quaker faith. And while dozens of Quakers abandoned that belief to join the rebellion, Gould later insisted that he never did believe that violence was the solution to the colony's political problems. He was sure that no matter how unsympathetic Bond Head was, they'd still be able to find some peaceful solution. In fact, he told Mackenzie as much, trying to talk him out of his armed insurrection at a secret rebel meeting just a week before it was scheduled to begin. In return, Gould was ridiculed. "I was taunted with cowardice," he complained, "because I refused to give encouragement or approval to violent measures." When the day came for the rebels to meet at Montgomery's Tavern, Gould found himself surrounded by about fifty of his friends who insisted that he join them. Otherwise, they told him, he would be a hypocrite and a coward. In the end, he felt he had no choice. "They were determined to go, and there was nothing else left for me, but to take my place amongst them."

By the time they arrived at the tavern, the rebellion was nearly over. The march down Yonge Street had already failed. And soon an army, filled with friends and neighbours who were now their mortal enemies, was spotted marching north. James FitzGibbon led a force of twelve hundred men. Bond Head was riding a big white stallion; Reverend Strachan was there, too, wrapped in a black cloak. They'd made their way up from the city to the sound of marching bands and cheers from their supporters, who leaned out windows and climbed up on rooftops, waving the Union Jack. The Battle of Montgomery's Tavern was about to begin.

Gould and a few others grabbed their weapons, some of them armed with nothing but pikes and pitchforks, rushing south along Yonge Street to meet the approaching army. As they did, a group of militiamen headed into the forest, trying to cut around them and reach the tavern. Gould and his companions raced into the woods after them. They scrambled over dead trees and climbed over the underbrush, until they found themselves within range of the government's biggest weapons: two small field guns. There, in the forest near Yonge and Eglinton, the artillery opened fire. Gould could see that one of the guns was controlled by a friend, who launched grapeshot high into the hemlock trees above their heads, bringing dead branches crashing all around them. A shot from the other gun smashed into the ground near Gould's feet, nearly blinding him with a shower of sand. A third shot struck a tree, sending shards of bark and splinters of wood slicing through the air and into his face. One rebel was shot through the shoulder. A second fell dead.

Meanwhile, the rest of the government army had reached the tavern, opening fire on the rebels' makeshift fortress. Cannonballs smashed through the dining room window. Chimneys came crashing to the ground. Rebels rushed out of the building, some fleeing into the woods as the militia fired upon them with rifles and muskets. Some fell dead right there. Some were wounded and captured. Most escaped. The battle was over in a matter of fifteen or twenty minutes. The rebellion was crushed. The government had won. FitzGibbon ordered the tavern burned to the ground.

As the flames consumed the building, Gould and about six or seven other men kept themselves hidden in the forest, trapped on the wrong side of Yonge Street, with the militia standing between them and home. They would be forced to camp out in the woods for about a week, debating what route to take to the United States. As time wore on, they felt safe enough to build a campfire in a swamp. That was a mistake. The smoke was spotted; soon, they found themselves surrounded by militiamen. They were captured and taken south into the city.

By then, the Toronto Gaol was already full, overflowing not just with rebels but anyone who was suspected of supporting democratic reform and opposing the Family Compact. Some would be held for months on end without any charges being laid, dozens crammed into a single cell. So many had been arrested, the government was running out of places to put them. Rather than being thrown immediately into a jail cell, the Quaker rebel first found himself imprisoned inside the Legislative Council room. Many years later, when he got elected to the assembly, he would joke about the day he first "took his seat in Parliament."

His hearing came weeks later. He was found guilty. His life was spared, but he was condemned to exile. He seemed destined for the labour camps of Van Diemen's Land. He spent months inside the Toronto Gaol and at Fort Henry in Kingston, awaiting his dismal fate, expecting that at any moment he would be sent to the other side of the planet. And all the while, he longed for Mary James, knowing he might never again see the woman he loved.

That's when he made his box.

The whole thing started with just a few men carving away at scraps of firewood. Stuck in jail for months on end, the prisoners began to look for ways to pass the time. Since many of the rebels were skilled carpenters, they turned the pieces of firewood they were given into beautiful works of art: small decorative boxes they could send to their loved ones. Soon, scores of prisoners were sharing their skills, creating hundreds of boxes for their families and friends. Each of those boxes was inscribed with a message: some were memorials to their fallen comrades, some were defiant political declarations of their undying belief in Canadian democracy, and others were messages of love.

During his time in prison, Joseph Gould would make at least three boxes. One was dedicated to his sister, another to his future mother-in-law. But the very first box he made was for his fiancée, who, despite it all, he still hoped to marry. He might be on the very brink of being sent to a brutal Australian penal colony, but he hadn't lost hope or the conviction of his beliefs. There, in the Toronto Gaol, he inscribed his box with a message in ink:

To Miss Mary James

When liberty with all its charms
Shall comfort the distressed
Then I'll return with open arms,
And clasp you to my breast.

From Joseph Gould, in prison, June 1838

And there was indeed hope that he and his beloved might one day be reunited. The rebellion might have failed in its bid to overthrow the government, but it did spark gradual change. Far across the ocean in London, the British government was horrified by the violence. Bond Head was fired. He left Toronto a hated man. When the surviving rebels put a five-hundred-dollar price on his head, he was forced to cancel his plans for a grand departure through Halifax and sneak out through the United States instead. When the British picked a new governor general to oversee the Canadian colonies, they made sure they didn't make the same mistake again; they chose one of the most liberal politicians in England.

Lord Durham, they knew they could trust. He was the nephew of Earl Grey — the reform-minded prime minister Mackenzie had met with years earlier. Durham had fought for public education, for better working conditions for miners, and for the right of every man to vote, no matter his wealth. He'd even been one of the leaders of the reform movement in England. He was so liberal, in fact, they called him "Radical Jack."

When he arrived in Canada, Durham travelled across the country, listening to both sides of the conflict before submitting his findings to his bosses in England. The Durham Report recommended the thing the Reformers wanted the most: responsible government. Ministers, they argued, shouldn't answer to the governor and his colonial overlords in London, but to Parliament — to the elected representatives of the people. In other words, they wanted real democracy. And while the British would ignore the idea for now, the Durham Report laid the foundations for the changes to come.

By then, Durham had also made another grand gesture of reconciliation. One of his very first acts as governor general was to release nearly all the political prisoners. Only the most radical rebels would be sent into exile. The rest were to be set free, finally allowed to head home to their families.

And so, Joseph Gould was saved from the horrors of Van Diemen's Land. Nearly a year after the Battle of Montgomery's Tavern, the Quaker rebel was released from prison and allowed to return home to the woman he loved. They didn't waste any time. Just three months later, they headed to a friend's house at the corner of Yonge and Queen, not far from where he had been imprisoned for all those long months. And there, on New Year's Day of 1839, Joseph Gould and Mary James declared their love for each other, exchanged their vows, and were finally, happily married.

15
YOUR MOVEMENTS ARE WATCHED

The housekeeper listened closely. The Parliament buildings must have been quiet on that spring evening in 1838, with most of the politicians and staff already gone for the day. But Margaret Powell was used to being there at night; she was the housekeeper for the west wing. Over the course of that winter, she'd noticed George Markland was spending an awful lot of time in his office at night. And that he often wasn't alone in there.

Her curiosity had finally gotten the better of her, so on this particular night, she came to investigate. She found the door to Markland's office locked. But there were voices coming from the other side of the door, too quiet to make out. She could hear nothing more than a murmur, just enough to tell that one of the people speaking was Markland himself.

Then, other sounds started — the kind of sounds that convinced her Markland was in there with a woman. "No doubt remains upon my mind," she would later claim, "as to the nature of the noise I heard, and I was sure a female was in the room."

The housekeeper withdrew discretely and waited downstairs. Fifteen minutes passed before the door finally opened and someone came rushing down the stairs. But it wasn't a woman. Mary Powell was surprised to see she'd been wrong; Markland's visitor was a man. A drummer from the army.

She'd been growing suspicious for months, but this was the final straw. When Markland emerged from his office hot on the drummer's heels, she confronted him. "Well sir, these are queer doings from the bottom to the top." And the very next day, the housekeeper sent the politician a warning.

"Sir," her letter began, "I trust you will excuse the few lines I now address to you, which I do as a caution. Allow me, therefore, to tell you that your movements about this Building in the Evenings are watched, and have become the subject of conjuncture; I have been turning this step over in my mind for weeks, because I know that I [take] the Risk of Making you My Enemy ... but I write from pure Motives and Merely as a caution against circumstances that mitigate against you."

She was right. George Markland had enemies in Toronto. And they were ready to move against him.

He'd been born in Kingston, part of the very first generation of settlers to grow up in Upper Canada. He was educated by Reverend Strachan, served in the militia during the War of 1812, and made his way quickly up the political ranks of the province as a successful Tory. He was appointed to the Legislative Council and to the Executive Council, too. He helped start Upper Canada College and had an active role in the Anglican Church. He was even given the very same job that Alexander Wood once held: inspector general of public accounts. By the time he was in his midforties, he had established himself as one of the leaders of the Family Compact. In the years before the rebellion, George Markland was one of the most powerful men in Toronto.

But that's when his troubles began. It all started with the arrival of Bond Head. When the new lieutenant-governor first arrived, he'd chosen some leading Reformers to sit on his Executive Council as a symbolic olive branch. It quickly became clear, however, that it was an empty gesture; Bond Head had no interest in listening to his Canadian advisors from either side of the political divide. Frustrated by his refusal to take their advice, his entire Executive Council resigned in protest — Reformers and Tories alike. The crisis sparked a standoff that ended with the corrupt election of 1836, and would be remembered as an important milestone on the road to rebellion.

Markland was one of the Tories who quit the council in protest. And once the rebellion had been crushed, it seems that some members of the Family Compact may have been looking for revenge.

Markland's sexuality made him an easy target. He was married, but there had long been questions about his private life. Nearly twenty years earlier, John Beverley

Robinson described him as "a good fellow, and very friendly," but worried about the way he carried himself. "I prefer seeing a person at his age rather more manly and not quite so feminine either in speech or action." Nothing had come of it. Until now.

It was about a month after the housekeeper's warning that it all blew up. An anonymous letter — signed simply by "Toronto" — was sent to the lieutenant-governor's secretary. It took direct aim at Markland's career: "Can it be possible that the Government will continue to retain in office a man with such an indelible stain upon his character as the Honourable!! George H. Markland!" A second letter, sent directly to Lieutenant-Governor Arthur, built on the attack: "What an everlasting stigma and disgrace it will be upon the Government of this province if [Markland] is allowed to remain in office."

It was a serious accusation. As the British Empire spread across the globe, they'd brought laws against homosexuality with them. It's a legacy that has lasted well into the twenty-first century; today, more than half the countries where being gay is a crime are former British colonies. Upper Canada was no exception. Homosexuality was illegal. Sodomy was punishable by death and would be for another thirty years. Those laws weren't usually enforced — the most notable previous cases of men being convicted for being gay in Canada had occurred during the days of New France — but Markland could be forgiven for worrying his life might suddenly be in jeopardy.

As the dangerous rumours swirled, it was Markland himself who called for an inquiry. He hoped an official investigation into his private life would clear his name. "It would seem that I am suspected of what I declare myself wholly incapable of even imagining," he wrote to the lieutenant-governor, "and I unhesitatingly assert my innocence, which I can prove."

But things went off the rails from there. Markland asked that John Strachan — his lifelong friend and mentor — conduct the inquiry. Instead, it was the entire Executive Council who would examine his case. That summer, they dug deep into the details of his private life, calling a series of witnesses to give testimony about their relationships with the politician.

One after another, the young men called upon to testify described their encounters with Markland. Some had spent time alone with him in his office. Others had been to his house for dinner. At least one had gone for a sunset stroll with him along the waterfront. Markland had been having these kinds of meetings for years. And while all the men agreed that none of their experiences were so blatantly intimate as to call their own sexuality into question, they did claim his behaviour was enough to make them uncomfortable.

One law student remembered some of Markland's loaded comments. "On one occasion," he explained, "I was dining with Mr. Markland alone when I was much ashamed at Mr. Markland making the following observation: 'You have the most perfect figure of any one in town. Several people have remarked it.'"

And that student wasn't alone. A soldier from Fort York remembered physical contact during a walk: "He laid his hand on my arm as if he knew me and leaned on my arm. I was quite alarmed. I did not understand his behaviour. I thought Mr. Markland must have been out of his mind."

A third witness shared a story his brother had told him about a long walk along the water at dusk. "Mr. Markland had leaned upon his shoulder and had put his hand in an indecent manner on my brother's person. And that he, my brother, immediately kicked Mr. Markland on the body and immediately ran away."

We will, of course, never know the truth of what happened on those evening strolls along the lakeshore, or behind Markland's locked doors. The city's prejudice against anyone who didn't conform to accepted ideas about love and relationships provided plenty of reasons to keep those feelings private. For his part, Markland insisted there was nothing romantic about the encounters; they were, he claimed, simply meetings with young men he had taken under his wing, buying their discharge from the army or lending other professional and financial support.

William Lyon Mackenzie, beginning his life of exile in New York, rushed to Markland's defence. His newspaper dismissed the entire affair as a political witch hunt, claiming the Family Compact was simply looking for revenge against someone they believed had betrayed them. The housekeeper, Margaret Powell, Mackenzie's *Gazette* insisted, must have been bribed to lie about what she'd seen and heard on those infamous nights at the Parliament buildings.

In the end, the Family Compact won. As the testimony piled up, Markland made a deal: he resigned in return for the inquiry being dropped. His reputation in tatters, he fled from Toronto and would never hold public office again. And that wasn't the end of his suffering: he'd be investigated twice more over the next decade, accused of financial wrongdoing. For the most part, though, he lived a quiet life in Kingston. He made no further mark on the history of the province and he left little behind, a few letters he exchanged with his friends and colleagues, and a folder at Library and Archives Canada called "File M," which contains the records from the inquiry into his love life. Before the rebellion, he'd been one of the most powerful men in the province, with the full weight of the Family Compact behind him. But when he died in 1862, his passing was worth only a couple of lines in the newspaper. George Markland faded from history, the true details of his private life lost in time.

16
ADULTERY AT OSGOODE HALL

Elizabeth Stuart had fallen madly in love. But there was one major flaw with the man she'd fallen in love with: he wasn't her husband. His name was Lieutenant John Grogan, an Irishman in the British army. His unit had fought to put down the rebellion in Lower Canada, was even there for the massacre at Saint Eustache, when troops set fire to a church full of rebels, picking them off as they tried to escape before setting the whole town ablaze. Since then, they'd been stationed in the town of London, far to the west of Toronto, which had also seen a small rebel uprising. That's where Lieutenant Grogan and Elizabeth Stuart met and fell in love, starting an affair so shocking it would be debated and dissected in Parliament.

Lieutenant Grogan wouldn't be in London for long. Two years after he arrived, his regiment was sent away to Toronto, to take up residence in Osgoode Hall. Today, it's one of the oldest buildings in the city; the east wing was erected nearly two hundred years ago. Named after the colony's first chief justice, it was originally built as a home for the law society and a law school, given a prominent spot on the edge of town. Today, it stands between Osgoode Station and Nathan Phillips Square, hidden away behind a black iron fence and green trees. It's still home to provincial courts, the Law Society of Ontario, and a magnificent library. But there was a brief period when it wasn't home to lawyers and judges. In the wake of Mackenzie's rebellion, the building was leased by the army for a few years.

Osgoode Hall became a garrison on the edge of the troubled capital. Law students were kicked out in favour of soldiers — including Grogan's regiment. So soon after falling in love, Elizabeth Stuart and her lieutenant were going to be torn apart. And to make things worse, she was pregnant with his child.

That's when Elizabeth Stuart made a bold move. Leaving her husband and her three girls behind, she fled London and joined her lover in Toronto. She spent a night with him there at Osgoode Hall, daring to sleep with him in his quarters, a married woman defying one of the most rigid social conventions of her time.

The scandal would rock Toronto. And the affair was made all the more shocking by the fact that Elizabeth Stuart was a member of what had once been one of the most respectable families in the entire province.

Elizabeth Stuart had been born Elizabeth Powell. She was Anne Murray Powell's granddaughter.

In many ways, John Stuart must have seemed like a perfect match for her. They were both born into prominent families, both grandchildren of some of Upper Canada's early settlers. While Elizabeth was the granddaughter of a chief justice and the great Anne Murray Powell, John's grandfather had been the first Anglican priest to call the province home. On the surface, a marriage between Elizabeth and John must have seemed like a promising and appropriate union between two of Toronto's most storied families.

Anne Murray Powell, on the other hand, knew it was a mistake right from the very beginning. It had been nearly two decades since the matriarch of York had withdrawn from public society. She was nearing the end of her life now, almost eighty years old, but she still knew an approaching disaster when she saw one.

"Affection on her part is out of the question; and of [this] everyone who knows her is fully aware," Powell wrote before her granddaughter got married. And her opinion didn't change after the wedding. It was still very clear that Elizabeth didn't love her new husband — even *he* knew it: "Hers is a most ill assorted and unhappy match. He was aware of her indifference before marriage, and is not … calculated to excite affection. It is a forlorn prospect."

The old woman was right. As the newlyweds set off for London to begin their life together, they were headed toward marital doom. It was only five years later that Elizabeth left her husband to join her lover at Osgoode Hall. Her reputation was ruined, and her marriage with it. It was such a blatant and public insult her husband could hardly ignore it.

John Stuart began by suing Grogan for damages — and won. But that was only the initial step, a necessary prelude to what would come next.

A divorce was a hard thing to get in Upper Canada; the courts had no power to grant one. Instead, each individual case required an act of Parliament: a bill approved by both houses of the legislature. John Stuart was determined to get one. He petitioned Parliament soon after his wife left him, and the process began. First, a trial was held by a committee of the Legislative Council, complete with lawyers and witnesses, dissecting the details of Elizabeth Powell's adultery. They found in favour of Stuart, so it went on to the next stage: a vote in the Legislative Assembly, which he also won. But the idea of granting a divorce was so unusual in the early 1800s that the lieutenant-governor refused to sign the bill into law himself. Instead, it was sent all the way to England, where it finally received royal assent two years after that infamous night at Osgoode Hall. It was the only divorce ever granted in the entire history of Upper Canada — a period that covered half a century.

It was, by the standards of English law, an unusual divorce; while most forbade the guilty party from ever getting married again, this one let Elizabeth Powell have another wedding. It was held at St. James Church in the summer of 1841. She was finally free to spend the rest of her life with the man she loved.

But that life wouldn't be easy. Lieutenant Grogan was ruined by the lawsuit. The court had awarded Stuart nearly seven hundred pounds in damages, plus costs. Grogan was forced to sell his military commission in order to cover the debt, losing his livelihood. Disgraced by the scandal, the newlyweds were driven from Toronto. The Grogans shunned them and the Powell family was split in two; while some relatives supported Elizabeth, most refused to see her at all. When the penniless couple eventually returned and tried to re-enter society, Anne Murray Powell met them with the same steely resolve she'd used against Elizabeth Small all those decades earlier. "I would as soon receive a Housebreaker or a Murderer," she wrote, "as a Man who had inflicted indelible disgrace on a large and respectable family." She was sure Elizabeth was doomed to an unhappy life with an unfaithful man. "Her crime will be her punishment, for misery must attend a marriage with a noted profligate who tho' neither young nor even good looking has been the ruin of several *married women*; some of respectable connections."

Anne Murray Powell had spent her life trying to build a sterling reputation for her family. And she'd failed. Even now, her descendants were still letting her down. "I writhe under that which casts a stain upon my family," she wrote. "We are become subjects of scorn or of pity." She had seen her children convicted of piracy, drowned in shipwrecks, and tainted by scandal. Now, she'd lived long enough to see her granddaughter get Toronto's first divorce.

17

THE BLUE SCHOOL BOYS

James Hunter Samson was worried. It had been months since he'd gotten a letter from his best friend. And in that last message, Robert Baldwin had spoken of a new girl: his latest crush. That wasn't a good sign. Samson knew perfectly well that Baldwin was a hopelessly romantic teenager who devoured romance novels and longed to be swept up in a great love story of his own. Baldwin was only fourteen, but he was already falling head over heels for the girls of York on a regular basis, writing love poems to them, and waxing on about them at length in his letters to his friend. And so, as the silence grew longer and longer, Samson must have had a sinking feeling in his stomach. It seemed as if Baldwin might be falling in love yet again. And that was truly terrible news, because James Hunter Samson was sure *he* loved Robert Baldwin more deeply than any woman ever could.

Many years later, when they were both grown men, they would take their place among the most powerful politicians in Upper Canada, their relationship in tatters as they stood on opposite sides of the vicious fight over Canadian democracy. One them would change the country forever. But it all began when they were boys in a blue schoolhouse in 1818.

Samson was born in Ireland and had sailed across the ocean as a young teenager — his father was a soldier sent to fight in the War of 1812. When the war ended, the family stayed in the Canadian colonies, with Samson aspiring to become a lawyer. He was eighteen when he arrived in York to attend the most prestigious school in the province. The Home District Grammar School stood on a square near St. James Church; it was two storeys high, held about fifty students, and had such a distinctive paint job that it became known as the Blue School. (It would eventually evolve into today's Jarvis Collegiate.) The students learned to develop moral character, to love the British monarchy, and to be devoutly religious Protestants. And since the school was run by none other than Reverend John Strachan, Samson's classmates included the sons of all the most respected families in Upper Canada.

Robert Baldwin was one of them. His life had been intertwined with the history of Toronto since the day he was born. He'd been part of the very first generation of settlers raised in York, born in the same house where the Mackenzies would later live: the one where the Types Riot happened. He grew up at Russell Abbey, where John White had died after his New Year's duel. On the day the

Americans invaded, Robert was nine years old, fleeing up Yonge Street with his mother. He heard the great explosion that killed Zebulon Pike and saw the plume of smoke rise into the air. His father was one of the town's leading citizens: William Warren Baldwin was a doctor, lawyer, and one of the original architects of Osgoode Hall. He'd also married one of the Willcocks sisters, so he was there the day Eugenia married Augustin Boiton de Fougères, brandishing his rifle to scare off the revellers at that night's charivari.

And while William Warren Baldwin was a leader of the Reform Party, passionately opposed to Reverend Strachan's politics, that didn't stop him from giving his son the best possible education. When he was old enough, Robert Baldwin was sent to the Blue School just like all his most privileged peers.

It was there at the schoolhouse that the two boys must have met for the first time. Baldwin was a few years younger than Samson, but they still quickly hit it off. Within months, they'd become best friends. But one of them seems to have longed for more than simple friendship.

Samson didn't live in York for very long. His year at the Blue School complete, he was sent off to continue his education by serving in the office of one of the most successful lawyers in the province. It was a great opportunity. Christopher Hagerman was a major figure in the Family Compact; in fact, he was one of the Tories that Mackenzie got fired during his trip to London. But taking that great opportunity also meant that Samson had to move to Kingston, which must have seemed a long way from York and his dear new friend — in those days it took a steamship to get there, or a long stagecoach ride over punishingly rough roads. Still, distance wouldn't weaken their bond; in 1819, Samson and Baldwin sent a flurry of letters up and down Lake Ontario.

In their messages, they talked about everything from juicy gossip to politics and literature. Baldwin came from a proudly literary family — his grandson Robert Baldwin Ross would one day have his own great love affair with Oscar Wilde — and he fancied himself something of a poet. He kept his friend up to date on all his latest crushes by sending him love poems dedicated to a pantheon of teenage girls.

Samson was incredibly supportive of his friend's writing. He was constantly encouraging him, acting as his editor, even suggesting they collect their poems together into a homemade book. When one of Baldwin's pieces was criticized, Samson rushed to his defence by slamming the critic: "[H]e knows as much about poetry as a horse does about his grandfather." But he clearly didn't like hearing about all the enchanting young women Baldwin was spending his time with. Samson suggested that his friend focus on his studies instead of his crushes. He wanted Robert to himself. "His letters show Samson as articulate, sensitive, fond of poetry, hard-working, and ambitious," historian Gerald E. Boyce once explained, "but also insecure, subject to fits of depression, and extremely jealous of anyone who threatened to come between himself and Baldwin."

"I love and esteem you with my whole soul," Samson once confided to his friend. As with Alexander Wood and George Markland before him, it's impossible to know now exactly how romantic Samson's feelings really were. But his letters suggest those feelings were intense and that he was deeply worried that Baldwin didn't feel the same way. When his friend fell suddenly silent, it must have seemed as if that fear had been confirmed.

Every day, Samson walked to the post office "tortured by anxiety and suspense." And every day, he was disappointed: there was no letter waiting for him. He sent his own messages off to York, pleading with Baldwin not to choose a girl over his best friend. "Believe me," he warned him, "she cannot love or esteem you more than I do."

But Baldwin was always falling in and out of love. It had already happened at least ten times by Samson's count. And this new crush would eventually pass, as well. It would be a few years before James Hunter Samson's greatest fear really did come true. In 1825, Robert Baldwin fell deeply and irreversibly in love.

Her name was Elizabeth Sullivan. Baldwin was in his early twenties when they fell for each other. She was only fourteen or fifteen, but he was charmed by everything she did. She was the one person that he felt he could truly confide in — much to Samson's chagrin. But in the end, it wasn't his jealous friend who would prove to be the biggest obstacle to Baldwin's new relationship; it was his family.

That's because it was her family, too. Robert and Eliza were cousins. Their relatives didn't approve of the incestuous match or the worrying age difference. Eliza was banished to New York City; the family hoped that with a little time apart, the young love would fade. But they were wrong. For more than a year, Eliza and Robert exchanged their own flurry of love letters. He wrote poems about her. Had dreams about her. Longed for her as the scent of lilacs drifted through the air at Russell Abbey, reminding him of their time together. On the first day of every month, they had a set hour when they would both think of each other, knowing the other was doing the same. If anything, their love was growing stronger. "Be assured," he promised her, "every day increases my affection."

And so, with every passing day, Samson's hopes were fading. In the end, Robert and Eliza's parents gave up. She was allowed to return home to York and to marry Robert at a modest ceremony at St. James Church in front of their reluctant relatives.

Samson was there, too. He stood at Robert's side, serving as his groomsman, but he'd been deeply wounded by the news. "It seemed to me," he wrote, "as if I were losing some portion of that, to which I had prior claim." In that moment, as the ceremony was performed, he must have felt a greater distance between himself and his best friend than ever before, his heart breaking as he watched Robert pledge his undying love to Eliza instead of to him.

As soon as the wedding was over, the Baldwins excitedly began building their new life together. For a while, they lived at the family's summer residence — Spadina House — and then settled into an elegant brick home on the corner of Front and Bay Streets. They had three children together. Robert's career began to take off. It was a blissful life. "I wish every one was as happy as I am," Eliza wrote.

In the years to come, Baldwin and Samson — once such close friends — would do more than just drift apart. They would become political foes.

After the wedding, Samson retreated to his own new home in Belleville. The city was just a village back then, home to only a few hundred people. Samson had become their first lawyer and was a leader in the small community. When cholera swept through the Canadian colonies during the summer of 1832, he helped to pay for the construction of the town's first hospital. He sat on the local board of health, and on the village council, too.

He even got married. And he married well. Alicia Fenton Russell was the niece and ward of Sir John Harvey, a hero of the War of 1812 who would go on to become lieutenant-governor of all three Maritime provinces, and civil governor of Newfoundland, too. Samson and his new wife would never have any children, but the impressive match did undoubtably help cement his public reputation. Just a few months after getting married, he ran for a seat in the Legislative Assembly. And he won.

But if he thought his new career would provide a distraction from an aching heart, he was sorely mistaken. He would now have to travel to York on a regular basis to take his seat in Parliament. And soon, Baldwin would be there waiting for him.

Six months after Samson took his seat, John Beverley Robinson resigned from his. He'd been appointed as chief justice of Upper Canada, finishing his climb up to the very top of the legal profession in the province. That meant Robinson was leaving the Legislative Assembly. There would be a by-election to pick his replacement. The riding of York, the capital itself, was suddenly up for grabs.

The Reformers saw a huge opportunity. Robinson had held that seat for nearly a decade, using it to consolidate the power of the Family Compact. If they could win in his old riding, it would be a major symbolic victory: the leader of the Family Compact replaced by a Reformer, a sure sign that popular support was beginning to swing away from the Tories. And the candidate the Reformers picked to perform this miracle was Robert Baldwin.

It was a tough race. He and his Tory opponent were neck and neck right to the very end. Baldwin was running against William Botsford Jarvis, a leading member of the Family Compact and who was serving as sheriff at the time. He had co-founded the village of Yorkville, and his country estate would one day become the affluent neighbourhood of Rosedale. In a few years, he'd be leading the militiamen who faced down Mackenzie's army on Yonge Street. And yet even with the support Jarvis enjoyed, when the dust had settled, Baldwin had done it. Barely. He had won by only nine votes.

It was the beginning of a transformative political career. Over the next twenty years, Baldwin would be in the thick of the battles over Canada's future. While he was a moderate who opposed Mackenzie's violence, he still found himself caught up in the rebellion crisis. It's thought he was the one who convinced George Markland and the rest of the Executive Council to resign with him in protest when Lieutenant-Governor Francis Bond Head refused to heed their advice. On the day Mackenzie marched his army down Yonge Street, Baldwin was there trying to arrange a truce. After the rebellion was crushed, it was Baldwin who represented Samuel Lount and Peter Matthews in court as their defence attorney, convincing them to plead guilty in the vain hope that John Beverley Robinson would show mercy and spare their lives. And in the years to come, with all the most radical Reformers dead, imprisoned, or driven into exile, it was the moderate Baldwin who would find himself the undisputed leader of the Reformers and the struggle for responsible government.

James Hunter Samson, on the other hand, would spend his entire political career opposing almost everything Robert Baldwin believed in.

When Samson first took his seat in Parliament, he claimed to be a moderate, too. But that was far from the truth. His days as a student under John Strachan and Christopher Hagerman seem to have rubbed off on him — and the heartbreak he suffered at Baldwin's hands can't have helped. He soon proved himself to be one of the most radically conservative Tories in all of

Upper Canada, opposing the Reformers at every turn. William Lyon Mackenzie despised him, putting him on his "Black List" of Family Compact villains, calling him "a selfish illiberal creature." Samson retaliated by suing Mackenzie. He dismissed his opinions as "gross, scandalous, and malicious libels — intended and calculated to bring this House and the Government of this Province into contempt." It was Samson who introduced the motion to have Mackenzie thrown out of Parliament, sparking the crisis that led to the rebel mayor's mission to London.

While Baldwin believed wholeheartedly in democratic reform, Samson simply couldn't understand why anyone thought change was needed in Upper Canada. "We have less cause of complaint," he argued, "than any people on earth." And for a while, it seemed as if it was Samson's vision for the future that would win out: as if ultimate power in the hands of the British lieutenant-governor and his bosses in England forever; and as if Canada would never embrace democracy.

Robert Baldwin might have been destined for great things, but his political career got off to a rough start. Just a few months after his big by-election victory, tragic news arrived: King George IV had died. The monarch's death meant a new election was automatically called. Samson won his seat again; in fact, he'd hold it for the rest of his life. But Baldwin lost. It was Sheriff Jarvis and the Tories who won the riding of York — as well as the entire election. Support was swinging back toward the Family Compact.

Baldwin had never really liked politics. He wasn't a particularly good speaker or at all charismatic. He was perfectly happy to return to his private life, focusing on his thriving legal career, and his love for Eliza and their children. But that blissful existence was about to suffer a much greater loss than any election could ever deliver. Heartbreak was coming for Robert Baldwin, too.

Giving birth in the early 1800s was a life-threatening ordeal. And Eliza's fourth labour proved to be difficult, requiring a Caesarean section. The wound never fully healed. It slowly and painfully killed her over the course of the next two years.

Robert was devastated. He'd be deep in mourning for the rest of his life. During the fight for responsible government, Baldwin suffered bouts of severe depression. He was plagued by nightmares and insomnia. There were days he couldn't muster the energy to complete even the most simple tasks. He kept Eliza's room untouched: a shrine to her memory, one that only he was allowed to enter. He kept her love letters in his pocket wherever he went. On the day of their wedding anniversary, he could be found wandering the streets of Toronto like a ghost, visiting the landmarks of their relationship. A devoutly religious man, he longed for the day when he would finally be reunited with his lost love.

It finally came in 1858. A thousand mourners attended Toronto's first state funeral, following the horse-drawn hearse as it made its way up from the new St. James

Cathedral to Spadina House. There, Robert Baldwin was taken into the family tomb and laid to rest beside his beloved Eliza.

It was a month later that they found the note, tucked away in a pocket of one of his vests: a list of his final wishes. Most of them were fairly ordinary, touching requests. He wanted to be buried with Eliza's love letters, and with a brooch she'd given him as a gift. But some of them were much more bizarre. Baldwin had never lost the sense of romantic drama he'd shared with James Hunter Samson through those teenage love poems all those years ago.

On a chilly winter day in 1859, three of Robert Baldwin's closest relatives descended into the family tomb to crack open his casket. They brought a doctor with them. There inside the tomb, the physician took a scalpel to the corpse, splitting Baldwin's stomach open, giving him a Caesarean section like the one that had killed his wife. Then they closed the coffin and chained it to Eliza's, so that in death the two lovers would never be apart.

By then, James Hunter Samson had been dead for more than twenty years. The heartbroken Tory never fully recovered from the loss of his cherished relationship with Baldwin. As their political views diverged, the two old friends were driven further and further apart. When Samson's father died, it left him even more bereft. At the very same time that Eliza Baldwin's health was spiralling toward death, so, too, was his. Samson sank into alcoholism and despair. Eventually, he was unable even to attend Parliament. The state of his mental health became fodder for the press. Ravaged by his drinking, plagued by depression, he lived only a few weeks longer than Eliza did. He died at the age of thirty-six.

He didn't live to see the Family Compact lose their fight, or to see the man he'd once loved so dearly change the course of Canadian history.

It was just a matter of weeks after Eliza died that Robert Baldwin was dragged back into politics for the first time since his lost election. Bond Head arrived to take his post as lieutenant-governor and quickly appointed the respected Reformer to his Executive Council. Baldwin, still overwhelmed by grief, tried to decline, but was eventually worn down. And so, the series of events that would lead to Mackenzie's rebellion were set in motion.

In the wake of the uprising, the British forced Upper and Lower Canada to unite as the "Province of Canada." It was a naked attempt to stamp out French Canadian culture, which they blamed for the rebellions that had swept across both provinces. They assumed all the Anglophones would stick together and outvote the Francophones. But the new leader of the Reformers had a better idea. He saw an opportunity to lay the foundation for a new kind of multicultural nation.

Robert Baldwin cemented an alliance with the leader of the Quebecois reformers: Louis-Hippolyte LaFontaine. By uniting all those who believed in responsible government — Anglophones and Francophones, Protestants and Catholics alike — they would have the power they needed to defeat the Tories.

Together, Baldwin and LaFontaine would accomplish what Mackenzie had been unable to do with an entire army at his back. In 1848, they ran on a platform demanding responsible government. They were elected by such an overwhelming majority that the British had little choice. The following year, for the first time in Canadian history, the governor general signed a bill into law, even though he and the Tories disagreed with it. With that stroke of the pen, he was acknowledging for the very first time that it wasn't his will that should rule over Canada, but the will of Canadians themselves.

The Tories were so enraged, they burned down the Parliament buildings in Montreal. But when the riots died down, it was clear the Reformers had won.

There was still much more work to be done. It would be many decades before Canadian women were able to cast a ballot. Chinese Canadians would be stripped of the right to vote for decades beyond that. First Nations voters wouldn't be allowed to cast a ballot without giving up their status under the Indian Act until the 1960s, which is when ballot boxes were finally brought to Inuit communities, too. But after decades of struggle, of violence, and of rebellion, a landmark victory had finally been achieved. Robert Baldwin had won. James Hunter Samson had lost. Responsible government was a reality. Canada really was a democracy.

THE BOOMING
METROPOLIS

18

ESCAPE FROM KENTUCKY

The painting hangs on the wall of the Canadian Gallery in the Royal Ontario Museum: a small oil displayed in a golden frame. It was painted nearly two centuries ago by a fairly obscure local artist called John Gillespie. It shows a bustling King Street on a beautiful day in the middle of the 1840s. The soaring spire of the new St. James Church — the immediate precursor of to-day's grand cathedral — reaches up into the bright blue sky toward a few wisps of cloud. The wide sidewalks are filled with life: women in bonnets and long dresses pass from shop to shop; men in top hats stroll along the store-fronts; a pair of First Nations people chat by the entrance to the old St. Lawrence Market while two soldiers do the same nearby in their bright red uniforms and fuzzy black bearskin hats. Horses and riders trot by in the street. It's an idyllic scene of a metropolis just beginning to grow into its own, home to twenty thousand people. It depicts the young city as the great British author Charles Dickens described it just a few years earlier: "[T]he town itself is full of life and motion, bustle, business and improvement."

There, in the centre of the painting, surrounded by the commotion of King Street, is a yellow carriage. It's heading away from us, disappearing down the street. The driver, perched atop the cab, has his back turned to us. We can't see his face. You can barely tell he's there at all: a few indistinct strokes of grey lost in the bright chaos of the streetscape.

But that patch of grey paint represents a harrowing tale of bravery. Sitting on top of that carriage is a man who was willing to risk everything for freedom — and for love.

Thornton Blackburn was born into slavery, but within sight of freedom. He grew up in Kentucky, living right alongside the Ohio River. The blue waters marked the official boundary between the slavery of the American South and the free states of the North. On his side of the river there was bondage and captivity; on the other side, liberty.

But crossing that river was a dangerous proposition. Those who were caught trying to escape slavery were often brutally punished. Some were beaten or whipped, some had their faces branded with a red-hot iron, some had ears cut off or limbs amputated, while others were castrated. It was a death-defying risk that might even lead to your execution.

And yet, Blackburn was about to try. He was in danger of losing the woman he loved — more than enough reason to make the perilous journey across the Ohio River.

He was a teenager when he met her. They were both living in Louisville; Ruthie was enslaved just a few doors down the street. She'd been born in the Caribbean — maybe even in Haiti, taken from the island as a child by some of the French refugees who fled the revolution just as Jeremiah Powell was about to arrive — before ending up in Kentucky. She and Thornton fell in love and got married, allowed to spend a little time together every weekend: from Saturday night to early Monday morning before their work began.

But now even those few hours were under threat. Ruthie was being sold down the river into the Deep South, where the back-breaking labour of the cotton fields would likely be accompanied by sexual abuse. The Blackburns' only chance to stay together was to sneak across the river and escape Kentucky into freedom.

They made their move on a July day in 1831. At first, everything went to plan. They caught a ferry across the river using forged papers in case they were questioned. It was risky gambit; they were well-known in these parts and anyone who spotted them would be legally obligated to capture them and turn them in. But the ferry ride went off without a hitch. They made it across the river into Indiana.

But that was just the first step. Indiana was a free state, but it wasn't entirely safe. Slave catchers prowled the North looking to capture runaways and return them for a bounty. The Blackburns would need to keep moving, getting as far from Kentucky as they could, if they were going to stay free.

So, it was time for the next step in their plan. They waded out into the water and flagged down a steamboat as it pulled away from the Louisville docks. The captain was deeply suspicious, questioning them closely, looking for any sign they might be fleeing slavery. But they'd appeared from the Indiana side of the river and their papers seemed to be in order. One day, he would be put on trial for believing them, but believe them he did. The Blackburns were allowed to book passage upriver, steaming away from Louisville, leaving their life of slavery behind.

In Cincinnati, they grabbed a stagecoach heading north, bumping along the rough roads of Ohio until they reached the shores of Lake Erie. Then, they caught a second stagecoach to Detroit. It was there, right across the river from Upper Canada, that the Blackburns planned to live their new life of freedom.

Detroit was still a small town: about two thousand people living on the edge of the frontier; the last stop before the Indigenous lands to the west. There, finally, the Blackburns were able live together as husband and wife. Thornton got a job as a stonemason, making his own money as a free man for first time.

But this new life didn't last long.

It all began to unravel with a chance encounter. One day, while walking down the street, Thornton bumped into a man who used to work at the very same store in Louisville where he'd been enslaved. They had a pleasant conversation, catching up, and Thornton told him he'd been given his freedom. But when the man finally returned home to Kentucky, the lie was uncovered. The Blackburns might have been living hundreds of kilometres from the South, but they still weren't safe — not even in a free territory like Michigan. The law said anyone anywhere in the United States who was found to have escaped slavery had to be sent back. The Blackburns were arrested and thrown into the Detroit Jail, waiting to be shipped to Kentucky in chains.

But the people of Detroit weren't going to let them go without a fight.

Over the weekend, a crowd began to gather in the fields and forests around the jail: the town's Black residents and their white abolitionist allies. They came armed with everything from pistols and swords to clubs and sticks. They were going to do everything in their power to make sure the Blackburns weren't returned to slavery. Even if that meant violence.

Eventually, two women came forward out of the crowd. They asked if they could at least visit with Ruthie for a while before she was hauled away. They spent the rest of the day inside her cell, plenty of time to enact their plan. One of them switched clothes with Ruthie. And when two women emerged from the jail that evening, veils drawn over their faces in sorrow, handkerchiefs wiping away their tears, the sheriff didn't notice that one of them was his prisoner. By the time he realized what had happened, Ruthie Blackburn had already slipped across the border into Upper Canada. Into freedom.

One prisoner down. One to go.

Thornton's escape wouldn't be as easy. It came down to the very last minute, as he was led down the steps of the jail by armed guards, chained and manacled, heading toward a waiting carriage. But the crowd stood in the way, at least two hundred angry citizens ready for a fight.

Blackburn convinced the sheriff he could make peace: if he were allowed to address the crowd, he could talk them into leaving and he would go without a fight. But when he stepped forward to begin speaking, someone in the crowd tossed him a pistol with the cry, "Shoot the rascal!" Suddenly, the prisoner was armed.

Blackburn wheeled on the sheriff. He pointed the pistol right at him before raising it into the air. He fired a shot into the sky. As he did, the crowd surged forward, and while the guards disappeared back inside the safety of the jail, the sheriff was pulled to the ground, knocked unconscious by a blow to the head.

Nearby, church bells began to ring out in alarm. Now another angry mob was on the way: white citizens coming to the defence of their sheriff. In the violence that followed, one young Black man was shot in the chest, his lung pierced; he would eventually die from the wound. In the chaos and confusion, Thornton Blackburn was bundled onto a waiting wagon and rushed away toward the border.

It was the beginning of a dramatic cart chase. With a posse hot on their heels, dogs barking and alarm bells ringing out, Blackburn's rescuers rushed toward the Detroit River, urging their driver and his blind horse to go faster and faster. When they reached the river, they paid a boatman with a gold watch to take Blackburn across the water into Canada, where freedom and Ruthie were waiting.

Tensions in Detroit would remain high for weeks. In the wake of that night's violence, nearly every Black resident was rounded up and thrown in jail; the others were placed under a strict curfew and not allowed to go anywhere near the river. A night watch was established to make sure those new rules were followed. There were protests, and the stables next to the jail were burned down; in retaliation, more than forty Black homes were torched. White citizens attacked Black citizens in the streets. The army was called in and martial law was declared. Before long, nearly all the Black residents of Detroit had fled across the river into Canada. The Blackburn Riots were the first race riots in the history of Detroit. The town had paid a heavy price, but the Blackburns were finally free.

For a few hours. Later that same night, they were arrested by the Canadian authorities, and thrown into a Canadian jail.

John Graves Simcoe hated slavery. As a member of Parliament in England, he'd given abolitionist speeches in the House of Commons. When he was picked to be lieutenant-governor of Upper Canada, he made it clear: he saw no place for slavery in his new province. "The principles of the British Constitution do not admit of that slavery which Christianity condemns," he wrote before he officially took his post. "The moment I assume the Government of Upper Canada, under no modification will I assent to a law that discriminates by dishonest policy between natives of Africa, America or Europe."

By then, slavery had already been abolished in England — a court decision had ended it fifteen years earlier. But hundreds of people were enslaved by the colonists of Upper Canada, many of them brought north by the Loyalist refugees as they fled the revolution in the United States. The British government had officially condoned the practice. So, if Simcoe wanted to get rid of slavery in Upper Canada, he was going to have to pass a new law to actively abolish it.

He didn't wait long to act. In the summer of 1793, just weeks before he founded Toronto, Simcoe introduced a bill to abolish slavery. He'd been inspired by the horrifying tale of Chloe Cooley — a Black woman enslaved at Niagara who'd loudly resisted being sold across the river into the United States, kicking and screaming as she was rowed across the border. But actually getting that bill passed into law wasn't going to be easy. Simcoe would need support. The bill would have to pass through the Legislative Assembly and then through the Legislative Council. Both of those bodies were full of slaveholders. And that, in part, was thanks to Simcoe himself.

The Legislative Assembly was an elected body, but the members of the Legislative Council were hand-picked by Simcoe himself — and he'd packed it full of slaveholders. At least five of the nine members were either slaveholders or from slaveholding families. They formed a majority. Simcoe, determined to abolish slavery in Upper Canada, had made it almost impossible to do.

In the end, he was forced into a compromise — the exact thing he had promised never to do. His new law didn't abolish slavery immediately; instead, it would be gradually phased out. No enslaved person could be brought into Upper Canada, but all those already there would spend the rest of their lives in bondage. Their children would be born into slavery, too; they wouldn't be free until they turned twenty-five.

And so, while the "Act Against Slavery" was the first bill to abolish slavery ever passed anywhere in the British Empire — introduced more than seventy years before the Emancipation Proclamation in the United States — it was still legal when Toronto was founded. During the city's founding years, fifteen people were enslaved within its borders, as well as another ten just across the Don Valley. Some of Toronto's slaveholders are still familiar names in the city: William Jarvis, James Baby, Peter Russell, and John Denison all have streets and neighbourhoods named after them to this day, while the Kanien'keha:ka chief Joseph Brant — who enslaved dozens of people outside the city — is remembered in the name of a school in Scarborough.

The Blackburns fled Detroit four decades after Simcoe's bill became law, but slavery still wasn't illegal in Upper Canada. It was another year before the practice was officially abolished across the entire British Empire.

And there were still plenty of questions left to be settled concerning people who escaped American slavery by coming to Canada. The Blackburns weren't safe yet. Their struggle wasn't over.

They'd made it across the river into Canada, where they should have been free. Simcoe's law made it clear: only people who were already enslaved in Upper Canada could be enslaved there; no one from outside the province. But the American authorities weren't going to give up that easily. They wanted the Blackburns extradited back to the United States to face trial for their involvement in the riots. So, just hours after Thornton slipped across the border, the Blackburns were arrested and held in a Canadian jail while the government leaders in York figured out what to do.

Thankfully, they had some rather unexpected allies. It was the early 1830s and the Family Compact still ruled Upper Canada. And their hatred of all things American included a hatred of slavery. The law was clear, with a recent precedent set by the top judge in the province: John Beverley Robinson. As soon as someone set foot on Canadian soil, they were given the full protection of British law. That meant people who escaped slavery would not be sent back south.

But it suddenly seemed as if things might not be that simple. The Blackburns weren't just being accused of escaping slavery, they were being accused of other crimes, as well. It wasn't clear what would happen. As they awaited their fate, the question hung over them: Would Canada send them back to be tried in the United

States even though it was perfectly clear they would be returned into slavery whether or not they were found guilty? Powerful abolitionists in York, like Reverend Strachan, leapt to the Blackburns' defence, advising the new lieutenant-governor to refuse the extradition request. In the end, after an agonizing few weeks, that's just what he did. The Blackburns were released. They were finally, truly free.

With their liberty finally secured, the Blackburns settled in Toronto. There was even a pleasant surprise waiting for them there: Thornton's brother Arthur had escaped slavery and made his way north, too. The Blackburns stayed with him for a while, but eventually built a small farmhouse just a block away — not far from the Don Valley, at what's now the corner of Sackville Street and Eastern Avenue. It was a modest home, with just three little rooms and a cellar, but they had a wonderful view out over the lake, with the iconic Gooderham & Worts windmill towering above the shore. The kept a big vegetable garden and a small orchard of fruit trees, while fishing and hunting in the nearby valley and the sprawling Ashbridge's Marsh. Ruthie gave herself a new name for her new life in freedom: she was now Lucie Blackburn.

The couple would become community leaders in Toronto. They helped to found Little Trinity Church on King Street, which still stands there to this day. And when William Lyon Mackenzie launched his rebellion, just a few years after the Blackburns arrived, they were ready and willing to protect the government that had once protected their freedom. When a group of rebels tried to cross a bridge across the Don River and attack the city from the east, they were met by a single Black man who stood on the bridge, blocking their path — believed to have been Thornton Blackburn or his brother. Years later, the front door of the Blackburns' home would still be riddled with bullet holes put there by rebel muskets.

Their fight against slavery wasn't over, either. There were still millions of people enslaved in the United States — including some of their own loved ones. Soon, Thornton would risk his life again, heading all the way back to Kentucky so he could track down his mother and bring her back with him to Toronto. And she was only one of countless people the Blackburns helped.

Their own legal case had cemented Upper Canada's reputation as a safe haven for those fleeing slavery. And as American laws around people escaping from slavery grew even more draconian, tens of thousands would flee north to Canada.

The Blackburns played a major role in helping turn Toronto into one of the most important destinations at the end of the Underground Railroad. When they arrived in the city, Thornton got a job at Osgoode Hall, working as a waiter in the dining room. After a few years, the Blackburns had saved enough money to start their own business. They had a horse-drawn taxicab built for them, painted it yellow and red, and called it "The City." It had enough room for four passengers inside the carriage, with their luggage and the driver — Thornton Blackburn — perched on top. Many decades later, its yellow and red paint job would inspire the colours of the Toronto Transit Commission.

The City was the first taxi in Upper Canada, and it made the Blackburns wealthy. Before long, they began to buy up property in a new neighbourhood called Macaulaytown — where city hall and Nathan Phillips Square now stand. It would one day become known as "The Ward" and gain a reputation as the city's most notorious "slum," but back in the middle of the 1800s, it was a largely Black neighbourhood, providing a new home for many who escaped on the Underground Railroad. The Blackburns rented out their houses at discount rates to many of those newcomers, helping them to establish themselves in their new city. Some, they even welcomed into their own home — including one mother and her seven children, one of whom would grow up to become Toronto's first Black postal worker, Albert Jackson.

The Blackburns didn't stop there. They were active in anti-slavery societies and supported a whole new settlement for those who'd escaped on the Underground Railroad. In the town of Buxton, they helped fund new businesses and industries that would allow its residents to prove they were just as capable of looking after themselves as white settlers were.

They helped turn Toronto into a vital bastion in the fight against slavery — an emerging metropolis just across the lake from the United States, where leading abolitionists could feel safe meeting, planning, and coordinating their fight. There was plenty of racism in Toronto, too, of course, but it was a far cry from the burning hatred that ruled in so much of the United States. Many of the city's leaders — Tories and Reformers alike — were passionately opposed to slavery. Torontonians were known to drive slave catchers out of town. And when the brand new St. Lawrence Hall opened on King Street in 1850, not only was its first event an abolitionist lecture, it would bring anti-slavery leaders from across the United States, Britain, and Canada together at the historic North American Convention of Colored Freemen later that same year.

The climax in the fight came with the American Civil War. Despite Toronto's abolitionist history, a disturbing number of people in the city supported the Confederate cause. When the South won an important early battle, the Legislative Assembly gave three cheers. A visiting Union soldier was jeered in the streets. The Queen's Hotel on Front Street became a hotbed of Confederate spies and refugees, who rented out all the rooms and hung around the lobby and the bar in their tattered grey uniforms. From Toronto, Confederate agents planned fire-bombings in New York City and plots to kidnap the vice president, to seize a Union warship, and to assassinate President Abraham Lincoln by sending him clothes infected with yellow fever. George Denison — the wealthy grandson of one of York's old slave-owning families — even helped buy them a steamship so they could launch raids on the northern states just across the Great Lakes.

But most Torontonians supported the Union. Tens of thousands of Canadians headed south during the war to take up arms in the fight against slavery — many of them Black. Some included the Blackburns' own friends. Dr. Anderson Ruffin Abbott, the first Black Canadian to graduate from medical school, ended up running a hospital in a refugee camp in Washington, DC, and became friends with Abraham Lincoln. And when the American president began planning for life after the war, he sent a delegation to Canada to learn more about how people freed from slavery were able to live in peace and prosperity.

Finally, after four years of bloodshed and centuries of suffering, the war was won. The Blackburns had lived long enough and fought hard enough to see their dream come true. Slavery had finally been abolished across the United States.

By the time the American Civil War ended, Toronto was a very different city than it had been when the Blackburns first arrived. It was now a booming metropolis. The population was skyrocketing. New businesses and industries were opening all the time. The taxi business had changed with it. The city now had its first horse-drawn streetcar service. Big companies operated whole fleets of cabs, where once the Blackburns had been the only game in town. With times changing, Thornton Blackburn decided to retire, spending more of his remaining days at home with Lucie.

The view out their window had changed drastically over the last thirty years. The iconic old Gooderham & Worts windmill had come down, replaced by a distillery — an entire complex of factories that would produce more whiskey than any other in the world. The land around their property had been developed; it was now home to so many Irish immigrants employed by the distillery that the area had become known as Corktown. Even the Blackburns' own backyard had been swallowed up by the city, expropriated to build a new school for local children.

Soon the schoolyard would swallow up the rest of the Blackburns' land, too. They died as the 1800s drew to a close, laid to rest in the Necropolis cemetery. Their house was demolished and their story began to fade from history, the details of their lives forgotten for a century. It wasn't until an archaeological dig uncovered the ruins of their home that interest in their remarkable tale of bravery and love would be sparked once again. In recent years, they've been resurrected with an award-winning biography — Karolyn Smardz Frost's *I've Got a Home in Glory Land* — and countless articles. A nearby conference centre now bears their names and a few Torontonians even know that a colourful echo of the city's first taxicab still lives on in the red paint of every TTC streetcar.

The Blackburns spent their final years there, together, at home, sitting on their porch, watching the city grow up around them. Two old Torontonians who'd risked everything to make it to the city, who'd fought hatred at every turn, who'd helped play their own small part in bringing an end to one of the most vile institutions the world has ever known, and who now, finally, could rest in peace. And in freedom.

19

THE SUSPICIOUS OYSTER SHOP

There was something suspicious happening at the oyster shop. Long after it closed up for the day, customers continued to arrive. It was still busy deep into the night, carriages pulling up until two in the morning, the sound of their horses' hooves ringing out as they trotted down King Street and stopped outside. One after another, carriage drivers would descend from their cabs — Thornton Blackburn presumably among them on occasion — and approach the entrance, even though it was well after hours. They would knock on the door with their whip and, in response, it would crack open to admit their passengers, some undoubtably boisterous and already more than a little drunk. The whole process made for quite a disruption in the quiet night, and loud arguments could sometimes be heard coming from inside. It was getting to be annoying. Grumpy neighbours were kept awake into the wee hours.

They all knew exactly what was going on: they lived next door to Daniel Bloxsom's brothel.

This was the spring of 1847. Toronto was growing quickly. Twenty thousand people now lived in the city; new immigrants were arriving all the time. But in a lot of ways, it was still a rowdy frontier town. Toronto wasn't exactly living up to Simcoe's dream of a thoroughly respectable British capital. It had plenty of sin; moralizing leaders were horrified by the drunkenness, violence, and adultery that could be found in every corner of their city. By 1850, there were a hundred and fifty taverns in Toronto — more than one for every three hundred residents — and two hundred beer shops on top of that. Blood was spilled in the streets on a regular basis thanks to riots and brawls. And brothels like Bloxsom's could be found across the city, too — shadowy establishments where lustful passions were indulged behind closed doors.

It's hard to know exactly how many of these "Palaces of Sin" were operating in Toronto at the time. Sex work was illegal, so the industry was forced to operate in secrecy. Seemingly respectable businesses like hotels, boarding houses, restaurants, and laundries acted as fronts. To escape detection, many brothel keepers adopted aliases and changed locations. The wonderfully named Mary Anne Trebilcock, for instance, ran a number of Toronto brothels over the years, each with a different address, and she used at least three different names. But records of court proceedings suggest there were, at least, dozens of "bawdy houses" operating in the city. Of the hundreds of charges laid against women for various offences during a typical year, the vast majority would be laid under laws generally used to prosecute sex workers.

But even those police raids did little to slow the industry down. Brothel keepers who ran prosperous establishments could easily afford to pay a fine, avoid prison time, and return to work that very same day. Trebilcock was arrested more than a dozen times, often brought down by an informant who spied on her for the police, but it clearly didn't stop her. Some bawdy houses were even tipped off before raids. Getting a brothel shut down for good wasn't easy.

The exhausted residents of King Street East must have known that going to the police was unlikely to provide a permanent solution to the problem of the oyster shop. So, they tried another approach; they talked to Bloxsom's landlord instead. The man who owned the building just so happened to be one of the most respectable and powerful men in the city.

His name was William Henry Boulton. He was the mayor of Toronto.

Boulton had been born into power. His grandfather was a chief justice. His uncle was John Beverley Robinson. He grew up in one of the most splendid mansions in the city: the Grange is now a National Historic Site and part of the Art Gallery of Ontario. He would eventually inherit the distinguished house himself, taking his place among the leaders of the Family Compact. As a successful Tory politician, he opposed Robert Baldwin in the Legislative Assembly and had also been elected to city council, chosen by his fellow councillors and aldermen to serve as mayor for the last three years in a row.

The oyster shop's neighbours approached him with their problem, explaining the situation: the carousing at all hours, the restless nights, their long suffering. As a respectable Conservative, he would *surely* be shocked by the depravity being unleashed at one of his own properties. He would *have* to leap into action and shut it down. Then they would finally be able to get a good night's sleep.

But it wouldn't be so easy. It was powerful landlords like Boulton who stood to gain the most from sex work. They charged brothel keepers like Daniel Bloxsom inflated rents and rarely faced any consequences. Even if the police did raid the property, the landlords could plausibly deny they'd known anything untoward was happening, letting more vulnerable people take the fall.

When it came to sex work in Toronto, it was often those from marginalized communities who bore the brunt of society's disapproval. For a while, Canadian law would specifically target Indigenous sex workers and those who hired them, imposing stricter limits and higher penalties in their cases. Black brothel keepers like Daniel Bloxsom seem to have been more likely to face repercussions, too. And when one of Thornton Blackburn's properties in The Ward was found to house a brothel, he was charged in a situation where most landlords went unnamed.

Most often, it was the sex workers themselves who paid the cost. They couldn't always afford to buy their way out of jail. It was often poverty that had driven them into sex work in the first place. They were usually young — nearly half of those arrested in 1845, for instance, were under the age of nineteen — and recent immigrants. In fact, the vast majority came from one country in particular.

At the very same time the oyster house was kicking up a racket on King Street, the Great Famine was ravaging Ireland. As a potato blight devastated the island's staple crop, typhoid fever swept through the weakened population. Half-hearted British relief efforts did little to help, while British landlords evicted starving tenants. The Great Famine would claim a million lives and drive another 2.5 million to flee the country, many of them heading to the Canadian colonies. That summer, nearly forty thousand Irish refugees arrived in Toronto, twice the city's population. Many of them were sick and dying, taken to temporary fever sheds on King Street. And even those who somehow survived the crossing in relatively good health were in desperate need of work, having left their livelihoods behind in Ireland.

Some Torontonians welcomed the new arrivals with open arms. But others were dead set against them. The Family Compact wasn't the only formidable group of Protestant Tories in the city. Toronto was a stronghold for the Orange Order, too.

The organization had been founded in Northern Ireland. It was named after William of Orange, the Protestant king who seized the British throne from the Catholic king. The Orange Order was proudly British and violently anti-Catholic. And it found fertile ground in the thoroughly Protestant metropolis of Toronto.

By the middle of the 1800s, the Orange Order had been part of life in the city for decades, but as the Family Compact began to wane, the organization was securing its own stranglehold on power — sometimes by force. Riots between Protestants and Catholics became a regular occurrence in Toronto's streets. Things got so bloody, the St. Patrick's Day parade was banned for more than a century, all the way up to 1988. The annual Orange Parade on the twelfth of July was practically an official holiday: Protestants got the day off work to celebrate, while Catholics hid inside. Orangemen would come to dominate city hall, the civil service, the fire brigades, and the police force. Catholics had a hard time getting any good job at all. The Orangemen running the city weren't about to help those refugees get settled in their new home.

Many of the Irish women arriving in the city must have had little choice but to work in the sex industry. (And some men, too, though in much lower numbers.) Even twenty years after the famine the vast majority of women arrested on sex work–related charges were Irish. Most of them were Catholics. They were dragged into the courthouse on Adelaide Street (it's an Italian restaurant today) where, if they couldn't pay their fines, they were sentenced to a month of hard labour.

Some would spend their entire lives bouncing back and forth between brothel beds and the Toronto Gaol. Catherine O'Hem, for instance, was arrested for the first time at the age of nineteen. Over the next twenty-five years, she would serve seventy-seven sentences in that jail, and her daughter would follow in her footsteps.

Her customers, on the other hand, had little to worry about. Men were barely ever arrested in the raids on Toronto brothels. While hundreds of sex work–related charges might be laid against women during a typical year, only about a dozen charges would be laid against the men who availed themselves of their services. Never mind the men who profited off the industry from behind the scenes — like William Henry Boulton.

Mayor Boulton knew perfectly well that the police weren't about to give him any trouble over the oyster shop. It wasn't just that he was a leader of the Family Compact, or a powerful Tory, or even the mayor. He was also a leading Orangeman, on his way to becoming deputy grand master of the entire Canadian Orange Order — an impressive feat in a country that at one point boasted more Orange lodges than all of Northern Ireland. It was his support within the order that helped him get elected in the first place; he was an Orange hero for helping to overturn a ban on the political parades where Orange mobs clashed with Catholics and Reformers.

Since the police were Orangemen, too, Mayor Boulton knew he had nothing to worry about. They had a proven history of looking the other way when their fellow Orangemen committed crimes. When the residents of King Street came to him complaining about the noise at the oyster shop, Boulton turned them away. Over and over again. He could do what he liked, he told them.

In the end, they felt they had only one option left. They would go public with his name, hoping to embarrass him into shutting the brothel down.

When the news broke, it sparked a scandal. "Utterly disgraceful," the *Globe* called it. Reformers on city council took up the cause, pressuring Boulton to respond. Eventually, the police were forced to act. But, of course, it wasn't the mayor who would pay the price; it was Daniel Bloxsom who was arrested. His trial was far from fair. The judge was Boulton's own uncle, John Beverley Robinson, and Boulton himself was there sitting next to him as his associate. They fined Bloxsom ten dollars. "We confess [the trial was] the most indecent thing we have seen yet in Canada," the *Globe* complained.

Boulton does seem to have suffered a bit of fallout. He wouldn't be chosen as mayor for a fourth term the following year. But he was re-elected to the Legislative Assembly and, a decade later, he was back in the mayor's office once again. It would take a clash with another influential Orangeman to finally bring him down.

Samuel Sherwood was the chief of police, a proud Orangeman with a history of violence. Years earlier, he'd helped organize an attack on a Reform Party parade; one Reformer was shot and killed. His fervour and loyalty were eventually rewarded when he was put in charge of the city's police force. He was a fairly lax leader: his men didn't wear uniforms, were known to be "slovenly," and tended to join the riots they were sent to quell. Now,

Sherwood was embroiled in his own sex work–related scandal.

One summer night in 1855, some clowns from a visiting circus headed to Mary Ann Armstrong's brothel at King and John Streets. They were, by all accounts, a pretty tough crew. And while they were there, they got into a brawl with some other customers: a group of firefighters from the Hook & Ladder Firefighting Company.

While the clowns won that night's battle, leaving two firefighters seriously injured, they'd picked the wrong fight on the wrong night. In those days, there was no central, public, government-run fire department. When a blaze broke out, all the nearby brigades rushed to the scene with their horse-drawn engines to call dibs. Just a couple of weeks earlier, the Hook & Ladders had arrived at a fire on Church Street at the same time as another brigade. The two crews battled in the street as the building burned. The firefighters were no strangers to violence.

They were also Orangemen. They'd been at the brothel that night celebrating the biggest day on the Orange calendar: the twelfth of July, the day of the big parade. So, the next day, a crowd began to gather around S.B. Howes's Star Troupe Menagerie & Circus. An angry, Orange crowd.

When Chief Sherwood was told about the approaching trouble, he dragged his feet for as long as he could. By the time his men got there, the violence had already started. People were hurling stones at the circus performers. While the clowns, acrobats, and carnies were able to hold the mob off for a while, it couldn't last. Eventually, the crowd overwhelmed them. And when the Hook & Ladders arrived, all hell broke loose. They stormed the circus with pikes and axes, overturned wagons, and pulled down the tents and the big top and set fire to them. They beat clowns to a pulp. Circus folk ran for their lives. Some dove into the lake for safety. It was mayhem. The mayor was eventually forced to call in the militia.

The police had done pretty much nothing. They just watched. Chief Sherwood eventually made a personal appearance but did little other than stopping the rioters from setting fire to the cages of the animals. Of the seventeen people charged in the riot, only one was ever convicted. All the police who were at the scene claimed they couldn't remember any of the Orangemen who'd been there — just as they'd done a few weeks earlier after the Firemen's Riot.

That cover-up wasn't Sherwood's last. After yet another riot between Protestants and Catholics ended with a Catholic stabbed to death with a pitchfork, Chief Sherwood's memory was yet again suspiciously fuzzy as far as Orangemen were concerned. Not long after that, he was under fire again, for freeing a suspect who'd been accused of robbing a bank.

By then, Boulton was mayor again. And that was a bridge too far, even for him. An inquiry was called, but Sherwood refused to cooperate. Boulton responded by trying to have him fired and replaced. But when it came to a vote, city council took Sherwood's side. Defeated and embarrassed, Boulton resigned. Without his traditional Orange support, he would lose the next election — the first in which voters picked the mayor directly.

Chief Sherwood's days were numbered, too. For the first time in more than twenty years — since Mackenzie's rebellion — a Reformer was elected mayor. City council called for big changes to the way the police force was run. The provincial government agreed. Another inquest was launched, and in the end, the whole system was overhauled. Every single police officer in the city was fired, and a new force was created from scratch. Thanks in part to the brothel brawl, the foundations of the modern police force had been laid.

But it was only a tiny step. Even without Boulton in office, the systems that had kept him there were still in place. The Orange Order would have a stranglehold on power for another century, ruling over the city into the middle of the 1900s. For the next hundred years, nearly *every* mayor of Toronto would be an Orangeman. And the police force stayed Orange, too.

Despite the overhaul, half the old constables would end up being rehired. And in the years to come, Toronto's police force would be used more aggressively than ever before to enforce strict limits on love in the city. They would be recast as defenders of public virtue, used as a tool to crack down on drinking, sex work, homosexuality, and anything else the city's leaders decided was a vice. The Toronto Police Morality Squad was on the way.

20
THE WINTER ACCIDENT

It was the dead of winter: the first week of January 1854. Somewhere on the snowy country roads far to the northeast of Toronto, a horse-drawn sleigh rushed away from the city. On board were two old friends. Jeanie Hall was in her early twenties, energetic and a bit of a tomboy, the daughter of a politician. Over Christmas and New Year's, she had come to Toronto to visit family friends — including a promising young engineer called Sandford Fleming. Now, with the holidays over, he was escorting her back home to Peterborough in a small, elegant sleigh with just enough room for the two of them to bundle together against the cold.

But as they slid across the snow, they were, perhaps, going a bit too fast. Somewhere outside the town of Lindsay, the sleigh hit a bump in the road hidden by the snow. The curved runners were pitched off balance. The sleigh toppled over. The two passengers were thrown into the road. Jeanie wasn't hurt, but Sandford slammed into the stump of a tree and was knocked out cold. She rushed to his side, watching over him as he lay there in the snow, unconscious.

That accident was about to change both of their lives.

They'd first met nine years earlier — back when they were teenagers. Fleming had left Scotland with his brother at the age of eighteen, sailing across the stormy Atlantic in search of a new life in Canada. He settled in Peterborough, living with his father's cousin and family in a grey stone house that is still standing today (now run as a museum called Hutchison House).

Jeanie Hall lived next door. Her father was a prominent figure in the community; he served time as the mayor, a member of Parliament, and the sheriff. He also owned a store, and when the adventurous young Scot moved in next door, the Halls offered Fleming a job working behind the counter until he found his bearings.

And so, Sandford and Jeanie began to spend time together. But it wasn't love at first sight. Jeanie was just fourteen when they met, and Fleming was looking ahead to his ambitious professional plans. He would soon leave Peterborough for Toronto, where he quickly established himself as one of the city's most promising young intellectuals. He apprenticed as a surveyor and co-founded the Royal Canadian Institute — one of the country's leading scientific societies. Within a few years, he'd worked his way up to becoming the chief civil engineer for the city's very first railway. The Ontario, Simcoe & Huron Railway connected Toronto with Collingwood and the ships that sailed the upper Great Lakes, bringing wheat and timber from the West. The new railroad helped to cement Toronto's central role in the Canadian economy.

It had only been a few years since he'd left Scotland, but Fleming had already made a mark. He was twenty-six years old and quite a catch: a tall and adventurous young man, with long hair, an impressively bushy beard, and a wildly successful career.

That's certainly how Bessie Mitchell saw him. By the summer of 1853, she and Sandford were courting, taking frequent walks together around Toronto. It looked like things might be getting serious. But Fleming had gnawing doubts. He clearly cared for her, but he wondered if she was really the woman he wanted to spend the rest of his life with. As a decision about their future loomed, Fleming decided that he didn't want to decide at all. Instead, he would leave things up to fate.

One autumn evening, he invited Mitchell on a long walk. As they strolled out north of the city toward the village of Yorkville, he revealed his bizarre plan. Their future would be decided by a sunset. In exactly four weeks, on the evening of November 2, they would have their answer. If the sunset was clear and bright, they would get married. If it was cloudy and overcast, they would break up. Mitchell was appalled by the idea, but she went along with it.

Four weeks later, the fateful evening arrived. Fleming recorded the results in his diary. "Cloudy all day, drizzly rain, sun never appeared," he wrote. "Poor Bessie!!! ... I had fully made up my mind for either way. Hope she has. Indeed, it may be best for both parties — we must hope so!"

Bessie Mitchell was heartbroken. She returned his love letters and cut off all contact. Meanwhile, Fleming was free to pursue a new romance and to see what fate had in store for him next.

The holidays arrived just a few weeks later. And so did his old friend Jeanie Hall. They'd kept in touch over the years; she was a regular visitor to Toronto; they hung out when she was in town, sometimes visiting with mutual friends or taking walks together (on the nights he wasn't already seeing Bessie).

It was during the last few weeks of 1853 that their friendship grew into something more. They saw a lot of each other over the holidays that year, attending Christmas Day services together at St. James Cathedral, going to the same dinners and parties. By the time the year drew to a close, it was obvious something had changed in the way they felt about each other. But even then, it wasn't entirely clear what that something was. Fleming was feeling cautious, still reeling from his bad breakup with Bessie.

On New Year's Eve, he made another entry in his diary. "An intimacy growing up with Miss Hall of Peterboro," he wrote. "How it may terminate I don't know. An amiable well-bred woman with her own peculiarities. Poor Miss Mitchell but it cannot be helped — have done everything for the best."

As it turned out, fate would make this decision for him, too.

With the new year underway, it was time for Jeanie to return home to Peterborough. Sandford offered to escort her. They took a train partway and then, for the next leg of their journey, hired a horse and cutter. Sleighs had long been popular with Canadians during the winter months, when the rough and muddy roads were transformed by a thick blanket of snow, making travel much easier. With the harvest done for the year and the frigid nights getting longer, settlers were free to spend more of their time having fun. They headed out in their sleighs to visit family and friends, threw parties and dances, drank and laughed and sang until the spring came, the snow melted away, and the roads became nearly impassable once again.

But the young couple's cutter would prove to be more than just a mode of transportation. When it hit that bump outside Lindsay, it changed the course of its passengers' lives. As Fleming regained consciousness in the snow, he found Jeanie hovering over him, worried. His chest had been seriously wounded; it would take a while to heal. Jeanie helped him to a nearby farmhouse, where they called for a physician. The doctor took Fleming home with him to Uxbridge, where the patient spent a week recovering from the crash. And all the while, Jeanie stayed by his side, helping to nurse him back to health.

It was during that long week together that Sandford Fleming and Jeanie Hall fell truly and deeply in love. For someone who clearly believed in the power of signs as much as he did, the overturned sleigh must have been a blatant omen. When he returned home to Toronto, Sandford wrote a letter and sent it off to Peterborough; in it, he asked Jeanie to marry him. She wrote back quickly; her answer arrived in the very next post. She said yes.

They were married a year later — nearly on the exact anniversary of their wintry accident. They began their honeymoon by heading back out onto the snowy roads, heading to the doctor's house where they'd fallen in love. On their way, they passed the same fateful stump where their sleigh had overturned. When he spotted it, Fleming stopped their horses and leapt from their wagon, a saw in his hand.

He began to cut away at the stump. But it wasn't easy work; the stump was stubborn. It was very slow going. As Fleming sawed away, his bride teased her new husband. "Sandford, why on earth are you wearing yourself out on that wretched stump?"

"Be patient, Jeanie," he promised, "I'll have a use for it, I expect."

It took him an hour to finish, but he finally did defeat the stump that had once defeated him. And with the wood safely secured in their wagon, the newlyweds continued on to their honeymoon and then to their new life together in Toronto.

It would be a happy one. Soon, Fleming's work had made him famous not just in Toronto, but around the world. He helped build the railway across Canada, designed the country's first stamp, and united the British Empire with a network of underwater telegraph cables stretched across the ocean floor. Most impressive of all: he convinced the world to divide the entire planet into time zones. He would eventually be knighted for his life's work; he would go down in history as *Sir* Sandford Fleming.

Through it all, he remained a devoted family man. He and Jeanie would have nine children together, and although two of those children died tragically young, the Flemings were a close and loving family.

It was years later, long after their wedding day and their fateful sleigh ride, that Sandford Fleming finally did find a use for that troublemaking stump. He carved it into a wooden frame, one of the world's most famous engineers using his hands to create a deeply personal ornament. Inside that frame, he placed one of their most precious possessions, still a rare and wonderous thing in those early days of photography: a picture of their children. And so, the family they built together stood forever framed by the stump that had made that family possible — a wooden souvenir from one truly lucky winter accident.

21

THE MOTHER OF CONFEDERATION

Five thousand people waited in the rain on a damp December night. It was Boxing Day 1862. But the miserable winter weather didn't stop them from crowding around the train station. They came in droves to the city's first Union Station, a modest collection of wooden buildings on Front Street — a block west of where the impressive modern transportation hub stands today. It was well after dark by the time the train chugged its way along the waterfront and slowed to a stop. It had been hired to make this single special trip, bringing one of Toronto's leading citizens home after months away — something of a belated Christmas gift for the city. As the crowd erupted into cheers, one of Canada's most beloved politicians stepped down onto the platform. George Brown was back. And he wasn't alone.

Since the 1840s, when Robert Baldwin and Louis-Hippolyte LaFontaine had won their battle for responsible government, a new generation of political leaders had taken over. Younger, more radical Reformers wanted to push change even further: they demanded that more people be given the right to vote, that inheritance laws be overhauled, and that copyright be abolished, among many other things. They drove Baldwin into retirement and formed a powerful faction within the Reform Party: the Clear Grits. Eventually, they would evolve into the Liberal Party. And George Brown was their leader.

By then, he was already a successful public figure. He was the founder of the *Globe* newspaper — the forerunner of today's *Globe and Mail* — owned a cattle farm near Brantford, and was a leader in the fight against slavery. As the co-founder of the Anti-Slavery Society of Canada, he was one of the Blackburns' most powerful and dedicated white allies.

But as he basked in the crowd's warm welcome on that cold December night, some deeply challenging years laid ahead.

The 1860s were a nervous time for the Canadian colonies. Half a century after the War of 1812, the United States still posed a monumental threat. The American Civil War was proving just how much terror it could unleash. And as if to drive the point home, Irish-American armies would invade the Canadian colonies once the war was over; Fenian revolutionaries hoped their attacks would pressure the British into leaving Ireland. Meanwhile, Canada's own political system was grinding to a halt. United together as the "Province of Canada," the old territories of Upper and Lower Canada were now mired in political deadlock. Laws couldn't get passed. Nothing could get done.

In response, a new idea emerged. They called it Confederation. If the Province of Canada joined with the Maritime provinces, the deadlock would be broken and they would be united against any threat coming from south of the border. The Dominion of Canada would still be part of the British Empire, but it would be an independent country — bigger, stronger, and more resilient.

Still, making Confederation a reality was going to be a monumental challenge. In order for Canada to become a country, its most powerful politicians would need to work together. They'd have to put aside a lifetime of rivalry and deeply conflicting views.

That might be a problem for George Brown. He wasn't exactly known for his collaborative charms. His whole life, he'd been direct and dogmatic, sometimes even authoritarian. As the owner of the *Globe*, he could be something of a tyrant. In a few years, when his printers went on strike demanding safer working conditions and a nine-hour day, he would crack down hard, throwing the organizers in jail and forcing his employees back to work even though ten thousand people — 10 percent of the city's entire population — marched on Queen's Park in solidarity. He broke the strike, but in response, unions were legalized in Canada. And the march inspired the Labour Day holiday still celebrated across North America every September. Years later, Brown would meet his end by being murdered by one of his own disgruntled employees. He might have been a respected champion for reform, but he wasn't always easy to work with.

And when he'd left Toronto for a trip to Britain, things hadn't been going well for the curmudgeonly politician. He'd lost his seat after a decade in Parliament. He was in his forties now and his health was failing him; he'd just been forced to spend two months in bed. His trip was meant to be refreshing and restorative. And that's exactly what it was, thanks to a woman he met in Scotland.

Anne Nelson was the sister of an old friend. She was about ten years younger than Brown, more worldly, and better educated than he was. She'd travelled across Europe, studied in Germany, and lived in Paris as a young woman. She spoke three languages. And she was charming, too: lively, good-natured, and loving. Brown was transformed in her presence. His stern facade melted. It was five weeks later, during an evening walk along the River Clyde, that Brown proposed. They were married just two months after they met.

It must have seemed as if the whole city of Toronto had come out to welcome the newlyweds when they pulled into Union Station on that Boxing Day. For at least one evening, the city's divisions were forgotten. The crowd of five thousand well-wishers included Tories, Reformers, Clear Grits, Catholics, and Orangemen alike. As a carriage bore the beloved politician and his new bride through the streets of Toronto, the crowd followed.

Bands played. Fireworks lit up the night. People leaned out of their windows along their route, waving handkerchiefs and cheering them on.

"I feel more than ever," Brown had told the crowd at the train station, "the necessity for Upper Canadians of all shades of political opinion to unite heartily in advancing the great interests of our country — to forget the minor differences which have so long separated us." And as he prepared to pass through the front door of his home on Church Street and begin his new life with Anne, he turned back to them once again. "I trust … that whenever the great interests of Canada are at risk, we will forget our merely political partisanship and rally round the cause of our country." That, he promised, would be his new motto.

And indeed, by all accounts, he was a new man. Happy and in love, with Anne at his side giving him valuable political advice, he was now warmer, more patient, and more conciliatory. Another leading figure in Confederation, Sir Oliver Mowat, once congratulated her on the transformation she'd inspired in her husband. "Since you became his wife," he wrote, "the softer side of his nature has been developed under your loving influence — himself becoming an increasingly gentle, kind and considerate person."

Now that George Brown was in love, compromise didn't seem so terrible after all. Suddenly, he was willing to join forces with his political foes. Together, they formed "The Great Coalition."

It was an unlikely crew. There was Conservative leader John A. Macdonald (Brown's greatest enemy), former Irish revolutionary Thomas D'Arcy McGee (who once proudly called himself "A Traitor to the British Government"), and Quebecois champion George-Étienne Cartier (whose influence Brown had spent years trying to diminish). George Brown might have been anti-conservative, anti-Catholic, and anti-French, but now he was allied with them all, building an alliance of thirty-six Canadian politicians who would be remembered as the Fathers of Confederation.

Together, they would establish a new country stretching from the Great Lakes to the Atlantic Ocean — with a little help from the $13,000 worth of champagne they brought with them to the first round of talks. The negotiations would take three years, but it wasn't all business. Balls and dinners played a vital role building trust and camaraderie, wives and daughters helping to cement the new bonds being forged between the Canadian leaders.

Anne supported her husband the whole way through, even when they were apart, guiding him and offering him advice. As the politicians hammered out the framework for a new nation, the Browns sent countless letters back and forth to each other. The couple's correspondence would provide a valuable historical record of the negotiations. Anne's influence on her husband was so strong that one historian has suggested, "Perhaps the real father of Confederation was Mrs. Brown." Indeed, some remember her as the Mother of Confederation.

In the end, all the effort was worth it: New Brunswick and Nova Scotia agreed to join with the Province of Canada. On July 1, 1867, the Dominion of Canada officially came into being. There were celebrations all across the newly formed country of four million people. The festivities in Toronto began at midnight as church bells rang with joy, led by the singing spire of St. James Cathedral. Bonfires lit up King Street while fireworks burst into the night air. Drunken revellers belted out patriotic songs. People kept the party going all through the next day, woken by a twenty-one-gun salute from Fort York. An entire ox was roasted at dawn, and there were more light shows and fireworks to come.

George Brown spent that night writing, hard at work in his sweltering office on King Street while the party raged outside. Hour after hour, he wrote, well past dawn, penning a gargantuan celebratory article that would cover the entire front page of the *Globe*. And then, his work done, he finally headed home through the exuberant city. The Mother of Confederation would be waiting for him.

22

THE TOMB IN HIGH PARK

You'll find it standing at the top of a hill high above Grenadier Pond, erected in a small clearing ringed by trees. It's a massive monument, a towering pile of boulders topped by a marble cross, surrounded by a black iron fence. The cairn is there to protect the bones of one Toronto's most prominent Victorian couples. This is where you'll find the Howards.

John Howard was Toronto's leading architect in the middle of the 1800s, the man who designed part of Osgoode Hall, the Provincial Lunatic Asylum (at 999 Queen Street, where the Centre for Addiction and Mental Health stands now), plus banks and houses and elegant office blocks. But he did far more than just design buildings. He was an accomplished artist who taught at Upper Canada College. He was a justice of the peace and an associate judge. He was a militia member who fought against Mackenize's rebels. And he was an engineer who once took a young Sandford Fleming under his wing, and who laid out Toronto's first sidewalks and sewers, as well as many new streets and bridges. Two centuries later, Torontonians still live in a city John Howard helped create.

But he didn't do it alone. While he worked himself to the point of exhaustion, helping transform Toronto into a thriving metropolis, his wife, Jemima, was right there by his side. They'd left England together to come to Canada in 1832. She was a painter herself, made copies of his plans and drawings, kept him organized, and even helped write his diary. They had a house downtown near King and York Streets, and together they bought a big country estate to the west of the growing city: an expanse of hills, forest, and creeks that ran all the way from the lakeshore up to Bloor Street. Howard designed a second home for them there: Colborne Lodge, a museum today. They moved in just a few weeks after Howard helped put down Mackenzie's rebellion. The picturesque cottage had a commanding view from the top of the hill it was built on — a view that inspired Jemima to call their estate High Park.

In many ways, it must have been a rewarding life: spending part of their time in the heart of the city they were helping to build, and part of it enjoying the rural pleasures of High Park. They kept much of their property as natural as possible — Howard was no fan of the carefully cultivated lawns and fountains that surrounded so many English manors — with just a few orchards and gardens near the house. Howard even hunted deer and quail on the property.

The couple didn't keep all of these natural wonders to themselves. They welcomed visitors: soldiers from

Fort York fished in Grenadier Pond, there was curling and skating in the winter, the city's elite came to enjoy carriage rides and long walks through the trees. There were charity picnics, and even tenant farmers who harvested wheat and alfalfa from the slopes of a big hill overlooking the pond. The Howards always wanted to share High Park with the people of Toronto.

But their life wasn't quite as peaceful and uncomplicated as it must have seemed on the surface. John Howard had a secret. The respected architect had a second family.

For years, Howard had been sleeping with another woman. Mary Williams was from Northern Ireland, and it seems that she was just a teenager when their affair began, while Howard was in his late thirties. But the relationship was more than just a casual tryst. Howard and his mistress had three children together. He gave them financial support, built a house for them, chipped in with ideas for Christmas celebrations, and collected his children's drawings. He made sure that when he died, they were included in his will.

But we don't know much beyond those few details. It was, of course, a scandalous secret. It wasn't the kind of relationship that would have been publicly acceptable in a city where the Church had enormous moral power, a place whose strict, conservative values were about to be immortalized in the nickname "Toronto The Good." And so, it's maybe not surprising that near the end of his life, Howard burned many of his personal papers in the fireplace, leaving little evidence behind. The autobiography he donated to the Toronto Public Library makes no mention of his affair. Historians have been left to cobble together whatever they can from the few hints available. Howard pencilled notes about his second family into his diary sometime after he and Jemima completed the first draft together. We can see that he had a suspicious habit of leaving the house at night right around the time he and Mary must have conceived their youngest child. Some suspect that Williams may have been a servant in the Howards' household when the affair first began.

Still, to this day, no one is entirely sure whether Jemima knew what her husband was up to — in a city as small as Toronto was then, it's quite possible she did. Given that she and John never had any children, there's a chance it could even have been an arrangement they openly agreed upon. Or, at the very least, that he abided by the patriarchal conventions of the time: failing to be faithful, but ensuring his wife was never publicly embarrassed by his wandering ways.

Whether or not she knew about her husband's affair, Jemima stayed with him for the rest of her life. And when her end began to draw near, John did everything he could to protect his wife. In life and in death.

Jemima Howard was seventy-three when she was diagnosed with breast cancer. She suffered terribly. The opiates she took as a painkiller were powerful. She began to be clumsy and forgetful — sometimes, it seems, she didn't recognize her husband at all. She was known to disappear — she was found wandering in the woods. The doctor at the Provincial Lunatic Asylum didn't think she belonged there. So, instead, Howard hired a pair of nurses and customized the guest room at Colborne Lodge, where they were now living full time in their retirement. He installed an extra door just outside her room, with no inside doorknob, so Jemima wouldn't be able to wander off into danger.

She was coming to the end of her life. But Howard wasn't just planning to keep his wife safe while she was alive. He was already working on a plan to keep her safe in death, too. He was well aware of the morbid threat that awaited Toronto's dead.

As the city grew, so did the demand for fresh corpses. Toronto's first medical school had opened in the 1840s, and cutting open cadavers was an important part of a student's education. The province passed an Anatomy Act, allowing for the unclaimed bodies of those who died in government-run hospitals and poorhouses to be used for anatomical dissections — as long as what was left of the remains were respectfully buried once the students were done. But over the course of a few decades, the number of those studying to become doctors grew from dozens to hundreds. As the city boomed, there weren't enough unclaimed people dying to meet the demand.

The solution: some medical students became grave robbers. They snuck around cemeteries at night, digging up newly buried bodies to be carried off for dissection. By the time Jemima fell ill, bodysnatchers had been a problem in Toronto for decades. During the 1800s, the city was plagued by horror stories of empty coffins and missing corpses. Of farmers chasing medical students down Yonge Street trying to get their loved ones back. Of sentries posted to the military graveyard at Victoria Memorial Square near Fort York, protecting dead soldiers from shadowy men bearing spades, picks, and body bags. Of trunks oozing blood, shipped by train to Union Station.

To protect his wife's corpse, Howard began to build a fortress of a tomb. It was a massive stone cairn: a pile of granite boulders weighing ten tons, topped by a marble Maltese cross. It would present quite a challenge to any medical student looking to get his hands on the Howards' cadavers.

And he didn't stop there. The tomb would also be protected by an iron fence with a storied past, one much older even than the city itself. Howard would have it shipped across the ocean from one of the most famous churches in the world.

St. Paul's Cathedral had stood in London, England, since medieval times — but it was destroyed by the Great Fire in 1666. In the wake of the blaze, the renowned architect Sir Christopher Wren was tasked with the job of rebuilding the church into the great domed landmark it is today. And Wren didn't just design the church itself. He also designed a black, iron fence to surround the cathedral.

The fence protected the new St. Paul's for more than a century. But when the cathedral grounds were being renovated, the old fence was going to be destroyed.

When Howard heard the news, he was appalled. He decided to save the historic fence. He bought it and arranged to ship it across the Atlantic, all the way up the St. Lawrence to Lake Ontario, so he could use it as an additional layer of protection for his wife's fortified tomb.

But the journey from London to Toronto was a perilous one. As it sailed into the narrowing mouth of the St. Lawrence, the steamship carrying the fence ran into a terrible storm. It was wrecked on the rocks and sank to the bottom of the great river — taking the fence down with it.

Howard refused to leave it there. He spent two years working on a plan to salvage the fence from the muddy bottom of the St. Lawrence, paying a small fortune for divers to go down and get it. The rescue operation cost even more than shipping the fence across the ocean had. And the diving team could only recover part of it. The portion they did manage to bring up to the surface was severely damaged; when it finally arrived in Toronto, what was left of the mangled fence was repaired at a foundry before taking its place in the shadow of the stone cairn.

By the time it was finished, the tomb had cost more than three thousand dollars to build (tens of thousands in today's money). But it was ready and waiting when Jemima passed away in 1877, just a few months after the Howards' fiftieth wedding anniversary. Three long years of suffering were over; she could finally rest in one of the best-defended graves in Toronto.

John was devastated when she died. As he prepared to inter his wife under the towering pile of stones, he wrote a heartbreaking poem for her. He called it "The Tomb in High Park":

> A rustic cairn on hallowed ground,
> Surmounted by a Mystic Cross;
> O'ershadowed by some lofty oaks —
> The sun's bright rays through foliage pass;
>
> Which lighting up the Mystic Cross,
> Brings forth the symbol from the shade;
> The rustic cairn all clothed with moss,
> A glimmering light o'er it pervades.
>
> But what of this to the old man
> Who mourns the loved one laid below —
> Those rustic stones so stately piled
> To mark the spot where he must go!
>
> For years, altho' her mind was gone.
> The dear one still was left with him;
> Tho' often times she knew him not,
> Still was the ruin dear to him.
>
> And why should he now cling to life —
> Now all worth living for is gone:
> With nothing left but care and strife,
> But man, they say, was made to mourn.

John Howard would live another decade before he joined his wife beneath the stones, still taking the time to visit with Mary Williams and their only surviving child — though there's no evidence they ever joined him at Colborne Lodge, or that they were there the day he was laid to rest in the tomb.

By then, the great stone cairn stood in the middle of a park. The Howards had given their country estate to the people of Toronto. Years before they died, they gifted their land to the city to be turned into a public park for everyone to enjoy. They simply asked to be allowed to live out their final years at Colborne Lodge with a yearly pension. They asked that the park be kept in a natural state, that alcohol never be allowed within it, and that it should always be known as High Park.

Finally, they asked that, in return for their remarkable gift, their resting place be taken care of forevermore — that their tomb would stand in Toronto as long as Toronto stands.

Today, High Park is one of the jewels of the city's parks system — one of the most famous green spaces in the country — an expanse of forests and creeks surrounded by a buzzing metropolis. Countless Torontonians and tourists enjoy it every day, jogging and walking their dogs, fishing and skating on the pond, visiting the cherry blossoms or feeding the ducks. And as they do, the Howards are still there high on that hill next to Colborne Lodge, resting beneath their granite fortress, safe from grave robbers and the ravages of time. A century and a half after they were placed in their imposing tomb, John and Jemima Howard continue to keep watch over the park where they once lived.

23

THE SECRETS OF JALNA

With the jingle of sleigh bells came the first hint her life was about to change forever. Right up until that moment in the winter of 1886, Maisie had been a very lonely little girl. Her father was a travelling salesman, rarely home. Her mother was desperately ill, confined to her bed after a crippling case of scarlet fever, her chronic sickness hanging over the house like death. Even when they were all living there at her grandparents' house in Newmarket, with plenty of adults around, little Maisie was mostly left to her own devices. She became a voracious reader, devouring books like *Through the Looking Glass*, *Oliver Twist*, and *Little Women* (though she liked *Little Men* better), and spent long hours developing her own rich fantasy world. She called it "The Play": a fictional universe populated by pirates, explorers, and soldiers; a detailed dream world she would act out every day, bringing the characters to life all by herself, making those lonely hours a little less lonely. But that changed with the sound of the sleigh bells. A bay mare trotted up the snowy driveway pulling a big red sled, and her uncle George walked through the front door carrying something bundled up in shawls.

That something, it turned out, was another little girl. Her cousin, Caroline Clement.

"Although I did not realize it at the time," Maisie would write decades later, "or for many years afterward, that January day was the most important day of my life."

Clement would become her adopted sister and her best friend, welcomed into her fantasy world. "I have a secret," Maisie told her on the first day they met. "My play I call it. But now it must be *our* play."

There were six characters at first, all men and boys, but in time the dream world expanded to include more than a hundred different people, all meticulously imagined down to the smallest detail. They became a second life for the girls. "As we grew to know them better, we ceased to *act* them," Maisie explained in her autobiography. "We *were* them. When surrounded by other people we strained toward the moment when we could be alone together. Then, at once, magic enveloped us. The outside world became unreal. The vivid reality was our Play."

Their imaginations helped bond the two youngsters for life, even as they and their families moved around Ontario, eventually settling in Toronto. Bound together as girls, they became inseparable partners for the rest of their lives.

Maisie Roche's imagination continued to fuel her through her teenage years. And even as adults, she and Caroline kept building upon their fictional world. Eventually, it fed into Maisie's work. By 1927, they were living in a boarding house on Yorkville Avenue as she put the finishing touches on her latest novel. Maisie Roche had become an author, giving herself the more poetic name of Mazo de la Roche.

Her new novel was the story of the Whiteoaks, a rich Ontario family who lived on a thousand-acre estate called Jalna. The book built upon the fictional world she and Clement had created as children, and borrowed details from their real lives. The Whiteoaks' estate is said to have been inspired by a grand old manor called Benares, which still stands in Mississauga to this today, operated as a museum. At Jalna, the Whiteoaks lived a life akin to that of the English aristocracy, echoing Simcoe's original vision for Upper Canada as an oasis of British class and sophistication. But behind the Whiteoaks' refined exterior, the family kept secrets. They had scandalous thoughts and feelings, erotic dreams, illicit affairs, and passionate obsessions.

De la Roche used the book to play around with gender and sexuality. She'd never identified strongly with the female characters she created; when she and Clement played as children, it was the men de la Roche felt kinship with. "I always wished I were a boy," she admitted. And so, in *Jalna* it wasn't the heroine she saw as a reflection of herself, it was the swashbuckling male hero. "Renny appeals to me partly because he is someone for whom I have understanding and sympathy," she once explained. "Never have I been completely at one with any female characters of mine. I might love them, suffer with them, but they were they and I was I."

In the book, Renny has fallen deeply in love with the woman of his dreams. But his feelings are forbidden. He's in love with his brother's wife, Alayne — a character who was clearly based on Caroline Clement, with her shimmering hair, blue eyes, diminutive frame, and a mouth like a spring flower. They're tempted by each other, and things get steamy. "The next moment, she found herself in his arms with his lips against hers, and all her sensations crushed for the moment into helpless surrender," de la Roche writes of the characters she'd based on herself and her Caroline. "She felt the steady thud of his heart and against it the wild tapping of her own."

"I had," she once said of *Jalna*, "put the essence of myself into it."

With the finishing touches on the novel finally done, de la Roche sent it away to be entered into an international writing competition held by the *Atlantic Monthly*. It was one of the most prestigious literary prizes in the world, not something a Canadian was supposed to win. But that's exactly what happened.

The ten-thousand-dollar prize was a fortune at the time, a life-changing amount of money, but even more transformative than that, the victory launched de la Roche into superstardom. *Jalna* was a global hit; she was suddenly a literary giant. From the moment the news of her big win broke, splashed across the front page of the *Toronto Star*, she became an international sensation. The phone rang off the hook; knocks at the door brought a shower of flowers and telegrams. Reporters wanted to know everything about her.

But she wasn't going to tell them. Mazo de la Roche had her secrets, too. With her fame exploding, de la Roche remained fiercely protective of her privacy. As the public appetite for revealing details about her life grew, she actively worked to keep those details secret. She liked to play games with the press, lying and evading questions. "Those whose work lies in the field of imagination," she explained, "have no need to explain their actions, or failures, except to themselves." Her own autobiography further obscured the truth, blurring the line between fact and fiction, as much a work of imagination as an intimate confession. Even the story of the day she met Clement, of the jingle bells and the red sleigh, seems to be twisted and embellished. The dates and details don't match up, leaving historians to wonder how much of the tale was invented as a romantic founding myth for their relationship. When it came to Mazo de la Roche, you couldn't take anything on face value.

To this day, historians can't be sure about the true nature of her relationship with Caroline Clement. There's no question the two cousins were soulmates. "I usually try to conceal how perfect I think she is," the author once admitted. They spent their entire lives together. Clement was there at her side through all their most difficult days: the lean years before the author became famous; the depressions and electroshock therapy that followed her success. And when Clement nearly married a man, engaged to him for a few years, de la Roche was beside herself with jealously. "If I had broken with Mazo," Clement admitted, "she would never had written another word."

She broke off her engagement. The two women stayed together.

Passionate female friendships were not uncommon at the time. Many women lived in what became known as "Boston Marriages" — a reference to the ambiguous relationship between two female characters in the Henry James novel *The Bostonians* — spending their lives together without marrying a man. Some, to be sure, were just close companions at a time when intense friendships between women were encouraged; others were lesbians forced to hide their sexuality.

A century after the city was founded, Toronto was still a very conservative place — and, in some ways, getting more so. The very same year that de la Roche remembers meeting Clement, the city elected a new mayor. William Holmes Howland was a member of the Orange Order, the son of a Father of Confederation, and a deeply conservative man. His campaign slogan would become an unofficial motto for the city: "Toronto The Good." As the former head of a temperance society running in an election against a brewery owner, he promised to crack down on the consumption of alcohol. That message resonated with the public, especially women who saw booze as a root cause of poverty, drunken husbands, and domestic violence. For the first time in that 1886 election, some Toronto women were allowed to vote — as long as they owned property or were wealthy renters. With their help, Howland won.

But once he was in office, the new mayor wouldn't just reduce the number of liquor licences; he'd also promised to strengthen law enforcement. Howland established the notorious Toronto Police Morality Squad to crack down on all kinds of vice. Initially led by the big Irish constable David Archibald — nicknamed "The Moral Man" — they would spend the next century stamping out "immorality" wherever they found it: drunkenness, sex work, and homosexuality were just a few of their targets. Once, they even shut down a play because the actors onstage kissed for too long. Toronto wasn't an easy place to challenge notions of sexuality and gender.

But in her books, de la Roche was able to do just that. With the sequel to her big hit, she got even more bold. In *Whiteoaks of Jalna*, the black sheep of the family develops a relationship with another man. But Finch is bullied by his older brothers when they discover what seems to be a love letter between the two. "I'm disgusted with you," one of them tells him, driving him to tears. The encounter leaves a troubling question ringing in Finch's head: "What am I?"

"Finch was my alter ego," de la Roche explained. "I was one with Finch. For he and I have much in common."

Whiteoaks of Jalna was just the first of fourteen sequels. In the 1920s and '30s, the series was everywhere: a major multimedia franchise and a household name. As the *Jalna* empire grew bigger, de la Roche and Clement grew even more inseparable, sharing the most important parts of the author's life and career. Caroline seems to have become her uncredited co-author, fleshing out Mazo's ideas as she typed up the writer's handwritten pages. They even adopted a pair of children together: a little girl and a baby boy. To this day, it's not clear where the children came from, or how, back in the 1930s, two women were able to adopt them. While rumours swirled, de la Roche stuck to her usual secrecy, sharing different stories with different people. She refused to tell anyone, even the children themselves, the truth about their origins.

But one thing, at least, was clear. Clement would forever be the centre of de la Roche's world. She'd made it clear she had no interest in ever leaving her for a man. "It was not in me to be the sort of female who knows no boredom, no fatigue, as long as she can trail after the man she fancies," she explained in her autobiography, adding, "An attempt at handholding, a hand stealing toward my waist, was enough to make me fiercely withdraw.... There were insipient affairs of the heart [but] I retained a dislike of being touched.... I looked on sex as rather silly. There was so much that was more interesting."

But to the readers of *Jalna*, there was no doubt Mazo de la Roche had an intimate understanding of passion and romance. "Only a few people ever know anything about love," she once explained. "For the rest of them, they marry, bring up their children, and die. What they call love is nothing more than a habit. Real love is tremendous: tremendous in its power, tremendous in its force. It is a terrible thing that seizes you in its grip.... Love throbs into life within you. It overpowers your senses. Your being is aflame with it. It is of such love that I have written in *Jalna*."

Clement stayed with her to the end. They spent their final years living together in Forest Hill — in a big

Tudor-style mansion just across the street from Group of Seven painter Lawren Harris. By the time Mazo de la Roche died there as an old woman, her books had sold eleven million copies, had been translated into ninety-three languages, and had been adapted into movies, television programs, and a Broadway play. She was, without a doubt, one of the most successful Canadian authors who had ever lived.

Her secrets, she took with her to the grave. After de la Roche died, Caroline Clement performed one last act of love, fulfilling the final request of the woman she'd spent her life with. She gathered up the old writer's papers: the diaries where she shared her innermost thoughts, the answers to all the questions everyone had ever wanted answered. And then she burned them. On a summer day in 1961, the secrets of Mazo de la Roche went up in flames.

24

"A CRY FROM AN INDIAN WIFE"

It had been a long night. The audience was growing restless. The Young Men's Liberal Club was gathered in the lecture hall of an art school on King Street, packing the room on a frigid January night in 1892. They had come to enjoy "An Evening with Canadian Authors": the impressive bill was filled with some of the leading lights of the Canadian literary scene. But so far, the event had been deadly dull: just one dry poetry recitation after another. Despite the promising lineup, the night threatened to be a disappointment. But then, someone new appeared onstage.

Pauline Johnson was the only woman invited to read that night. She slipped out in front of the crowd in the pale grey of a silk gown, white gloves reaching up her arms, and took her place at the centre of the stage. She stood there motionless, a statue, her eyes cast upwards as she waited for the chatter of the audience to die down.

And then, only then, when silence finally filled the hall, did she begin to speak. She began to tell a love story.

Pauline Johnson had grown up in the territory of the Six Nations. Her mother was an English gentlewoman; her father was a Kanien'keha:ka chief. Johnson was raised in both cultures. While her mother schooled her in the intricacies of colonial etiquette, her grandfather told her the oral histories of the Haudenosaunee. Even her name was a reflection of her multicultural heritage: her great-great-grandfather had been the godson of William Johnson, the old superintendent of Indian affairs back in the 1700s, and inherited the name from him. (She would later adopt her grandfather's Kanien'keha:ka name, as well: Tekahionwake.) One of her first successes was a poem written for the unveiling of a statue of Joseph Brant that still stands in Brantford to this day.

Johnson had plenty of experience with love growing up: there were romantic canoe rides along the Grand River and flirtatious picnics in the summer, quickened pulses and hands inching tentatively toward each other. She was thirty years old as she stood on that stage on King Street and had already been proposed to many times. She'd broken hearts and had hers broken, too. For the rest of her life, she would wear a silver locket around her neck; inside was a photograph of a handsome and mysterious young man she refused to ever talk about. But the tragic tale she chose to recite that night in Toronto wasn't a personal lament of her own lost loves. Instead, she told the audience a story unlike any they'd ever heard.

> My Forest Brave, my Red-skin love,
>   farewell;
> We may not meet to-morrow; who can tell
> What mighty ills befall our little band,
> Or what you'll suffer from the white
>   man's hand?

It was a love poem, but instead of a romantic ode to beauty and youth, it was a tale of war and of heartbreak. And it was told not from the perspective of a brave British soldier, but from the point of view of an Indigenous woman, a wife worried about her warrior husband as he headed off to battle against Canadian soldiers.

Her reading of "A Cry from an Indian Wife" was like nothing else the audience had seen that evening — or any other evening for that matter. Johnson didn't actually read it at all, she performed it. Unlike the other poets, she could recite her work from memory. Instead of staring down at a piece of paper, she connected directly with her audience. She had theatrical experience, and she used every ounce of it, bringing her poems to life with passion and flair.

> Here is your knife! I thought 'twas
>   sheathed for aye.
> No roaming bison calls for it to-day;
> No hide of prairie cattle will it maim;
> The plains are bare, it seeks a nobler game:
> 'Twill drink the life-blood of a soldier
>   host.

> Go; rise and strike, no matter what the
> cost.

In time, she would develop her theatricality even further, using her wardrobe to full advantage. For half of her performance, she would appear onstage in all the finery of a typical English gentlewoman. In the other half, she would emerge in a costume she'd created herself: fringed leather, beads, fur, and a necklace of claws combined to produce the stereotypical image of an "Indian princess." Playing with her audience's own prejudices gave her the freedom to deal with subjects — like war and sex — that were considered improper for most women to broach. And by slipping from one culture into another, she was able to reach an audience of colonizers with tales told from an Indigenous perspective.

This was an era of westward expansion. In the years since Confederation, the new Canadian government had pushed beyond the Great Lakes, looking to expand its empire across the Great Plains. It turned the Prairies into a battleground. The Canadian forces were met by Indigenous resistance, most famously led by Métis leader Louis Riel. Métis and First Nations warriors, along with some early white settlers, fought back: first with the Red River Resistance (at what's now Winnipeg) and then with the North-West Resistance (in what's now Saskatchewan and Alberta). Sir John A. Macdonald, who'd been elected as the country's first prime minister, responded by sending troops west to crush Riel's resistance and bring the Prairies under Canadian control.

They but forget we Indians owned the land
From ocean unto ocean; that they stand
Upon a soil that centuries agone
Was our sole kingdom and our right
    alone.
They never think how they would feel
    to-day,
If some great nation came from far away,
Wresting their country from their hap-
    less braves,
Giving what they gave us — but wars
    and graves.

Many of the soldiers who fought against Riel were militiamen from Toronto. On the day the Queen's Own Rifles boarded a train out of Union Station, bound for the Prairies, thousands of their fellow Torontonians were there to see them off. When they returned, a cheering crowd of a hundred thousand people welcomed them home. The *Toronto World* called it "the greatest day Toronto ever witnessed." Even now, a monument dedicated to the soldiers who fought against Riel stands on the lawn outside Queen's Park.

Johnson knew her audience. In the poem, the Indigenous wife is torn between fear for her husband's life and defiance in the face of genocide, going back and forth between encouraging her sweetheart to fight and begging him to stay home. But she also hesitates because she can see both sides of the conflict. She thinks of the settler wives in cities like Toronto who were worried about their own husbands heading off to fight on the other side of the same battles.

> Yet stay, my heart is not the only one
> That grieves the loss of husband and of
> son;
> Think of the mothers o'er the inland seas;
> Think of the pale-faced maiden on her
> knees;
> One pleads her God to guard some sweet-
> faced child
> That marches on toward the North-West
> wild.
> The other prays to shield her love from
> harm,
> To strengthen his young, proud uplifted
> arm.
> Ah, how her white face quivers thus to
> think,
> *Your* tomahawk his life's best blood will
> drink.

When the *Globe* reviewed the event, they reserved their greatest praise for Johnson — though they couldn't resist including some condescending racism: "Miss E. Pauline Johnson's may be said to have been the pleasant-est contribution of the evening. It was like the voice of the nations that once possessed this country, who have wasted away before our civilization, speaking through this cultured, gifted, soft-faced descendant."

Soon, she would be famous. She toured across the country, and was a hit in England, too. Today, she's remembered as one of the greatest of all Canadian poets. Her work is taught in schools across the country; her "The Song My Paddle Sings" is one of the most famous Canadian poems ever written. Her childhood home on the banks of the Grand River, Chiefswood, is a National Historical Site.

And that night in Toronto, as Johnson reached the final stanzas of her poem, the audience was hanging on every word, drawn in by her dramatic performance. It was a rare moment: a crowd of Victorian Torontonians paying rapt attention to an Indigenous voice reminding them of the pain and suffering caused by their colonial exploits, asking them to see things from the other side.

> She never thinks of my wild aching
>   breast,
> Nor prays for your dark face and eagle
>   crest
> Endangered by a thousand rifle balls,
> My heart the target if my warrior falls.

But hers wasn't the only vision presented onstage that night. Douglas Campbell Scott was on the bill, too. He was already hailed as one of the country's greatest writers — one of the "Confederation Poets," whose work helped to establish a national identity at the time when the country was being stitched together through politics and railroads.

But he was also a government bureaucrat, destined to become one of the most notorious civil servants in Canadian history. A decade after that night in Toronto, he would become the leading architect of the residential school system. He was responsible for Indigenous children being torn away from their parents, forcing them to be educated far from home in an attempt to erase their culture and forcibly indoctrinate them as English-speaking, god-fearing "Canadians." Scott made no secret of the fact that he wanted to wipe out Indigenous society entirely — just like the missionaries who'd first arrived in the Great Lakes centuries before. "I want to get rid of the Indian problem," he once explained. "Our objective is to continue until there is not a single Indian in Canada that has not been absorbed into the body politic and there is no Indian question, and no Indian Department."

It was Douglas Campbell Scott's vision of Canada that would dominate the century to come. By the time Johnson spoke on that stage, the rebellions on the Prairies had already been crushed. Louis Riel had been hanged. Manitoba had been brought into Confederation. The Indian Act had been passed. The first residential schools had been opened. Indigenous traditions like potlatches and the sun dance had been banned. There wasn't a single plains bison left anywhere in Canada. Vast numbers of Indigenous people were dying of starvation and tuberculosis.

In the end, Johnson's "Indian wife" chooses resistance.

> O! coward self I hesitate no more;
> Go forth, and win the glories of the war.
> Go forth, nor bend to greed of white
>   men's hands,
> By right, by birth we Indians own these
>   lands,
> Though starved, crushed, plundered,
>   lies our nation low ...
> Perhaps the white man's God has willed
>   it so.

She was done. The poem was finished; the performance was over. For a moment, the crowd was stunned into silence. And then, as Johnson's final words hung in the air and she turned to leave the stage, they erupted into a roar of applause, calling for an encore, demanding more.

25
THE QUEEN OF HEARTS

She smelled of ammonia. Her feet were big. She looked at least ten years older than she actually was. Her hands were stained with ink, and so were her clothes: maybe a wrinkled old blouse or a drab dress, sometimes a man's smoking jacket. Her hair, which was red and curly, she wore up, just because it was more practical that way. "I simply detest fashion," she once declared. She had a temper. Some said her face was hard and cruel. Her writing, certainly, could be blunt and without mercy. She was sharped-tongued and quick-witted. Kit Coleman did not suffer fools lightly.

But for decades, she was also the reigning expert on Canadian hearts, the author of the country's first "advice for the lovelorn" column. Every week, she dispensed her romantic wisdom to thousands of readers. She got bags full of letters asking her to help win a heart or solve marital woes. In her own life, she would marry three men and attract proposals from at least five more.

They called her the Queen of Hearts.

Still, while Kit Coleman may have once been among the country's most famous journalists, it's not easy to trace her personal history. She was a public figure but a private woman; much like Mazo de la Roche, she was prone to mixing lies with the truth when it came to her own past. She lied about her age and about her family background. She burned most of her letters and diaries, openly encouraging her readers to do the same. Even her gender could be something of a mystery; when her androgynous name led some readers to accuse her of being a man, she toyed with them, refusing to give a straight answer.

What we do know is that she was born in a small Irish village during the winter of 1856, to a middle-class farming family in the hard years that followed the Great Famine. To secure her future, her family arranged a marriage for her; whether she liked it or not, she was going to marry a wealthy landowner. Some sources say she was just sixteen years old at the time. The marriage was destined to be short and loveless. Her husband was much older — some say by a full forty years. He was unfaithful. And their life together was marked by tragedy: their young daughter died in childhood. Her husband followed close behind. Just eight years after their wedding day, he fell off his horse during a fox hunt and was killed. His money went to his mother, leaving Coleman with practically nothing — a penniless widow in her twenties.

The time had come, she decided, to take control of her life.

With her husband dead and his fortune gone, she would leave Ireland behind. She sold enough furniture to get to England. From there, she planned to book passage to South Africa. Or maybe Australia. But the next ship out of Liverpool wasn't heading to either of those places. And she couldn't bear to wait. That's how Kit Coleman ended up on a ship bound for Canada.

In her new country, it didn't take long for her to meet a new man; when she got a job as a secretary, her boss quickly fell in love with her. But the travelling salesman from Toronto was no better than her last husband. He was an alcoholic who slept around. Coleman's second marriage was just as doomed as her first. Some historians suggest that when she demanded a divorce — still a rare and controversial process in Canada requiring an act of Parliament for every new request — she learned that he had a second wife in England. Another version of the story says he died — that she was thirty-three years old and already a widow twice over. Either way, only five brief years after arriving in Canada, Coleman found herself alone yet again. This time as a single mother with two children.

That's when she decided to write.

Coleman had grown up surrounded by intellectuals. Her parents might have been farmers, but they were also part of the Irish literary community: her father had an impressive library; their friends were writers and artists. Her uncle was one of the most respected and liberal priests in Ireland, preaching to overflowing crowds. Her first husband, though a terrible match, had sent her to one of the better schools in Dublin. Now, she put all that experience to work. Her own writing was good enough to soon land her a job as Canada's first full-time editor of a women's page.

The *Toronto Mail* was one of Toronto's leading newspapers. It was the brainchild of prime minister Sir John A. Macdonald, founded a decade earlier to support his federal Conservative Party. The new paper got off to a quick start; it immediately drove the *Toronto Telegraph* out of business, with the *Toronto Leader* following a few years later. Soon, the *Mail* had a fancy new building on the corner of King and Bay. But in recent years, the newspaper had declared its independence from the Conservative government — beginning with its opposition to the execution of Louis Riel. It was a risky move. Macdonald responded by starting a new Tory paper: the *Toronto Empire*.

The *Mail* now had more fearsome competition than ever before, making it an important time to attract new readers. Under general manager Christopher William Bunting — he'd gotten his start by setting printing type for George Brown's *Globe* — the newspaper set out to redefine itself. It embraced modernity by introducing photographs and hired exciting new columnists.

And there was one particularly big audience Bunting wanted to attract: women.

Women, it was generally agreed by all the most learned men, didn't read newspapers. Bunting was looking for someone to prove them wrong. As he imagined it, "Woman's Kingdom" would be a half-page of domestic tips, recipes, and fashion advice — he believed it was the kind of soft news women would buy the *Mail* to read.

And having enjoyed one of her first articles, he hired Kit Coleman to write it.

It was quite a bold career move for her. There were barely any women working as journalists in Canada — only about thirty-five, compared to more than seven hundred and fifty men. Journalism wasn't considered a respectful profession for a woman — just a step or two above sex work. But Coleman threw herself into it. She spent her days writing while her children were at school, hunched over a rolltop desk for hours on end, her near-sighted eyes just a few inches from the page. Meanwhile, her white rat, Patsy Brannigan, scampered around the unkempt apartment. Once a week, when her scribbling was finally done, she would venture out on her bicycle or by streetcar, making her way over to the *Mail* building at King and Bay to deliver her column in time for the Saturday edition.

But the column that rolled off the press wasn't ex-actly the column Bunting had imagined. Coleman had plans of her own. "Woman's Kingdom" was more than just domestic tips and fashion advice. She wrote about politics, literature, business, religion, science, and many other fields traditionally considered the domain of men. "I think it is paying us women a poor compliment," she explained, "to imagine we cannot take an interest in the highest and the very deepest questions of the day."

"Woman's Kingdom" became an instant success. It proved to be one of the most popular features in the *Mail,* driving the paper's sales up by a third. She would eventually expand her column to a full page, writing an average of six or seven thousand words a week. Even the new Liberal prime minister Wilfrid Laurier was a devoted follower, known to buy the conservative paper just so he could read Coleman's pieces.

To find her stories, she was willing to travel far beyond the borders of Toronto. Coleman had been an eager and determined traveller ever since she was a girl. As a youngster, she had disguised herself as a boy so she could join her uncle, the preacher, on his tours through the Dickensian slums of London. Now, at a time when a woman travelling alone was still a scandalous sight, she was equally willing to dress as a man to explore places thought to be unfit for a woman. She traced the steps of Jack the Ripper through the back alleys of Whitechapel and explored the ruins of San Francisco after the Great Earthquake, just as she covered the Chicago World's Fair and Queen Victoria's Diamond Jubilee. In Cleveland, she landed a breathtaking scoop by slipping into the prison cell of the Canadian woman who'd conned American banks out of millions of dollars by claiming she was the daughter of the wealthy Andrew Carnegie. In New York, she attended the infamous murder trial of a jealous millionaire who'd shot a renowned architect on the roof of Madison Square Garden in front of hundreds of witnesses — the first trial ever called "The Trial of the Century."

When war broke out in Cuba between Spain and the United States, Coleman decided she was going to cover that, too. The fact that no woman had ever been accredited as a war correspondent wasn't about to stop her. Neither was the American military's outright ban on women journalists.

Convincing the *Mail* she should cover the Spanish-American War wasn't much of a challenge; they signed on, thinking the novelty would help sell papers. But when Coleman headed to Washington and barged her way in to meet with the U.S. secretary of war, he burst into laughter when she told him why she was there. "I hate awfully to have you go down into that frightful country," he explained. "Why, the men may pitch the camp almost anywhere, in any kind of rough place, and there, where the heat is so great, they will be lounging about half-dressed. It would be no place at all for a lady."

Coleman wasn't about to take no for answer. She returned to his office over and over again until he finally said yes. One hundred and thirty-five journalists were given accreditation to cover the war. Coleman was the only woman.

But as it turned out, even that official permission did her little good. When her ship sailed for Cuba, filled with reporters, Coleman wasn't on board. The captain had refused to take her. And when she managed to find room on a medical ship instead, that fell through, too; the founder of the Red Cross hated her on sight. Coleman was stuck in Florida for weeks, trying to find her way onto a boat. Even while she was stranded, though, she got to work, digging up scoops, uncovering secret arms shipments to Cuban rebels, all while trying to find her passage south.

"I'm going through to Cuba," she wrote, "and not all the old generals in the old army are going to stop me. I beat them in Washington and I'll beat them here."

She finally talked her way aboard an old American supply ship, arriving in Cuba just in time to witness the final battles of the war. She wrote about dead bodies lying in the streets under the hot summer sun. Surveyed battered troops from the back of a mule. Visited wounded Spanish soldiers in a field hospital — "living ghosts of men." Examined the charred hulks of warships half-sunk off the beaches.

"Awful was the ruin everywhere," she wrote about those ships. "You would think an army of demons had been let loose from hell to twist and smash and batter the ships, to torture and burn and wreak impish cruelties on the men and beasts. What the Spanish soldiers must have suffered on that July day in the smoke and heat and stress of this terrible battle cannot be told by human lips, nor written by any hand."

Coleman was in Cuba for a month, eating where she could, bathing in streams and well water, suffering through a case of malaria, and sending vivid dispatches back to Toronto. When the month was done, she returned to the United States on an American troopship, tending to the wounded soldiers on board.

By then, Coleman was known around the world: her experiences in Cuba had made newspaper headlines far beyond Toronto. The secretary of war, who had laughed in her face just weeks earlier, was now deeply impressed. He tried to convince her to go on an American tour as "the world's first female war reporter." She refused. "If I tell the women of the United States the awful things I have seen," she said, "you will have riots on your hands."

She did, however, agree to give one single lecture in Washington, DC. And while she was there, her thoughts turned back to love.

For a while now, a Canadian doctor by the name of Theobald Coleman had been ardently wooing her. He'd been very persistent: one of the many men who could see past her gruff exterior to recognize how warm she could be, admire the beauty of her sherry-brown eyes, or be struck by her resemblance to the famous red-headed actor Sarah Bernhardt, as well as her prodigious talents. After the utter failure of her first two marriages, she must have been reluctant to pursue another romance. "Is love eternal?" she once wrote in response to a reader's question. "Pray, how should I know? My experience of it has been that it is as ephemeral as the daily newspaper — and not as useful for it will not light kitchen fires. But then one is only an ordinary, middle-aged woman and such do not inspire love. My fairy prince, Little Woman, turned into a pumpkin stalk so long ago that I begin to believe he never existed as a prince, but was always a weed."

Despite her reluctance, in the end Kit couldn't resist Dr. Coleman's insistent charms. In Washington, they were finally married, and then they returned home to Canada. Their life together wouldn't be filled with burning passion and Kit did have her complaints, but he was a far better man than her first two husbands: kind, soft-spoken, and good with her children. Kit's third marriage was destined to be the one that lasted for the rest of her life. And it gave her the family name we remember her by.

Her own experiences with love and heartbreak — and her professional life — undoubtedly helped her give advice to her women readers. The end of the 1800s was a time of radical change in gender relations. The "New Woman," as the new feminists were called, was demanding more and more control over her own life, challenging the strict gender conventions that had ruled the Victorian era. To the horror of many, she rode a bicycle — giving her a new kind of freedom. She smoked. Demanded the right to attend university. She maybe even had a job, so she wouldn't have to depend on a husband. And as the century came to a close, an increasing number of suffragists were organizing in support of women's right to vote.

The implications for romantic relationships were staggering, leaving many disoriented. But they did, at least, have Kit Coleman doling out her weekly advice on love and marriage in the "Our Letter Club" section of "Woman's Kingdom." She got so many questions every week — hundreds of them came in the mail — she didn't even have room to print them, just her responses. And while the column wasn't always on the cutting edge of feminism — Coleman did still believe in traditional gender roles within marriage and publicly condemned homosexuality — many of her columns sound remarkably modern. She demanded she get paid the same as a man and supported the idea of equal pay in her column. She wrote about women's working conditions. She co-founded the Canadian Women's Press Club and served as its first president. And she tried to help her readers wrestle with issues of gender, sexuality, and romance.

To one reader, she wrote, "Every girl should respect her own body absolutely. She should never permit herself to be kissed and embraced even by a man old enough to be her great-grandfather. Faugh!"

To another, "No man has any right to shower a girl employee with gifts or flowers or candy, or ask her to go out to the theatre with him and accept his attentions unless he is prepared to go to the length of asking that girl to be his wife."

And to a third, "You make rather sweeping assertions. A pretty face does not necessarily imply 'no brains.' The old idea that clever girls are dowdy, plain and untidy must surely be exploded by now. Have you travelled much?"

Her readers were dear to her heart — she called them her "paper children" or her "shadow children" — but she didn't pull her punches. She was just as happy to call them "foolish woman," "silly chap," or "a soursoul-pickled misanthrope." Her advice was as blunt as it was witty. "How could you think of marrying such a flabby poltroon?" she responded to one woman. "I am afraid that you will not be very much better than him if you do. Perhaps this is for the best, as then you will be well-mated."

In response, Coleman was adored by her readers. When she was too sick to write a column, her editor's office would be flooded with gifts: flowers, chocolates, home remedies — one follower even gave her some cheese, worried she might not be well enough to shop for Patsy Brannigan that week.

And her readers were there in the moment she needed them most. In 1895, the *Mail* merged with the *Empire* to become the *Mail and Empire* (which would later merge with the *Globe* to become the *Globe and Mail*). Her new bosses demanded a change; they wanted Coleman to stick to the domestic tips and fashion advice of a typical women's page. But Kit wasn't about to throw away the freedom she'd won, and the loyal following she'd built. She asked her readers what they believed. "I want the candid, honest opinions of Canadian women," she wrote. "Do you enjoy fashion articles more than other kinds of writing?" The response was overwhelming. They say Coleman dumped the flood of letters on her editor's desk and kept writing what she wanted to write.

It wasn't the last time she'd have to fight for her editorial freedom. She was willing to risk everything for it. Years later, when her boss threatened to cut "Our Letter Club" entirely while refusing to give her a raise, it was the last straw. She quit. If they weren't going to let her write what she wanted and pay her what she deserved, she would go it alone. She began to sell her weekly feature herself — becoming Canada's first syndicated columnist — and refused to let the *Mail and Empire* publish her writing ever again, no matter how much they offered to pay. She made even more money in syndication than she had when she was on staff.

As a young woman, Coleman hadn't had much control over her own life, married off to a man she didn't love. But over the course of her six decades on earth, the world began to change — and she helped change it. She fought relentlessly for the freedom to make her own decisions: whether it was the words that appeared on her page of the newspaper, or the events she travelled around the world to witness, or the man she shared her life with. And in the hundreds of thousands of words she wrote, she helped the women of Toronto navigate that same evolution. In her column and in the way she lived, Kit Coleman helped lead a new generation of women who challenged the conventions of the past and seized control over their own lives, their own careers, and their own hearts.

THE GREAT
WARS

26

A FIVE-DOLLAR DATE

Billy Bishop was a popular young man. He grew up in Owen Sound, on the rugged shores of Georgian Bay just a few hours north of Toronto. He was a cute sixteen-year-old boy, confident, with a swagger and a slight, charming lisp. He was even a good dancer — took lessons and everything. The girls of Owen Sound were enchanted. Bishop was so popular, in fact, that he and his younger sister Louie came to an arrangement: he would take her friends out on dates in exchange for five dollars. It was a lucrative racket.

But even that grew old for a boy as popular as Bishop. By the time Margaret Burden arrived from Toronto to spend some time at her family's summer home, Billy already had his hands full. When Louie asked him to accompany Burden to a dance that Saturday night, he declined. "I don't need any more girls," he told her.

But Margaret was no ordinary girl. When she came over for tea one day, Bishop secretly peeked out to catch a glimpse of her as she sat on the veranda. He was stunned.

She was beautiful, with dark hair and hazel eyes. Bishop fell for her instantly: love at first sight.

Suddenly, he changed his tune. He told Louie that he *would* be willing to take Burden out after all — although he would still insist on charging the usual five dollars.

By the time their date was over that Saturday night, he knew this was it. Bishop returned home from the dance and announced to his parents that he had met the girl he was going to marry.

Making that happen, however, wouldn't be easy. Margaret Burden belonged to one of the richest and most respected families in Canadian history. Billy Bishop had fallen in love with an Eaton; his crush was the granddaughter of Timothy Eaton, a Toronto business tycoon who had turned his dry goods shop on Yonge Street into a department store empire stretching across the country, with an iconic mail-order catalogue and thousands of employees. The Eatons were such a revered national institution they've been called "Canada's royal family."

And as far as the Eatons were concerned, Billy was nowhere near good enough for their Margaret. He was the son of an ordinary town registrar and more than a little rough around the edges. He got into fights. Didn't like rules. Had poor grades and no plans for his future; he certainly wouldn't be going to university. Worse still, there was a great war looming; Burden's parents were sure a ruffian like Billy wouldn't make it out alive. If he died, their daughter would be left heartbroken and alone.

But there was little they could do as they watched their daughter fall in love. During that romantic summer of 1910, the two teenagers began to spend all their free time together. They attended dances and went for long walks, with Bishop pointing out all the beautifully coloured birds you could never see in Toronto. At the end of their dates, Burden would come home eager to tell her family all about the boy who was winning her heart. But still, they were unconvinced. Her father repeatedly tried to keep the two apart.

It would take a lot for Billy Bishop to prove him wrong. He tried and failed for years, struggling through military school as the war loomed. But thanks to that coming war, and an utterly bizarre coincidence, he would meet a woman who could make that impossible task very possible, indeed.

To begin, all Billy Bishop needed to do was to fall down a flight of stairs.

One spring day in 1916, he woke up in the hospital. The First World War had been raging for nearly two years. The quick, sweeping movements of the conflict's opening stages had settled into a brutal stalemate. A vast line of trenches had been dug across France and Belgium, miserable ditches where men died by the thousands just to gain a few muddy, blood-soaked metres, where they were cut to pieces by a hail of bullets and artillery, choked by sickly clouds of poison gas.

Bishop joined the fight in its opening weeks, having spent a few years as a student cadet at the Royal Military College in Kingston. He enlisted in Toronto, joining a cavalry unit — trained to ride his horse into the onslaught of German machine guns. It was a spectacularly dangerous job. Cavalry had once been a powerful weapon, but it was quickly becoming clear the days of men riding horses into battle were over, thanks to the machinery of modern warfare — especially when they were forced to ride over the crater-filled moonscape of the Western Front.

Bishop didn't even make it that far. He was miserable on the ground, stuck in the rain and mud. After just a few weeks of training, he requested a transfer to the Royal Flying Corps. It would be incredibly dangerous, too — the average life expectancy for a rookie pilot was only eleven days — but as Bishop put it, "I'll bet you don't get any mud or horseshit on you up there. If you die, at least it would be a clean death."

He got his transfer. His request was accepted before he saw any action on horseback. But his dream of becoming a pilot would have to wait. He was given a less glamorous assignment: he would serve as an observer, sitting in the plane as it flew over the front lines, taking notes on German positions.

And yet, still, he managed to get wounded. Mostly in impressively unheroic ways. First, he got into a truck accident. Then, he was hit in the head while working on an airplane and was knocked out for two days. When he recovered, he promptly injured his knee during a failed takeoff — his airplane ploughed through a hedge and into a neighbouring field. On leave in England, he hurt his knee again — this time, he got drunk and fell off a gangplank. Through it all, he refused to see a doctor. It wasn't until he fell down the steps of London's Savoy

Hotel that he finally found himself at Lady Carnarvon's Hospital for Officers.

Today, the building is a prep school overlooking lovely Bryanston Square, but back in the days of the First World War, it was a private home turned into a temporary military hospital. It was founded by one of the most famous aristocrats in England: Lady Carnarvon, the secret, illegitimate, but still-very-wealthy daughter of a Rothschild. And as such, Lady Carnarvon's hospital was far from your typical military institution. There were butlers and footmen to serve breakfast in bed and bring the wounded men the newspaper. The beds were made up with fine linen. Patients were fed with fresh food from the gardens. It was like something out of *Downton Abbey*. And that was no coincidence; the hospital helped inspire the television show. The programme was filmed at Lady Carnarvon's country home, where she first opened the hospital before moving it to London.

And she wasn't the only famous woman who volunteered her time and energy to help the war's wounded men. As Bishop woke from his slumber on that spring day in 1916, he found another one of the most influential women in England sitting at his bedside.

Lady St. Helier was at the heart of social life in London. She was a baroness, a writer, a philanthropist, even an alderman on the city council. The parties she threw at her home were *the* place to be in the early years of the 1900s. She played host to many of the greatest writers and most important politicians of the age, like Thomas Hardy, Edith Wharton, David Lloyd George, and W. Somerset Maugham. She even introduced Winston Churchill to his future wife — her niece — and then hosted their wedding reception.

But Billy Bishop didn't know any of that. They'd never met before and he didn't recognize her. As a Canadian, her name meant nothing to him. But she, by an exceptionally strange coincidence, knew exactly who *he* was.

"I saw your name on the hospital register," she explained. "And I was sure that someone named William Bishop from Canada must be the son of my friend Will Bishop. And when I looked at you, I was sure of it."

Amazingly, she was right. Once, during a trip to Ottawa years earlier, she'd been a guest at a reception held by Prime Minister Laurier. Bishop's father — the humble town registrar in Owen Sound, but also a graduate of Osgoode Hall and an ardent Liberal Party supporter — was there, too. He made enough of an impression that, years later, Lady St. Helier still remembered him fondly. And when she visited Lady Carnarvon's hospital, the Bishop name stood out.

That coincidence changed Billy Bishop's life.

Suddenly, he was a very well-connected young officer. Lady St. Helier invited him to spend the rest of his convalescence at her own home. The two became very close. Before long, she was introducing him as her grandson — and he, in turn, called her "Granny." When his father had a mild stroke back in Canada, Lady St. Helier pulled some strings to get Bishop a leave from the military and a ticket on a ship back home. Thanks to her, he was able to spend a few months visiting with his father in Owen Sound and with Margaret Burden in Toronto. That trip may very well have saved his life — back in Europe, his squadron was being cut to pieces at the Battle of the Somme.

When he returned to England, Bishop was still determined to become a pilot. But his application was being ignored. So once again, Lady St. Helier pulled some strings. And before he knew it, Bishop was in flight school.

That was a stroke of luck for the Royal Flying Corps. By the end of Bishop's first week as a pilot, he'd already shot down five German planes and earned the title of "ace." A few months later, he'd been awarded the Victoria Cross, faced off against the Red Baron, and set the record for the most enemy planes shot down by any pilot in the service of the British Empire.

And whenever Bishop was back in London, away from the front lines, he was staying at Lady St. Helier's, drinking and dancing with the most powerful people in England. By the time he got another leave to visit Canada during the autumn of 1917, he was an international celebrity.

It seemed Billy Bishop might be good enough to marry an Eaton after all.

It had been about six years since their five-dollar date, but Billy was still very much in love with Margaret. They kept in close touch while he was away at war. He sent hundreds of letters to his beloved sweetheart at her home on Avenue Road. And now, finally, his dream was going to come true. He would make good on the prediction he'd made to his parents all those years before. Billy Bishop and Margaret Burden were engaged.

"It is wonderful to think of those glorious days coming in our lives when night and day I can hold you in my arms and love, love, love you!" he wrote. "To every morning awaken to kiss you first thing and to feel your warm lips on mine and hear you say, I love you. To even write this thrills me, my darling.… Margaret, with all my heart and soul I love you, love you as a girl was never loved before."

There was now no way Burden's family could stop them. Bishop was lauded in Parliament and celebrated with public rallies in Toronto, Montreal, Ottawa, and Kingston. He exploits in the skies above Europe had made him a national hero.

They were married at Timothy Eaton Memorial Church on St. Clair Avenue West — in what the *Toronto World* declared "the most interesting wedding which has ever been celebrated in Toronto." Burden wore a simple and elegant white dress, a necklace, and a veil. He wore his uniform, medals on his chest. They emerged from the church to cheers — a crowd of onlookers had gathered to wish them well as they walked down the church steps under a canopy of raised swords. Then, they were off on their honeymoon in the Catskills before Bishop returned to his deadly work.

Their marriage together wouldn't quite be the fairy tale it promised to be on that autumn day. For one thing, the war was taking a psychological toll on Bishop. "You have no idea how bloodthirsty I've become," he wrote in a letter to the love of his life, "and how much pleasure I get in killing Huns." After one battle, he's said to have tried bringing back a German corpse as a trophy. His enemies started calling him "Hell's Handmaiden" and "The Blue Nosed Devil"; one fighter squadron put a bounty on his head.

But there was also Bishop's infidelity. He was never a faithful husband. He kept a mistress in France during the war. And that was far from his only affair — some say he even had a fling with the actor Rita Hayworth. Margaret was well aware of her husband's wandering eye. In fact, whenever she was able to figure out who Billy's new mistress was, she would invite the woman to a mischievously awkward lunch. And then watch her husband squirm.

Margaret, too, seems to have had her admirers. Many years later, when her granddaughter asked her about a lovely silver pig she used as a centrepiece, Burden admitted it was given to her by a gentleman friend during an intimate dinner, while "Billy was off somewhere giving speeches." She and her mysterious admirer drank champagne right out of the hollow pig.

Still, the marriage would survive it all. Margaret Burden and Billy Bishop would spend the rest of their lives together, more than thirty years of it.

But the fame that had brought them together would also bring an end to Bishop's flying career. It wasn't long after he started shooting down enemy planes that he was so famous the Canadian government began to worry:

What would happen to morale if the great Billy Bishop were shot down? They decided to ground him before it was too late. With the war still raging in the summer of 1918, the British Empire's greatest ace was pulled out of action and ordered away from the front lines.

Bishop was beyond frustrated. On his last day, he ran one final solo mission, downing five more planes in fifteen minutes. It gave him a total of seventy-two, making him the third most successful ace of the First World War — just eight victories behind the Red Baron.

Billy Bishop was famous enough to marry Margaret Burden. But he'd never fly a plane into action again.

27
LONGBOAT'S WIDOW

The best man did everything he could to keep it secret. Tom Flanagan also served as the groom's manager, so he was well aware this was no ordinary wedding. If the public were told where the ceremony was being held, they would show up in droves to celebrate the happy couple. "I'm not going to make the place public," Flanagan told the newspapers, "because I do not want the church besieged.… A wedding ceremony is a sacred thing." But somehow, scores of people figured it out anyway. Long before the couple arrived, a crowd began to gather in the cold. It was a dark December night — just a few days after Christmas in 1908 — but of course that didn't keep them away. Nothing could. They thronged beneath the brick spire of St. John the Evangelist — an old church on Portland Street, where soldiers from Fort York came to pray. The fans hoped to catch a glimpse of the bride and groom, to wish them well on their wedding day.

They finally got what they wanted at seven o'clock. The carriages of the wedding party arrived. The bride wore a white satin dress, with a veil and a long train; the groom was tall and striking in his tuxedo. They entered the church through a shower of confetti.

The wedding wouldn't go entirely smoothly. It had been a bit controversial to begin with: Toronto's Anglican archbishop nearly banned his priests from performing the ceremony, worried about the groom's recent and reluctant conversion from his own Haudenosaunee beliefs. And now, the lovebirds waited impatiently as the best man rushed back to his hotel, a horse-drawn cab galloping through the streets so he could grab the marriage licence he'd forgotten. But in the end, the couple was finally married. They emerged from the church to another shower of confetti and an even bigger crowd.

The public party was held at Massey Hall. The big, red-brick theatre was a little more than a decade old and had rarely seen an occasion as joyful as this one. There were bands, singers, comedians, acrobats, and more than a thousand spectators who streamed through the doors to celebrate the marriage. They cheered and applauded as the newlyweds kissed and then waited for a chance to shake their hands and give them their best. There at the centre of it all was Lauretta Maracle, the petite Kanien'keha:ka bride in her white dress, standing next to her tall husband. Tom Longboat, the greatest runner in the world, had just gotten married.

The marathon was both a very old and a very new event. Its roots stretch all the way back to antiquity. According to ancient scholars, the first marathon was run by a Greek messenger named Philippides, who rushed all the way from the battlefield of Marathon to the city of Athens to report a victory over the invading Persian army. He burst into the assembly, reported the news, and promptly died of exhaustion.

The second marathon was run two thousand years later. When the Olympic Games were resurrected at the end of the 1800s, the organizers were looking for a big, high-profile event to cap things off. Something that would draw spectators and reflect the ancient glory of Greece — a connection between the modern games and the original, ancient ones. They decided on a long-distance race: a gruelling run to commemorate that legendary sprint to Athens.

It was an instant success, becoming one of the most popular sports in the world. And nearly immediately, a runner from Canada established himself as the greatest marathon runner of all.

Tom Longboat, Cogwagee, was born in the territory of the Six Nations as a member of the Onondaga nation, growing up along the Grand River just a generation after Pauline Johnson did. His family lived in poverty, raising a few animals on a small plot of land. That's how Longboat learned to love running: by chasing down and herding cows.

His first big race came when he was eighteen years old: a long dash around Hamilton Harbour against some of the best runners in the country. The teenaged upstart crushed his competition, nearly setting a new course record even though he'd briefly gotten lost along the way. He quickly followed that with more victories, including the Ward Marathon in Toronto, racing through High Park and along the lakeshore with his trademark long, low strides and his hands held at his hips. With each victory, his future grew brighter.

It wouldn't be an easy road. The gruelling demands of the marathons were matched by the exhausting burdens of racism. Longboat had been taken from his parents as a child and sent to the Mohawk Institute Residential School on the outskirts of Brantford. It had been open for decades, the first residential school in Canada. There, he was forbidden from speaking the Onondaga language. His hair was cut. His clothes were thrown away. He was forced to wake up at five thirty every morning and work the fields until school began in the afternoon. At night, he was made to pray to the Christian god. The children ate porridge for nearly every meal; so much, they nicknamed their school "The Mush Hole." Some were beaten and abused. At one point, the students set fire to the building, trying to burn it down. Longboat ran away, was caught and returned, and then ran away again. This time, for good. Years later, when he was asked to give a speech at the school, he refused. "If I had my way," he explained, "I wouldn't even send my dog to that place."

He remembered those years at the residential school as the worst of his life. But the racism would never end. It didn't seem to matter that he was a world-famous runner and one of the most successful athletes in Canadian history. Even the favourable press he received was full of condescension and racist nicknames. A newspaper in

Boston, finding themselves without a photo of him, just ran an image of another Indigenous athlete instead. One of Canada's most respected sportswriters, Lou Marsh, who sometimes worked with and supported Longboat, also published more than one piece filled with racist drivel about him. "In my time, I've interviewed everything from a circus lion to an Eskimo chief, but when it comes to being the original dummy, Tom Longboat is it. Interviewing a Chinese Joss or a mooley cow is pie compared to the take of digging anything out of Heap Big Chief T. Longboat." And rumours of alcoholism followed him for the rest of his life, despite historians suggesting that there is no real evidence he drank more than anyone else.

Adversity found him on the track, too. At a Christmas Day race in Hamilton, a cart was sent crashing into Longboat and one of his fellow athletes — sabotage from a group who'd bet on another runner. When he ran at the 1908 Olympics in London, he collapsed before the finish line, complaining of a severe headache. There were rumours that Tom Flanagan — his own manager and best man — had poisoned him with strychnine. Some thought it had been an accident, that Flanagan was trying to give Longboat an illicit boost with a small dose of the dangerous stimulant — many runners used a cocktail of strychnine and champagne in an attempt to give themselves an edge. Others thought he'd done it on purpose to win a big bet against his own runner.

But no matter how much adversity he faced, Longboat kept winning races across Europe and North

America — including a few at Hanlan's Point Stadium on the Toronto Islands. When he ran the Boston Marathon, he didn't just win the race, he smashed the record by five minutes, even though it was snowing and he kept having to dodge eager fans. When he arrived home at Union Station after his big win, he was welcomed by a parade up Bay Street to Old City Hall where the mayor, a band, fireworks, and thousands of fans were waiting for him. It was the biggest reception the city had ever seen.

At the height of his fame, he was compared to Babe Ruth and Man o' War — an undisputed champion. And Lauretta was there at his side through all those glorious years. When Longboat was lagging during one famous race at Madison Square Garden just a couple of weeks before their wedding day, Flanagan even convinced her to stand right next to the track, waving a handkerchief every time her fiancé passed by. It gave Longboat the strength he needed to surge in front and win the race.

He was still the greatest runner in the world when the Great War came.

Longboat signed up in January 1916. Tom Flanagan had co-founded a new battalion and was convincing his Toronto friends to enlist — many of them from the sporting world. The runner would eventually become one of the biggest names in this "Sportsmen's Battalion."

At first, the new outfit was less of a fighting unit than a way of entertaining the troops — with Tom Longboat taking centre stage. But as the war wore on, he found himself in the trenches. He dug ditches and laid wire, and he did what he did best: he ran.

The First World War was fought in a time before radio technology was advanced enough to be used on the front lines. And telephone wires were both difficult to string all the way to the battlefield and easily cut by the enemy. While terrible new machinery was being invented to do the killing, communication was still left to old-fashioned technology: much of it done by carrier pigeon and on foot. As one of the greatest runners the world had ever seen, Tom Longboat was too valuable an asset to waste on entertainment. The army was going to put his legs to use as an instrument of war.

Longboat didn't talk much about his experiences on the Western Front. When he did, it was usually to crack a joke. But we know he was there at Vimy Ridge and at Passchendaele — two of the most brutal battles of the entire war. His unit was sent up to the front lines for construction projects and repairs. On some nights, they'd be sent out into no man's land to lay barbed wire. Longboat must have sprinted through the muddy, blood-soaked trenches, dodging sniper fire as shells whizzed by his head. He must have raced through sickly yellow-green clouds of poison gas. As thousands of soldiers were killed all around him, Longboat ran and ran and ran.

More than once it seemed as if he might never make it home. The first time a shell exploded nearby, he thought it was the end. "I thought I'd never see Canada again," he admitted. Later, a rumour spread that he'd been caught in a hail of artillery fire and buried by the bombardment, spending six days living underground with some other men before they were rescued. In some interviews, Longboat played along, claiming it was the only time he got a decent sleep during the entire war. But more often, he denied the story — while some of the men in his battalion had been buried in the barrage, Longboat wasn't one of them. Either way, while he suffered from knee and back pain for the rest of his life, he survived the war. Tom Longboat had outrun death itself.

As the war came to an end, he returned to Toronto. After years surrounded by horror, he was finally heading home to be reunited with his dear Lauretta. He could finally resume his old life.

Or, at least, that's what he hoped. But when he got home to Toronto, he was in for a shock. In the chaos of war, even the army had gotten confused. Somehow someone had believed one of the rumours that spread through the trenches, or they'd checked the wrong box on a form. While Longboat was racing through the poison clouds of Flanders, a notice had been sent to Lauretta. The message regretfully informed her that her husband had been killed. And if she'd somehow managed to keep hope alive, refused to believe the terrible news, convinced herself that her husband had survived and would make it back home someday … that hope can't have survived the second message. Another regretful notification of his death. Another mistake.

By the time Tom Longboat got home to Toronto, Lauretta had given up. She'd married another man. The life the runner had left behind when he went off to war didn't exist anymore. He was furious, but there was little he could do. His wife had fallen in love with someone else. Longboat filed for divorce. Lauretta carried on with her new husband.

There were more hard days to come. With his sore knees and his bad back, Longboat's running career was just about over, and he'd failed to save much of his winnings. After a brief stint as a farmer out West, he got a series of less glamorous jobs in Toronto. The world's greatest runner worked at a rubber plant, as a truck driver, a street cleaner, and a garbage collector. Some even say he got a job as a custodian at Old City Hall, cleaning the building where he'd once been celebrated as a hero by thousands of proud Torontonians.

But at the very least, Tom Longboat wasn't alone. He found love once again. Martha Silversmith was from Six Nations, just like him, a Seneca woman whose brother would become famous in his own right: Jay Silverheels played Tonto on *The Lone Ranger*. Silversmith had been a fan of Longboat's for years, regularly making the trip to Hamilton or Buffalo to watch him race and cheer him on. Twelve years after his first wedding day, Tom Longboat got married again. And this time, they would be together until the day he *really* died.

28

HEMINGWAY HATES TORONTO

A train pulled into Union Station. It had been travelling overnight from New York City, bringing the British prime minister to Toronto as part of his North American tour. His stop in the Big Apple had been big news. Reporters flocked to cover the event, including a young journalist from the *Toronto Star* by the name of Ernest Hemingway. Soon, he'd be one of the most celebrated authors in the world, but at the time he was making do with a modest salary from the newspaper. He was coming back to town on the very same train as the visiting prime minister, spending much of the sixteen-hour journey leisurely drinking and joking around with the other reporters. But as the train came to a stop at Union Station, he rushed down the steps onto the platform. He'd just received word, a few kilometres back: his wife, Hadley, had given birth to their first child. He needed to get to the hospital as quickly as he could.

Toronto had built a new train station in the decades since George Brown's triumphant return to the city. The second Union Station was an opulent building with three grand towers; the biggest train station in Canada when it first opened. It stood on the south side of Front Street, overlooking the lake, next to the spot where the modern Union Station stands today. Toronto Western Hospital, where Hadley was recovering with their new baby, was a couple of kilometres away. Hemingway was in a hurry.

But as he raced through the station, he was stopped by a fellow reporter, a colleague from the newspaper who'd been sent by his editor to collect him. He was under strict orders to head straight to the *Toronto Star* headquarters, a distinguished four-storey building on King Street. Hemingway had missed a scoop while he was in New York and his boss was furious. According to another paper, the deputy mayor of New York had insulted Britain; big news in British Toronto. But Hemingway didn't care. He had bigger things to worry about right now. He stuffed his notes into the hands of the reporter and rushed away.

He'd met his wife at a party in Chicago a few years earlier. He was the most handsome man there — at least as far as Hadley Richardson was concerned. He was nearly a decade younger than she was — just twenty while she was twenty-eight, already at risk of becoming an aging spinster by the standards of the time. For years, she'd been living a half-life, nursing her dying mother. But now that her mom had passed way, Richardson was ready for love. And she found it there in that handsome young writer wearing an Italian cape.

He proposed within weeks. The engagement was far from uncomplicated: Richardson wasn't the only woman in love with Hemingway; his other admirers included the mutual friend who'd introduced them. But their bond was strong. He wrote her so many love letters he worried he would be ruined as a letter writer forever, "Like a pitcher with a dead arm." And she wrote more than a thousand pages back. "You're absolutely a flame of love," she told him, "and sweetness and understanding and strength and my I love you beyond anything. Why you're *All*." They were married on a September day in Michigan in 1921.

Two years later, in Toronto, when the contractions started, Hadley didn't realize what was happening. Not right away. She was distracted, hanging out at their friends' house, when the labour pains began. It was almost midnight by the time she understood, and nearly too late as he rushed down Bathurst Street to the hospital. "We got there in the nick of time," she remembered. "Of course, I missed Ernest terribly. He should have been there with me, suffering." But it went quickly after that. Just a couple of hours later, she gave birth to a healthy baby boy.

Hemingway was elated when he finally arrived to meet his new son. It's why they'd come to Canada in the first place, taking a break from their beloved Paris because they heard Toronto had the best doctors. And in that moment, it must have all felt so worth it as they gazed down at their new baby boy: John Hadley Nicanor Hemingway — or Mr. Bumby, as they would call him. At the sight of his first child, Hemingway broke down in delight, exhausted and relieved to be reunited with his wife. That joy wouldn't last forever. Soon, they'd be back in Paris, and Hemingway would fall in love with another woman; their marriage would end in heartbreak and betrayal. But for now, in that moment, they were truly happy.

The next day, Hemingway reported to his editor's office at the *Star*. His boss tore into him for missing the scoop and for heading directly to the hospital to see his wife and child instead of straight to work. Hemingway was enraged. He was already frustrated by his heavy workload, which too often kept him from writing his fiction, and by the fact that his editor had shipped him off to New York when Hadley was nine months pregnant and due to give birth any day. His complaints would eventually drive him into a legendary act of defiance. There are many different versions of the story, but some remember Hemingway as being so incensed that he angrily typed out a venomous, sixteen-page screed against his boss. He then taped it together and pinned it to the office notice board for all to read. It was so long the pages curled up on the floor.

Hemingway was out of patience. He'd always hated Toronto. He first moved to the city in 1920. He'd been invited by a wealthy Canadian who saw him give a talk to a women's group in Michigan. He showed up in his military cape and medals and told harrowing tales of his adventures during the First World War — complete with the war wound he'd earned as an ambulance driver on the Italian front. Many of those tales were completely imaginary — he'd only served for two months and the cape was new — but Harriet Connable didn't know that. Hemingway was a good storyteller. She was so impressed she offered him a job: hanging out with her son, who was introverted and had a disability, in their mansion near Casa Loma. She hoped the adventurous Hemingway would rub off on her teenager. That job in Toronto led to Hemingway's gig with the *Star*, and the paper eventually sent him to Paris as a foreign correspondent, writing dispatches back to Canada from the cobblestoned streets of France with his new wife, Hadley, by his side.

It wasn't until she got pregnant that they came back to Toronto, living in a tiny apartment on Bathurst, a few blocks north of St. Clair, in a building now known as "The Hemingway." It wasn't much. While they did manage to squeeze in a grand piano for Hadley to play, there wasn't even enough room left over for a full-sized bed; instead, they had to pull a Murphy bed down from the wall every night.

But Hemingway's dislike for Toronto was the product of more than his cramped living conditions. This was 1923. Toronto was still deeply conservative, staunchly British, and thoroughly reserved. Boring, according to many. It was a city where hotels weren't allowed to rent rooms to unmarried couples. Where on a Sunday, it was illegal to shop, to swear, or to ride a toboggan. Drinking was illegal on any day of the week: Prohibition was still years away from being repealed in Ontario. Toronto wasn't exactly the ideal home for one of history's most infamous alcoholics.

While he praised the TTC — "No city in the world has a better-run and more comfortable streetcar system than Toronto" — and wrote lovingly about the old trees in Queen's Park, Hemingway was miserable in the city. In his letters to the poet Ezra Pound, Hemingway called Canada a "fistulated asshole" and claimed, "The people are all merde." To Sylvia Beach, owner of the Shakespeare and Company bookstore, he wrote, "Canadians are all tapettes [pansies] at heart under all the big free open spaces.… It is a dreadful country." Thanks to the blow-up with his boss, he was done with the *Star*. That meant he was done with Toronto, too. He was determined to leave the city as soon as possible.

On Boxing Day 1923 — the day after he secured his Christmas bonus — Hemingway quit the paper. But there was still one hitch: the lease on their tiny Bathurst Street apartment. If they simply tried to move out of the building, they'd be caught by the landlord, who would certainly call the police. So, Ernest and Hadley hatched a plan. Every time a friend stopped by to say goodbye, they asked them to take a single piece of furniture out with them when they left. Ever so slowly, one belonging at a time, they secretively moved out of the apartment. When the place had finally been emptied out, they made their move. They slipped away, undetected, and headed south to Union Station.

Not three months after he arrived on that train from New York, Hemingway was waiting for a train to take him back. From there, they would catch a steamship to France. They were leaving Toronto forever, heading home to their beloved Paris, back to the artists and the cafés, back to their famous friends. In Europe, without his work for the *Star* to distract him, Hemingway would finally have time to finish his first novel. *The Sun Also Rises* was published just two years later, dedicated to Hadley and their Toronto-born son. But by the time the book went to press, their marriage was coming to an end. Fame was waiting for Ernest Hemingway in Paris, but so were the days of betrayal, heartbreak, and divorce that would haunt him to the end of his life.

29
THE GREAT STORK DERBY

It all started on Halloween in 1926. That's the day Charles Vance Millar died. He was a rich Toronto lawyer and financier — best known for modernizing a stagecoach company out West, replacing horses with automobiles. He amassed quite an impressive fortune during his life, but he never got married or had any kids. So, when he rushed up some stairs that Halloween and it proved to be too much for his seventy-three-year-old heart, there was no one to inherit his fortune. He left no close relatives behind.

What he did leave behind was a bizarre Last Will and Testament. Millar had always loved practical jokes and he found a way to turn his death into the biggest prank of all.

To seven Protestant ministers who supported Prohibition, Millar left shares to the O'Keefe brewery. He also gave some of those stocks to every Orange Lodge in Toronto — leaving the Catholic-hating Orangemen with an investment in the Catholic O'Keefe's. To a couple of

Ontario's most ardent opponents of horse racing, he left memberships in the Ontario Jockey Club. And to three local lawyers who absolutely despised each other, Millar left joint ownership of a vacation home in Jamaica.

But those bequests were nothing compared to the strangest and most controversial clause: Millar declared that the rest of his fortune would be left to the woman in Toronto who gave birth to the most children over the course of the next ten years.

And so began the Great Stork Derby.

No one seems to be entirely sure what Millar was thinking. Some say his final prank was meant as a satirical comment on the provincial law banning birth control. Or on the absurdity of a judicial system that would uphold such a ridiculous will. Others wondered if he just wanted to show how far people were willing to go for money. One newspaper pointed out that he was "a bachelor almost to the point of being a misogynist"; the result, it seems, of a bitter, broken heart. As a young, struggling lawyer, he'd been rejected by the woman he loved when his modest salary proved too little to impress her rich family.

His will gave little explanation and, at first, people had trouble believing it was even real. When Millar's old law partner found it, he assumed it was a joke, not a legal document. When it became clear Millar was serious, many people were outraged. Millar's distant relatives launched legal challenges. *TIME Magazine* worried the prize might be won by "mental defectives" or by immigrants. The Ontario government called the Stork Derby "a fiasco," "a racket," and "the most revolting and

disgusting exhibition ever put on in a civilized country."
(This is the same Ontario government that had recently
taken the Dionne quintuplets away from their family to
be raised as a tourist attraction.) They tried to pass legislation against the contest and failed. Millar had been a
good lawyer; the will he wrote was airtight. One legal
challenge after another was defeated. Even the Supreme
Court of Canada ruled the Stork Derby was valid. As
one judge put it, "I cannot find that reproduction of the
human race is contrary to morals."

In fact, the contest was picking up steam. Millar died
in the middle of the Roaring Twenties, the prosperous
days of flappers and jazz. But just a few years later, the
stock market crashed. By the time the contest was finally
drawing to a close, Toronto was in the grips of the Great
Depression. The unemployment rate hit 30 percent. Even
those who were lucky enough to still have a job found
average wages cut by more than half. A quarter of the
city was on government relief. And with poverty everywhere, the prize money meant more than ever.

Meanwhile, the Millar fortune kept growing. While
most people's investments were going up in smoke, his
were still paying off long after he died. A two-dollar
stake in a proposed tunnel between Detroit and Windsor
turned into hundreds of thousands of dollars when the
tunnel opened in 1930. By the time the Derby deadline
arrived, Millar's estate was worth nearly a million dollars — more than ten million in today's money.

Most Torontonians decided the Great Depression
wasn't the right time to build a family. The number of

people getting married in the city was cut nearly in half, and the birth rate plummeted, too. All over the world, the fertility rate was dropping faster than at any other time in recorded history. It's been called "The Baby Bust."

But now, some Toronto families were racing to have as many babies as they could, making a desperate bid for Millar's fortune. As the contest drew to a close, the city's most fertile women came forward to make their claims. That sparked even more controversy and intolerance. Many of the mothers were from poverty-stricken families. Some had risked their lives giving birth to their children. Others had seen them die as infants — and were disqualified because of it. *TIME* even reported that a Stork Derby baby had been killed by rats. One woman, Grace Bagnato, was disqualified because her husband was an undocumented Italian immigrant. (She was also an important pioneer of Torontonian multiculturalism who could speak seven languages; she has her own historical plaque in Little Italy.) Another mother was disqualified because five of her ten children were conceived out of wedlock — the law discriminated against "illegitimate" children.

In the end, after more than a year spent sorting it all out, the prize money was split evenly between four mothers. Their children were all "legitimate," properly registered, and still alive. Annie Smith, Alice Timleck, Kathleen Nagle, and Isobel MacLean had all given birth to nine babies in ten years. Each mother was awarded $125,000. Two more settled out of court for smaller amounts. The money was, according to later accounts, invested wisely in businesses, securities, and homes. The mothers and their families retreated from public view. The controversy and excitement faded. Procreation went back to being the dreary, ho-hum task it has always been.

That is, at least, until 1945. Thomas Foster had been mayor of Toronto when the Stork Derby began — and he thought the contest was a wonderful idea. So, when he died at the age of ninety-three, the whole thing started all over again.

30
THE INCORRIGIBLE VELMA DEMERSON

There was a knock at the door. It came on a quiet spring morning in 1939. Velma Demerson and her fiancé, Harry, were having breakfast in their apartment downtown. Right up until that moment, it seemed as if she was about to begin a wonderful new life. She was eighteen years old, engaged to be married to the man she loved, looking forward to their wedding day and to the baby they had on the way. They were happy and in love.

But that was all about to change. When they opened the door, they found Velma's father standing on the other side — along with the police. They'd come to arrest her.

Velma was led out of her apartment and into the back of a waiting police car. She would spend the next week living behind the bars of a jail cell with nothing but a wooden bench to sleep on. She would be questioned about her religion, about her past relationships, and about her sexual history. She told them everything they wanted to know. All she was hoping to do, she told them, was to return home, marry her fiancé, and begin their life together as a family. It seemed like such a modest request. "She loves him," she heard one police officer ask another. "Why won't they let her marry him?" And yet, still, she languished in jail.

Demerson was scared and alone. Her parents refused to visit her, and it was far too dangerous for Harry to come. "The separation from my fiancé consumes me," she wrote. "I imagine I see him at every turn." As the days passed, she began to despair. In her bleakest moments, she even began to hope for a miscarriage.

Finally, at the end of that lonely week, Demerson was brought to trial. It didn't last long. She was found guilty, convicted of being "incorrigible," and given a one-year sentence. Her crime was simple: Velma Demerson was a white woman who had fallen in love with a Chinese Canadian man.

It was a dropped fork that brought them together. Demerson was out for dinner with her fortune-teller mother and some friends — one of the rare joyful occasions during those hard years of the Great Depression. It was fun. They were laughing, eating, and drinking. There was a hint of excitement in the air.

The first time she accidentally dropped her fork, the waiter picked it up for her. The second time, there he was again. He was quite attractive, she thought, in his waiter's white shirt and tie. So, when he asked her out, she said yes.

Everyone there assumed they were joking. But the very next day, Demerson headed back to the restaurant to meet Harry Yip for their first date. They hung out at his place — a modest room on the third floor of an old house near Yonge Street — drinking vermouth out of whisky glasses, smoking, and chatting until he had to go back to work. As he rose to leave, he asked if he could kiss her. She said yes.

They spent a year together, taking walks on summer days, visiting the best restaurants in Chinatown, or hanging out alone in his apartment. They both felt like outsiders: he was a Chinese immigrant; her parents were divorced, and her father was Greek. That was enough to leave them both ostracized in such a conservative town. "Maybe that's what attracts us to each other," she suggested in her autobiography. "My fiancé and I are lonely people who have found each other. We share the same enemies."

By the spring of 1939, they had a plan: it didn't matter what their families thought; they would elope and spend the rest of their lives together. But there was a costly hiccup. Yip was a gambler. And when he lost all his money, they were forced to delay those plans. She didn't blame him; she was confident they'd get married as soon as they could. But that's when the knock came at the door.

The 1930s were an incredibly difficult time for anyone who fell in love with someone who didn't look like them. The decade opened with an attack on an interracial couple by the Ku Klux Klan. It was carried out in Oakville — just outside Toronto. A mob of seventy-five men in white hoods burned a cross in the middle of a downtown street and a second outside the couple's home, dragging them off in separate cars and warning them that if they were ever seen together again, the Klan would be back. The mayor of Oakville responded by praising the KKK. "Personally, I think the Ku Klux Klan acted quite properly in the matter," he told the *Toronto Star.* "The feeling in the town is generally against such a marriage. Everything was done in an orderly manner. It will be quite an object lesson." Only one man was ever convicted for the attack. He got three months in jail.

Meanwhile, the federal government had a policy of official racism toward Chinese immigrants. The Chinese Exclusion Act banned nearly all Chinese people from moving to Canada. In a quarter century, only fifteen Chinese immigrants were accepted into Canada. And those Chinese Canadians who were already in the country faced terrible prejudice. In Toronto, just as in cities across Canada, Chinese men were demonized and accused of corrupting white women, even of luring them into the sex industry. Toronto police were known to arrest white women just for being found inside a Chinese restaurant at night. And much of the city's first Chinatown in The Ward would disappear as the community was driven out of businesses and homes in order make way for a new city hall.

Demerson wasn't about to let racism stop her, however. "I know that going out with a Chinese man is socially unacceptable," she wrote. "There may be disapproving looks from passersby, but I don't care. It's the first time I look forward with such eagerness to a date." But she would soon learn just how much hatred could be found in Toronto. It wasn't just disapproving looks.

The Ontario government had passed a law called the Female Refuges Act. It gave anyone the power to have a woman under thirty-five brought in front of a judge for "leading an idle and dissolute life." Parents could drag their daughters into court, too; if they were under twenty-one and the judge agreed they were "unmanageable or incorrigible," women could be institutionalized. The law was frequently used to punish them for their sexual choices. And in Toronto, living with a Chinese Canadian man and being pregnant with his child provided plenty of grounds for a conviction.

That's how Velma Demerson found herself at the Andrew Mercer Reformatory for Women.

It was an ominous sight. A gothic mountain of red brick rising up from King Street. A tall steeple towered above the main entrance; turrets rose from both wings. At first glance, it might have seemed like a private school or a university building, but this was a more sombre, foreboding place. If you looked closely, you could see bars on the windows. Demerson would remember it as "a dark formidable fortress pencilled black against the white sky."

By the time she arrived, the Andrew Mercer Reformatory for Women was already more than half a century old. It was the first women's prison to open anywhere in Canada. The Mercer was home to a mix of women incarcerated for a wide variety of offences: everything from murder to drunkenness to being a pregnant teenager who'd fallen in love with the wrong man.

This is where Demerson would spend the next nine months of her life, locked away inside a tiny cell behind iron bars with little more than a wire cot and a pail for a toilet. The room was barely big enough to lie down. Demerson, like the other inmates, spent twelve hours a day confined inside her cell, forbidden from talking to her neighbours, not even allowed to lie down until bedtime when the bare bulb in the ceiling would finally be turned off.

"I never become used to my cell," she wrote. "Each morning I open my eyes and feel despair. Drab grey and hard surfaces have replaced the colour and texture of former surroundings."

Many of the brief hours she was allowed to spend outside her cell were filled with work. The Mercer was founded on the idea that labour would help reform "fallen" women. Demerson was assigned to a half-broken sewing machine, expected to work in silence for nine hours a day while earning less than a cent an hour. She made a grand total of six dollars during her entire stay.

"It's becoming horribly clear," she wrote, "that my life is forfeit to a still unknown but punitive monster — the state. All movement, all time, even my very thoughts are being consumed. I feel naked, shamed, and defenseless."

Worse still was the medical "care" she received.

Dr. Edna Guest was a respected physician: a pioneer in her field. She'd graduated from medical school at the University of Toronto back in 1910 — a time when only three of the hundred and fifty graduates were women. She did her postgraduate studies at Harvard, was a missionary professor in India, and served as a doctor on the Western Front during the First World War. In Toronto, she co-founded Women's College Hospital. She would eventually be named to the Order of the British Empire. To this day, McMaster University gives out an annual athletic award named in her honour. An avid feminist, cancer researcher, and campaigner against venereal disease, she'd been overseeing the medical treatment at the Mercer for nearly twenty years. But she was interested in more than just her patients' health.

Dr. Guest was a passionate supporter of eugenics. She believed strongly in the idea that "undesirable" citizens should be sterilized, while the most successful should be encouraged to procreate, leading to the creation of a stronger race. Canada was about to fight a war to end that kind of thinking in Nazi Germany, but for the moment there were still plenty of respected Canadians who believed in it — including celebrated feminist pioneers like Nellie McClung and Emily Murphy, and the champion of public health care, Tommy Douglas. Both Alberta and British Colombia had passed laws allowing patients in mental health institutions to be sterilized against their will.

Only a few weeks after she arrived at the Mercer, Demerson fell under Dr. Guest's knife. Her treatment was excruciatingly painful. Without being told what was happening or what she was being treated for, her groin was cut open with scissors; she believed the wounds were cauterized with acid. Week after week, she was brought back to have the procedures performed again. In between, she was kept in solitary confinement. Her fear only grew stronger as her groin turned black.

In the face of such torture, even Yip became a fading memory. "Love, now so distant," Demerson wrote, "appears to me as a luxurious fantasy compared to my life of physical fear.... I don't think about my fiancé anymore; my loyalties have dissolved in a sea of turmoil. I am still in shock. I will never think of sexuality.... My environment has taken over my entire being — there is no spirituality, no romance, only pragmatism."

It wasn't until many decades later that she would finally understand what happened. According to Demerson's autobiography, Dr. Guest was using the patients at the Mercer as unwilling subjects in her medical experiments. The doctor believed "incorrigible" behaviour in women was caused by overactive sex glands. If she could prove it, she would prove that women weren't inherently inferior, as so many men claimed — just those with the faulty glands. The doctor thought she was advancing the cause of equality.

It was in the middle of these horrifying experiments that Demerson went into labour.

She was taken to Toronto General Hospital to give birth. It went well: she had a bouncing baby boy she would name Harry Yip Jr. But she was terrified by the prospect of returning to the Mercer and its medical experiments. So, she seized her opportunity to escape.

She fled the hospital in the dead of night, escaping out the delivery entrance, running toward Bay Street in nothing but her hospital gown, slippers, and a sheet she'd wrapped around herself. Getting a ride from a stranger, she discovered her fiancé wasn't home. She had little choice but to go to her mother for help.

Her mom hadn't visited her in the hospital; she was so offended by Demerson's relationship she couldn't bring herself to meet her grandson. And when her daughter arrived at her doorstep in the middle of the night, begging for help, pleading with her to save her from the Mercer, she refused.

Demerson would be forced to return to her house of horrors, so desperate she used a pair of scissors to stab herself in the stomach. If only, she thought, she could injure herself enough to get sent back to the hospital, she would win a little more time outside the reformatory. It didn't work. But the end of her sentence, thankfully, was beginning to draw near. The day would come when she was finally released and allowed to return to the outside world — and to the man she loved.

They were married not long after she was released. It wasn't a particularly celebratory occasion. They simply brought a couple of friends with them to a church and had a Chinese Protestant minister perform the ceremony. Demerson didn't wear a wedding dress; Yip headed right back to work after they signed the register. It was more practical than anything else. Demerson still wasn't twenty-one years old. They worried she might get arrested again if they didn't get married right away. But at least they could finally be together. The little family settled into a second-floor apartment on Gerrard Street, just a few blocks from Chinatown, with a small balcony looking out over the sidewalk.

Their life wasn't an easy one. It took them a while to get custody of Harry Jr. He'd been taken away from his mother and admitted to the Hospital for Sick Children for treatment of asthma and chronic eczema. No one had told them where he was or why he had been taken away. And while Demerson was deeply scarred by the year she spent at the Mercer, she didn't feel she could confide in her new husband: she never spoke of her experiences, worried it would make Yip even more worried about their son's health. Meanwhile, Yip's gambling problem continued. He lost all their money again. Their love affair was doomed. It just couldn't survive everything they'd been through.

"Suddenly I'm overcome with despair," Demerson wrote, "I get up from the table and go out on the veranda and cry. My dreams are crashing down. The poverty, isolation, and my son's illness have disheartened me and I've lost respect for the man I love. He can't offer protection to the baby and me. My stay in the Mercer has ruined my spontaneity. The world looks grim." She was twenty-two years old.

Velma Demerson was in her sixties by the time she began her search for answers. She started digging through archives and enlisted the help of a lawyer. Together, they began to uncover the truth about her months at the Mercer and the things that had been done to her there. It wasn't until 2003 — when she was eighty-two years old — that the provincial government officially apologized for what happened. The following year, she finally reclaimed her Canadian citizenship — it had been stripped from her after she married Yip. Even then, she kept fighting, knowing how many others had suffered a similar fate to hers. She would keep raising awareness and pushing for justice until the day she died — at the impressive age of ninety-eight.

By then, the Andrew Mercer Reformatory for Women had been gone for decades. The imposing brick building was demolished in 1969. Tales of torture, abuse, and medical experiments had become a recurring theme. Women had been resisting the poor treatment they received at the Mercer since the 1800s. One notorious sex worker and petty criminal, Lizzie Lessard, had even retaliated against a two-week stint in solitary by stabbing a warden repeatedly with a pair of scissors, making sure to infect them with her own case of syphilis first. In 1948, the prisoners rose up in protest, staging a riot. Years later, a grand jury was convened to investigate. The *Toronto Star* ran front page stories about the horrors found inside the institution. The Mercer was finally shut down and destroyed. Alan Lamport Stadium replaced it.

But the place where so many women once suffered is still remembered in the name of the neighbourhood where it stood. Both the Mercer and the Toronto Central

Prison, just down the road, faced onto the same street. Prisoners who were released from either institution would take their first steps of freedom on that road — so it was given an appropriate name, one which, many decades later, would be adopted for the entire neighbourhood as it filled with condos, restaurants, and bars. They called that street Liberty Street, and the neighbourhood Liberty Village.

31
THE CLAY LADIES

The column towered over the mouth of the Humber River, where once the Rousseaus had lived and the cornfields of the Mississaugas covered the land. It stretched high into the sky above the entrance to the brand-new Queen Elizabeth Way. It was topped by a crown, adorned with a relief of the king and queen, and there at the base — just beginning to rise to his feet — stood an impressive stone lion. It was one of Toronto's most famous monuments — so well-known many simply called it *the* Monument.

It was unveiled in the first year of the Second World War to celebrate the city's newest highway. The beautiful Queen Elizabeth Way stretched from the Humber River around the western end of Lake Ontario to Niagara Falls. Now a roaring strip of asphalt and concrete, the QEW was born as a pleasant drive through farmers' fields and cherry trees. And it was named after the queen whose face graced the column at its entrance. Queen Elizabeth, better remembered as the Queen Mother, was the wife of King George VI and the mother of the future Queen Elizabeth II. She was even there for the dedication ceremony that summer. The royal couple's Canadian tour was a landmark event: the first time a reigning monarch had visited the country — or any other Dominion for that matter — and a way of rallying the British Empire as war loomed.

And so, the new monument symbolized many things. It celebrated the new road, commemorated the royal visit, and promised Canada would do its part in the fight against the Nazis. But it was also a testament to its creators and to the love that bound them together as partners — in art and in life. The Monument was a monument to Frances Loring and Florence Wyle.

They were two of the most respected sculptors in Canadian history, but they met in the United Sates. That's where they'd both been born and raised. Their paths first crossed as students at the Art Institute of Chicago. The two young women made something of an unlikely pair. Florence Wyle was from a conservative family, with a father who made it clear her place was inside doing housework while her twin brother played outdoors. They lived on a farm; Wyle grew up tending to wounded animals, interested in the life all around her. That's what turned her into an artist. She enrolled in medical school, where she took an anatomical drawing class that eventually led her to sculpture.

Loring, on the other hand, found sculpture in Europe. Her father made his money on Wall Street and in mining. But his fortune was wiped out by a stock market crash right in the middle of the family's trip to Europe. He suddenly couldn't afford the return ticket. So, while he headed home to save up enough money to bring his wife and children back to the United States, a teenaged Frances Loring spent seven years living in France, Italy, Germany, and Switzerland.

There, she explored the great museums and galleries, enrolled in prestigious Parisian art schools, and was exposed to a more liberal way of life than the one she had known back home. During one visit, her father took her to the Moulin Rouge, where she was transfixed by the scantily clad dancers. "Is this a place ladies can come?" she asked him. "Certainly," he told her. "A lady can go anywhere." Loring would spend the rest of her life trying to prove that was true.

When she enrolled at the Art Institute of Chicago, she and Wyle hit it off immediately. "It seemed amazing how congenial [we] were," Wyle would later remember, "how [our] ideals merged." They shared a love of sculpture, feminist ideas, and a way of seeing the world. When they were apart, they exchanged letters. And though Florence was in love with one of her professors for a while, he wasn't the one she would spend the rest of her life with.

Before long, the two young women had moved to New York, sharing a studio in Greenwich Village, at home in that neighbourhood's booming bohemian scene, getting to know their artist neighbours like Georgia O'Keeffe and Gertrude Vanderbilt Whitney. It was the beginning of their lives together. They shared the same kind of ambiguous Boston Marriage that Mazo de la Roche and Caroline Clement were about to start living in Toronto.

Their parents didn't approve. One day in 1913, Loring's father shut down the studio and offered to move the pair to Toronto. He thought he would be able to keep an eye on them in Canada — and hoped the city's conservative values might rub off on them. Instead, it was the other way around.

When the young sculptors arrived in Toronto, the Morality Squad was still at the height of its powers. Love was strictly regulated. We'll never know whether Loring and Wyle had a physical relationship, because if they did, they certainly couldn't feel comfortable being open about it in "Toronto The Good." The city's first lesbian bars were still a couple of decades away; it wasn't until the 1940s and '50s that places like the Continental and the Rideau began the long, hard work of carving out a safer space for queer women. But even as the Morality Squad stalked the streets of Toronto, the foundations of a more progressive, inclusive city were beginning to be laid. And Loring and Wyle would play a leading role.

The sculptors brought a slice of bohemian life to stodgy Toronto. They eventually settled into a rundown converted church in Moore Park (near Mount Pleasant Road and St. Clair Avenue), which is still there today. "The Church," as they called it, would become not just home to the women and their work, but the closest thing Toronto had to the famous salons of Paris.

Loring and Wyle became friends with the most important artists, musicians, architects, and intellectuals in the city. Their Saturday night parties became the thing of legend, going on long into the night; guests warmed by the big, red-brick fireplace, surrounded by half-finished sculptures and an assortment of cats. The artists of the Group of Seven and the Nobel Prize–winning doctor Sir Frederick Banting, who helped discover insulin, were particularly close friends, but the guest lists were long and filled with notable names.

The Church has been called "the hub of all that was vital and exciting in the Toronto art world of the twenties and thirties ... one of the most fascinating gathering places in the country." Their good friend A.Y. Jackson, one of the members of the Group of Seven, called it "the art centre of Toronto ... a most colourful place.... What wonderful parties they put on!" A young Timothy Findley grew up nearby; his father pointed Loring and Wyle out to him. "One day," his father said, "you will remember those two women, and you will understand how wonderful they are." And since they were in the habit of handing out lumps of clay to children around the neighbourhood, those children started calling them "The Clay Ladies."

Their contributions went far beyond social gatherings. At a time when female sculptors were dismissed and passed over for commissions — they were too frail for such physical work, some claimed — Loring and Wyle not only pioneered the place of sculpture in modern Canadian art, but the place of art in modern Canadian culture.

When the Clay Ladies first arrived in Toronto, Canadian art wasn't taken seriously, not even by Canadians.

Loring and Wyle set about changing that attitude — even while some Torontonians were busy gossiping about their sexual orientation. They co-founded groundbreaking artistic organizations, like the Sculptors Society of Canada and the Federation of Canadian Artists, pushing for the policies that would eventually lead to the creation of the Canada Council for the Arts. Loring in particular dedicated much of her time and energy to public causes and education; she was a familiar face at meetings and art openings, and her voice was often heard on the CBC.

By the time the QEW opened, Loring and Wyle were already well known for their war-related work. During the First World War, they had been commissioned to produce a series of statues about workers on the Home Front. Those sculptures had made them famous. Since then, Wyle had concentrated on smaller pieces while Loring developed a taste for large, monumental work. So, she was an obvious choice for the lion that would sit at the base of the column on the QEW; Wyle was chosen to carve the much smaller king and queen in relief.

It was an architect who designed the monument, but Loring and Wyle who would bring it to life. And that was a daunting task; the Lion was one of the most challenging pieces Loring would ever tackle. Given its prominence and meaning, the work came with strict, nationalistic requirements. The limestone would have to come from a Canadian quarry, even though it was of a lesser quality. And that was only the beginning of the trouble. A stone carver would be required to complete

Loring's design, but every stone carver she suggested was rejected. They all had Italian or German heritage; as far as some Canadian government officials were concerned, they were the enemy.

In the end, Loring was stuck with an Englishman she had never worked with before — and who, as she soon discovered, resented taking direction from a woman. When she discovered he had made a change to the design of her lion without her permission, Loring fired him on the spot. She would complete the stonework herself, despite the fact she had never done stonework on that scale before. Already in her fifties, but unfazed, she climbed the scaffolding up the column on an island in the middle of the highway, protected from Lake Ontario's bitter November winds by only a thin tarpaulin. As she chipped and chiselled away in the cold for weeks on end, her fingers were seized by arthritis. It would plague her for the rest of her life.

And yet, despite the obstacles, when Loring and Wyle's work was finally finished, it was a triumph. Loring's stylized lion rose from his rest, snarling and defiant, ready to face the Nazi threat and the brutal travails of the Second World War. She was praised for her artistic mastery: "a balance of tension that could be sensed running from the powerful paws to the end of the tail." The great cat has been hailed as "one of the finest pieces of outdoor sculpture in Canada" and "the finest piece of architectural sculpture in the country."

The Lion became a landmark for Torontonians. It was impossible to miss as they drove along the lakeshore in and out of the heart of the city. Children were particularly enthralled by the stone beast, keeping an eye out for the big cat as their parents drove along the highway. They called it the Lucky Lion. It was a powerful part of the city's public imagination. Loring and Wyle had cemented their place in the lore of their adopted home.

But then came the Gardiner Expressway. Twenty years after the opening of the QEW, another highway was built along the lakeshore, and some of Toronto's most recognizable landmarks were destroyed to make way for it. The old Dufferin Gate at the CNE was demolished. So was most of the Sunnyside Amusement Park. South Parkdale disappeared. Fort York was barely saved. And with the new highway and a booming population driving more and more traffic toward the QEW, the older highway would need to be expanded. In 1974, it was widened to twelve lanes. The island where the Monument stood was removed. The plan called for the Lion to be demolished.

In response, there was an outpouring of public support for the Monument. Torontonians loved their Lion. In the end, the government relented and promised to save it. But many hoped for more than that: not only did they want the Lion saved, they wanted it to be given a new home where it would remain an important part of Toronto's cultural consciousness. The *Globe and Mail* published an editorial declaring, "A country which sweeps aside its past and its art for ribbons of concrete is going nowhere of any importance."

The sculptor Rebecca Sisler, who had followed in the pioneering footsteps of Loring and Wyle and would later pen their first biography, wrote a letter to the paper: "Surely The Monument represents something rare in the annals of Canadian achievement: a synthesis of artistic excellence, historic significance, and public affection. Is this province so poverty-stricken, spiritually and financially, that funds cannot be allocated to preserve our best-known monument?" She, too, wanted it kept in a prominent location. "Are there no sites in the core of Ontario's capital where the column and its splendid Lion could be re-erected in the mainstream of everyday life where it can continue to stir public imagination?"

In the end, there was a compromise: the Monument was moved to a nearby location on the waterfront: in Sir Casimir Gzowski Park. It survived — it's still there today — but its importance was greatly diminished. Cars passing on the Gardiner Expressway can barely see the tip of it; the Lion is part of the mainstream of everyday life only for those who pass through that quiet section of the park or pay particularly close attention as they speed by on Lake Shore Boulevard. Over the last few decades, the Lion has faded from the minds of most Torontonians. As have Loring and Wyle.

They ended their lives in Newmarket living on separate floors of the same nursing home. They were both in their eighties by then, frail and suffering from dementia. Having spent sixty years living and working together, they now seemed to barely remember each other at all; as their minds slipped away, they rarely asked about one another, even though they were still so close. They died within three weeks of each other at the beginning of 1968.

Their work, however, lives on. Their sculptures can be found all over Toronto — all over Canada, in fact: chiselled into some of the country's finest buildings; on display at Osgoode Hall, the Art Gallery of Ontario, and the National Gallery of Canada in Ottawa; standing on Parliament Hill; and preserved among the old ruins that grace the gardens of the Guild Inn high atop the Scarborough Bluffs. Whether Torontonians realize it or not, they are surrounded by the sculptures Loring and Wyle hammered and chiselled into existence. "They are," as Wyle once put it, "our immortality."

32

HEARTBROKEN SPIES

Frank Pickersgill had a plan. It was December 1941. He'd been locked up by the Nazis for months, shipped from one internment camp to another. Starving and sick, he'd been forced to exist on nothing more than hot water, mouldy potato soup, and bread. He'd seen horrors, witnessed fellow prisoners murdered, and lost forty pounds off an already thin frame. But now, there was hope. Frank Pickersgill was going to escape.

His days as a student at the University of Toronto must have seemed like a distant dream. He'd been in Europe for a while now, having continued his studies in France, doing his postgraduate work at the Sorbonne, living the life of a young, struggling writer in the cafés of Paris when the war broke out. He hadn't left right away, had tried to stick it out during the first few quiet months of the war. He'd written the first English translation of Jean-Paul Sartre's new novel *Nausea*, and helped pay his bills by working as a milkman.

By the time he decided to leave, it was too late. The Germans were approaching. The Canadian authorities had already evacuated; they couldn't help. So, as the black smoke of Nazi war machines reached the City of Love, Pickersgill climbed onto his bicycle and raced off into the French countryside, joining the endless lines of refugees heading south out of Paris as German tanks rumbled into the city from the north. He pedalled endlessly through the French countryside, looking for a way out. The last ships to England had already left. Frightened villagers were suspicious of strangers: some nearly killed him, thinking he must be a German spy. In the end, as Hitler's forces took control of France, Pickersgill was rounded up like most of the Canadians and other British subjects who were still stuck in the country. Now, he was back in Paris, at the St. Denis Internment Camp.

But if he had his way, he wouldn't be there for long.

The first step: he got assigned to cleaning duty. That meant he worked one day a week in the administrative buildings. They were outside the barbed wire. There was nothing between him and freedom but a big brick wall.

Next: he needed to get access to the censor's office. It had a barred window that looked out onto the street. Luckily, one of the German officers was a bit careless with his key. When he forgot it in the lock, all it took was a few moments. Pickersgill's co-conspirator kept a lump of clay in his pocket. They pressed the key into it, making a perfect mould of its shape, and then put the key back where they found it. When Pickersgill got a visit from a friend, he secretly passed the mould on to him, and when the friend returned, he had a brand-new key ready to pass back to Pickersgill. A perfect copy.

Then: they had to wait for the office to be empty. They'd done their research: the censor spent every weekend with his mistress. They simply waited until the end of the day on Saturday and slipped right into his office with their copy of his key. He wouldn't be back until Monday.

Finally: they had to deal with the bars on the window. They had a plan for them, too. Pickersgill's accomplice got so much mail from friends and family that the guards at the post office had stopped searching his packages. They didn't notice when a friend mailed him a loaf of bread with a hacksaw and three blades baked inside. It took four hours of loud sawing, every moment excruciating as they expected to be discovered, but in the wee hours of the morning, the bars finally fell free.

They waited until morning, when the streets were full of people, then slipped out the window, put the bars carefully back in place, and melted away into the crowd. It would be weeks before the Germans finally figured out how they'd escaped.

The very next day, Frank Pickersgill was on his way out of Paris. For the next six months, through the summer of 1942, Pickersgill would live in the French countryside. There, he found plenty of people willing to help: to welcome him, conceal his true identify, and give him shelter — including a couple of Ernest Hemingway's old Parisian friends, the famous writer Gertrude Stein and her partner Alice B. Toklas. He was even able to find work with the French Resistance, translating anti-Nazi propaganda.

But Pickersgill was determined to do more. He'd fallen in love with France during his time in Paris. The thought of his beloved city suffering under Nazi occupation was too much to bear. Even before he'd been captured, he'd been driven to pitch in. "I am so full of shame and disgust that I must do something," he wrote in French, "if I don't, I could never come back."

He was still weakened and thin as a result of his months in captivity, but he was desperate to do something substantial — to a make a real, concrete contribution. "I was in the war up to the neck," he wrote, "and I think I should have died of spiritual starvation had I been wrenched away from it. In others words I suppose in a sense I had become a fanatic." Refusing to return home all the way to Canada and safety, he worked instead to get himself onto a flight bound for England. There, he was sure, he would find the opportunity he was looking for: a chance to join the fight.

And he was right. The day after he got off the plane in England, he was approached by officials from the British government. He was a scholar from a prominent diplomatic family who had survived Nazi internment camps, escaped captivity, and worked with the French Resistance. He was exactly the kind of person the Allied secret services were looking for. Frank Pickersgill was going to be a spy.

So was Ken Macalister. He was doing it for love. He'd once been one of the most promising young law students at the University of Toronto. So promising, in fact, he became a Rhodes Scholar, given a scholarship to study at Oxford University in England. But Macalister's interest in the origins of Canadian law wasn't just limited to its British roots. He wanted to know about its French origins, too. So he convinced the Rhodes Trustees to let him study at the Sorbonne for a while. And it was there in France that he met Jeannine.

A bit of luck brought them together. Looking to improve his French, Macalister arranged to spend the summer of 1939 living with a professor and his family in Normandy, so he could be fully immersed in the language. Jeannine was the professor's daughter. And as they spent those long summer days together near the coast of France, the two quickly fell in love. They were married before autumn arrived, ready to spend their lives together.

But then, just weeks later, the war began — and German tanks wouldn't be far behind. Macalister had promised the Rhodes Trustees he would immediately return to the safety of England when war broke out, but now he fought for every moment with Jeannine. He lied repeatedly, made up excuses, and dragged his feet, all so he could stay in France as long as possible. He even tried to enlist in the French army, but was rejected because of his poor eyesight. Even still, he was determined to do his part to keep France — and his new wife — safe from the Nazis. So, in the end, he made a heart-wrenching decision: he would return to England as he'd promised, leaving Jeannine behind, and try to join the British army.

Those days in London were an incredibly difficult time for the young law student. He was rejected from the military again. And his separation from Jeannine soon became even more rending; she was pregnant, expecting their first child that spring, and he wouldn't be able to see her. They could barely communicate at all, able to exchange only a few letters sent through the Red Cross or smuggled out of France. In spring, terrible news arrived: Jeannine's labour had gone poorly. She was okay, but the baby hadn't survived. And with Germany launching its invasion of France just weeks later, there was no safe way for Macalister to join his wife and console her. She would soon be trapped behind enemy lines.

The Canadian was more determined than ever. He would to do everything in his power to join the effort to liberate France — and Jeannine with it.

That's when he was presented with an unusual opportunity.

They called it "The Firm." Its official name was the Secret Operations Executive (SOE). It was created in the summer of 1940, in the terrifying months after Hitler's forces had swept across Europe and the Nazis began to bomb Britain in anticipation of an invasion. The Firm would be responsible for strengthening anti-Nazi resistance in the occupied countries of Europe through sabotage and death. Winston Churchill called the ministry overseeing it "The Ministry of Ungentlemanly Warfare." Its mission, as he put it, "was to set Europe ablaze."

Thousands of secret agents would be parachuted into Nazi-occupied territory over the course of the war, where they assumed false identities and recruited sympathetic locals. They carried out sabotage against the Germans, planned assassinations, and prepared secret armies of resistance fighters ready for the day when the Allies returned to liberate their countries.

In Prague, they assassinated a leader of the SS. In Scandinavia, they sabotaged atomic research facilities. In Italy, they would capture the entire city of Genoa. One German commander would later estimate that The Firm shortened the war by six months.

But it was incredibly dangerous and difficult work. Many of the spy networks were uncovered. Many agents were captured, tortured, and executed.

Canadians played an important role in the secret service right from the very start. One of the organizations that evolved into the SOE was founded by a newspaper magnate from Montreal: Sir Campbell Stuart. And one of Britain's most successful spymasters was an industrialist from Winnipeg: William Stephenson — said to have inspired the character of James Bond. With his help, a secret spy school was built on the shores of Lake Ontario. Camp X stood just outside Toronto, on the border between Whitby and Oshawa. Hundreds of recruits were trained there — including the children's author Roald Dahl and maybe even James Bond's creator, Ian Fleming. Graduates of Camp X would become spies for the SOE, the FBI, and the forerunners of the CIA. Today, the place where it once stood is a public park called Intrepid Park, in honour of William Stephenson's code name.

And Canadians weren't just working behind the scenes. Some were signing up to become spies themselves. When Ken Macalister was approached to join the SOE, he leapt at the opportunity. In the secret service, his poor eyesight wouldn't be as much of a liability as it was in the regular army. In fact, his thick glasses would help his disguise. It was settled: he would become a secret agent, join the fight against the Nazis, liberate France, and free his wife.

Little did he know the terrible truth: he would never see Jeannine again.

Frank Pickersgill was about to fall in love, too.

Training for The Firm was a thoroughly rigorous process, designed to weed out all the candidates who weren't up for such a demanding assignment. They learned how to fire guns and explode grenades; they ran obstacle courses and climbed ropes; and they learned sabotage, Morse code, and how to sneak up on a sentry and kill him quietly, even while drunk. They practised their French, studied maps, and carried out elaborate practice missions.

The Firm had some worries about Pickersgill. The Germans knew what he looked like thanks to the long months he'd spent in their prisons. And even if they'd forgotten, the story of his escape had been published in his hometown Winnipeg newspaper along with a photo — the Nazis might have seen it. He also had a terrible habit of talking in his sleep — in English. Not ideal for a man going undercover as a French citizen.

But he was also clearly driven, with a sense of purpose and a deep dedication to the cause. He wrote about his training with unbridled enthusiasm. "I'm enjoying it as I've never enjoyed anything in my life before.... I've been in a permanent state of exhilaration [since my escape] on the crest of a wave which kept getting higher and higher as each frontier was crossed, and which now, instead of subsiding, seems to be going on up. I don't know where it's going to land me, but it's damned good while it lasts."

He would be partnered with Ken Macalister, the two graduates of the University of Toronto taking on the Nazis together. Their training complete, there was nothing left to do but wait for the phone to ring with the details of their mission. And it was while they were waiting that Frank Pickersgill would fall in love with Alison Grant.

She was from an influential Toronto family: her relatives included famous academics and philosophers; her uncle was the governor general, Vincent Massey. Her background was a lot to live up to, and she took the responsibility that came with her heritage seriously; she was determined to make a real difference. Having moved to England to attend art school, she found herself in London as the war began, living with a couple of other young women in a perfectly ordinary-looking apartment above a dairy. But apartment 54A wasn't an ordinary apartment at all. It was a safe house.

Grant now worked for MI5. Her flatmates worked for The Firm. The two new Canadian spies would stay there until they got their phone call.

When he arrived at 54A, Pickersgill was nursing a broken heart. His escape from occupied France had taken him through Lisbon, where he'd coincidentally met another woman named Grant. Jacqueline Grant had also escaped from France after spending time in a Nazi internment camp. And during those brief but exciting days together in Portugal, the two fell in love. By the time he left for England, Pickersgill was confident they would soon be married — he simply wanted to make sure he could afford it before he officially proposed.

It wasn't until Jacqueline joined him in England that they realized their relationship wasn't quite as profound as they'd hoped — the thrill of their escape made their feelings seem stronger than they actually were. "We didn't have much in common to talk about," she would later admit. After a long and difficult conversation, hours of painful discussion, they decided to break it off.

That was good news for Alison Grant. When she first met Pickersgill, she described him as "terribly thin and hollow-eyed," still recovering from his ordeal, "but with such a sparkle in his eye." When he was back to full health, he was incredibly strong and tall, with the offbeat charm of an academic and rumpled clothes. He was excited about politics, philosophy, and ideas. And it was far from just talk; he was about to parachute into France to fight the Nazis.

He was smitten, too. "Alison is a frightfully good thing and terribly amusing," he wrote in a letter back home just after meeting her. "She is certainly one of the most amusing people I've ever met," he added later, "and we have a riotous time making New Yorkerish surrealist jokes at one another." Within a couple of months, they were truly and deeply in love.

The five of them — the three Canadians and the women who'd taken them in — became inseparable during the six months they were together, waiting for the phone to ring. They spent their nights dancing, going to the movies, or sitting at home around the fireplace deep in conversation. Grant helped them pick out clothes for their French disguises — rubbing them in dirt and ripping up the lining to make sure they looked authentically worn.

But all the while, the threat of death hung over them. They knew the men would soon be called away on their dangerous mission. Once, when Grant and Pickersgill went to a movie that featured a double agent, things got a bit too real for her. But he was resolute. "Frank knew exactly what he was doing and getting into.… [The movie] got pretty grim, and I began to feel uncomfortable, and suggested we leave. Frank said quite coldly: 'If I can stand it surely you can.' That was that." All they needed to do was survive the war. Then, they were sure, they would spend the rest of their lives together.

The telephone finally rang. It was time for the spies to begin their mission. Grant saw Pickersgill off, saying goodbye to him on a street corner, watching him walk away in his disguise. It was the last time she would ever see him.

On a moonlit night in June 1943, the two Canadian spies floated down out of the sky above France. Their plane had taken off in England, flying low over the English Channel to avoid detection, heading toward a field outside the French town of Blois. Signal lanterns marked the spot where the Canadians were meant to land. In those early morning hours, they leapt from the plane into the empty sky, their parachutes bursting open and bringing them gently toward the ground. It must have been an exhilarating moment. "Absolute peace and silence" is how Pickersgill described the experience during his training jumps. "It's the nearest thing to a perfect dream that could be imagined."

For a moment, all seemed to be going exactly to plan. Macalister would twist his ankle a bit on landing, but it was nothing serious. And the two French spies who would serve as their initial contacts were there waiting.

Pierre Culioli started the war with a motorcycle unit, but was wounded and captured — only to be released on compassionate grounds when his wife was killed by Italian bombers, giving him the chance to rejoin the fight as a secret agent. His partner was Yvonne Rudelatt, a forty-seven-year-old divorcee and grandmother, who'd been recruited while working at a club in London frequented by members of the secret service. Together, they pretended to be a married couple who'd been bombed out of their home and forced to become refugees. She had a knack for sabotage. He was skilled at organizing drops, just like the one that was now bringing the Canadians floating out of the sky.

Culioli and Rudelatt were meant to help the Canadians get started. The Firm had already established a large spy network in the region. Upon their arrival, Pickersgill and Macalister would set up a new subcircuit, codenamed "Archdeacon." Pickersgill would be the organizer, tasked with making new contacts, sussing out the people he met, and then bringing those he absolutely trusted into his confidence — and into his spy network. Macalister would be his radio operator, their vital link to the outside world and their only way of communicating with their bosses in London.

Even if everything went exactly to plan, it would be an incredibly dangerous mission. And it soon became clear that things wouldn't go to plan at all. In fact, things had begun to go horribly wrong before they'd even hit the ground.

Just days before the two new secret agents were scheduled to arrive in France, the British parachuted in a shipment of explosives to be used in sabotage. The drop was a disaster: the explosives detonated when they hit the ground. The Germans heard it. They would soon send more than two thousand troops into the region to investigate and search for spies. An agent on the ground sent The Firm an urgent message: they should abort the upcoming drop; it was too dangerous for the Canadians to parachute in.

But the message was either ignored or was never even received in the first place. The Canadians were sent anyway, dropping into an area that was about to become thick with German soldiers on the alert for anyone who seemed suspicious.

After months of preparation, the mission would last less than a week.

The spies laid low for a few days, until they decided it was safe enough to catch a train to Paris. But on their way to the station, they were pulled over at a checkpoint. While the soldiers bought the story Culioli and Rudelatt told them, the two Canadians weren't so lucky. They were taken inside the town hall for questioning.

It was a tense moment. Culioli and Rudelatt waited in the car, motor running, hoping their colleagues would somehow be able to convince the Germans they were just ordinary Frenchmen — despite their iffy command of French. There's no way to know what happened inside that town hall, but when the Germans came out and called for Culioli and Rudelatt to follow them, they assumed the Canadians had been found out. Culioli floored it, peeling out of town and away across the country roads, trying to outrun the three German cars that followed.

They didn't make it far. A roadblock loomed up ahead, and as Culioli sped forward to ram it, the guards opened fire. One bullet sliced through Culioli's hat. Another wounded Rudelatt in the head. He swerved, aiming for a brick house, trying to kill them both and destroy the car in a ball of flame that would burn all the evidence and equipment in the trunk. Instead, the car glanced off the house and landed in a field. All four spies were taken into custody.

The Canadians would spend months being interrogated, tortured, and beaten in prisons, Gestapo headquarters, and concentration camps across France and Germany. But they refused to give up any secrets. When the Germans tried to bribe Pickersgill with a lavish meal in Paris, he responded by grabbing a bottle of wine off the table, smashing it into a jagged weapon, slitting the throat of his guard, escaping into the hallway, killing another soldier who tried to stop him, and then jumping out the second-floor window into the street below, breaking his elbow in the process. As he hobbled away down the road, he was brought down by a shower of German bullets. He survived but was thrown back into prison.

Still, even without the Canadians' help, the Germans had a lot to go on. They used the information they found in the trunk of the car to launch their own covert operation. They had agents assume the identities of the Canadians, pretending to set up the spy ring as planned, and then arresting anyone they were able to lure into it. They even met with one of the greatest of all British spies. Noor Inayat Khan met with the two German operatives who were pretending to be Pickersgill and Macalister, barely avoiding capture. It was the beginning of the end for her; now the Germans knew what she looked like. She was betrayed and arrested soon after.

And that wasn't all the Germans found in the trunk of the car. They also had Macalister's radio. They sent messages to England, pretending the dispatches were coming from the Canadians. They were convincing enough that the British kept parachuting in money, weapons, supplies, and spies — which were all seized by the Germans as soon as they hit the ground. It wasn't until The Firm asked the women of apartment 54A if they'd like to send their Canadian friends a message for the holidays that they began to get suspicious. They sent a playful greeting: "The tea samovar is still bubbling at 54A." When the answer came, it was painfully dry and generic: "Thank you for your personal message." The women knew it couldn't possibly have come from the light-hearted Canadians. They must have been captured.

The realization must have come as a crushing blow to the women those secret agents had left behind. Germans weren't in the habit of showing mercy to Allied spies. They can't have known it for sure, and must have held out hope, however faint. But with that impersonal message, the truth began to reveal itself. They would never see Frank Pickersgill and Ken Macalister ever again. Jeannine Macalister would never remarry. Alison Grant would fall in love again. She would marry a diplomat called George Ignatieff, who would one day become the chancellor of the University of Toronto. Their son Michael would eventually grow up to become the leader of the federal Liberal Party.

Pickersgill and Macalister would spend more than a year in Nazi prisons. But as the end of the war drew near, they continued to insist they would never give their captors any help. That meant they weren't needed anymore. In the summer of 1944, as the Allies pushed the Germans back across the continent, the Canadians were taken to Buchenwald. They would spend their few remaining weeks surrounded by the horrors of one of the Nazis' most notorious concentration camps.

The end came on a September afternoon. They and fourteen other men were marched to the crematorium, their guards shoving them down the steps into the base-ment: a long, concrete room lined with big hooks known as "the corpse cellar." The executioner was waiting for them. He ordered their hands bound and a noose of thick wire wrapped around each of their necks. It was there in that basement that Frank Pickersgill and Ken Macalister were hanged, dangling from the hooks until they died. Then their bodies were fed into the ovens.

A big stone tower was built at the University of Toronto after the First World War. The Soldiers' Tower stands next to Hart House, a memorial to the students and staff who'd fought and died. And with the end of the Second World War, a new wall was added to the arch that passes through it. More room was needed for the names of the dead, hundreds of them chiselled into the stone. The names of Frank Pickersgill and Ken Macalister can still be found among them. And next to the tower, a small garden was planted: a flowering tribute to two Canadian spies who gave their lives trying to free Europe from the Nazis and return to the women they loved.

33
MIRIAM'S JUDAICA

It's easy to miss the shop if you're not looking for it. It blends into the other storefronts, one of many Jewish businesses that line Bathurst Street. It's been standing there for more than fifty years. A plain blue sign lists the wares inside — books, seforim, gifts — and displays the name of the store itself: Miriam's Judaica.

It doesn't seem to be particularly remarkable. It's a store like any other store. But the Miriam in Miriam's Judaica is Miriam Rosenthal.

Her story began in the town of Komárno, where she was born. It stands on the banks of the Danube River, in what's now Slovakia, right on the border with Hungary. She had a good childhood, the youngest of more than a dozen children in an Orthodox Jewish family. "I was spoiled," she once remembered. "I had a beautiful life."

When she was twenty-two years old, her family allowed her to get married — something she'd long been looking forward to. She went to a matchmaker to find her husband, flipping through the pages of a catalogue when her eye was caught by a man with the movie star good looks of Clark Gable. Bela Rosenthal was the son of a cattle broker; he lived on the Hungarian side of the border. Before long, they were engaged to be married.

But this was April 1944. Darkness had descended on Europe. The Slovaks had been allied with the Nazis since the early days of the Second World War; the persecution of the country's Jewish population began immediately. Two years before Miriam and Bela got engaged, the first trainload of Jewish prisoners had left Slovakia for the Nazi camps. Komárno had been turned into a major military hub for the Germans; as the young couple planned their wedding, all of the Jewish residents of Miriam's hometown — nearly three thousand of them — were being deported. Some of her brothers had already been sent off to labour camps.

Still, she was determined to go through with the wedding. She used false papers and wore a cross as she slipped across the border, taking a train to meet her fiancé in Hungary. They were married just a few hours after she arrived. As the rabbi performed the ceremony, bombs began to fall; the wedding party rushed underground, finishing the ceremony in the basement. "The rabbi insisted," Miriam explained years later, "bombs or no bombs." The young bride wore a red rose pinned to her lapel to cover her yellow star.

The newlyweds barely had any time to build their new life together. Just two weeks after the wedding, they were rounded up into a ghetto and separated, likely never to see each other again. They had only just met and their love story was already abruptly cut off. A few weeks later, the Nazis came for them again. Bela was sent to a slave labour camp. Miriam was sent to Auschwitz.

More people would die at Auschwitz than at any other Nazi concentration camp: more than a million were killed in the four years the gas chambers and the ovens were in operation. As Rosenthal and the other new arrivals were herded off their trains, Dr. Joseph Mengele — "the Angel of Death" — was waiting for them. By then, they were already weakened by their journey, worn down by untold hours spent crammed together in cattle cars without room to sit or food to eat. Many died along the way. Now, Dr. Mengele scrutinized them, his eyes coldly assessing them from beneath the brim of his black cap, the skull and crossbones of the SS emblazoned on the front. He divided them into two groups, their fate determined by a wave of his gloved hand or a flick of his cane: left or right. Those he deemed unfit for work — more than 80 percent of them — were sent to the left: straight to the gas chambers. The others were sent to the right, to a life of slavery inside the concentration camp. Rosenthal watched as her mother, her sister, and her one-year-old niece were all sent to the left, to death. But she made it through.

And it was there, just a few weeks later, trapped within the horrors of Auschwitz, that Miriam Rosenthal realized she was pregnant.

* * *

The Nazis didn't spare Jewish children. They killed more than a million of them during the Holocaust. The leader of the SS, Heinrich Himmler, repeatedly justified and defended the slaughter in chilling speeches to his fellow party members. "I am not a bloodthirsty person," he once told a group of generals, "on the other hand, I have such good nerves and such a developed sense of duty ... that when I recognise something as necessary I can implement it without compromise. I have not considered myself entitled ... to allow the children to grow into the avengers who will then murder our children and our grandchildren. That would have been cowardly."

At Auschwitz, many children were immediately gassed, but a few were allowed to live. Some were kept as fodder for horrifying medical experiments carried out by Dr. Mengele and his staff. When he was done performing his bizarre tortures, he would kill some of them himself, injecting chloroform into their hearts and then dissecting them to study their organs. On other occasions, death came more casually: Mengele is said to have once drawn a line along the wall of the children's barracks about five feet from the ground — any child shorter than that line was promptly sent to the gas chambers. Sometimes children were thrown straight into the ovens, burned alive.

Pregnant women weren't given the chance to give birth. They, just like young mothers, were usually declared unfit for work and quickly murdered.

There was no question: Rosenthal would hide her pregnancy for as long as she could. "Not a word," one of her fellow prisoners advised her. "Not a single word. If not, you'll end up at the crematorium."

One day, the SS called for all the pregnant women to step forward. They were, the officers told them, going to be given double their usual ration of bread. But it was a lie, a trap.

"Can you imagine?" Rosenthal asked a reporter from the *National Post* many years later. "Even women who were not pregnant stepped forward." But she stayed put. "Two hundred women stepped forward and two hundred women went to the gas chamber. And I don't know why I didn't step forward.... I have asked rabbis. I have asked some big people and no one can give me an answer.... I have asked myself this question so many times as I lay in bed upstairs."

Declared fit for work, she was soon transferred out of Auschwitz and eventually sent to a factory in Augsberg, where she was forced to make airplane parts for the Luftwaffe. Things there were slightly easier: the prisoners were given clean clothes and a little more food, allowed to grow their hair long for the first time since they'd arrived in the camps.

But all the while, Rosenthal's pregnancy was progressing. She was beginning to show. It was only a matter of time before the SS would notice.

The dreaded day came during the winter of 1944. Two SS officers arrived at the factory with angry German shepherds; they demanded any woman who was pregnant immediately identify herself. This time, there was no hiding.

"I had to raise my hand," she explained. "I was showing, and if I didn't put up my hand all those other women would be killed. How could I not put up my hand?"

The SS officers were furious. "You bitch!" they barked. "You're coming with us — to Auschwitz."

"I said goodbye to my friends," she remembered, "who were crying, but it was a relief for me. The suffering would be over, as well as the fear of what would happen to my baby." Rosenthal resigned herself to death.

She was taken out into the snow with nothing to protect her from the bitter cold but the dress she'd been wearing in the factory. The SS loaded her onto a train. This time, strangely, it wasn't a freight train packed full of prisoners, but a regular passenger train. There were civilians on board, seemingly oblivious to the genocide taking place all around them. One woman was shocked to see Rosenthal in her emaciated state. "Frau, what is with you?" she asked the prisoner. "You don't have hair. The clothes you are wearing. What are you, from a mental hospital?"

"She didn't have a dream, this German woman," Rosenthal remembered, "of all the horrible things the Germans were doing. I told her I am not from a mental hospital; I am going to Auschwitz — I am going to the gas. She looked at me like I was crazy, opened her purse, and gave me some bread. I ate it so fast. I was so hungry."

She was twenty-two years old and seven months pregnant.

* * *

Now that the Nazis knew Rosenthal was carrying a child, she was certain that she would be taken to Auschwitz, where she would meet almost certain death. But that's not where the SS took her. The Russians, they told her, had just bombed Auschwitz, so instead they were headed toward another one of the most notorious concentration camps: Dachau.

By then, the war was going very poorly for the Nazis. The Allies had landed at Normandy six months earlier and begun their push across Europe. That year, the British and the Americans dropped more bombs on Germany than in the entire rest of the war combined — hundreds of thousands of tons of them. In response, the Nazis were moving their facilities underground. Near Dachau, in a town called Kaufering, they established eleven smaller sub-camps and used the slave labour of the prisoners to build giant subterranean airplane factories. There, they were put to work making Hitler's new "miracle weapon": the Messerschmitt Me 262, the world's first fighter jet.

Rosenthal was taken to one of those sub-camps: Kaufering I. It held thousands of prisoners, the vast majority of them Jewish, half of them doomed to die. The guards took her below ground and left her there in a dark room. It was hard to see. Only a single bulb cast dim light in the subterranean prison. But there were voices: other women, speaking Hungarian. "Where are you from?" they asked. "What happened to you?" There were six of them, they told her. And they were all pregnant. They would be known as the "Schwanger Kommando" — the "Pregnant Commando."

"We started to cry and we just cried and cried," Rosenthal remembered. "It was like we were all sisters. We had no one else in the world. We hugged each other. We kissed each other."

With the end of the war approaching, some of the Nazis were beginning to realize there would be consequences for their war crimes. They were starting to worry. The killing was far from over, but it seemed as if some things were beginning, ever so slightly, to change — if only so the Nazis could save their own skins.

The seven pregnant women were eventually taken above ground, to a small wooden hut that would serve as meagre shelter against the most terrible winter Europe had seen in the last fifteen years. What little heat they had came from a stove smuggled in for them by a fellow prisoner — one of the "kapos" who agreed to help oversee the camps in return for special treatment. She had taken a great risk getting it for them. When the guards discovered the stove, they took it away and beat the kapo bloody. The next day, she brought it right back.

The SS officers brought them a doctor, too — one of the prisoners in the camp had been a gynecologist in Hungary before the war. But there was only so much Dr. Vadasz could do for them. He broke down in tears when he saw the seven women, all of them now very far along in their pregnancies. He begged the Nazis to give him the equipment he would need for the deliveries. "I have no instruments! I need hot water! Towels! Soap!" But he would have to make do.

Within days, the first of the women went into labour.

And in the weeks to come, the others would follow, one after another, suffering terribly as they gave birth on a hard, wooden bunk without anaesthetic or the necessary medical equipment. Dr. Vadasz, terribly weakened himself, was given nothing but a bucket of hot water to use.

Still, one by one, the first six mothers did what seemed to be impossible: they gave birth in a concentration camp. Six new babies were brought into the world. Six new lives in the middle of all that death.

Eventually, it was just Miriam Rosenthal who had yet to give birth to her child. She finally went into labour during the last week of February. But as she struggled through the contractions, it was clear her delivery wasn't going as smoothly as the others had. There were complications. She was growing weak.

Dr. Vadasz urged her on. "Miriam, push, push, you must help me. I can't do it on my own. He's going to die." Her strength was failing her. "Miriam, please try, try, try, try …"

"I couldn't keep going any longer," she later remembered, "but all of a sudden the baby is out.… And what a beauty. With blond, beautiful hair; big, blue eyes. The other women were crying. Dr. Vadasz was crying. Everyone was crying."

On February 28, 1945, Leslie Rosenthal was born.

It was a miracle. But they weren't safe yet. The Allies were still fighting their slow way across the continent. The war against Germany wouldn't end for another ten weeks.

And those ten weeks would be hard weeks. An outbreak of typhoid tore through the camp. Prisoners were still dying everywhere. And even as they recovered from the strain of childbirth, the new mothers were forced to keep working, washing prisoners' clothing and unloading dead bodies.

Rosenthal was in especially poor shape. After the delivery, her placenta had never emerged. It was another life-threatening complication. "After a week, I started to bleed," she remembered. "The blood was flowing like water from a tap." Dr. Vadasz warned the others that Rosenthal wasn't going to make it. "If you die," one of them promised her, "I will take Leslie."

Rosenthal kept fighting, and eventually recovered. But death was still a constant threat. When Leslie was just two weeks old, the camp's head physician signed an order to have all the new mothers and their babies sent to Bergen-Belsen to be gassed. His order, for some unknown reason, was never carried out.

Meanwhile, the Allies were getting closer; by the end of March, they were across the Rhine, marching through Germany itself, pushing on toward victory. Soon, the Soviets were on the outskirts of Berlin, shelling the capital. Hitler had retreated into his bunker, never to emerge again. In just a few days, he would put his gun to his head and end his own life.

As the Third Reich collapsed, the SS officers at the Kaufering camps were debating what to do. Some were determined to kill as many Jewish prisoners as possible and destroy as much evidence as they could before the end. As the Americans approached, the Nazis set fire to some of the barracks. Hundreds of prisoners were too weak to escape the flames. They were burned alive.

Thousands of others — including the seven mothers and their babies — were evacuated, forced into a death march from the sub-camps of Kaufering toward Dachau itself, nearly sixty kilometres away. "Anyone who was unable to keep walking was shot on the spot," one of the other mothers remembered. "People were sick, weak, and malnourished. We had to march without shoes."

Rosenthal could barely keep moving, but if she stopped she knew she would be killed — and Leslie with her. So, she kept going, struggling on long enough to get loaded onto yet another train. But even the train wasn't safe. The American air force didn't realize it was filled with the people they had come to save — so they bombed it. As prisoners fled the wreckage into the surrounding woods, the SS opened fire. The forest was filled with bodies.

"I kept saying, 'Leslie, we're going home. God will help us.… Please God, please God. Help me, help me.'"

In the end, it took two days for the prisoners and their guards to make the journey from Kaufering to the main camp. Thousands of prisoners died in death marches around Dachau in the final few days of the war. But Rosenthal, the six other mothers, and all seven of their babies survived.

The morning after they arrived, they were lined up for one last roll call. A few hours later, the Americans arrived.

One solider began to sob when he saw Leslie. "We have seen only the dead, dead bodies in the crematorium, and here — a live baby!"

It was over. They were free.

He was there, in the distance, running toward her. Somehow, they had both survived — and they had both made their way back home to find each other. "I could see him coming, running from afar, and I shouted, 'Bela, Bela,'" she later remembered. "I wasn't sure it was him, and he was running and calling my name." He was stunned to see Leslie in Miriam's arms. He couldn't believe she'd gotten pregnant so quickly, in those two brief weeks before the Nazis tore them apart. He was overjoyed. "I can't describe that feeling of when he saw our baby," she remembered, "when he saw Leslie for the first time. We cried and cried and cried."

With the war over, they decided to leave Hungary behind and set out in search of a new life; they travelled through Bratislava, Prague, Paris, and Cuba before they finally reached Canada. For a while, Bela worked at a mattress factory. And then as a rabbi in Timmins and Sudbury. But in the end, they settled in Toronto, where they would spend the rest of their lives.

In 1965, the Rosenthals opened a shop on Bathurst Street at the corner of Caribou Road. They called it Miriam's Fine Judaica. They ran the store for more than four decades, and raised their growing family: three children, and then grandchildren, and great-grandchildren.

They would both live well into their nineties. They were married for sixty-four years.

At first, Rosenthal didn't tell her story to very many people outside her own family. She was still haunted by nightmares of SS officers coming to steal her newborn child. But in her later years, she began to share her extraordinary tale. "I believe," she told the *Star* in 1997, "as I get older, I think more and more about the Holocaust and my family.... I feel my memories more, but still I am not bitter."

In 2010 she was interviewed for an award-winning German documentary about the seven mothers and their children called *Born in a Concentration Camp*. A couple of years after that, a journalist from the *National Post* interviewed her for an article about her remarkable life.

Leslie was there, too. By then, Miriam and Bela's son was nearly seventy years old. As he arrived, Miriam proudly introduced him: "Here is my miracle baby now."

"And here," Leslie answered, "is my miracle mother."

34
THE BLIZZARD

It was the last winter of the Second World War. The first week of February 1945. Far away in Europe, the Nazi war machine was crumbling; the Soviets were closing in on Berlin; the Americans would soon be crossing the Rhine. The war would be over in just a few months. The Big Three — Churchill, Roosevelt, and Stalin — were already at Yalta, meeting to decide what the world would look like when the fighting was finally done.

Scott Young was one of the people doing that fighting. He was a reporter by trade — he would eventually author dozens of books and co-host *Hockey Night in Canada* for a while. He first went to Europe to cover the war for the Canadian Press. His dispatches were published in newspapers all over Canada. But he soon joined the Royal Canadian Navy instead, serving as a communications officer.

The war was taking a toll, though; Young was suffering from chronic fatigue and losing weight at an alarming rate. So, he was sent back to Canada for tests.

That meant he would get to make a brief visit home to Toronto, where he could spend a little time with his wife, Rassy, and their toddler, Bob.

When he got home, he found the city covered in snow. That winter was a terrible winter — one of the worst in the entire recorded history of Toronto. One infamous blizzard in December killed twenty-one people: one died in an overturned streetcar on Queen Street, more than a dozen suffered fatal heart attacks from shovelling half a metre of snow. All winter long, the temperature barely ever climbed above freezing, so the snow just kept piling up as the blizzards kept coming. By the time Young came home at the beginning of February, Toronto had already seen more than a metre and a half of snow.

There was yet another big storm coming. As the city braced itself for the blizzard, the Youngs spent the day visiting with friends who lived in a little house near Eglinton Avenue and Mount Pleasant. It was far on the outskirts of the city back then; a long way from downtown in the days before the subway. And so, as the storm descended, the Youngs decided to stay over. They dragged a mattress downstairs and set it up on the dining room floor.

Scott Young wrote about that night in his memoir: "I remember the street in Toronto, the wild February blizzard through which only the hardiest moved, on skis, sliding downtown through otherwise empty streets to otherwise empty offices."

The Youngs' love story wouldn't last forever. In the coming years, they would often fight; she drank, he had affairs. In the end, he fell in love with another woman and Rassy discovered their letters. Scott took their sons to an Italian restaurant on King Street and told them their parents were getting divorced. But on that stormy winter night in 1945, they were happy. A young wife and her new husband home on leave from the war.

"We were just past our middle twenties," Young remembered, "and had been apart for most of the previous year.... We were healthy young people, much in love, apart too much. It was a small house and when we made love that night, we tried to be fairly quiet, and perhaps were."

Nine months later, the war was over; peace had finally come. Scott Young was back home again. When Rassy went into labour, a neighbour drove them down to the fancy new wing of the Toronto General Hospital. It was early in the morning of a warm November day when the baby came. They named him Neil.

He would grow up to become one of the most famous rock stars in the world.

THE MODERN CITY

35
LITTLE GREEN

He was butchering the song. At least Joan Anderson thought so. She was a young musician, just twenty-one years old and starting out in her career. She'd moved to Toronto a few months earlier, attracted by the city's booming folk scene. The centre of that scene was Yorkville, which had become a magnet for musicians from across the continent; many of the neighbourhood's creaking old Victorian homes had been transformed into artsy coffee houses. Young people flocked to them, getting buzzed on caffeine, smoking cigarettes, and listening to some of the best music Canada had ever produced. And while she might have been young and new to the city, Joan Anderson had already found a place for herself in the scene. Thanks to her bittersweet folk tunes, she'd become a regular fixture onstage at the Penny Farthing; not yet popular enough to headline the big stage on the main floor, but a nightly guest in the cellar where local artists performed.

That's where she was on a March night in 1965 — at the Penny Farthing, getting ready to play a set — when a friend caught her attention. "That song you've been try-ing to learn? There's an American downstairs and he's singing it."

It had only been a matter of days since Bob Dylan had released his latest album. There were plenty of landmark tracks on *Bringing It All Back Home*, but few would prove to be as popular as "Mr. Tambourine Man." Anderson had already been trying to teach herself how to play it, so when she heard there was a folksinger playing his own cover of the new tune on the Penny Farthing's main stage, she rushed down to catch the end of the song.

But when she heard it, she was disappointed. Chuck Mitchell was playing his first ever gig outside of his home-town of Detroit, but he was still confident enough to change a few of Dylan's lyrics. He added some of his own words. And Joan Anderson didn't care for them at all. Later that night, she told him as much. They'd only just met and they were already fighting. But there was a spark.

It was the beginning of a life-changing romance. They spent the rest of that night together, braving the cold for a stroll through a nearby park before heading back to Anderson's tiny apartment. Mitchell was tall and sure of himself; Anderson was thin, with long blond hair — famously kind. By the end of their first thirty-six hours together, Mitchell had already proposed.

He was only half-serious when he suggested they should get married, but she quickly said yes. On a June day just a few months after they met, Chuck Mitchell and Joan Anderson found themselves standing in his parents' backyard in Michigan. She'd made her dress

herself, and ones for her bridesmaids, too; she held dai-
sies as she walked up the aisle. "There were trees and
birds," she'd later remember, "and streams and folksingers and baroque trios hiding in the bushes."

It was intimate and idyllic, but less romantic than
it might have seemed. As she walked down the aisle in
front of Mitchell's friends and family, Anderson had
major doubts. "I can get out of this," she told herself. She
hadn't agreed to marry Chuck Mitchell because she was
head over heels in love with him. She'd done it to save
her daughter.

Before Chuck Mitchell, there was Brad MacMath.
Anderson had met him at art school in Calgary; he was
a student there, too. She was nineteen years old, living away from home, and ready to try new things. All
her friends were already having sex; she figured it was
about time she joined them. She might not have been in
love with MacMath, but he was nice enough, handsome
enough, and *there*. So, in the spring of 1964, she slept
with him.

Months later, she realized she was going to have
a baby. "I got pregnant right out of the chute with my
friend," she would later confess. "It was my own stupid
fault. That was not even a romance. It was just that I was
the only virgin in art school, and I thought, 'What is this
all about?' And I got caught out and that was bad."

In the early 1960s, being pregnant and unmarried
was still considered to be shockingly scandalous. "That

was a terrible thing for a woman," Anderson remembered, "nothing worse. You may as well have killed somebody." Worried about what her parents would think back home in Saskatoon, she decided to keep her pregnancy secret for as long as possible. To spare them the humiliation, she would put two thousand kilometres between herself and her parents. She dropped out of art school and headed east, to Toronto.

She had a very good cover story. She was truly disappointed by art school, unmoved by the cold modernism that was all the rage at the time. Disillusioned with her studies, she'd spent more and more time indulging her love of music instead. As a young girl, she'd worn out her stockings dancing to jukebox rock 'n' roll. Forbidden from buying a guitar, she'd learned to play the ukulele instead, developing a passion for folk music. And now that she was old enough to teach herself guitar, as well, she'd begun to perform at folk clubs — undaunted by a left hand weakened by a childhood case of polio.

When she discovered she was pregnant, she realized her music gave her the perfect excuse to leave school. "I tried to spare my parents," she explained, "by going to the anonymity of a large city, under the ruse that I wanted to be a musician." And in 1964, there was no better place in Canada to be a musician than in Yorkville.

In at least one small corner of Toronto, the city was changing. The painfully boring British town that Hemingway so despised was finally beginning its transformation into a vibrant, cosmopolitan metropolis. In the years after the Second World War, Canada had welcomed hundreds of thousands of new arrivals who left the smouldering ruins of their European homelands behind. Many ended up in Yorkville, taking advantage of the low rents charged for the neighbourhood's crumbling Victorian homes. Some of them opened European-style cafés there, and when they did, they inadvertently sparked a local revolution.

Those coffee houses attracted young people from across the city and beyond. All through the 1960s, those few blocks near Yonge and Bloor were filled with beatniks and hippies, greasers and bikers, potheads and acid freaks, writers, artists, poets, and musicians. The neighbourhood became a place where the strange and experimental were welcomed, a safe haven for those who didn't feel like they fit in anywhere else, who didn't belong in the conservative "square" culture that had dominated so much of Canada for so long.

And so, when she realized she was pregnant, that's where Joan Anderson headed.

She arrived in Toronto with only sixty dollars to her name, just enough to pay for a few weeks of rent in a tiny attic. The drafty room made for a miserable home, providing little protection against the icy Canadian winter. Most of the railings from the stairs were missing — they'd been burned by the previous tenants for heat. She'd brought MacMath with her, but he didn't last very long. He left her pregnant, freezing, and worried about making rent.

It was a rough beginning. Anderson couldn't afford to join the musicians' union; her prospects were limited to the few "scab" clubs that welcomed non-union performers. With her money quickly running out, she was forced to get a retail job for a while, working in women's wear at the Simpson's department store. She bounced around from her attic to a boarding house to a friend's place.

But Anderson wasn't about to give up. She'd written her first original song on the train from Calgary to Toronto, inspired by the rhythms of the wheels. And her talent was obvious; her performances enchanted her audiences. "When she introduced her song," one of her fellow folksingers explained, "you would lean in and listen. That gorgeous, bell-like voice would take you away." She landed gigs at church clubs, YMCAs, and some of the most popular coffee houses in Yorkville.

She sang at the Purple Onion (where Buffy Sainte-Marie wrote "Universal Soldier"), at the Bohemian Embassy (where Margaret Atwood read poetry over the hissing cappuccino machine), and at the Village Corner (where Gordon Lightfoot's folk duo recorded a live album). She became friends with some of the scene's leading figures: she crashed at the same apartment as Neil Young, introduced him to his bandmate and future pop star Rick James, and lived across the hall from the Ojibwe poet Duke Redbird.

But even there, at the centre of one of the most exciting music scenes on the continent, her pregnancy was a constant worry. "It was a very sad and lonely time for her," Redbird explained. "I remember Joni being a very private person. I would hear her singing in that beautiful voice of hers, strumming her guitar behind the closed door of her room." All the while, her belly was growing bigger and bigger. Eventually, she couldn't even hold her guitar anymore, and was forced to switch to a tiple — a smaller stringed instrument — instead. Her due date was rapidly approaching. Eventually, she had to stop performing altogether.

The baby finally came two weeks later, on a day in the middle of February. Anderson headed to Toronto General Hospital, where she gave birth to a baby girl. As she held her in her arms, she fell deeply in love with the tiny new life she'd created. She named her Kelly Dale Anderson: *kelly* — an intense, pure green, like the green Canadian countryside in the summer, like her own mother, green with youth.

Joan Anderson was far from the only young woman in Yorkville facing a heart-wrenching decision. In the early 1960s, it was still illegal to sell birth control in Canada; even distributing information about it was technically still banned. Just a couple of years earlier, a Toronto pharmacist had been put on trial for selling condoms, convicted and fined. He was having them shipped from England in bulk, packaging them at his own dining-room table in Forest Hill, and then secretly mailing them out to the people who needed them.

Without easy access to birth control, countless Canadians were getting pregnant who didn't want to be. Abortion was illegal, too. And in a country where conservative social values were still a powerful force, those who got pregnant out of wedlock faced more than just scandal and ostracism. They also faced a crushing pressure to give up their child. In the first decades after the war, hundreds of thousands of new Canadian mothers were pushed into handing over their babies for adoption. It's been called the "Baby Scoop Era" (a similar term to the "Sixties Scoop," which specifically targeted Indigenous mothers).

Seen as "fallen women," they were told that they were unworthy mothers, that their child would be far better off without them. Doctors, social workers, and religious leaders believed that by going through the trauma of losing their child, women would learn the error of their promiscuous ways. "When she renounces her child for its own good," as Dr. Marian Hillard of Women's College Hospital put it, "the unwed mother has learned a lot. She has learned an important human value. She has learned to pay the price of her misdemeanor, and this alone, if punishment is needed, is punishment enough.... We must go back to a primary set of values." While some mothers, of course, might have made the same decision anyway, many felt like they were being bullied into giving up a child they loved.

Anderson's stay at the hospital was a deeply painful one — "traumatic," she would later call it. She had decided to give little Kelly Dale up for adoption. "I have no money," she told herself. "I have no home. I have no job. When I leave the hospital, I have no roof over my head." Far from being sympathetic, the hospital staff was cold and severe, clearly judging her harshly for her decision — and for being in that situation in the first place. There were additional tortures, too. After she gave birth, her breasts would be tightly and painfully bound to stop them from producing milk. It was, she said, "barbaric." In order to spare herself any further pain, she asked that the baby be taken away immediately — holding her newborn daughter would just be too devastating an experience.

But there were complications. The birth hadn't gone smoothly. So instead of leaving the hospital within a few days, Anderson was stuck there for more than a week. And during that time, she ended up holding Kelly Dale after all — some think it was a mix-up by the hospital staff. And once she held her baby daughter in her arms, Anderson began to have second thoughts. She fell in love with her beautiful, rosy-cheeked child. There, in her hospital bed, she changed her mind.

Instead of giving Kelly Dale up for adoption, Anderson decided she would put her daughter in foster care temporarily. Somehow, she would gather enough money to raise her herself. She put her new plan into action as soon as she was out of the hospital: looking for a job, playing shows, and trying to build the kind of life that would provide a safe and stable home for her daughter. It wasn't easy, but she was determined. "I kept trying to find some circumstance where I could stay with her," Anderson remembered.

And then along came Chuck Mitchell.

In the wake of the pregnancy, she landed a regular gig at the Penny Farthing. It stood right in the middle of the scene, on Yorkville Avenue. (The building is still there today, now home to a fashion boutique.) It was one of the best known of all the coffee houses, famous for its backyard pool and bikini-clad servers, where half-naked hippies slathered themselves in colour during a psychedelic "paint-in." Anderson started playing in the cellar every night, right up until that fateful evening when she met Chuck Mitchell and got into a fight over "Mr. Tambourine Man."

She did like him. But when he proposed to her just a couple of days into their relationship, the reason she said yes had little to do with love at first sight. Her decision was much more about her new daughter. With a husband, she'd have a better chance of raising Kelly Dale herself. She might have been filled with doubt on her wedding day, but it would all be worth it, if only she could keep her daughter.

The newlyweds made a new home for themselves in Detroit, not just living together but performing together as a folk duo, too. He was older — twenty-nine — and more successful than she was, so for a brief moment it must have seemed as if the new arrangement might work, that it might give her the stability and financial security she needed to get her daughter back.

But they still weren't making much money. As they travelled between the folk clubs of Michigan and Canada, they couldn't even afford to stay in hotel rooms. And all the while, the marriage was descending quickly into unhappiness. Mitchell could be condescending and paternalistic. He looked down on Anderson's Prairie roots. "My husband thought I was stupid because he had a B.A. in literature," she explained many years later. "He took me on as a trophy wife. He liked my body, but he didn't like my mind. He was always insulting me." His sense of humour could be vicious and cutting. "When you don't wear makeup and you smile," he told her, ridiculing her big teeth, "you look like a rhesus monkey." That fight about "Mr. Tambourine Man" was just the beginning. "Chuck Mitchell was my first major exploiter," she would later claim, "a complete asshole."

Thoughts of her daughter weighed heavily on her. As they drove from one folk club to the next, there were long silences; sometimes tears. It didn't take her long to realize her husband didn't share her vision for their future. While Chuck Mitchell later said he left the decision about the baby up to her, she knew he had no interest in becoming a father to her daughter. "The moment we were married," she said, "he intimated strongly that he had no interest in raising another man's child — so I was trapped."

It was quickly becoming clear her plan wasn't going to work. The time had come to make her heartbreaking decision. It wasn't long after their wedding day that the Mitchells took another trip back across the border to Toronto, paying a visit to the foster home where Kelly Dale was being raised. She was a few months old now. Her mother held her in her arms for a final time, saying a sad farewell. And then she signed the adoption papers.

Two years after they met at the Penny Farthing, the folksingers got divorced. But Joan Anderson did get at least one useful thing out of the marriage: a new name. She was now known as Joni Mitchell.

Laurel Canyon winds its way through the hills at the heart of Los Angeles. It's a land of pale browns and of deep greens, with houses scattered like jewels among the sunny slopes. It's a place where you can hear a coyote's howl at night, or a hooting owl ... or the chords of an acoustic guitar echoing through the starry sky. By the end of the 1960s, Laurel Canyon had become home to some of the greatest musicians in the world — including Joni Mitchell.

She and her ex-husband weren't the only ones inspired by "Mr. Tambourine Man." Just a few weeks after Dylan's song came out, a new band called The Byrds released their own version. It was a smash hit, racing all the way up to number one on the *Billboard* charts — more successful than any of Dylan's songs had ever been before. But The Byrds' version was very different: they took the acoustic folk tune and turned it into an electric rock song. It was the beginning of an entire new genre, combining the depth of folk music's poetic lyrics with the energy of rock 'n' roll. Folk rock was born. Soon, countless other acts were racing to follow in The Byrds' footsteps. And when the band moved to Laurel Canyon, others did, too. It quickly became the epicentre of the new sound, home to artists like Carole King, The Turtles, Carly Simon, and James Taylor — even members of The Monkees and The Doors lived there.

Joni Mitchell arrived in the spring of 1968. In the year following her divorce, her career had begun to take off — thanks in no small part to The Byrds. The band's guitarist, David Crosby, had seen her play in New York's Greenwich Village. "I walked into a coffeehouse and she was singing," he explained, "and she just floored me. She rocked me back up against the back wall of that place and I stood there just transfixed. I couldn't believe that there was anybody that good." Crosby immediately became a champion of her work, producing her first album. And just a few weeks after it came out, she made the move to Laurel Canyon.

She wasn't the only Toronto musician there. As the sixties came to a close, the Yorkville scene was dying. Toronto might be changing, but many of its residents weren't comfortable with that change. They were happy with the conservative city they'd always known. As sensationalized stories of sex and drugs filled the newspapers, many Torontonians wanted the hippies driven out of the neighbourhood. Among the many complaints were objections to public displays of affection and inter-racial couples kissing on street corners. Some wanted the hippies rounded up and sent off to work camps. A doctor interviewed by the *Toronto Daily Star* suggested they should be kept behind bars at the Riverdale Zoo. One provincial politician — former Toronto Maple Leafs hockey player Syl Apps — declared that Yorkville was "a festering sore in the middle of the city" that had to be "eradicated." City hall began to actively suppress the Yorkville scene, introducing new bylaws and regulations. There were police crackdowns. Real estate developers moved in. One coffee house after another fell under the wrecking ball. As Yorkville was transformed yet again — this time into a fancy shopping district — many of its most creative young people would spread out across the rest of the city, starting new scenes in new neighbour- hoods, helping turn Toronto into a more exciting and artistic place in the process.

But by then, many of the city's most promising musi- cians were already gone. There just wasn't enough sup- port for the music industry in Canada. There weren't enough record labels, recording studios, or airtime. The Canadian content regulations ensuring that Canadian artists get played on Canadian airwaves wouldn't be introduced until 1971. If a Canadian musician wanted to find success, it helped to leave Canada behind.

Many of Yorkville's biggest stars soon found them- selves in Laurel Canyon — just a few minutes' drive from the biggest record labels in the world. Mitchell's old friend Neil Young was there. He'd driven straight to L.A. from Toronto and immediately started a new band: Buffalo Springfield. By the end of that month, they were opening for The Byrds on tour. After they broke up, Young would join another new group: Crosby, Stills, Nash & Young featured Joni Mitchell's old producer David Crosby and her new boyfriend, Graham Nash.

Denny Doherty had played the coffee houses of Yorkville in a folk trio called the Halifax Three. But he was now part of a folk-pop quartet called The Mamas & the Papas. His house played host to some of the most debauched parties in the canyon.

The Hawks had been one of the most exciting rock bands in Toronto, playing the rough-and-tumble taverns of the Yonge Street Strip. But they changed their name when they shot to fame as Bob Dylan's new backing group. Now, they were calling themselves The Band and were recording their debut album just over the hill, at Sammy Davis Jr.'s house.

Jack London & The Sparrows had changed names since their Toronto days, too. They were going by Steppenwolf, now, writing songs like "Born to Be Wild" and "Magic Carpet Ride." When Mitchell's neighbour's house burned down, they showed up with a photographer, grabbing a photo in the charred ruins for the cover of their next album.

But there was no one in Laurel Canyon quite like Joni Mitchell. Her music had evolved in the years since she dropped out of art school. The folk songs she'd been writing since that train ride to Toronto now incorporated new influences: not only a bit of California rock 'n' roll, but the jazz sounds she'd picked up during her time in Detroit. Her songs were complex and unusual; she adopted strange guitar tunings that gave them a unique, otherworldly quality. Her voice was delicate but powerful, soaring into the clouds before plunging into the depths. Her lyrics were personal and poetic, as intimate as they were mysterious. And they were often filled with hidden messages for her lost daughter.

Over the next few years, those songs would make Joni Mitchell a superstar. Her most celebrated album, *Blue*, was filled with songs of love and loss: of her crumbling relationship with Graham Nash; of her fling with a hippie living in a cave on Crete; of her new romance with James Taylor. And one of the most powerful songs of them all was a tune called "Little Green."

She'd written it many years earlier, not long after that heartbreaking visit to the foster home in Toronto, when she said goodbye to her daughter for the last time. When the song was released, the lyrics left some reviewers baffled. *Rolling Stone* complained they were "dressed up in such cryptic references that it passeth all understanding." But once you know the story behind it, the song describes her sorrow in surprisingly honest terms.

The lyrics of "Little Green" include references to everything from Brad MacMath leaving her freezing and alone in Yorkville, to being a young mother hiding the truth from her parents back home in Saskatchewan, to the day she gave her baby up for adoption.

Blue helped make Joni Mitchell one of the most successful musicians on the planet. Her songs were being heard by millions. But even as her fame grew, she was haunted by heart-rending questions: What was her daughter like? What kind of life was she leading? What had happened to her Little Green?

Kelly Dale Anderson grew up as Kilauren Gibb, raised by her adoptive parents: teachers who lived in Don Mills. It was a comfortable childhood. They were successful enough to be members of the prestigious Donalda Golf & Country Club; to send her to the private, all-girls Bishop

Strachan School; and to take a tropical vacation every Christmas. She grew up to become a fashion model, gifted with her mother's striking looks. Some friends at the country club had always wondered whether she might be adopted, but her parents denied it. They'd even hidden away their son's baby photos so Kilauren wouldn't wonder where hers were. She was twenty-seven years old and pregnant with her own child before they finally told her the truth. The revelation sparked a five-year search for her birth mother.

She didn't have much to go on. She was eventually allowed to access some government records, but they only contained a few scraps of information: that her mother was originally from Saskatchewan, came from a northern European background, and had polio as a child. But there was one clue in particular that would prove to be intriguing: "Mother left Canada for U.S. to pursue career as folk singer."

Still, it would take a remarkable coincidence for everything to come together. Gibb had an old friend who was also adopted; he volunteered for the Children's Aid Foundation, helping bring adopted children together with their birth parents. When Gibb finally got her scraps of information from the government after years of waiting, she called him to let him know. The news was exciting enough that he repeated the words to himself out loud on the phone: "Your mother was from a small town in Saskatchewan and left for the U.S. to pursue her career as a folk singer."

His girlfriend, Annie Mandlsohn, was in the room. She overheard him.

Years earlier, Mandlsohn had been a grad student at York University, where she became friends with another, older student: Duke Redbird. The poet shared some stories with her from his Yorkville days, including a secret from the winter of 1964: "Never tell this to anybody, but I lived in the same house as Joni Mitchell; she had a baby and nobody knows." Nearly a decade later, as she listened to her boyfriend describe Kilauren Gibb's birth mother, it all suddenly clicked. She grabbed the phone.

"Your mother is Joni Mitchell!"

By then, Mitchell had launched her own search. After decades of keeping her painful secret, she'd gone public with her story: when a tabloid tried to catch her out during an interview, she simply responded honestly. She'd been making oblique references to her daughter in her songs ever since the day she'd given her up. Now, she could actively try to find her. Once word got out, her managers' office in Vancouver was inundated with phone calls: women who'd never known their own birth mothers hoped they might be the daughter of the famous folksinger.

Gibb was becoming ever more convinced. All the details in her file matched. The dates matched. She even looked a bit like Joni Mitchell, with her high cheekbones and blond hair. The more she learned, the more it seemed true: she really was Joni Mitchell's daughter.

Nothing about the reunion would be simple. Even getting through to her was a major challenge. She emailed Mitchell's managers for weeks on end, had to mail them her information, and then follow up every day by phone before they finally believed her. And even after they did meet, there would be rough days ahead; they were two strong-willed women sharing a complicated, emotional past. They didn't always get along. There were heated fights to come. But there would also be beautiful moments, moments like the ones they'd long dreamed of sharing.

It was on a March day in 1997 that Kilauren Gibb found herself on a plane, her young son at her side, flying to Los Angeles. They were picked up at the airport by a limousine, driven into the same hills where Joni Mitchell had first become famous so many years earlier. She lived in Bel Air now, still just a few kilometres from Laurel Canyon, in an old Spanish-style villa, the walls covered in her paintings, a courtyard at its heart. As the evening's darkness gathered, Gibb walked up to the front door, rang the doorbell, and waited.

And then, the moment arrived. "I heard a voice coming from above," Gibb remembered, "looked up, and there she was, like Juliet on her balcony."

Thirty-two years after Joni Mitchell held her baby in her arms for the last time, she had finally found her Little Green. She rushed downstairs to let her in.

36

I WOULDN'T HAVE IT ANY OTHER WAY

It was the summer of love: 1967. A crowd had gathered at the Saphire Tavern on a cool July night. Inside the bar, the air was thick with smoke and the sounds of soul music. One of the most exciting bands in the city was onstage. Frank Motley and the Hitchhikers swung with an irresistible blister of horns, guitar, and percussion. But they weren't the star of the show that night. No, the crowd wasn't there for the band. They'd come for the singer.

As the Hitchhikers reached the end of their first song — a raucous instrumental introduction that saw bandleader Frank Motley play not just one trumpet, but *two at the same time* — the moment had come. "It's just about that time," Motley announced to the crowd as the band continued to play, "for the star of our review, ladies and gentlemen: Little Jackie Shane!"

Shane had grown up in the musical mecca of Nashville, learning how to sing in church before becoming a staple of the local R & B scene. By the end of her teenage years, she was friends with Little Richard, and had toured with The Impressions and Jackie Wilson. It didn't take long for it to become clear that Shane was *too* good; Wilson's manager paid her to sit out the rest of the tour — she was upstaging the headliner.

She'd known she was a transgender woman for years: she began dressing as a girl at the age of five; by thirteen, she was wearing makeup to school and came out to her mother. "I was born a woman in this body," Shane explained many years later. "That's how it's always been. I'm not putting on an act. I could not be anyone else if I tried. It would be the most ridiculous thing in the world for me to try to be a male.... What I am doing, there is nothing wrong with it. The way others think doesn't mean anything to me. I'm not hurting anyone."

In the end, it wasn't just transphobia that would drive her out of Tennessee. It was racism, too. Nearly a century after slavery was abolished in the United States, the laws of Jim Crow still made segregation a state-sanctioned fact of life. Nashville might have been one of the musical capitals of the world, but it was also a deeply prejudiced place. The final straw for Shane came when she and a friend watched a group of white thugs on a rampage. The gang chased down a Black man, beat him bloody, and threw him in a Dumpster. Then, they dragged Black passengers off a bus and beat them, too. Shane was done with Nashville. "That's when I started to look for a home."

Her first step was to join a travelling carnival, performing alongside a snake dancer, a stripper, and a man who ate glass. When they paid a visit to Canada, she knew she'd found the home she was looking for. "I never felt that good before," she explained. "I felt so *free*. I just loved it." When the carnival headed back south across the border, Shane stayed.

It was while walking through the streets of Montreal one night that she found her new backing group, drawn into a club by the sound of soul music. Inside, she found Frank Motley and his band. Motley was a trumpeter from South Carolina who'd studied under Dizzie Gillespie. His unique ability to play two trumpets at once helped his band book regular gigs on both sides of the border. And as soon as they dragged Jackie Shane up onstage to sing with them, it was clear she was going to be touring with them from then on. "Man, let me tell you," the keyboardist remembered, "Jackie set that place on fire."

That's how Shane would end up in Toronto.

Yorkville wasn't the only neighbourhood where the city's conservative facade was beginning to crack. By the end of the 1950s, the Yonge Street Strip had earned a notorious reputation as a land of hard drinking and rock 'n' roll. It wasn't for the faint of heart: when The Band got their start playing taverns on the strip, they wore brass knuckles onstage, knowing they might have to fight their way out of the bar after their set was done. But those few blocks between Dundas and Gerrard were also an exciting place for anyone who cared about music.

Motley's band had been playing gigs in the city for years, and Shane fell in love with it. "You see," she would later tell the CBC, "one cannot choose where one is born, but you can choose your home. I chose Toronto. I love Toronto." And Toronto loved her.

As her songs climbed the local CHUM chart, Shane became a familiar face on the Yonge Street Strip. She played bars like the Hawk's Nest, Zanzibar, and the after-hours club where all the best musicians in the city gathered at the end of the night: Club Bluenote. But it was the Saphire Tavern, just around the corner from the strip, where she was most likely to hold court. Tucked into the ground floor of the old Confederation Life Building (which is still there today at the corner of Richmond and Victoria Streets), the Saphire became Shane's musical home. She played there for weeks on end, drawing enthusiastic crowds in a city that had never seen anything quite like her before.

"She had a lot of fire," one of her fellow soul singers, Eric Mercury, remembered. "We had never seen anything up close like that in Toronto. It was like a tornado coming through the place. She was brash. She was the centre of attention. She was authentic; she was for real and she was living her life out loud."

You can still hear it today: her shows at the Saphire Tavern during that week in the summer of 1967 were recorded for a live album. Half a century later, it's still recognized as a remarkable record, nominated for a Grammy Award when it was re-released in 2017 along with some of her other songs. After Motley's introduction, she took the stage — all confidence and grace, wearing a sequined pantsuit and false eyelashes. She was a singer who made every song her own, a performer electric with coiled energy, and an entertainer who knew damn well how to put on a show. In the quieter moments of her sets, her confessional banter allowed her to connect with an audience in an intimate way. Whoever they were — whoever they loved — she could make them feel like they weren't alone.

When she first started playing at the Saphire Tavern, she made sure her queer fans would feel welcome, talking to the owner to guarantee it. "In fact, I told Mrs. Stone," she remembered, "'Look, gay people must be able to come and see me. As long as they come just like everyone else and obey the rules and such, I don't want anyone kept from seeing me. I want them to come.' We had an understanding."

Shane drew audiences both queer and straight, Black and white — as well as everyone in between. And when they ventured inside the Saphire, they found her there onstage, blurring gender lines and talking openly about her sexuality. On the live album, her banter with the audience is filled with references to loving both men and women. "I'm going to enjoy the chicken," she told the crowd, using a slang term for young men, "the women, the chicken, and everything else that I want to enjoy. That's how I live. That's why I'm so happy all the time." And she took that message well beyond the confines of the Saphire. She played in high schools and YMCAs across the city, and toured communities all over southern Ontario. A curling rink in Scarborough. The town hall in Newmarket. A dance club on the shores of Lake Simcoe. As well as her adult fans, she reached countless queer teens who didn't have many public role models.

It wasn't always easy. People gawked and snickered, even in Toronto. "You know," she explained, "when I'm walking down Yonge Street, you won't believe this, but you know some of them funny people have the nerve to point the finger at me and grin and smile and whisper." She often presented as a gay man in drag. Local newspapers wrote columns speculating about her gender; at least one sent a journalist to ask her about it to her face.

Not that she would let that stop her. "So, now listen, baby," she told the crowd at the Saphire, "when you see Jackie walking down the street, or I walk into a restroom that you're in, I want you to laugh and talk and grin and point the finger at me because if I ever walked out and they didn't point and whisper about me, I'd go back in and look in the mirror and stick out my tongue because I thought I was sick or something, I done lost my touch.... Every Monday morning, I laugh and grin on my way to the bank."

Still, she would never become a major international star. When she was invited onto *The Ed Sullivan Show*, she refused — they wanted her to take her makeup off. When Dick Clark's *American Bandstand* came calling, she turned them down, too: they wouldn't let Black kids appear in their audience. And in the end, she would even disappear from the stages of Toronto. She slipped out of the city one night after a show in 1971 and wasn't heard from again for decades. There were rumours she'd been murdered. It would be forty years before a reporter finally tracked her down. In the last few years of her life, Jackie Shane would become a public figure once again, embraced by a city that was more ready than ever to celebrate her work. Today, she towers above Yonge Street as part of a twenty-two-storey mural commemorating the musical history of the Strip — and the remarkable decade when she graced the smoke-filled taverns of Toronto.

"I live the life I love," she told the crowd at the Saphire that night, "and I love the life I live. I hope you'll do the same…. As long as you don't force your will and your way on others, forget 'em baby, you don't need 'em." In a city where homosexuality was still illegal, where the Toronto Police Morality Squad still stalked the streets, where queer couples would have to worry about their safety for decades to come, Jackie Shane was setting an example. Up there on that stage, self-assured and unapologetic: a Black transgender woman who knew exactly who she was — and who wasn't afraid to show it.

At the end of the night, as the band settled into a slow and sultry rhythm, Shane began to sing her most famous song. Her biggest hit was an old soul tune called "Any Other Way." It would be recorded by several artists over the years. But the lyrics took on a deeper meaning when Jackie Shane was the one singing the words.

"Tell her that I'm happy," she sang. "Be sure and tell her this: tell her that I'm gay. Tell her I wouldn't have it any other way …"

37

ELIZABETH TAYLOR'S LOVE NEST

Cleopatra was a BIG movie. It told the story of one of the most spectacular love affairs of all time — the tragic romance between Roman general Mark Antony and Egyptian queen Cleopatra — and the film production matched the grandeur of the tale. It had lavish sets. Elaborate costumes. Thousands of extras. It ran more than three hours long. At the time, it was the most expensive film ever made. It won four Oscars, earned more money at the box office than any other movie in 1963, and *still* managed to lose tens of millions of dollars.

But nothing about *Cleopatra* was bigger than its stars. Elizabeth Taylor, hailed as one of world's most beautiful women, became the highest paid actress in Hollywood when she signed on to play the title role. Starring alongside her as Mark Antony was one of the most respected thespians of his time: Richard Burton.

To the joy of paparazzi everywhere, the two fell in love. They were gorgeous, tempestuous, alcoholic, and entertaining. Their director said working with them was "like being locked in a cage with two tigers." Every twist and turn in their relationship became international news.

It was less fun for their spouses. At the time, Burton had been married for more than a decade; Taylor, at twenty-eight years old, was already on her fourth husband. Neither marriage would last much longer. When Burton's wife saw the way he behaved with his co-star on the set of *Cleopatra*, she fled — not just the set, but the entire country. The couple was divorced by the end of 1963.

It wasn't an easy divorce. More than a hundred years after Elizabeth Powell and John Stuart were granted the first divorce in Toronto history, divorces were still exceedingly difficult to get — both in Canada and the United States. Burton and his wife had been forced to go to Mexico for theirs. Taylor's was taking even longer.

That was a problem. Burton needed to get to Toronto right away; he was set to star in a production of *Hamlet* directed by the respected Shakespearean actor John Gielgud. It would be playing at the O'Keefe Centre (later known as the Hummingbird Centre, the Sony Centre, and the Meridian Centre) before heading to Broadway. He'd been there for the red carpet grand opening of the flashy new theatre on Front Street just a few years earlier, starring with Julie Andrews in its first ever production: the world premiere of *Camelot*. Now, he was scheduled to make a grand return. There was absolutely no way he could possibly miss it.

But he also couldn't bear to be without Elizabeth Taylor. Which meant they would be living in Toronto. Together. For eight weeks. In sin.

They arrived in January 1964 and took over a five-room suite on the eighth floor of the King Edward Hotel. It was big news. "SHE'S HERE!" screamed the front page of the *Toronto Star* upon their arrival, alongside a photo of a Mountie escorting the hand-holding stars into a waiting car at the airport. The couple's Hollywood nickname, "Dickenliz," was thrown around liberally. And the paper reported gleefully on the crowd of fans filling the lobby of the hotel, packed so tight that when Prime Minister John Diefenbaker finished giving a speech in a ballroom, he couldn't find his way to the exit. They even printed a photo of Taylor's dogs when they arrived on a later flight.

The couple's marital status was big news, too. For many people, it was an outrageous scandal. There was no shortage of religious indignation in the early 1960s. The Vatican had already denounced Taylor's "erotic vagrancy." Judgmental teenagers showed up at the hotel to protest, brandishing signs with slogans like "Drink not the wine of adultery" and "She walks among your children." And while some have since suggested that at least a few of the teenagers were being satirical, there was no shortage of righteous scorn directed the couple's way. One congressman in the United States suggested that Burton's U.S. visa should be revoked.

But the moralizers were fighting a losing battle. There were more fans than picketers. The *Toronto Star* ran an editorial defending the couple. Times were changing.

And then one day, when Taylor came down from their suite to meet Burton for lunch, there he was, sitting at their usual table in the Sovereign Ballroom. It was strangely deserted; he'd reserved the entire room. That's when he proposed.

Nine days after Taylor's own Mexican divorce was finalized, the couple were married — in Montreal, since conservative Ontario wouldn't recognize their quickie, foreign divorces. A couple of days later, they were back in Toronto showing off their wedding rings. The minister who performed the ceremony would be getting angry phone calls for weeks.

A few days after they got back, Taylor and Burton were off to the United States; *Hamlet* was opening on Broadway. Over the course of the 1960s, they would make seven movies together and drink and fight and write passionate love letters declaring their undying devotion. He called her "a poem," "unquestionably gorgeous," "extraordinarily beautiful," and also "famine, fire, destruction and plague." They divorced in 1974. Remarried in 1975. Divorced again in 1976. That would be the last time; a few years later he was dead.

When she came home from the memorial service, there was one last love letter waiting for her in the mail. He'd written it three days before he died, asking her to give him one more chance. In one of the last interviews she gave before she passed away in 2011, she said it was still there, where she always kept it, in a drawer beside her bed.

38
THE NAPALM GIRL

It's one of the most notoriously disturbing photographs ever taken. It's a June day in 1972. The camera is pointing down a grass-lined road in Vietnam. In the distance, a curtain of dark smoke obscures the horizon. South Vietnamese soldiers are walking toward the camera, some carrying machine guns in their hands, all with helmets on their heads. A couple of photographers walk with them, one replacing the film in his camera. But none of that is where your eye is drawn. It goes immediately to the children. They run down the road before the soldiers. A boy holds his sister's hand as they flee. A toddler looks back toward the smoke on the horizon. A boy in the foreground cries, his mouth an open, black, despairing hole. And in the middle of them all: a girl, naked, running down the pavement with bare feet, crying, her arms outstretched, raw with pain as her skin burns from the napalm that was just dropped on her town.

The Pulitzer Prize–winning photo appeared in newspapers around the world. In the United States, it was published on the front page of the *New York Times* and gave even more momentum to the rapidly mounting peace movement, as protestors took to the streets demanding an end to the Vietnam War. The picture became a thorn in Richard Nixon's side; the president privately wondered if the whole thing had been staged just to erode his support. Finally, in 1975, nearly three years after the photo was taken, he reluctantly withdrew the last American troops from Vietnam.

Phan Thi Kim Phúc was nine years old when the photo was taken. She lived in Trảng Bàng, a town in South Vietnam, which had been invaded by the Communists in early June. Their troops dug in, waiting for the inevitable American and South Vietnamese retaliation, while Phúc and other civilians took refuge with some South Vietnamese soldiers in a nearby temple.

Two days later, a pair of South Vietnamese bombers appeared in the sky above the town. They circled and then dove, using eight napalm bombs to turn the ground below into a hellscape of liquid fire, mistakenly attacking their own troops and civilians fleeing from the temple. Phúc's clothes were burned completely off her. Her back and one of her arms were turned into a mess of blisters and peeling skin. Third-degree burns covered more than half her body. She ran, along with her brothers and the rest of the survivors, down the road out of town, naked, screaming, and burning.

That's when Nick Ut, a photographer with the Associated Press, snapped his infamous photo. He was standing a few hundred metres down the road with a handful of foreign journalists. When Phúc got to them, they gave her water to drink and poured some over her wounds. She passed out. Ut gathered her and some of the other children into his car and rushed them to the nearest hospital, in Saigon. He was sure she was going to die. So were the doctors. It would take fourteen months and seventeen operations before she was finally well enough to head back to a home that had been destroyed.

And her suffering wasn't over. When the war ended a few years later, Phúc found herself growing up in a communist country. She started studying medicine at university, but the government pulled her out of school so she could use her time to give interviews and pose for photos, used as a propaganda tool for the state. She hated it with a passion; thought about suicide. It took years before she finally convinced the government to let her continue her studies abroad. And even then, she was only allowed to move to another communist country. She attended the University of Havana in Cuba. While she was there, she looked for her chance to escape.

It would come on her honeymoon.

Phúc was convinced she would never find love. Before the bombing, she'd spent her childhood reading tales of romance and marriage, giggling with her best friend as they imagined their future husbands, playing "wedding" with cobs of corn as the bride and groom. "Together," she later remembered, "we dreamed of the moment when we would meet our long-awaited princes — oh, what beautiful brides we someday would be!" But after the bombing, scarred and in pain, she was sure she'd spend the rest of her life alone. Even that childhood friend shunned her.

"I made an agreement in those moments when the napalm scorched my clothing and … my skin and then the fat and muscle and other tissue," she wrote in her autobiography, "that because I would now and forever be seen as 'different,' I was unfit to be loved." It echoed as an endless refrain in her head. A vow. *I am unfit to be loved.* Even in the moment when the doctors told her she would be scarred forever and suffer from chronic pain for the rest of her life, what she heard was "You are unfit to be loved now, Kim." And as she grew older, the idea only became more firmly embedded in her mind. "After all," she worried, "who would desire a woman with a tragic past, with buffalo-hide skin, and with the inability to conceive?"

His name was Bui Huy Toan. She met him there at the university in Havana. He, like her, was a visiting Vietnamese student — one of four who volunteered to act as her assistants, doing the simple physical tasks she still found hard. They first met in a school cafeteria; he complimented her beautiful smile and carried her lunch tray for her. From then on, they saw each other every day, going for long walks together, sharing in their homesickness and their worry about what was happening back in Vietnam. He was an exuberant, gentle, and generous man. Within a few weeks, she realized she had fallen in love.

It wasn't always easy. He drank and smoked and didn't share her passionate belief in Christianity. She worried her family would reject him because he'd grown up in the Communist North. She was scared of rejection and scared of what he'd think when he finally saw her scarred body. She refused to let him do anything more than hold her hand or kiss her cheek. She turned down his first marriage proposal. When the subject came up again, she spent days deep in prayer. When he asked for a second time, she knew her answer. This time, it was yes.

Ten days later, they were standing before each other in the house of the Vietnamese ambassador, surrounded by flowers and friends as it poured rain outside, promising to spend their lives together. When they kissed on their wedding day, it was for the first time.

For their honeymoon, they were only allowed to visit another communist country. Even that was a concession: at first, they said only Toan could go; that she would have to stay behind as her husband went on their honeymoon alone. In the end, they chose Moscow, which turned out not to be the most romantic of destinations — it was cold and grey, and they were never allowed to be alone. Vietnamese officials monitored them at every turn.

That made it awfully difficult to discuss her plan. They were on the flight back home before they could really talk. On the long journey across the Atlantic, their plane would have to refuel. It would make a brief stop in Gander, Newfoundland — one of the most strategically placed airports in the world, there on the very edge of the North Atlantic. It would one day become famous for sheltering stranded passengers after 9/11. She told her husband that when their plane landed there, she would be getting off and never getting back on. She might have promised to spend the rest of her life with him, but she refused to do it in a communist country.

At first, Toan resisted. "Think of my family, Kim! And also of yours." It wasn't until they were sitting in the terminal at Gander, waiting for the plane to reboard, that he gave in and handed her his passport. "Do whatever she says to do," he told himself. "Do whatever you have to do *in order not to lose this girl.*"

Before long, they were on a train to Toronto.

It was the name that originally attracted her to the city; it reminded her of the Spanish word for grapefruit — *toronja* — and she loved grapefruit. Plus, she was told it was a multicultural place, a big city with a strong job market and a relatively moderate climate by Canadian standards. They spent their first nights at Henry's Motel on Kingston Road, amazed by the room service while watching reruns of *I Love Lucy*; she laughed so hard she cried. There were hard days ahead — they had little money and refugees weren't allowed to work — but they eventually made a new home for themselves in an apartment in Riverdale, in Toronto's eastern Chinatown.

At first, Phúc led a private life in the city, not wanting to relive the memories of the bombing and the shocking photo that changed her life. She avoided the journalists who waited outside her window, hoping to grab their own photograph of the famous "Napalm Girl." But when they finally did get that shot, and the *Toronto Sun* splashed it across the front page, she decided to use it as an opportunity to re-enter the public eye and do some good.

In the years since she's moved to Ajax, where she runs a foundation helping to find medical treatment and psychological counselling for children affected by war. She's given speeches and interviews, and has worked for the United Nations as a UNESCO Goodwill Ambassador. She even spoke to Vietnam War veterans at the Memorial Wall in Washington, DC, to let them know she forgave them all. Once, she was unfit for love. Now, she spreads it wherever she goes.

"Love," according Phan Thi Kim Phúc, "is more powerful than any weapon."

39
MAGGIE AT THE EL MO

It casts a colourful glow on a grey sidewalk on the edge of Chinatown, a bright beacon in the night. It's one of the most iconic signs in Toronto: a neon palm tree topped by a crescent moon. Along the trunk shine the words that have been keeping watch over this stretch of Spadina Avenue since the 1940s: El Mocambo. The club has been a staple of the city's nightlife for decades — with a history that stretches back even further than that. The building first opened as a music venue in the 1850s and is said to have given shelter to some of those who escaped slavery along the Underground Railroad. It was reborn as the El Mocambo in the wake of the Second World War, when bars and taverns were allowed to serve hard liquor for the first time since Prohibition. It became one of the city's first cocktail bars, classy enough to birth stories of Marilyn Monroe and Grace Kelly stopping by for a drink. When the city lifted a ban on live music at cocktail bars — though singing along was still strictly forbidden — the "El Mo" took advantage. Over the next couple of decades, it played host to a German dance club, a strip tease act, and blues legends like Muddy Waters and Buddy Guy. By the late 1970s, it had earned a reputation for supporting Toronto's up-and-coming young rock groups.

The band playing the El Mocambo on a rainy March night in 1977 seemed to be just another one of those local acts. No one had ever heard of The Cockroaches. But the name was a ruse, a cover story to hide the fact that that night the El Mo was playing host to one of the biggest rock bands in the world.

The Rolling Stones were having a very rough week. They had come to Toronto to record a live album, but things had been thrown into chaos from the moment they arrived. The band's guitarist, Keith Richards, had brought his son and his common-law wife along with him — as well as her twenty-eight pieces of luggage. Inside those bags, customs officials found ten grams of hashish and a spoon coated with traces of heroin. Her arrest was shortly followed by Richards's. When the RCMP showed up at the Harbour Castle hotel on the waterfront, where the band was staying, they found about four thousand dollars' worth of heroin in the guitarist's bathroom. Plus, some cocaine. "The Mounties always get their man," *Rolling Stone* magazine wrote, "and they damn sure have him."

Richards would eventually be let off with a light sentence: a promise to play a charity show. But at the time, of course, no one knew that was going to happen. Richards was facing a potential life sentence. For a while, it seemed as if The Rolling Stones might be done for good.

But that damp night in Chinatown, a limousine pulled up outside the El Mocambo. Out stepped the band's legendary front man: Mick Jagger. For now, at least, the Stones were carrying on, going ahead with their plan to play a pair of secret shows at the El Mo, their first club gigs in fourteen years, to be recorded for their *Love You Live* album. Even as the rumours swirled and the drug scandal made headlines around the world, The Rolling Stones were going to keep the party going.

And there, stepping out of the limousine right behind Mick Jagger, came the wife of the prime minister of Canada.

It was during a Christmas in Tahiti that Margaret Sinclair first met the man she was going to marry. She was there on holiday with her family, enjoying the green palm trees, white sands, and a bronzed Frenchman named Yves — the grandson of one of the founders of Club Med. But one day, as she relaxed on a raft, gently bobbing in the bay, another man swam over to join her for a while. He was much older than she was: she was nineteen; he was forty-eight. But she did like the look of his legs. There under the bright Tahitian sun, they talked about Plato, the history of the Roman Empire, and whether existence was just an illusion. He was a politician; she was the daughter of a former cabinet minister. They got along well enough that they spent some more time together, snorkelling through the waters of the South Pacific, before returning to their regular lives back home in Canada. She didn't think much of it: he was much too old and much too square for an aspiring hippie like her. But for his part, he was immediately smitten. At breakfast one day, while she ate at the far end of the table, he confided to his friends. "If I ever marry," he told them, "she's the one."

It would be a while before they met again. He'd been in Tahiti pondering one of the biggest decisions of his life: whether to run for the leadership of the federal Liberal Party. In just a few months, he'd be the prime minister of Canada. He was pretty busy. And so, a couple of years passed before Pierre Trudeau finally asked Margaret Sinclair out on a date.

By then, Trudeau had already begun to make his mark on Canada as one of the boldest and most controversial leaders the country has ever known. During his very first year as prime minister, he'd started to change the country's legal approach to love. In 1969 his government decriminalized birth control, legalized some abortions, and decriminalized homosexual acts between men — as long as they were both twenty-one years old and behind closed doors. "There's no place for the state in the bedrooms of the nation," Trudeau famously declared, echoing an editorial in the *Globe and Mail*. "What's done in private between adults doesn't concern the Criminal Code." It was far from a complete legal acceptance of gay rights. But it was a major step forward in a country where men had once been threatened with death if they fell in love with another man. As Trudeau put it, "It has knocked down a lot of totems and overridden a lot of taboos.… It's bringing the laws of the land up to contemporary society."

Canada was changing, and Trudeau was leading that change. While some Canadians reviled him, he was a hero to many. Since Margaret Sinclair had last seen him, Trudeaumania had swept the county. The young, bachelor prime minister had the aura of a rock star. Sinclair might not have been completely sold on the idea of dating a man nearly three decades her senior, but it was hard to turn him down.

Pierre and Maggie had their first date in Vancouver, dining at a restaurant high atop Grouse Mountain as they talked about student revolutions and the time she'd spent living in Morocco. By the end of the night, she'd fallen hard. When he casually suggested she might be interested in a government job, she dropped everything and headed for Ottawa. They began dating on and off at first; Pierre kept seeing a few other people, including Barbra Streisand; there were even rumours he'd proposed to the movie star. But he and Margaret were becoming closer and closer: having dinner together at 24 Sussex, hiking and skiing at the prime minister's retreat on Harrington Lake, and spending time at his cabin in the Laurentians. They got engaged under the palm trees of the Bahamas, during a vacation spent diving through the blue waters and living in a ramshackle hut on the beach.

The prime minister almost missed their wedding. He had to talk a ground crew into letting him fly through one of the worst blizzards Ottawa had seen in years. But he finally arrived at the little church in North Vancouver — only half an hour late. They were married as the setting sun streamed in through the windows, surrounded by yellow candles and garlands of spring flowers.

It was a small, private event, with only about a dozen guests. They didn't tell the press. But when news broke, they were suddenly the most popular husband and wife in Canada. "We were the golden couple … and everyone seemed to love us," Margaret Trudeau would later remember. To the public, their marriage had all the allure of a fairy-tale romance, a glamorous love affair that resonated with Canadians who could feel their country finally coming into its own. And that impression only got stronger when each of their first two children were born on Christmas Day. Baby Justin was destined to become prime minister himself when he grew up. One newspaper called them "The World's Most Glamorous First Family."

But, like so many fairy tales, this one wouldn't have a happy ending.

The first public sign of trouble came on the night of their sixth anniversary. Instead of celebrating together, the prime minister and his wife were hundreds of kilometres apart. Pierre was in Ottawa. And Maggie? Well, she was in Toronto, climbing out of Mick Jagger's limousine outside the El Mocambo. Instead of spending her wedding anniversary having a romantic dinner with her husband, she would spend the entire night in a grimy club in Chinatown partying with a rock band whose guitarist was facing a possible life sentence for heroin possession. And the next night, too. She'd stay up until five in the morning, talking, playing dice, and smoking drugs with the band in her hotel room.

Maggie Trudeau had always been a free spirit, uncomfortable with the traditional role she was expected to play as the prime minister's wife. Over the course of the 1970s, controversy seemed to follow her wherever she went. She smoked pot, drank, had an affair with Ted Kennedy, passed out at the Louvre, wore a scandalously short dress to the White House, and did peyote and broke into song at a state dinner in Venezuela. The list went on and on. "Margaret Trudeau did it again," was the lede on the front page of the *Globe and Mail* the day after the peyote state dinner. It was far from an isolated incident. One day, many years later, she would talk openly about the truth behind those scandalous stories: she'd been diagnosed with bipolar disorder. She would eventually become an advocate for mental health. "I wince when I look back at this really stupid, shameful behaviour," she would remember in her autobiography. "I was so lonely. I was so sad."

The headlines from her nights with The Rolling Stones were especially brutal, made all the more shocking by Keith Richards's arrest. "SEX ORGY IN PRIME MINISTER'S WIFE'S SUITE," one newspaper cried. Rumours she'd slept with Mick Jagger were everywhere. (In fact, she spent the night with guitarist Ron Wood.) And there would be more headlines to come when she turned up a few days later, living with a princess in New York City, attending the ballet with Mikhail Baryshnikov. And then again when she was photographed dancing at the notorious disco Studio 54 on the night her husband lost the next election. Some even worried her behaviour was going to cost him his career, and — in an era of rising Quebec separatism — that it would lead not just to the breakup of her marriage, but to the breakup of Canada, as well.

But the truth was that their marriage had been on the rocks for years, and had long been coming to an end. "I see now with clarity," she wrote many years later, "how opposites and contradictions can coexist in a human being, how a generous man can also be tight-fisted, how a husband can say adorable things one minute and hard things the next, how a sweet, sweet husband can turn on his wife."

Pierre Trudeau could be kind and charming, but he could also be mean, distant, and cheap. She felt isolated and controlled, like she didn't have a voice. "He literally wanted me barefoot, pregnant, and in the kitchen." He might have believed, intellectually, in gender equality, but, as she remembered it, "it was very hard for him to allow that freedom to me or to any women in his life." For years, he kept her from going back to school or even volunteering for charity. And the age difference was a problem, too. "He thought that by bullying me he could turn me into the perfect wife — in the way that a father might bully a recalcitrant teenager. Unfortunately, Pierre was not my father; he was my husband." And as prime minister, he was so busy that even their love life had to be tightly scheduled. "Reason over passion," was his favourite phrase.

They'd fallen out of love in 1974. And while there were still some good times, things had pretty much fallen apart. "The day came when I started to hate Pierre," she wrote later, "and I knew that if I didn't leave, I would go insane." The morning of their sixth wedding anniversary, just hours before Maggie turned up at the El Mocambo, the Trudeaus agreed to separate. That weekend, she wrote an entry in her diary: "March 6. Toronto. Done. I have left Pierre and the children in Ottawa and I am heading out into the world to seek my fortune. Either it will work or it won't."

By then, divorces were much easier to get than they had been in the days of Elizabeth Powell, or even Elizabeth Taylor — and that was thanks to Pierre Trudeau. His government had loosened the restrictions as part of the same big bill that changed the laws around birth control, abortion, and homosexuality. Adultery was no longer the only acceptable reason to end a marriage; now there were multiple grounds for divorce — you could even just both agree to end it after spending three years apart. For the first time since Toronto had been founded, couples weren't forced to stay together long after they'd fallen out of love. In 1984 the Trudeaus would make use of the new law, officially ending their marriage. Canada's fairy-tale couple got divorced.

And so, that night with The Rolling Stones wasn't a shocking betrayal of her marriage vows; it was Margaret

Trudeau's first step into a new life. She was on her way to New York, where she would begin to build an existence apart from her famous husband, and pursue a new profession: photography. That night in Chinatown, when The Rolling Stones took the stage in front of the El Mo's palm tree–covered backdrop, she had her camera in her hand. As the legendary rock group belted out some of their most beloved tunes — songs that had helped fuel the social revolution of the sixties, songs that helped usher in new attitudes toward love, songs that were the soundtrack of Margaret Sinclair's youth — she took photographs, hesitant at first, but more and more confident as the night wore on. "It was," she wrote, "an exhilarating start to my new career." She'd met her husband under the palm trees of Tahiti. She'd promised to marry him under the palm trees of the Bahamas. And now, under the palm trees of the El Mocambo, she was promising herself a new, better, happier life.

"It was a good night, and it was my new world."

40
THE MICHAELS

Michael Stark was walking around the block. It was a rainy Saturday night during the Victoria Day weekend of 1981. He was trying to build up his courage. There, just down a laneway, was the entrance to a gay bar called Buddies.

"I hadn't been out very long," he later explained, "and was nervous about someone seeing me go in."

Stark had been raised in a military family, spending most of his youth in small communities in the Maritimes before moving to Toronto to attend Ryerson University. The big city was a big shock. He was still just twenty-three, shy, and not yet entirely comfortable being open about his sexuality. That night, he was supposed to go see a movie with a friend, but when she cancelled, he decided to steel himself and head downtown instead. It took a few times around the block, but he finally gathered enough courage to head inside. And there in that underground bar at Church and Gerrard, he would find the love of his life.

Michael Leshner was a bit older, a lawyer in his early thirties. "Somehow our eyes must have met," he remembered about the moment he first saw Stark, "and I went over to introduce myself. Quickly, we realized there was a physical as well as an emotional connection. The bottom line was Mike was very cute, handsome, and radiated goodness." As the bar closed down for the night, the two Michaels headed off into the rain. They would spend most of that weekend together. And decades after that.

There was good reason for Stark to be nervous. Ever since the days of Alexander Wood and George Markland, queer Torontonians had been forced to keep their feelings secret, driven into the shadows by public prejudice and legal discrimination — sometimes quite literally. Unable to safely carry on their romances in the public eye, some men looked for connections by cruising in dark alleyways, parks, and public washrooms. There were "glory holes" in the bathrooms of the old Union Station by the end of the 1800s. In the early 1900s, spaces like Queen's Park and Albert Lane (on the edge of The Ward) were earning reputations as cruising grounds.

They became contested spaces. In the washrooms at Sunnyside Amusement Park, metal plates would be erected in the partitions between stalls to keep men from making holes in them. "Morality lights" were installed along Philosopher's Walk at the University of Toronto, bushes were cleared from Queen's Park, and many public washrooms were closed entirely. Even there, in the few marginal spaces where gay men could meet, the officers of the Toronto Police Morality Squad followed. Their first ever report, written back in 1886, listed sex between men as one of the priorities on the list of "vices" they were targeting. In the 1920s, the squad regularly spied on men using the public washroom at Allan Gardens — climbing a ladder so they could peer through a peephole into the stalls. Officers were known to burst into private parties, businesses, and bathhouses in their search for gay men to round up and drag in front of a judge.

And it wasn't just ancient history. The most notorious police raids against the gay community came a century after the Morality Squad was founded — just a few months before the Michaels met. The police called it "Operation Soap." At eleven o'clock on a winter night in 1981, two hundred officers in plain clothes, armed with sledgehammers and crowbars, burst into four gay bathhouses. Over the course of the night, they arrested more than three hundred men — at the time, it was the single biggest police roundup in the history of the city. Those who were targeted would later remember police officers hurling homophobic slurs, busting down doors, breaking into lockers, even taking photos of their naked prisoners. "I wish these pipes were hooked up to gas," one officer reportedly told a row of gay men as he lined them up against a shower wall, "so I could annihilate you all."

People had been fighting back against that kind of oppression for decades. Over the course of the 1900s, Toronto's LGBTQ+ communities had been carefully carving out more public space for themselves. Bars like the Continental and the Rideau began to welcome a lesbian crowd in the years after the Second World

War. Hanlan's Point on the Toronto Islands became a gay hangout, the beaches where Elizabeth Simcoe once found social freedom still serving a similar function two centuries later. By the 1950s, an annual Halloween drag ball was being hosted at the Nile Room, the Egyptian-themed basement of the Letros Tavern on King Street; the sidewalk outside served as a makeshift runway. In the 1960s, and '70s, as Canada's first gay rights groups were being founded, an increasing number of openly queer-themed books, plays, and films began to be released. And at the time the Michaels met in the early eighties, the country's airwaves were filled with a new wave hit from Toronto band Rough Trade: "High School Confidential" featured a woman singing about being attracted to another woman. While some radio stations censored the lyrics, that didn't stop the song from climbing the charts.

By then, the annual Halloween drag ball had migrated north. The St. Charles Tavern, an old Chinese restaurant on Yonge Street, was now a gay bar. So was the Parkside Tavern just down the street. The Glad Day Bookshop had opened, with the *Body Politic* magazine published out of its space. Buddies in Bad Times Theatre was putting on groundbreaking productions. The heart of the community would shift slightly eastward in time, centred on the intersection of Church and Wellesley. Countless queer romances would play out on the land where Alexander Wood's forest had once stood. The Church Street Village became the focal point of Toronto's LGBTQ+ communities.

The Michaels took things slow at first, not making any long-term plans. "Don't forget," Stark later explained, "back in the early 1980s, gay men and women didn't couple that frequently. There really wasn't any road map or any role models." Neither one of them had ever had a boyfriend. But they kept seeing each other every weekend. Before long, on weekdays, too. They were growing closer. "[It] felt very safe, natural, even carefree," Leshner remembered. "We enjoyed each other's company — going to movies, meeting my friends, and socializing with them with dinners, brunches and parties." After a couple of years, Stark got an apartment in Leshner's building on the fringes of the Village — and six months after that, they moved in together.

Building that kind of stable, long-term relationship already felt like an immense accomplishment. "To meet someone," Leshner once told *Xtra* magazine, "fall in love and grow old together. From our first consciousness we were taught we could never have that, that we're bad people not allowed to dream that dream."

But there was still a long way to go. Every year on Halloween, a crowd of hateful bigots would gather outside the St. Charles Tavern, hurling eggs and insults at the drag queens. It carried on all through the 1970s and there was still plenty of hate in the '80s. The first cases of AIDS were reported in Toronto the year after the Michaels met, unleashing a new wave of public homophobia. Just a few years later, a gay librarian was beaten to death by five teenagers in High Park. There was clearly a lot more work to be done.

The Michaels would become leaders in that struggle, joining countless others in the fight for gay rights.
Leshner wrote op-ed pieces in the *Toronto Star*, arguing
for equal employment benefits, the right to adopt children, and an end to homophobic legislation. When the
police service introduced gay sensitivity training for its
officers, he was there to observe the proceedings. He even
took the fight to his own employer. In 1988 he launched
a lawsuit against the Ontario government, where he
worked as a lawyer in the Ministry of the Attorney
General, demanding that gay and lesbian couples be
given the same pension rights as straight couples. When
someone died, he argued, the person they loved and
spent their life with should get the same benefits, no
matter what their gender or sexuality. His victory was a
landmark moment for gay rights in Canada, laying the
groundwork for even more progress.

When Leshner was passed over for a promotion,
despite a glowing recommendation from his boss,
he complained that it was a clear case of homophobic
discrimination. When he was reprimanded for talking
about it with the *Star*, he sued again. And won again.

All the while, he was resisted at every turn by conservative groups, Christian organizations, and those in
power. "You think if you're logical and rational," he explained, "the establishment will see the error of its ways.
You think that structural discrimination will end overnight. Guess what? It doesn't work that way. The people
with power hang on to their power, and if you want to
open up that status quo, you've got to fight."

It was a lesson the Michaels would take into their biggest battle of all. Decades after homosexuality began to be decriminalized, gay and lesbian couples in Canada still weren't allowed to get married, to officially and legally share their lives with the person they loved. The Michaels had been together for decades, but as far as the government was concerned, that didn't matter. They still didn't have the same rights as straight couples.

"There's no reason why I shouldn't be able to marry Michael," Leshner explained at their twentieth anniversary party. "I have three brothers and a sister, and I've attended all of their weddings. It would be nice for them to be able to attend mine. I've had the longest relationship of any of my siblings, yet I can't marry."

But that was finally about to change.

A modest, red brick church stands on a quiet residential street in Riverdale, just around the corner from Broadview and Gerrard. It's been there for more than a century, since the early 1900s, but the biggest moment in its history came much more recently.

It all started on a December Sunday in the year 2000. By then, the old building was home to a relatively new congregation. The Metropolitan Community Church was founded in California in the 1960s and came to Toronto a decade later; it's a Protestant denomination specifically created to welcome to LGBTQ+ parishioners. For more than twenty years, it bounced around the city, holding services everywhere from the Church of the

Holy Trinity to the Bathurst Street Theatre. But it eventually found a permanent home in that old building in Riverdale. And it was there the minister was planning to make history.

The church had always been involved in the fight for gay rights — and marriage was the next big battle. The senior pastor, Brent Hawkes, planned to open up a new front by using a loophole in Ontario's discriminatory laws. The reading of marriage banns is an ancient tradition stretching back nearly two thousand years, first adopted as part of the law of Upper Canada all the way back in the 1700s, when John Graves Simcoe was battling with Parliament over the legal definition of marriage. If Reverend Hawkes read out the banns on three successive Sundays, announcing a coming wedding and giving everyone in the community a chance to object, then the church didn't need an official licence. Gay and lesbian couples could get married without needing permission from the government.

One winter Sunday after another, Reverend Hawkes stood in front of the congregation and read out the banns for two Toronto couples. He announced that Kevin Bourassa and Joe Varnell were planning to get married. So were Elaine and Anne Vatour.

The first Sunday went off without a hitch. But by the second and third readings, conservative activists had heard what was going on. They arrived at the old church in Riverdale determined to block the plan. When the time came, they rose to make their objections — but the reverend dismissed each of them; their arguments, he explained, weren't rooted in the church's beliefs or in Ontario law. He carried on. The banns were read three times.

On the second Sunday of 2001, more than a thousand people crowded inside the church. Reporters and television crews came from around the world, camera shutters clicking away as Reverend Hawkes took his place before his congregation. He was wearing a bullet-proof vest hidden away under his robes: a bomb threat had been called in, he'd already been attacked at that morning's service, and a small group of protesters was gathered on the corner, hateful placards in hand. One woman tried to derail the proceedings, declaring herself to be a messenger sent by Jesus. But nothing would ruin that day. Despite the protests and distractions, the ceremonies were performed. The crowd cheered and applauded as the two newly married couples kissed.

The government of Ontario, as everyone expected, refused to recognize the weddings. And the Metropolitan Community Church launched a legal battle, uniting with seven other Toronto couples who applied for marriage licences and were denied by city hall — including the Michaels.

It took more than a year for the case to be heard, appealed, and the final decision to come back. But when it did, the Michaels were ready. They'd already bought their rings — their miniature schnauzer, Schmikey, threw up in the jewellery store — and the morning the decision was scheduled to come down, they got dressed in their suits before heading down to Osgoode Hall. An envelope was waiting there for them, the court's decision inside. They opened it to find the news they'd waited so long for. The Ontario Court of Appeal declared what so many already knew to be true: the law banning same-sex marriages was discriminatory. Gay marriage was now officially legal, effective immediately. The ceremonies performed at the old red church in Riverdale would now be recognized as legally valid. And new weddings were cleared to take place.

The race was on. The Michaels were worried the government might launch an immediate appeal, but they were sure the Supreme Court wouldn't overturn the decision if they were already married before the appeal was launched. So, they rushed over to city hall, just metres away, to get their marriage licence, and then scrambled back over to the nearby courthouse on University Avenue. A judge was waiting there to perform the ceremony. They weren't allowed to hold their wedding in an actual courtroom, so a cloakroom would have to do. There they stood in front of Leshner's mother, a crowd of journalists and cameras, a few lawyers, and some of the cleaning staff.

After all those years of struggle, it was finally happening.

"I Michael, take you, Michael, to be my lawfully wedded spouse. To have and to hold, from this day forward, whatever circumstances or experiences life may hold for us."

The Michaels were officially married.

* * *

The night after the bathhouse raids, people took to the streets. More than three thousand protestors marched down Yonge Street behind a banner declaring "ENOUGH IS ENOUGH! STOP POLICE VIOLENCE." And that was just the first in a series of protests. People in Toronto had been meeting for annual Pride events for years, stretching back to picnics held at Hanlan's Point on the islands. But the 1981 Pride, held just months after the raids, took on new urgency and momentum. A thousand people gathered in Grange Park and then marched on 52 Division, the nearby Toronto police station. That protest is now recognized as the first official Toronto Pride.

The Michaels were there that day in 1981, marching outside the police station, protesting the raids, and standing up for their rights. It was a big step for them. Just a few months earlier, Stark had been worried he would be spotted walking into a gay bar. Now, they were both proudly demonstrating in public. "Quite frankly, we didn't care if our bosses and coworkers learned of our participation. It was a very important first step in our public advocacy.... There was no turning back."

The Michaels would attend Pride every year after that, watching the protests grow and evolve. Even as progress was made, there was always a lot more work to be done — and there still is. Despite public apologies, periodic police raids against queer spaces have continued in recent years, a century and a half after the Morality Squad was formed. A serial killer preyed on gay men in the Village for nearly a decade while police turned a deaf ear to the community. Pride itself faced internal turmoil after Black Lives Matter organizers protested police involvement in the big Sunday parade. More than two hundred years after the city was founded, there are still plenty of people in Toronto who want to enforce strict limits on love.

But progress was being made. Important victories were being won. The event became more of a celebration with every landmark win, and as more and more Torontonians came out of the closet. By the time the fight for gay marriage had finally been won, the old bathhouse protests had been transformed into a massive, week-long party attracting throngs of people every year. Pride was not just a celebration of the progress that had been made, but a chance to proudly stand up in public, in full view, after centuries of being forced into the shadows. In time, the crowds grew from thousands to tens of thousands and then to hundreds of thousands. It's now one of the biggest events in the city.

The 2003 edition was a particularly special one. Pride came just two weeks after the big court victory on marriage. Scores of couples were flocking to Toronto from around the world, eager to get married in one of the few places on earth where those marriages were legally recognized.

It was a hot Sunday afternoon at the end of June when the big parade got underway. The sun beamed down on the huge crowds of people gathered along Yonge Street in the heat. The land that had once been home to Alexander Wood's forest was now draped in rainbows, alive with the sound of techno music. People danced, waved flags, and shot confetti, streamers, and water guns into the air. And there in the middle of the celebration, rolling down Yonge Street in the back of a blue convertible, their faces painted in a rainbow of colour, were Michael Stark and Michael Leshner. Newlyweds after twenty-two years.

Every time they kissed, the crowd cheered.

EPILOGUE: THE ONGOING HISTORY OF KISSING IN TORONTO

Chris Kay Fraser was riding the Queen streetcar when the idea came to her. It was a miserably grey spring day in 2011. She was grumpy and cold; the ride was slow and frustrating. But as the streetcar rumbled and screeched along the tracks, Fraser suddenly found herself transported back in time. "I glanced out the mud-splattered window and realized that we were passing a street corner ... where I'd had a ground-shaking kiss years and years earlier. I felt my whole body soften, remembering the tenderness of that moment. *God*, I thought. *If only I could always see the city that way.*"

That night, the writing teacher began a new project. She created a Google Map, using it to document her most memorable kisses in locations across the city. When she was done, she opened it up to others — anyone who wanted to contribute was welcome. The Toronto Kiss Map quickly filled with hundreds of anonymous entries:

first kisses, last kisses, hot and heavy make-out sessions. It became an interactive romantic survey of the city, tying stories of love, lust, and heartbreak to the places where intimate moments were shared.

"Escalator to the Subway," one entry begins, pinned to Bloor-Yonge station. "After our first date. I wasn't sure if you were going to go for it, so I rose up on my toes, leaned in and kissed you first. It was quick and electric. Then I skipped off through the turnstile, grinning like mad, and excited for what the future might hold."

Another kiss is pinned to the big hill in Riverdale Park. "I had no idea where this thing between us was going. I liked you. I could tell you liked me. But we were stumbling over stories and small talk with plastic take-out trays piled between us in the grass. Nervous. The sunset was just starting when you leaned in and whispered 'Wanna roll?' and then your arms were around me and we were careening down, down, laughing uncontrollably while the pink sky somersaulted over us again and again. At the very bottom, you kissed me. Soft and wild and perfect."

The city is covered in kisses. As the map shows, nearly everyone has their own mental atlas of romantic landmarks from their past: the bars, bedrooms, parks, and bus stops where their breath grew quick and their stomach fluttered as they leaned in for a kiss. It's the psychogeography of love. And it's nothing new. It's been happening ever since the city was founded, and for thousands of years before that.

Even the most famous public landmarks are intensely personal places; they've been the sites of tender moments for countless couples and become part of the romantic architecture of their relationships. Take Old City Hall, where the sex worker and petty criminal Lizzie Lessard was put on trial for the umpteenth time in 1905; on this occasion, she'd stolen a fur muff and some hats from the Eaton's department store. As she was led out of the courtroom for yet another stint behind bars at the Mercer Reformatory, she delivered a resounding smooch on the lips to one of her fellow prisoners: a kiss so prodigious it left the *Toronto Daily Star* amazed.

"There are kisses at weddings, there are kisses of farewell as the train is pulling out — but louder and more fervent than all of these was the smack to-day in court," the newspaper told its readers. "Some kisses are sweet as cider fresh from the bunghole, some kisses are like the report of an elephant pulling a foot out of the mud. Of the second variety was the kiss to-day in court. Smack!" The staff inspector was startled by the sound; he looked around as if a gun had just been fired. "But there was no gun — Lizzie Lessard had simply kissed her prison companion, John Kelly, as she bade him farewell in the dock, before leaving for the Mercer."

Just down Bay Street, Union Station may have witnessed more kisses than any other building in Toronto since it opened nearly a century ago. It's the busiest transportation hub in Canada, with hundreds of thousands of travellers passing through it every day. As a place of arrival and departure, it has been the scene of many joyful greetings and teary farewells. During the Second World War, soldiers gave their sweethearts one last kiss before their train headed off to Halifax, where a ship to the battlefields of Europe was waiting for them. And while some of them would never come home, many of those who did returned to Union Station, where their sweethearts were waiting to kiss them once again.

Those returning troops were soon followed by trains filled with young women: "war brides," most of them British, who'd fallen in love with Canadian soldiers and married them overseas. The Canadian Wives' Bureau was created to assist them, and the Red Cross was waiting for them at Union Station to give them a cup of tea and help them find their husbands. Some of the women didn't recognize their new Canadian spouses as they searched for them among the crowds, never having seen them out of uniform before. But when they were finally reunited, they must have kissed them with a potent mix of excitement and trepidation.

Some kisses have changed the city. During the winter of 1976, two men were arrested for kissing on the corner of Yonge and Bloor streets. Tom Field and Bill Holloway were being photographed for a newspaper article about homophobia when the police showed up. The men were found guilty of committing an indecent act and obstructing the sidewalk. When the verdict came down that summer, a "kiss-in" was held at the same intersection: twenty gay and lesbian couples marched and kissed in protest. A few years later, activists were thrown out of the provincial legislature at Queen's Park while kissing and holding hands in the public gallery as part of a "mince-in" for gay rights.

Two decades after that, the Michaels were featured on the front page of the *Star*, kissing at the press conference where they got engaged.

Romances have helped shape the city we live in. They've changed the course of its history. And the Toronto Kiss Map is a reminder of the fact that that history is still being written. More than two hundred years after John Graves Simcoe tried to ensure that only Anglicans could get married in his new province, the evolution of attitudes toward romance and sexuality continues. Toronto is now a place where many couples choose not to get married, where dating apps have changed the way people meet, where some are becoming more open about polyamory and open relationships, where there's a growing awareness of asexuality, and where the vital importance of consent and the dismantling of rape culture have become major topics of public discussion. More than ever before, people are recognizing that romance and sexuality mean something different to everyone. Everyone has their own unique love stories.

You can add your own kisses to the Toronto Kiss Map. You can share your own intimate memories of the places where your heart beat quick as your lips pressed up against someone else's. Your own love stories can take their place among those shared by hundreds of others. Everyone's tales of infatuation, devotion, and heartache are part of the romantic landscape of Toronto.

A city is a collective endeavour. And it's made of more than just bricks and mortar; it's also built of much more ephemeral things. It's made with high-school crushes and first dates, with Valentine's Day cards and anniversary gifts, with a swipe to the right on a dating app or a flirtatious text, with hands nervously inching toward each other over a movie-theatre armrest and the thrill of an undone zipper or an unclasped bra. "Imagine how it would create a new view of this city," Fraser wrote when she was just beginning her map, "not of cold and concrete, but as a place of connection, softness, and tiny moments of love."

Toronto is as much a city of romance, heartache, and passion as of skyscrapers, sewers, and roads. Newlywed Wendat villagers, lovestruck politicians, and adulterous movie stars have all left their mark. The city stands as a towering monument to the loves and lusts of those who've called it home. And it is still being built today, by millions of people, not just with cranes and bulldozers, but with every held hand, with every love letter, and with every kiss.

ACKNOWLEDGEMENTS

The Toronto Book of Love was written on and about the traditional territories of the Wendat, Haudenosaunee, and Anishinaabe (most recently the Mississaugas of the New Credit First Nation) Peoples.

It was also completed and edited during the spring and summer of 2020: historic months that were defined by the COVID-19 pandemic and Black Lives Matter protests. So, I'd like to express my heartfelt appreciation to the health care professionals around the world who have been hard at work saving lives, including my sister, Megan Bunch, at the Hospital for Sick Children. And to all those fighting for equality and justice.

I would like to sincerely thank everyone at Dundurn Press who has been so encouraging of this book and who have worked so hard to make it a reality. I would especially like to thank my editor, Dominic Farrell, as well as project editor Jenny McWha, associate publisher Kathryn Lane, art director Laura Boyle, and president and publisher Scott Fraser.

Researching during the COVID lockdown was a unique and sometimes frustrating experience. With libraries and museums closed, I wasn't always able to conduct research in person. So I'm very thankful to all those who took the time to answer my questions over email: John Shoesmith at the Thomas Fisher Rare Book Library, Beau Levitt at the Toronto Reference Library, Carolyn Wong and Kathryn Money with the Friends of Trinity Bellwoods Park, Karen Edwards at Spadina House, Amanda Gallagher and Pat Neal at the Uxbridge Historical Centre, Benjamin Wolff at the Canadian War Museum, and Nathan Parkinson at the Kim Foundation International.

I am deeply grateful to the Michaels — Michael Stark and Michael Leshner — for taking the time to share their story with me, to Lilian Rosenthal, who was kind enough to send me information about her miracle mother, and to Chris Kay Fraser for answering my questions about the Toronto Kiss Map.

This book owes a deep debt to all the librarians, archivists, researchers, heritage workers, and history writers whose work makes a project like this possible. *The Toronto Book of Love* simply wouldn't exist without the city's heritage community. Thank you in particular to Adrianna Prosser and Michael Shelbourne for tipping me off to Anne Powell's tragic shipwreck, to Mark Osbaldeston for adding some detail to the story of the protests outside Elizabeth Taylor's love nest, to Richard Fiennes-Clinton for his excellent lecture about John Howard's secrets at Colborne Lodge, to Linda Grandfield for sharing her knowledge of war brides, to Chris Tindal for bringing my attention to the romantic history of the

Wendats, and to Natasha Henry for her vital research into the history of slavery in Toronto.

I am eternally grateful to *Spacing* magazine and its co-founders, Shawn Micallef and Matthew Blackett, for giving my writing about the history of the city, including a few stories that appear in this book, an early home. And I'm terrifically lucky that I get to work with storytellers as passionate and dedicated as Ashley Brook and Kyle Cucco on our *Canadiana* documentary series.

The last few hours before the COVID lockdown began were a mad scramble to borrow as many library books as possible from branches across the city. Carmen Cheung and Nicholas Van Exan aren't just wonderfully supportive friends, they also borrowed some books on my behalf during those final hours. *The Toronto Book of Love* contains some facts I wouldn't have known otherwise. Thank you to Melissa Hughes for her feedback on a few of the stories I've included, to Laurie McGregor, Cody McGraw, Matthew Ivanowich, and Christina Ivanowich for their friendship and support during the writing of this book, and to Maximus Peppercorn Brown and George Van Cheung, too.

It's from my family that I learned to love books, storytelling, and history. And so, I give a huge, loving thank you to my mom and dad, and to all the Bunches and Masseys who've shared their stories in the reading room every Christmas Eve since I was little. And to Mr. Boyd, Mr. Mackenzie, Ms. Kapour, and Mr. Scott, who helped to develop that interest in history.

And finally, to my own love: Amy Brown. As you are very well aware, no one has had to listen to me ramble on about the stories in this book more than you have. You've given me invaluable advice and feedback every step of the way; you've helped make this book what it is. You've kept me sane and happy while writing and editing day after day during one of the most challenging years in recent human history, locked up together inside for so much of it. I love you. And I can think of no better way to thank you than this: *The Toronto Book of Love* is, now and forever, dedicated to you.

SELECTED BIBLIOGRAPHY & FURTHER READING

INTRODUCTION

"Relics of ages ago." *Globe and Mail*, December 15, 1908.

Scrivener, Leslie. "The Enigma of Lake Ontario's 11,000 year-old Footprints." *Toronto Star*, November 23, 2008. Accessed June 3, 2020. thestar.com/news/insight/2008/11/23/the_enigma_of_lake_ontarios_11000yearold_footprints.html.

Williamson, Ron F., ed. *Toronto: A Short Illustrated History of Its First 12,000 Years*. Toronto: James Lorimer, 2008.

Williamson, Ron, and Robert I. Macdonald. "A Resource Like No Other: Understanding the 11,000 year-old Relationship Between People and Water." In *HTO: Toronto's Water from Lake Iroquois to Lost Rivers to Low-flow Toilets*, edited by Wayne Reeves and Christina Palassio, 42–51. Toronto: Coach House, 2008.

1. A TORCH IN THE NIGHT

Canadian Museum of History. "The Explorers: Louis-Armand de Lom d'Arce, Baron Lahontan 1684–1689." Accessed April 6, 2020. historymuseum.ca/virtual-

museum-of-new-france/the-explorers/louis-armand
-de-lom-darce-baron-lahontan-1684-1689.

Hayne, David M. "Lom d'Arce de Lahontan, Louis-Armand de,
Baron de Lahontan." *Dictionary of Canadian Biography.*
Accessed May 24, 2020. biographi.ca/en/bio/lom_d_arce_de_
lahontan_louis_armand_de_2E.html.

Labelle, Kathryn Magee. *Dispersed But Not Destroyed: A History
of the Seventeenth-Century Wendat People.* Vancouver: UBC
Press, 2013.

Lahontan, Louis Armand de Lom d'Arce, baron de. *New voyages to
North-America: giving a full account of the customs, commerce,
religion, and strange opinions of the savages of that country with
political remarks upon the courts of Portugal and Denmark and
the present state of the commerce of those countries.* London: H.
Bonwicke, 1703.

Lizars, Kathleen Macfarlane. *The Valley of the Humber 1615–1913.*
Toronto: W. Briggs, 1913.

Plummer, Kevin. "Historicist: Unearthing the Alexandra
Site's Pre-Contact Past." *Torontoist*, November 22,
2008. Accessed April 6, 2020. torontoist.com/2008/11/
historicist_unearthing_the_alexandr.

Sioui, Georges E. *Huron-Wendat: The Heritage of the Circle.*
Vancouver: UBC Press, 1999.

Smith, Dennis. "Toronto Feature: Huron-Wendat Village."
Canadian Encyclopedia, February 4, 2015. Last modified July 2, 2015. Thecanadianencyclopedia.ca/en/article/
obert-feature-huron-wendat-village.

"Thomas Fisher Rare Books Library." University of Toronto
Libraries.Accessed May 24, 2020. fisher.library.utoronto.ca.

Tindal, Chris. "The Sex-Positive Huron-Wendat." *Acres of Snow.*

February 11, 2017. Accessed April 6, 2020. acresofsnow.ca/
the-sex-positive-huron-wendat.

Trigger, Bruce G. *The Children of Aataentsic: A History of the Huron
People to 1660*. Montreal: McGill-Queen's University Press,
1987.

Williamson, Ron F., ed. *Toronto: A Short Illustrated History of Its
First 12,000 Years*. Toronto: James Lorimer, 2008.

2. SCANDALS OF THE FRENCH EMPIRE

Canadian Museum of History. "The Explorers: Louis Hennepin
1678–1680." Accessed May 28, 2020. Historymuseum.
ca/virtual-museum-of-new-france/the-explorers/
louis-hennepin-1678-1680.

Costain, Thomas B. "The Mad Visions of La Salle." *Maclean's*,
September 15, 1954. Accessed May 23, 2020. archive.macleans.
ca/article/1954/9/15/the-mad-visions-of-la-salle.

Dupré, Céline. "Cavalier de la Salle, René-Robert." *Dictionary of
Canadian Biography*. Accessed March 15, 2020. Biographi.ca/
en/bio/obertr_de_la_salle_rene_robert_1E.html.

Dupré, Céline. "Roybon d'Allonne, Madeleine de." *Dictionary of
Canadian Biography*. Accessed May 22, 2020. Biographi.ca/en/
bio/roybon_d_allonne_madeleine_de_2E.html.

Eccles, William John. "René-Robert Cavalier de la Salle."
Canadian Encyclopedia, January 7, 2008. Last modified
March 4, 2015. Thecanadianencyclopedia.ca/en/article/
rene-robert-cavelier-de-la-salle.

Eccles, W.J. "Buade, Louis de, Comte de Frontenac et de Palluau."
Dictionary of Canadian Biography. Accessed March 6, 2020.
Biographi.ca/en/bio/buade_de_frontenac_et_de_palluau_
louis_de_1E.html.

———. *Frontenac: The Courtier Governor.* Lincoln: University of Nebraska Press, 2003.

Fischer, David Hackett. *Champlain's Dream: The European Founding of North America.* New York: Simon & Schuster, 2008.

Fox, Haleigh. "Teiaiagon: History of a 17th Century Haudenosaunee Village." *First Story.* Accessed May 16, 2020. firststoryblog.wordpress.com/2013/10/30/teiaiagon-history-of-a-17th-century-haudenosaunee-village.

Levine, Allan. *Toronto: Biography of a City.* Vancouver: Douglas & McIntyre, 2014.

Lizars, Kathleen Macfarlane. *The Valley of the Humber 1615–1913.* Toronto: W. Briggs, 1913.

Marsh, James H. "Toronto Feature: Teiaiagon Seneca Village." *Canadian Encyclopedia*, February 4, 2013. Last modified July 2, 2015. thecanadianencyclopedia.ca/en/article/toronto-feature-teiaiagon-seneca-village.

Muhlstein, Anka. *La Salle: Explorer of the North American Frontier.* Translated by Willard Wood. New York: Arcade, 1994.

Ontario Heritage Trust. "Samuel de Champlain: Perspectives." Accessed August 12, 2020. heritagetrust.on.ca/en/pages/our-stories/exhibits/samuel-de-champlain.

Osler, E.B. "Tonty, Henri (de)." *Dictionary of Canadian Biography.* Accessed May 28, 2020. biographi.ca/en/bio/tonty_henri_2E.html.

Parkman, Francis. *Count Frontenac and New France under Louis XIV.* Boston: Little, Brown, 1877.

Quinn, David Beers. "Henri Quatre and New France." *Terrae Incognitae* 22 (1990): 13–28.

Robinson, Percy James. *Toronto During the French Regime: A History of the Toronto Region from Brule to Simcoe, 1615–1793*. Toronto: University of Toronto Press, 1965.

Tindal, Chris. "Life in Wendake vs. Life in France." *Acres of Snow*, December 10, 2017. Accessed August 12, 2020. acresofsnow.ca/life-in-wendake-vs-life-in-france.

Trigger, Bruce G. *The Children of Aataentsic: A History of the Huron People to 1660*. Montreal: McGill-Queen's University Press, 1987.

Wencer, David. "Historicist: The Village of Teiaiagon." *Torontoist*, June 20, 2015. Accessed December 15, 2015. torontoist. com/2015/06/historicist-the-village-of-teiaiagon.

Wien, Tom, and Suzanne Gousse. "Filles du Roi." *Canadian Encyclopedia*, December 6, 2011. Last modified February 24, 2015. thecanadianencyclopedia.ca/en/article/filles-du-roi.

Wilson, William R. "Louis de Buade, Comte Frontenac." *Historical Narratives of Early Canada*. Accessed March 6, 2020. uppercanadahistory.ca/finna/finna4a.html.

3. FOUR WEDDINGS & A FUR TRADER

Arthur, Eric. *No Mean City*. Revised by Stephen A. Otto. Toronto: University of Toronto Press, 1986.

Benn, Carl. "Fort Rouillé an Outpost of French Diplomacy and Trade." *Fife and Drum* 22, no. 1 (April 2018).

Carlos, Ann M., and Frank D. Lewis. "The Economic History of the Fur Trade: 1670 to 1870." *EH.net*. Accessed April 30, 2020. eh.net/encyclopedia/ the-economic-history-of-the-fur-trade-1670-to-1870.

Cataraqui Archaeological Research Foundation. "Molly Brant." Accessed May 16, 2020. carf.info/kingston-past/molly-brant.

Conn, Heather. "Mary Brant (Konwatsi'tsiaiénni)." *Canadian Encyclopedia*, January 30, 2008. Last modified August 20, 2019. thecanadianencyclopedia.ca/en/article/mary-brant.

Edwards, Peter. "Shrugs Greet Historic $145 Million Toronto Land Claim Settlement." *Toronto Star*, June 8, 2010.

Freeman, Victoria Jane. "Toronto Has No History!: Indigeneity, Settler Colonialism and Historical Memory in Canada's Largest City." Ph.D. diss., University of Toronto, 2010.

Gaudry, Adam. "Métis." *Canadian Encyclopedia*, January 7, 2009. Last modified September 11, 2019. thecanadianencyclopedia.ca/en/article/metis.

Graymont, Barbara. "Koñwatsi'tsiaiéñni." *Dictionary of Canadian Biography*. Accessed May 16, 2020. biographi.ca/en/bio/konwatsitsiaienni_4E.html.

———. "Thayendanegea." *Dictionary of Canadian Biography*. Accessed May 16, 2020. biographi.ca/en/bio/thayendanegea_5E.html.

Hall, Anthony J. "Royal Proclamation of 1763." *Canadian Encyclopedia*, February 7, 2006. Last modified July 23, 2015. thecanadianencyclopedia.ca/en/article/royal-proclamation-of-1763.

Haudenosaunee Confederacy. "The League of Nations." Accessed April 30, 2020. haudenosauneeconfederacy.com/the-league-of-nations.

Haudenosaunee Confederacy. "Who We Are." Accessed April 30, 2020. haudenosauneeconfederacy.com/who-we-are.

Hemmings, David F. *Fort Niagara — 1759–1815*. Niagara: Niagara on the Lake Museum, 2012. Accessed April 30, 2020. nhsm.ca/media/02FortNiagara.pdf.

Johnston, Charles M. "Rousseaux St John, John Baptist." *Dictionary of Canadian Biography*. Accessed April 5, 2020. biographi.ca/

en/bio/rousseaux_st_john_john_baptist_5E.html.

Karcich, Grant. "Jean Baptiste Rousseau's Trading Posts on Lake
    Ontario." *Ontario Professional Surveyor* (Summer 2018).

Levine, Allan. *Toronto: Biography of a City.* Vancouver: Douglas &
    McIntyre, 2014.

Lizars, Kathleen Macfarlane. *The Valley of the Humber 1615–1913.*
    Toronto: W. Briggs, 1913.

Louis Riel Institute. "Women of the Fur Trade." Accessed May 16,
    2020. louisrielinstitute.com/women-of-the-fur-trade.php.

MacIntosh, Robert M. *Earliest Toronto.* Renfrew, ON: General Store:
    2006.

Robertson, John Ross. *Robertson's Landmarks of Toronto.* Toronto:
    John Ross Robertson, 1908.

Robinson, Percy James. *Toronto During the French Regime: A History
    of the Toronto Region from Brule to Simcoe, 1615–1793.* Toronto:
    University of Toronto Press, 1965.

Scadding, Henry. *Toronto of Old.* Toronto: Adam, Stevenson, 1873.

Smith, Donald B. "Jones, Augustus." *Dictionary of Canadian
    Biography.* Accessed May 16, 2020. biographi.ca/en/bio/jones_
    augustus_7E.html.

Stones. "Molly Brant." Accessed May 16, 2020. stoneskingston.ca/
    indigenous-history/molly-brant.

Turner, Glenn. *The Toronto Carrying Place: Rediscovering Toronto's
    Most Ancient Trail.* Toronto: Dundurn, 2015.

Walden, Keith. *Becoming Modern in Toronto: The Industrial
    Exhibition and the Shaping of a Late Victorian Culture.* Toronto:
    University of Toronto Press, 1997.

4. THE FIRES OF ELIZABETH SIMCOE

"An Ancient Valentine." *The Canadian Antiquarian and Numismatic Journal*, 3 (1874).

Archives of Ontario. "Travels with Elizabeth Simcoe: A Visual Journey Through Upper and Lower Canada." Accessed May 4, 2020. archives.gov.on.ca/en/explore/online/simcoe/index.aspx.

Brunger, Alan G. "Talbot, Thomas." *Dictionary of Canadian Biography*. Accessed November 3, 2019. biographi.ca/en/bio/talbot_thomas_8E.html.

Firth, Edith G. "Gwillim, Elizabeth Posthuma (Simcoe)." *Dictionary of Canadian Biography*. Accessed January 2014. biographi.ca/en/bio/gwillim_elizabeth_posthuma_7E.html.

Fowler, Marian. *The Embroidered Tent: Five Gentlewomen in Early Canada*. Toronto: House of Anansi, 1994.

Fryer, Mary Beacock. *Elizabeth Postuma Simcoe, 1762–1850: A Biography*. Toronto: Dundurn Press, 1989.

Fryer, Mary Beacock, and Christopher Dracott. *John Graves Simcoe, 1752–1806: A Biography*. Toronto: Dundurn Press, 1998.

Grazley, Robin Christine. "Nothing 'Improper' Happened: Sex, Marriage, and Colonial Identity in Upper Canada, 1783–1850." Ph.D. diss., Queen's University, 2010.

Jameson, Anna. *Winter Studies and Summer Rambles in Canada*. London: Penguin, 1838.

Kilmeade, Brian, and Don Yeager. *George Washington's Secret Six: The Spy Ring That Saved the American Revolution*. London: Penguin, 2013.

McLaughlin, Florence. *First Lady of Upper Canada*. Burns & MacEachern, 1968.

Mealing, S.R. "Simcoe, John Graves." *Dictionary of Canadian Biography*. Accessed January 2014. biographi.ca/en/bio/simcoe_john_graves_5E.html.

Mealing, Stanley R. "John Graves Simcoe." *Canadian Encyclopedia*,
    February 7, 2006. Last modified February 1, 2017.
    thecanadianencyclopedia.ca/en/article/john-graves-simcoe.

Parker, Ann Gwillim. *The Extraordinary Lives of Elizabeth Posthuma
    Gwillim & John Graves Simcoe*. Whitchurch: Whitchurch
    Parochial Church Council, 2004.

Rathner, John. "Remembering a Master Spy at Home." *New York
    Times*, December 15, 1985.

Raynham Hall Museum. "American's First Valentine." Accessed
    April 4, 2020. raynhamhallmuseum.org/history/first-valentine.

Simcoe, Elizabeth. *Mrs. Simcoe's Diary*. Edited by Mary Quayle
    Innis. Toronto: Macmillan, 1965.

Simcoe, John Graves. *Letter to Sir Joseph Banks, (President of the Royal
    Society of Great Britain) Written by Lieut.-Governor Simcoe, in 1791,
    Prior to His Departure from England for the Purpose of Organizing
    the New Province of Upper Canada; to Which Is Added Five Official
    Speeches Delivered by Him at the Opening or Closing of Parliament
    in the Same Province*. Edited by Henry Scadding. Toronto: Copp
    Clark, 1890.

Tasker, L.H. *The United Empire Loyalist Settlement at Long Point,
    Lake Erie*. Toronto: W. Briggs, 1900.

Villemaire, Tom. "First Valentine's Card Courtesy of John Simcoe."
    Simcoe.com. February 14, 2018. simcoe.com/community-
    story/8122563-first-valentine-s-card-courtesy-of-john-simcoe.

Wainwright, Kaitlin. "Historicist: Elizabeth Simcoe, A Toronto
    Pioneer." *Torontoist*, July 30, 2016. Accessed May 4, 2020.

Wesley, Bathsheba Susannah. "Finding the Sublime: Assessing
    Elizabeth Simcoe's Fires as an Art Practice." M.A. thesis,
    Concordia University, 2008. spectrum.library.concordia
    .ca/976091/1/MR45353.pdf.

Wilson, William R. "John Graves Simcoe." *Historical Narratives of Early Canada*. Accessed April 4, 2020. uppercanadahistory.ca/simcoe/simcoe1.html.

5. THE NEW YEAR'S DUEL

Bercham, F.R. (Hamish). *The Yonge Street Story, 1793–1860*. Toronto: Dundurn Press, 1996.

Fiennes-Clinton, Richard. "John Small, John White & The Fatal Christmas Party of 1799." *Toronto Then and Now*, December 24, 2015. Accessed January 6, 2018. torontothenandnow.blogspot.com/2015/12/64-john-small-john-white-fatal.html.

"First Treasurer John White Killed in a Duel." *Law Society of Ontario*. Accessed January 6, 2018. lso.ca/about-lso/osgoode-hall-and-ontario-legal-heritage/exhibitions-and-virtual-museum/historical-vignettes/people/first-treasurer-john-white-killed-in-a-duel.

Firth, Edith G. "White, John." *Dictionary of Canadian Biography*. Accessed January 6, 2018. biographi.ca/en/bio/white_john_1800_4E.html.

Kieman, Victor. *The Duel in European History: Honour and the Reign of Aristocracy*. London: Zed, 2016.

Levine, Allan. *Toronto: Biography of a City*. Vancouver: Douglas & McIntyre, 2014.

Lost Rivers. "First Parliament Buildings." Accessed January 6, 2018. lostrivers.ca/points/firstparliament.htm.

McKenna, Katherine M.J. *A Life of Propriety: Anne Murray Powell and Her Family, 1755–1849*. Montreal: McGill-Queen's University Press, 1994.

Mealing, S.R. "Small, John." *Dictionary of Canadian Biography*. Accessed January 6, 2018. biographi.ca/en/bio/small_john_6E.html.

Riddell, William Renwick. "The Duel in Early Upper Canada." *Journal of Criminal Law and Criminology* 6, no. 2 (1915): 165–76.

6. A DANGEROUS CHARIVARI

Beauchamp, Zack. "Why Are the French Always Protesting? Blame Unions and History." *Vox*, July 6, 2015. Accessed May 15, 2020. vox.com/2015/7/6/8887667/france-protest.

Combis, Hélène. "De la Monarchie de Juillet à François Fillon, Petite Histoire de la Casserole Comme Outil Politique." *France Culture*, March 3, 2017. Accessed May 15, 2020. franceculture .fr/histoire/de-la-monarchie-de-juillet-francois-fillon-petite-histoire-de-la-casserole-comme-outil.

C.W. Jeffreys. "The French Royalist Colony." Accessed November 16, 2019. cwjefferys.ca/the-french-royalist-colony.

Davis-Fisch, Heather. "Lawless Lawyers: Indigeneity, Civility, and Violence." *TRIC/RTAC* 35.1 (Spring 2014): 31–48.

Dooner, Alfred. "The Windham or 'Oak Ridges' Settlement of French Royalist Refugees in York County, Upper Canada, 1798." *The Canadian Catholic Historical Association*, Report 7 (1939–1940).

Firth, Edith G. *The Town of York 1793–1815: A Collection of Documents of Early Toronto.* Toronto: University of Toronto Press, 1962.

———. "Willcocks, William." *Dictionary of Canadian Biography.* Accessed November 16, 2019. biographi.ca/en/bio/willcocks_william_5E.html.

Gabbatt, Adam. "Montreal's 'Casseroles' Cook Up a Storm over Quebec's Anti-Protest Law." *Guardian*, May 26, 2012. Accessed May 15, 2020. theguardian.com/world/2012/may/26/montreal-casseroles-student-protests.

Grazley, Robin Christine. "Nothing 'Improper' Happened: Sex, Marriage, and Colonial Identity in Upper Canada, 1783–1850." Ph.D. diss., Queen's University, 2010.

Greenhill, Pauline. "Make the Night Hideous: Death at a Manitoba Charivari, 1909." *Manitoba History*, no. 52 (June 2006).

———. *Make the Night Hideous: Four English-Canadian Charivaris, 1881–1940*. Toronto: University of Toronto Press, 2010.

Jaenen, Cornelius J., ed. *Les Franco-Ontariens*. Ottawa: University of Ottawa Press, 1993.

Janetsky, Megan. "Kitchenware Cacophony: How 'Cacerolazos' Became the Symbol of Colombia's Anti-Government Protests." *The World*, November 26, 2019. Accessed May 15, 2020. pri .org/stories/2019-11-26/kitchenware-cacophony-how-cacerolazos-became-symbol-colombia-s-anti-government.

Molina, José Carpintero, Fernanda Canofre, and Mong Palatino. "From Brazil to Kosovo to the Philippines, Confined Citizens Protest from Their Windows." *GlobalVoices*, April 14, 2020. Accessed May 15, 2020. globalvoices.org/2020/04/14/from-brazil-to-kosovo-to-the-philippines-confined-citizens-protest-from-their-windows.

Moodie, Susanna. *Roughing It in the Bush*. Toronto: Maclear, 1871.

Palmer, Bryan D. *Marxism and Historical Practice: Interpretive Essays on Class Formation and Class Struggle,* vol. I. Leiden: Brill, 2015.

Paradkar, Shree. "Why the COVID-19 Pandemic Has Pots and Pans Clanging with the Sounds of Defiance." *Toronto Star*, March 23, 2020. Accessed May 15, 2020. thestar.com/opinion/2020/03/23/why-the-covid-19-pandemic-has-pots-and-pans-clanging-with-the-sounds-of-defiance.html.

Robertson, John Ross. *Robertson's Landmarks of Toronto*. Toronto:

John Ross Robertson, 1908.

Scadding, Henry. *Toronto of Old*. Toronto: Adam, Stevenson, 1873.

Scherck, Michael Gonder. *Pen Pictures of Early Pioneer Life in Upper Canada*. Toronto: W. Briggs, 1905.

Thorning, Stephen. "Elora Woman Left Town After Two-Day Charivari." *Wellington Advertiser*. Accessed May 15, 2020. wellingtonadvertiser.com/elora-woman-left-town-after -two-day-charivari.

7. SHIPWRECKS & DISGRACE

Brode, Patrick. *Courted and Abandoned: Seduction in Canadian Law*. Toronto: University of Toronto Press, 2002.

———. "Powell, Anne." *Dictionary of Canadian Biography*. Accessed March 23, 2020. biographi.ca/en/bio/powell_anne_6E.html.

Craig, Gerald M. *Upper Canada: The Formative Years, 1784–1841*. Don Mills: Oxford University Press, 1963.

Firth, Edith G. "Murray, Anne (Powell.)" *Dictionary of Canadian Biography*. Accessed March 23, 2020. biographi.ca/en/bio/ murray_anne_7E.html.

Jones, Donald. *Fifty Tales of Toronto*. Toronto: University of Toronto Press, 1992.

Lost Rivers "Caer Howell." Accessed April 26, 2020. lostrivers.ca/ content/points/caerhowell.html.

McCalla, Douglas. "Quetton St George, Laurent." *Dictionary of Canadian Biography*. Accessed March 28, 2020. biographi.ca/ en/bio/quetton_st_george_laurent_6E.html.

McKenna, Katherine M.J. *A Life of Propriety: Anne Murray Powell and Her Family, 1755–1849*. Montreal: McGill-Queen's University Press, 1994.

Mealing, S.R. "Gore, Francis." *Dictionary of Canadian Biography*.

Accessed March 23, 2020. biographi.ca/en/bio/gore_francis_8E
.html.

———. "Powell, William Drummer." *Dictionary of Canadian
Biography.* Accessed March 23, 2020. biographi.ca/en/bio/powell
_william_dummer_6E.html.

Mills, David. "Sir John Beverley Robinson." *Canadian Encyclopedia*,
January 22, 2008. Last modified March 4, 2015.
thecanadianencyclopedia.ca/en/article/sir-john-beverley-robinson.

Powell, Anne Murray. *Letters of Mrs. Wm. Drummer Powell,
1807–1821.* Niagara: Times Print, 1905.

Riddell, William Renwick. *The Life of William Drummer Powell.*
Lansing: Michigan Historical Commission, 1924.

Robertson, John Ross. *Robertson's Landmarks of Toronto.* Toronto:
John Ross Robertson, 1908.

Saunders, Robert E. "Robinson, Sir John Beverley." *Dictionary of
Canadian Biography.* Accessed March 23, 2020. Biographi.ca/
en/bio/robinson_john_beverley_9E.html.

Selin, Shannon. "The Wreck of the Packet Ship *Albion*." Shannon
Selin: Imagining the Bounds of History. Accessed May 14, 2020.
shannonselin.com/2017/04/wreck-packet-ship-albion/.

Thomas, R. *Interesting and Authentic Narratives of the Most
Remarkable Shipwrecks, Fires, Famines, Calamities, Providential
Deliverances, and Lamentable Disasters on the Seas, in Most Parts
of the World.* New York: Ezra Strong, 1837.

8. THE INSPECTOR GENERAL OF PRIVATE ACCOUNTS

Adamson, Ryan. "Complicating Queer Space in Toronto: How
the Development of Toronto's LGBTQ2I Space Fits within Heteronormative and Homonationalist Scripts." York
University, 2017.

Bredin, Simon. "Meet Alexander Wood, the Pioneer of
    Toronto's Gay Village." *Torontoist*, June 29, 2016.
    Accessed March 3, 2020. torontoist.com/2016/06/
    meet-alexander-wood-the-pioneer-of-torontos-gay-village.

Craig, G.M. "Strachan, John." *Dictionary of Canadian Biography.*
    Accessed March 4, 2020. Biographi.ca/en/bio/trachan_john_9E
    .html.

Firth, Edith G. "Wood, Alexander." *Dictionary of Canadian
    Biography.* Accessed March 3, 2020. Biographi.ca/en/
    bio.php?id_nbr=3734.

Goldie, Terry. *In A Queen Country: Gay & Lesbian Studies in the
    Canadian Context.* Vancouver: Arsenal Pulp, 2001.

Idlewild, Astrid. "From Molly Wood's Bush to the Gaybourhood:
    a Historical Narrative." *Accozzaglia*, June 21, 2016. Accessed
    March 4, 2020. accozzaglia.ca/essay/research/geography/
    from-molly-woods-bush-to-the-gaybourhood.

Jackson, Ed. "Alexander Wood: The Invention of a Legend." In
    Any Other Way: How Toronto Got Queer, edited by Stephanie
    Chambers, Jane Farrow, Maureen FitzGerald, Ed Jackson, John
    Lorinc, Tim McCaskell, Rebecka Sheffield, Tatum Taylor and
    Rahim Thawer, 91–95. Toronto: Coach House, 2017.

Lyons, Michael. "Molly Wood's Bush: Deconstructing the Legend
    of Alexander Wood." *Xtra*, March 2, 2014. Accessed March 4,
    2020. Dailyxtra.com/molly-woods-bush-58425.

Powell, William Drummer. *A Letter from W.D. Powell, Chief Justice, to
    Sir Peregrine Maitland, Lieutenant-Governor of Upper Canada,
    Regarding the Appointment of Alexander Wood as Commissioner for
    the Investigation of Claims.* Edmonton: University of Alberta, 1986.

Proulx, Shaun. "Tall, Bronzed Man Moves to Gay Village." *Globe and
    Mail*, May 21, 2005. Accessed March 3, 2020. theglobeandmail

.com/news/national/tall-bronzed-man-moves-to-gay-village/
article981131.

Ward, Peter W. *Courtship, Love, and Marriage in Nineteenth-Century
English Canada*. Montreal: McGill-Queen's University Press,
1990.

9. THE MYTH OF THE STIRRUP CUP

Berton, Pierre. *The American Invasion of Canada*. Toronto: McClelland
and Stewart, 1980.

Edgar, Matilda Ridout. *General Brock*. Toronto: Morang, 1904.

Fixico, Donald. "A Native Nations Perspective on the War of 1812."
PBS. Accessed April 4, 2020. pbs.org/wned/war-of-1812/essays/
native-nations-perspective.

Grodzinski, John R. "Capture of Fort Niagara." *Canadian
Encyclopedia*, March 24, 2011. Last modified March 4, 2015.
thecanadianencyclopedia.ca/en/article/capture-of-fort-niagara.

Hammond, M.O. "Brock's Ride." *Maclean's*, May 1, 1915. Accessed
April 4, 2020. archive.macleans.ca/article/1915/5/1/brocks-ride.

"How Brockamour Got Its Name." Brockamour Manor. Accessed
October 5, 2019. brockamour.com/history.

Laxer, James. *Tecumseh and Brock: The War of 1812*. Toronto: House
of Anansi, 2012.

Lost Rivers. "Oak Hill." Accessed April 1, 2020. lostrivers.ca/content/
points/oakhill.html.

MacDonald, Cheryl. *Isaac Brock: Canada's Hero in the War of 1812*.
Toronto: James Lorimer, 2012.

Marsh, James H. "Isaac Brock: Fallen Hero." *Canadian Encyclopedia*,
October 12, 2013. Last modified March 4, 2015.
thecanadianencyclopedia.ca/en/article/isaac-brock-fallen-hero
-feature.

Mealing, S.R. "Shaw, Aeneas." *Dictionary of Canadian Biography.*
Accessed April 1, 2020. biographi.ca/en/bio/shaw_aeneas_5E
.html.

Mortimer, Abráham. "Sobbing Sophia Haunted Niagara-on-the-
Lake." *Nightmares Fear Factory.* Accessed October 5, 2019.
nightmaresfearfactory.com/blog/sobbing-sophia-haunted-niagara-
lake.

Ridler, Jason. "Battle of Queenston Heights." *Canadian Encyclopedia*,
August 29, 2013. Last modified March 1, 2019.
thecanadianencyclopedia.ca/en/article/battle-of-queenston
-heights.

Robertson, John Ross. *Robertson's Landmarks of Toronto.* Toronto:
John Ross Robertson, 1908.

Scadding, Henry. *Toronto of Old.* Toronto: Adam, Stevenson, 1873.

Stacey, S.P. "Brock, Sir Isaac." *Dictionary of Canadian Biography.*
Accessed April 4, 2020. biographi.ca/en/bio/brock_isaac_5E.html.

Symons, John. *The Battle of Queenston Heights: Being a Narrative of
the Opening of the War of 1812 with Notices of the Life of Major-
General Sir Isaac Brock, K.B., and Description of the Monument
Erected to his Memory.* Toronto: Thompson, 1859.

Taylor, Alan. *The Civil War of 1812: American Citizens, British
Subjects, Irish Rebels, & Indian Allies.* New York: Vintage, 2010.

Tolan, Eva Elliott. "Reminders of the Past: Sophia Shaw." Niagara
Falls Public Library. November 15, 1958. Accessed October 5,
2019. nflibrary.ca/nfplindex/show.asp?id=314108&b=1.

Turner, Wesley B. *The Astonishing General: The Life and Legacy of Sir
Isaac Brock.* Toronto: Dundurn Press, 2011.

Whitfield, Carol. "The Battle of Queenston Heights." Parks Canada.
Last modified October 24, 2006. parkscanadahistory.com/
series/chs/11/chs11-1d.htm.

"Who Started the War of 1812?" *Ideas*. Toronto: CBC Radio, June 18, 2012.

Wilson, William R. "A Man of Exquisite Charm." *Historical Narratives of Early Canada*. Accessed April 4, 2020. uppercanadahistory.ca/brock/brock1.html.

10. SHOULD I FALL

Calvert, Patricia. *Zebulon Pike: Lost in the Rockies*. New York: Marshall Cavendish, 2005.

Cumberland, Barlow. *The Battle of York: An Account of the Eight Hours' Battle from the Humber Bay to the Old Fort in Defence of York on April 27, 1813*. Toronto: William Briggs, 1913.

Doak, Robin S. *Zebulon Pike: Explorer and Soldier*. North Mankato: Capstone, 2005.

Grogan, Mick, dir. *Explosion 1812*. Toronto: Yap Films, 2012.

Harris, Matthew L., and Jay H. Buckley, eds. *Zebulon Pike, Thomas Jefferson, and the Opening of the American West*. Norman: University of Oklahoma Press, 2012.

Malcomson, Robert. *Capital in Flames: The American Attack on York, 1813*. Montreal: Robin Brass, 2008.

———. "The Refugees at York: What Happened to the Families When the Americans Invaded?" *Fife and Drum* 12, no. 4 (December 2008): 3–4.

Matthews, George R. *Zebulon Pike: Thomas Jefferson's Agent for Empire*. Santa Barbara: ABC-CLIO: 2016.

Orsi, Jared. *Citizen Explorer: The Life of Zebulon Pike*. Oxford: Oxford University Press, 2013.

"War Events: Or, Matters Belonging to the Late War." *Niles' Weekly Register* 9 (October 28, 1815).

"York In Flames." *Ideas*. Toronto: CBC Radio, April 26, 2013.

11. FITZGIBBON'S LEAVE

Anderson, A.J. "Stuart, George Okill." *Dictionary of Canadian Biography*. Accessed October 5, 2019. biographi.ca/en/bio .php?id_nbr=4733.

Bonikowsky, Laura Neilson. "Laura Secord." *Canadian Encyclopedia*, March 24, 2011. Last modified March 24, 2015. thecanadianencyclopedia.ca/en/article/laura-secord.

Dale, Ronald J. "Battle of Beaver Dams National Historic Site." *Canadian Encyclopedia*, October 19, 2011. Last modified March 4, 2015. thecanadianencyclopedia.ca/en/article/ battle-of-beaver-dams-national-historic-site-of-canada.

Documents, Selected from Several Others, Showing the Services Rendered by Colonel FitzGibbon, While Serving in Upper Canada, Between the Years 1812 and 1837. Windsor: W. Whittington, 1859.

Duncan, Dorothy. *Hoping for the Best, Preparing for the Worst: Everyday Life in Upper Canada, 1812–1814.* Toronto: Dundurn Press, 2012.

FitzGibbon, Mary Agnes. *A Veteran of 1812: The Life of James FitzGibbon.* Toronto: W. Briggs, 1894.

McKenzie, Ruth. "FitzGibbon, James." *Dictionary of Canadian Biography*. Accessed October 5, 2019. biographi.ca/en/bio/ fitzgibbon_james_9E.html.

———. *James FitzGibbon: Defender of Upper Canada.* Toronto: Dundurn Press, 1996.

Ridler, James. "Battle of Beaver Damns." *Canadian Encyclopedia*, October 19, 2011. Last modified March 4, 2015. thecanadianencyclopedia.ca/en/article/battle-of-beaver-dams.

Zavitz, Sherman. "Siege of Fort Erie, War of 1812." *Canadian Encyclopedia*, March 3, 2011. Last modified December

14, 2013. thecanadianencyclopedia.ca/en/article/
siege-of-fort-erie-war-of-1812.

12. THE REBEL ISABEL

Armstrong, Frederick H. and Ronald J. Stagg. "Mackenzie, William
Lyon." *Dictionary of Canadian Biography.* Accessed August 17,
2016. biographi.ca/en/bio.php?BioId=38684.

Atkinson, Logan. "The Impact of Cholera on the Design and
Implementation of Toronto's First Municipal Bylaws, 1834."
Urban History Review 30, no. 2 (2002): 3–15.

Gates, Lilian F. *After the Rebellion: The Later Years of William Lyon
Mackenzie.* Toronto: Dundurn Press, 2012.

Goddard, John. *Inside the Museums: Toronto's Heritage Sites and Their
Most Prized Objects.* Toronto: Dundurn Press, 2014.

Gray, Charlotte. *Mrs. King.* Toronto: Penguin, 1997.

Kilbourn, William. *The Firebrand: William Lyon Mackenzie and the
Rebellion in Upper Canada.* Toronto: Dundurn Press, 1956.

Levine, Allan. *Toronto: Biography of a City.* Vancouver: Douglas &
McIntyre, 2014.

Lindsey, Charles. *The Life and Times of Wm. Lyon Mackenzie,
With an Account of the Canadian Rebellion of 1837, and the
Subsequent Frontier Disturbances, Chiefly from Unpublished
Documents.* Toronto: P.R. Randall, 1862.

Lost Rivers. "The Baldwin/Mackenzie House." Accessed December
27, 2019. lostrivers.ca/content/points/baldwinmackenzie.html.

Luno, Nancy. *A Genteel Exterior: The Domestic Life of William Lyon
Mackenie and His Family.* Toronto: Toronto Historical Board, 1990.

Mackenzie, William Lyon. *The History of the Battle of Toronto, with
Illustrations and Notes, Critical and Explanatory, Exhibiting the
Only True Account of What Took Place at the Memorable Siege
of Toronto.* Rochester: n.p., 1839.

Morgan, Henry James. *Types of Canadian Women and of Women Who Are or Have Been Connected with Canada*. Toronto: William Briggs, 1903.

Raible, Christopher. "'A Journey Undertaken Under Peculiar Circumstances': The Perilous Escape of William Lyon Mackenzie December 7 to 11, 1837." *Ontario History* 180, no. 2 (Fall 2016): 131–55.

Robertson, John Ross. *Robertson's Landmarks of Toronto*. Toronto: John Ross Robertson, 1908.

Terry, Andrea. "'Living History in Canada: Representing Victorian Culture in the Multicultural Present." Ph.D. diss., Queen's University, 2010.

Wilson, William R. "Upper Canada's Lieutenant-Governors and the Colonial Office." *Historical Narratives of Early Canada*. Accessed December 10, 2019. uppercanadahistory.ca/pp/pp5 .html.

———. "William Lyon Mackenzie Part I." *Historical Narratives of Early Canada*. Accessed December 27, 2019. uppercanadahistory.ca/tt/tt4.html.

13. NO PITY FOR THE BLACKSMITH

Buckner, Phillip. "Arthur, Sir George." *Dictionary of Canadian Biography*. Accessed December 20, 2019. biographi.ca/en/bio/ arthur_george_8E.html.

Charles, Ashok, and Randall White. "Lount and Matthews Commemoration Salon." Active History. Accessed December 20, 2019. activehistory.ca/2013/04/ lount-and-matthews-commemoration-salon.

Dent, John Charles. *The Story of the Upper Canadian Rebellion*. Toronto: C. Blackett Robinson, 1885.

Duffy, Dennis. "Historicist: Fixing the Broken Column." *Torontoist*,
    October 28, 2017. Accessed December 20, 2019. torontoist
    .com/2017/10/historicist-fixing-broken-column.

Kilbourn, William. *The Firebrand: William Lyon Mackenzie and
    the Rebellion in Upper Canada*. Toronto: Dundurn Press, 1956.

Lindsey, Charles. *The Life and Times of Wm. Lyon Mackenzie,
    With an Account of the Canadian Rebellion of 1837, and the
    Subsequent Frontier Disturbances, Chiefly from Unpublished
    Documents*. Toronto: P.R. Randall, 1862.

Lount, Elizabeth. "Open Letter to John Beverley Robinson, Chief
    Justice of Upper Canada." *Pontiac Herald*, June 12, 1838.

Mills, David. "Sir John Beverley Robinson." *Canadian Encyclopedia*,
    January 22, 2008. Last modified March 4, 2015.
    thecanadianencyclopedia.ca/en/article/sir-john-beverley
    -robinson.

M'Leod, Donald. *A Brief Review of the Settlement of Upper Canada
    by the U.E. Loyalists and Scotch Highlanders, in 1783: And of the
    Grievances Which Compelled the Canadas to Have Recourse to
    Arms in Defence of Their Rights and Liberties, in 1837 and 1838:
    Together with a Brief Sketch of the Campaigns of 1812, '13, '14*.
    Cleveland: n.p., 1841.

Morgan, Cecilia. "'When Bad Men Conspire, Good Men Must
    Unite!': Gender and Political Discourses in Upper Canada,
    1820s–1830s." *Gendered Pasts: Historical Essays in Femininity
    and Masculinity in Canada*. Edited by Kathryn McPherson,
    Cecilia Morgan, and Nancy Forestell. Toronto: University of
    Toronto Press, 2003.

Saunders, Robert E. "Robinson, Sir John Beverley." *Dictionary of
    Canadian Biography*. Accessed March 23, 2020. biographi.ca/
    en/bio/robinson_john_beverley_9E.html.

Stagg, Ronald J. "Lount, Samuel." *Dictionary of Canadian Biography.*
    Accessed December 20, 2019. biographi.ca/en/bio/lount_
    samuel_7E.html.

Thompson, Samuel. *Reminiscences of a Canadian Pioneer for the Last
    Fifty Years: An Autobiography.* Toronto: Hunter Rose, 1884.

Wilson, William R. "Samuel Lount and Peter Matthews." *Historical
    Narratives of Early Canada.* Accessed December 20, 2019.
    uppercanadahistory.ca/tt/tt10.html.

14. A BOX FOR MARY JAMES

Dillon, Moya. "Founded in Fellowship: a Brief History of Uxbridge."
    Uxbridge Times Journal, July 1, 2017. Accessed December 30,
    2019. durhamregion.com/news-story/7367646-founded-in-
    fellowship-a-brief-history-of-uxbridge.

Fuller, Sarah McCann. "An Account of Ezekiel James, Jr., (1782–1870)
    of Uxbridge and the Murder of his Son, Isaac James, in 1828."
    Canadian Quaker History Journal, no. 69–70 (2004–2005): 39–47.
    Accessed December 30, 2019. cfha.info/journal69-70p39.pdf.

Goddard, John. *Inside the Museums: Toronto's Heritage Sites and
    Their Most Prized Objects.* Toronto: Dundurn Press, 2014.

Higgins, W.H. *The Life and Times of Joseph Gould.* Toronto: C.
    Blackett Robinson, 1887.

"Joseph Gould the Rebel." *Uxbridge Cosmos,* April 26, 2012. Accessed
    December 30, 2019. thecosmos.ca/wp-content/uploads/2015/11/
    COS0010426.pdf.

Kilbourn, William. *The Firebrand: William Lyon Mackenzie and
    the Rebellion in Upper Canada.* Toronto: Dundurn Press,
    1956.

Raible, Chris. "'Confined in Toronto Gaol for High Treason,
    July 19th, 1838': Loyalties in Conflict in Upper Canada: An

Address Given at the Canadian Friends Historical Association Annual General Meeting Held in Toronto, 21 September 2013." *Canadian Quaker History Journal* 78 (2013). Accessed December 30, 2019. cfha.info/journal78p1.pdf.

———. "'*We Witness'd from our Massv Grate / These Two Martyrs Meet Their Fate*': 1837 Rebellion Prisoners Mourn the Deaths of Samuel Lount and Peter Matthews." *York Pioneer* (2018).

Raible, Chris, John C. Carter, and Darryl Withrow. *From Hands Now Striving to Be Free: Boxes Crafted by 1837 Rebellion Prisoners.* Toronto: The York Pioneer and Historical Society, 2009.

Stagg, Ronald, J. "Gould (Gold), Joseph." *Dictionary of Canadian Biography.* Accessed December 30, 2019. biographi.ca/en/bio/gould_joseph_11E.html.

15. YOUR MOVEMENTS ARE WATCHED

Burns, Robert. "'Queer Doings': Attitudes Toward Homosexuality in 19th Century Canada." *Our Image: The BP Review Supplement* 6 (December 1976–January 1977).

Burns, Robert J. "Markland, George Herchmer (Herkimer)." *Dictionary of Canadian Biography.* Accessed March 16, 2020. biographi.ca/en/bio.php?id_nbr=4568.

Burns, Robert J. "Queer Doings." *Canada's History*, June 12, 2019. Accessed March 16, 2020. canadashistory.ca/explore/politics-law/queer-doings.

The Canadian Centre for Gender and Sexual Diversity. "Queer Canadian History Timeline – Pre-Colonization to Present." July 2018. Accessed March 16, 2020. ccgsd-ccdgs.org/wp-content/uploads/2018/09/Canadian-History-Timeline.pdf.

Copley, Hamish. "George Herchmer Markland." The Drummer's Revenge: LGBT History and Politics in Canada, August 3, 2017.

Accessed March 16, 2020. thedrummersrevenge.wordpress
.com/2007/08/03/george-herchmer-markland.

Henderson, Jarett. "File M and the Straightness of the Settler State in
Early Canada." *Borealia: Early Canadian History*, January 18,
2016. Accessed March 16, 2020. earlycanadianhistory.ca/
2016/01/18/file-m-and-the-straightness-of-the-settler-state-in-
early-canada.

———. *File M — The 1838 Markland Investigation: Sexual Freedom
and Colonial Rule in British North America*. Accessed March 16,
2020. markland1838.wordpress.com/no-23.

Jackson, Ed, and Jarrett Henderson. "Sex, Scandal, and Punishment
in Early Toronto." In *Any Other Way: How Toronto Got
Queer*. Edited by Stephanie Chambers, Jane Farrow, Maureen
FitzGerald, Ed Jackson, John Lorinc, Tim McCaskell, Rebecka
Sheffield, Tatum Taylor, and Rahim Thawer. Toronto: Coach
House, 2017.

Westcott, Ben. "The Homophobic Legacy of the British Empire."
CNN. Last modified September 12, 2018. cnn.com/2018/09/11/
asia/british-empire-lgbt-rights-section-377-intl/index.html.

16. ADULTERY AT OSGOODE HALL

Abbott, Elizabeth. *A History of Marriage: From Same Sex Union to
Private Vows and Common Law, the Surprising Diversity of a
Tradition*. New York City: Seven Stories, 2011.

Firth, Edith G. "Murray, Anne (Powell.)" *Dictionary of Canadian
Biography*. Accessed March 23, 2020. biographi.ca/en/bio/
murray_anne_7E.html.

Grazley, Robin Christine. "Nothing 'Improper' Happened: Sex,
Marriage, and Colonial Identity in Upper Canada, 1783–1850."
Ph.D. diss., Queen's University, 2010.

Honsberger, John. *Osgoode Hall: An Illustrated History*. Toronto: Dundurn Press, 2004.

McKenna, Katherine M.J. *A Life of Propriety: Anne Murray Powell and Her Family, 1755–1849*. Montreal: McGill-Queen's University Press, 1994.

Statutes, of Her Majesty's Province of Upper Canada, Passed in the Fifth Session of the Thirteenth Provincial Parliament of Upper Canada (and an Act Passed in the Fourth Session, Thirteenth Provincial Parliament, to Which the Royal Assent Was Subsequently Promulgated) by Authority the Right Honourable C. Poulett Thomson, Governor-General. Toronto: Robert Stanton, 1840.

17. THE BLUE SCHOOL BOYS

Boyce Gerald E. *Belleville: A Popular History*. Toronto: Dundurn Press, 2009.

———. "Samson, James Hunter." *Dictionary of Canadian Biography*. Accessed May 23, 2020. biographi.ca/en/bio/samson_james_hunter_7E.html.

Courtney, John C. "Right to Vote in Canada." *Canadian Encyclopedia*, March 18, 2007. Last modified February 15, 2019. thecanadianencyclopedia.ca/en/article/franchise.

Craig, G.M. "Strachan, John." *Dictionary of Canadian Biography*. Accessed March 4, 2020. biographi.ca/en/bio/strachan_john_9E.html.

Cross, Michael S. *The Morning Star of Memory: A Biography of Robert Baldwin*. Don Mills: Oxford University Press, 2012.

Cross, Michael S., and Robert L. Fraser. "'The Waste That Lies Before Me': The Public and the Private Worlds of Robert Baldwin." *Historical Papers* 18, no. 1 (1983): 164–83.

Cross, Michael S., and Robert Lochiel Fraser. "Baldwin, Robert."
    Dictionary of Canadian Biography. Accessed December 26,
    2016. biographi.ca/en/bio/baldwin_robert_8E.html.

Fraser, Robert L. "Baldwin, William Warren." *Dictionary of
    Canadian Biography.* Accessed December 26, 2016. biographi
    .ca/en/bio/baldwin_william_warren_7E.html.

Lost Rivers. "The Blue School." Accessed July 31, 2020. lostrivers.ca/
    content/points/blueschool.html.

Lucas, Sir C.P., ed. *Lord Durham's Report on the Affairs of British
    North America.* Toronto: Henry Frowde, 1912.

Murray, Heather. "'And Every Lawyer's Clerk Writes Rhyme': Robert
    Baldwin as Poet, York, 1819–20. *Canadian Literature* 188
    (Spring 2006): 63–84.

Ryan, Elana Laurel Aislinn. "A Medieval New World: Nation-
    Making in Early Canadian Literature, 1789–1870." Ph.D. diss.,
    University of Toronto, 2015.

Saul, John Ralston. *Louis-Hippolyte LaFontaine and Robert Baldwin.*
    Toronto: Penguin, 2010.

Stewart-Robinson, Tristan. "The Man Who Had a C-Section."
    Tomorrow, June 30, 2012. Accessed May 2, 2020. tomorrow.is/
    yesterday/the-man-who-had-a-c-section.

18. ESCAPE FROM KENTUCKY

Caulfield, Jon. "The Imagined Cities of Three Canadian Painters."
    Urban History Review 20, no. 1 (June 1991): 3–14.

Frost, Karolyn Smardz. "A Fresh Start: Black Toronto in the 19th
    Century." In *The Ward: The Life and Loss of Toronto's First
    Immigrant Neighbourhood.* Edited by John Lorinc, Michael
    McClelland, Ellen Scheinberg, and Tatum Taylor. Toronto:
    Coach House, 2015.

————. *I've Got A Home in Glory Land: A Lost Tale of the Underground Railroad.* New York City: Farrar, Straus and Giroux, 2008.

Henry, Natasha. "Brought in Bondage: Black Enslavement in Upper Canada." Myseum. Accessed April 29, 2020. myseumoftoronto .com/programming/black-enslavement-in-upper-canada.

Henry, Natasha L. "Black Enslavement in Canada." *Canadian Encyclopedia*, June 16, 2016. Last modified June 9, 2020. thecanadianencyclopedia.ca/en/article/black-enslavement.

————. "Chloe Cooley and the Act to Limit Slavery in Upper Canada." *Canadian Encyclopedia*, October 30, 2013. Last modified January 5, 2016. thecanadianencyclopedia.ca/en/article/ chloe-cooley-and-the-act-to-limit-slavery-in-upper-canada.

————. *Talking About Freedom: Celebrating Emancipation Day in Canada.* Toronto: Dundurn Press, 2012.

Higginbotham, A. Leon. *In the Matter of Color: Race and the American Legal Process, The Colonial Period.* Cary, NC: Oxford University Press USA, 1980.

Marsh, James. "Anti-Slavery Lecture Opens Hall." *Toronto in Time.* Accessed May 31, 2020. citiesintime.ca/toronto/story/ anti-slavery.

Muir, Elizabeth Gillan. *Riverdale: East of the Don.* Toronto: Dundurn Press, 2014.

Plummer, Kevin. "Historicist: Confederates and Conspirators." *Torontoist*, May 21, 2011. Accessed May 18, 2020. torontoist .com/2011/05/historicist_sympathizers_and_spies_in_the_ confederate_cause.

Read, David Breakenridge. *The Lieutenant-Governors of Upper Canada 1792-1899.* Toronto, William Briggs, 1900.

Riddell, William Renwick. "The Slave in Upper Canada." *Journal of Law and Criminology* 14, Issue 2 (1923).

———. "Upper Canada-Early Period." *Journal of Negro History* 5, no. 3 (July 1920). Accessed April 29, 2020. jstor.org/stable/2713625.

Shadd, Adrienne, Afua Cooper, and Karolyn Smardz Frost. *The Underground Railroad: Next Stop, Toronto!* Toronto: Natural Heritage Books, 2002.

Wiens, Mary. "Archeologist Unearths Epic Story of Slavery and Freedom in Toronto." *CBC News*, February 26, 2017. Last modified February 26, 2017. cbc.ca/news/canada/toronto/steal-away-home-1.3998495.

Winks, Robin W. *The Blacks in Canada: A History.* Montreal: McGill-Queen's University Press, 1997.

19. THE SUSPICIOUS OYSTER SHOP

Bertram, Laurie. "The Madam Who Shot The Mountie." *University of Toronto Magazine*, June 25, 2019. Accessed August 1, 2020. magazine.utoronto.ca/research-ideas/culture-society/the-madam-who-shot-the-mountie.

Bertram, Laurie K. "Sex Work in the Queen City: Mapping Prostitution in Toronto, 1865–1915." *The University of Toronto.* Accessed June 1, 2020. utoronto.maps.arcgis.com/apps/StoryMapBasic/index.html?appid=434765ad4688479d80ae67a841aef5ee.

Blackhouse, Constance B. "Nineteenth-Century Canadian Prostitution Law Reflection of a Discriminatory Society." *Social History* 18, no. 36 (November 1985): 387–423.

"The Bloxsom Affair." *Globe*, May 26, 1847.

Bradburn, Jamie. "'Dereliction of Duty': The Rise and Fall of Toronto's First Police Force." *TVO*, June 20, 2020. Accessed August 1, 2020. tvo.org/article/dereliction-of-duty-the-rise-and-fall-of-torontos-first-police-force.

————. "Historicist: Read of the Fifty Days." *Torontoist*, February
    6, 2010. Accessed August 1, 2020. torontoist.com/2010/02/
    historicist_read_of_the_fifty_days.

Kealey, Gregory S. *Workers and Canadian History*. Montreal:
    McGill-Queen's University Press, 1995.

McLaren, John. "Recalculating the Wages of Sin: The Social and
    Legal Construction of Prostitution, 1850–1920." *Manitoba Law
    Journal* 23, nos. 1 and 2 (1995): 524–55.

Metzger, Patrick. "How a Fight with Clowns Led to the Birth of
    Modern Policing in Toronto." *Torontoist*, September 12, 2013.
    Accessed April 2, 2020. torontoist.com/2013/09/how-a-fight-
    with-clowns-led-to-the-birth-of-modern-policing-in-toronto.

Muir, Elizabeth Gillan. *Riverdale: East of the Don*. Toronto: Dundurn
    Press, 2014.

Phillips, Catherine. "Story of Toronto's 19th-Century Sex Trade
    Uncovered by Professor, Students." *Globe and Mail*, May 13, 2016.
    Accessed June 1, 2020. theglobeandmail.com/news/toronto/
    story-of-torontos-19th-century-sex-trade-uncovered-by-
    professor-students/article30020414.

"Police Intelligence: The Riot at the Circus Ground." *Globe*, July 14,
    1855.

Roberts, H. Julia. "Taverns and Tavern-Goers in Upper Canada, the
    1790s to the 1850s." Ph.D. diss., University of Toronto, 1999.

Senior, Hereward. "Boulton, Henry William." *Dictionary of
    Canadian Biography*. Accessed August 1, 2020. biographi.ca/en/
    bio/boulton_william_henry_10E.html.

Smyth, William J. *Toronto, The Belfast of Canada: The Orange Order
    and the Shaping of Municipal Culture*. Toronto: University of
    Toronto Press, 2015.

University of Toronto Libraries. "Canada's Oldest Profession: Sex

Work and Bawdy House Legislation." Accessed June 1, 2020. exhibits.library.utoronto.ca/exhibits/show/bawdy.

Vronsky, Peter. "Toronto Police in the 1850s: The Gangs of Toronto and the Call for Reform." Crime and Punishment in Canada. Accessed April 2, 2020. russianbooks.org/crime/cph4.htm.

20. THE WINTER ACCIDENT

Blaise, Clark. *Time Lord: Sir Sanford Fleming and the Creation of Standard Time*. New York, Vintage, 2002.

Cole, Jean Murray. *Sir Sandford Fleming: His Early Diaries, 1845–1853*. Toronto: Dundurn Press, 2009.

Croft, Frank. "The Forgotten Whirlwind Who Put the World on Time." *Maclean's*, December 1, 1954. Accessed December 2, 2020.

Hutchison House. Accessed December 4, 2020. hutchisonhouse.ca.

Trecartin, F. Whitman, and Matthew Trecartin, dir. 2002. *The Canadians: Sandford Fleming*. Halifax: Tri Media Productions.

Ward, Peter W. *Courtship, Love, and Marriage in Nineteenth-Century English Canada*. Montreal: McGill-Queen's University Press, 1990.

21. THE MOTHER OF CONFEDERATION

Andrew-Gee, Eric. "The Globe on Confederation Day: Read the Fine Print of George Brown's Letter to a New Nation." *Globe and Mail*, June 25, 2017. Accessed May 20, 2020. theglobeandmail.com/news/national/canada-150/globe-confederation-day-edition/article35407019.

"Anne Brown — THE Mother of Confederation." *University of Alberta Faculty of Law: Faculty Blog*, February 17, 2017. Accessed April 27, 2020. ualbertalaw.typepad.com/

faculty/2017/02/anne-brown-the-mother-of-confederation.html.

Archives of Ontario. "Meet the Browns: A Confederation Family." Accessed April 2, 2020. archives.gov.on.ca/en/explore/online/ familyties/index.aspx.

Baker, Nathan. "Anti-Slavery Society of Canada." *Canadian Encyclopedia*, February 13, 2018. Last modified March 5, 2019. thecanadianencyclopedia.ca/en/article/ anti-slavery-society-of-canada.

Careless, J.M.S. "Brown, George." *Dictionary of Canadian Biography*. Accessed April 27, 2020.

———. *Brown of the Globe: Statesman of Confederation, Vol. II.* Toronto: Dundurn, 1989.

English, John R., and David A. Wilson. "The Great Coalition of 1864." *Canadian Encyclopedia*, February 7, 2006. Last modified October 11, 2019. thecanadianencyclopedia.ca/en/article/ great-coalition.

Goodspeed, D.J. "Blow by Blow: The Day Canada Became a Nation." *Maclean's*, December 1, 1962. Accessed May 20, 2020. archive.macleans.ca/article/1962/12/1/blow-by-blow-the-day -canada-became-a-nation.

Lewis, John. *The Makers of Canada: George Brown*. Toronto: Morang, 1906.

Marsh, James H. "Editorial: The Charlottetown Conference of 1864 and the Persuasive Power of Champagne." *Canadian Encyclopedia*, August 29, 2013. Last modified January 13, 2020. thecanadianencyclopedia.ca/en/article/charlottetown- 1864-the-persuasive-power-of-champagne-feature.

Mills, David. "Clear Grits." *Canadian Encyclopedia*, February 6, 2006. Last modified December 16, 2013. thecanadianencyclopedia.ca/ en/article/clear-grits.

"Mothers of Confederation." *Canadian Encyclopedia*, January 15, 2016. Last modified October 15, 2015. thecanadianencyclopedia.ca/en/article/mothers-of-confederation.

Skikavich, Julia. "Anne Brown." *Canadian Encyclopedia*, May 21, 2015. Accessed May 20, 2020. thecanadianencyclopedia.ca/en/article/anne-nelson-brown.

22. THE TOMB IN HIGH PARK

Belli, Flavio. "The Story of a Fence." In "Human History of Toronto's High Park." High Park Nature. Last modified December 7, 2017. highparknature.org/article/human-history-year-by-year/.

Fair, Ross. "Historicist: Body Snatchers, Grave Robbers, and Night Ghouls." *Torontoist*, November 14, 2015. Accessed October 4, 2019. torontoist.com/2015/11/historicist-body-snatchers-grave-robbers-and-night-ghouls.

Francis, Deepa. "Bodysnatching in Canada." *Canadian Medical Association Journal* 164, no. 2 (February 21, 2001).

Franklin, Jill. "John Howard's Secret Children." *High Park: A Park Lover's Quarterly* 2, no. 2 (Summer 1995).

Goddard, John. *Inside the Museums: Toronto's Heritage Sites and Their Most Prized Objects*. Toronto: Dundurn Press, 2014.

Howard, John G. *Incidents in the Life of John G. Howard, Esq. of Colborne Lodge, High Park, Near Toronto; Chiefly Adapted from His Journals*. Toronto: Copp, Clark, 1885.

Keefe, Katherine. "John and Jemima Howard." High Park Nature. Last modified December 7, 2017. highparknature.org/wiki/wiki.php?n=History.JohnAndJemimaHoward.

MacGillivray, Royce. "Body-Snatching in Ontario." *Canadian Bulletin of Medical History* 5 (1988): 51–60.

"Rangers Howard Dead." *Toronto Daily Mail*, February 4, 1890.

Rankin, Matthew. "Anatomically Incorrect: Bodysnatching in the 19th Century." *Canada's History*, October 31, 2017. Accessed October 4, 2019. canadashistory.ca/explore/science-technology/anatomically-incorrect-bodysnatching-in-the-19th-century.

Wencer, David. "Historicist: John Howard's Enduring Monument." *Torontoist*, December 7, 2013. Accessed October 1, 2019. torontoist.com/2013/12/historicist-john-howards-enduring-monument.

23. THE SECRETS OF JALNA

Bradburn, Jamie. "Meet a Toronto Mayor: William Holmes Howland." *Torontoist*, April 2, 2014. Accessed May 9, 2020. torontoist.com/2014/04/meet-a-toronto-mayor-william-holmes-howland.

de la Roche, Mazo. *Jalna*. Toronto: Macmillan, 1927.

de la Roche, Mazo. *Ringing the Changes: An Autobiography*. Toronto: Macmillan, 1957.

de la Roche, Mazo. *Whiteoaks of Jalna*. Toronto: Macmillan, 1929.

Givner, Joan. *Mazo de la Roche: The Hidden Life*. Toronto: Oxford University Press, 1989.

"Heritage Houses." Mississauga. Accessed May 9, 2020. culture.mississauga.ca/collection/heritage-houses.

Kirk, Heather. *Mazo de la Roche*. Toronto: Dundurn Press, 2006.

Gallus, Maya, dir. *The Mystery of Mazo de la Roche*. Toronto: Red Queen Productions, 2011.

Plummer, Kevin. "Historicist: Revealing Fictions." *Torontoist*, June 28, 2014. Accessed May 9, 2020. torontoist.com/2014/06/historicist-revealing-fictions.

Strange, Carolyn, and Tina Merrill Loo. *Making Good: Law and Moral Regulation in Canada, 1867–1939*. Toronto: University of Toronto Press, 1997.

Wuorio, Eva-Lis. "Mazo of Jalna." *Maclean's*, February 1, 1949. Accessed
    May 9, 2020. archive.macleans.ca/article/1949/2/1/mazo-of-jalna.
York, Lorraine Mary. *Literary Celebrity in Canada*. Toronto:
    University of Toronto Press, 2007.

24. A CRY FROM AN INDIAN WIFE

Beal, Bob, and Rod Macleod. "North-West Rebellion." *Canadian
    Encyclopedia*, February 7, 2006. Last modified July 30, 2019.
    thecanadianencyclopedia.ca/en/article/north-west-rebellion.
Bumstead, J.M. "Red River Rebellion." *Canadian Encyclopedia*,
    February 7, 2006. Last modified November 22, 2019.
    thecanadianencyclopedia.ca/en/article/red-river-rebellion.
Daschuk, James. *Clearing the Plains: Disease, Politics of Starvation,
    and the Loss of Aboriginal Life*. Regina: University of Regina
    Press, 2013.
Eshet, Dan. *Stolen Lives: The Indigenous People of Canada and
    the Indian Residential Schools*. Toronto: Facing History &
    Ourselves, 2015.
Gadacz, René R. "Potlach." *Canadian Encyclopedia*, February 7, 2006.
    Last modified October 24, 2019. thecanadianencyclopedia.ca/en/
    article/potlatch.
Gray, Charlotte. *Flint and Feather: The Life and Times of E. Pauline
    Johnson, Tekahionwake*. Toronto: HarperFlamingo Canada, 2002.
———. "The True Story of Pauline Johnson: Poet, Provocateur and
    Champion of Indigenous Rights." *Canadian Geographic*, March
    8, 2017. Accessed December 4, 2019. canadiangeographic.ca/
    article/true-story-pauline-johnson-poet-provocateur-and
    -champion-indigenous-rights.
Johnson, E. Pauline. *Tekahionwake: E. Pauline Johnson's Writings on
    Native North America*. Peterborough: Broadview, 2015.

McDougall, Robert L. "Duncan Campbell Scott." *Canadian Encyclopedia*, August 11, 2008. Last modified January 18, 2018. thecanadianencyclopedia.ca/en/article/duncan-campbell-scott.

McRae, Matthew J. "Remembering Rebellion, Remembering Resistance: Collective Memory, Identity, and the Veterans of 1869–70 and 1885." Ph.D. diss., University of Western Ontario, 2018.

Miller, J.R. "Residential Schools in Canada." *Canadian Encyclopedia*, October 10, 2012. Last modified January 15, 2020. thecanadianencyclopedia.ca/en/article/residential-schools.

Plummer, Kevin. "Historicist: Toronto Troops in the Northwest Rebellion of 1885." *Torontoist*, July 13, 2013. Accessed April 28, 2020. torontoist.com/2013/07/historicist-toronto-troops-in-the-north -west-rebellion-of-1885.

Rose, Marilyn J. "Johnson, Emily Pauline." *Dictionary of Canadian Biography*. Accessed December 4, 2019. biographi.ca/en/bio/ johnson_emily_pauline_14E.html.

25. THE QUEEN OF HEARTS

Beaven, Brian P.N. "Bunting, Christopher William." *Dictionary of Canadian Biography Online*. Accessed June 22, 2019. biographi .ca/en/bio/bunting_christopher_william_12E.html.

Bradburn, Jamie. "Historicist: Delivering the *Mail*." *Torontoist*, November 22, 2014. Accessed June 22, 2019. torontoist.com/ 2014/11/historicist-delivering-the-mail.

———. "Historicist: Kit's Kingdom." *Torontoist*, November 23, 2013. Accessed June 24, 2019. torontoist.com/2013/11/ historicist-kits-kingdom.

———. "Historicist: Of *Mail and Empire*." *Torontoist*, December 20, 2014. Accessed June 22, 2019. torontoist.com/2014/12/ historicist-of-mail-and-empire.

Buzwell, Greg. "Daughters of Decadence: The New Woman in
    the Victorian Fin de Siècle." British Library, May 15, 2014.
    Accessed June 24, 2019. bl.uk/romantics-and-victorians/
    articles/daughters-of-decadence-the-new-woman-in-the-
    victorian-fin-de-siecle.

Der, Lauren. "The Pioneering Kit Coleman." *Ryerson Review of
    Journalism*, August 11, 2018. Accessed June 22, 2019. rrj.ca/
    the-pioneering-kit-coleman.

Ferguson, Ted. *Kit Coleman: Queen of Hearts*. Toronto: Doubleday,
    1978.

Freeman, Barbara M. "Ferguson, Catherine." *Dictionary of Canadian
    Biography Online*. Accessed June 22, 2019. biographi.ca/en/bio/
    ferguson_catherine_14E.html.

Giddens, Tara. "'Which Is Kit?': Discovering Kathleen Blake Coleman."
    Irish Women's Writing (1880–1920) Network, June 20, 2018.
    Accessed June 24, 2019. irishwomenswritingnetwork.com/
    2018/06/20/which-is-kit-discovering-kathleen-blake-coleman.

Jones, Donald. *Fifty Tales of Toronto*. Toronto: University of Toronto
    Press, 1992.

"Kathleen Coleman." *Canadian Encyclopedia*, March 24, 2015.
    Accessed June 22, 2019. thecanadianencyclopedia.ca/en/article/
    kathleen-coleman.

Lang, Marjory. *Women Who Made the News: Female Journalists in
    Canada, 1880–1945*. Montreal: McGill-Queen's Press, 1999.

Marshall, Tabitha. "Kathleen Coleman." *Canadian Encyclopedia*,
    January 23, 2008. Last modified March 24, 2015.
    thecanadianencyclopedia.ca/en/article/kathleen-coleman.

McMullen, Lorraine, ed. *Re(dis)covering Our Foremothers:
    Nineteenth-Century Canadian Women Writers*. Ottawa:
    University of Ottawa Press, 1990.

Sandford, John. "Queen of the Sob Sister." *Maclean's*, January 15, 1953. Accessed June 24, 2019. archive.macleans.ca/article/1953/1/15/queen-of-the-sob-sister.

Smith, Vivian. "All the Resistance That's Fit to Print: Women Print Journalists Narrate Their Careers." Ph.D. diss., University of Victoria, 2012.

Stewart, Chuch, and F. Whitman Trecartin, dir. *The Canadians: Kit Coleman*. Edmonton: Great North Productions, 2001.

Vann, Jerry Don, and Rosemary T. VanArsdel, eds. *Periodicals of Queen Victoria's Empire: An Exploration*. Toronto: University of Toronto Press, 1996.

Youngberg, Gail, and Mona Holmlund. *Inspiring Women: A Celebration of Herstory*. Regina: Coteau Books, 2003.

26. A FIVE-DOLLAR DATE

Bishop, Diana. *Living Up to a Legend: My Adventures with Billy Bishop's Ghost*. Toronto: Dundurn Press, 2017.

Bradburn, Jamie. "Historicist: Wedding Bells Are Ringing." *Torontoist*, October 19, 2013. Accessed November 3, 2019. torontoist.com/2013/10/historicist-wedding-bells-are-ringing.

Greenhous, Brereton. *The Making of Billy Bishop*. Toronto: Dundurn Press, 2002.

Kilduff, Peter. *Billy Bishop VC: Lone Wolf Hunter: The RAF Ace Re-Examined*. London: Grub Street, 2014.

Library and Archives Canada. "William Avery 'Billy' Bishop." Last modified August 7, 2018. bac-lac.gc.ca/eng/discover/military-heritage/first-world-war/100-stories/Pages/bishop.aspx.

McCaffery, Dan. *Air Aces: The Lives and Times of Twelve Canadian Fighter Pilots*. Toronto: James Lorimer, 1990.

———. *Billy Bishop: Canadian Hero*. Toronto: James Lorimer, 2002.

————. *Billy Bishop: Top Canadian Flying Ace*. Halifax: Formac, 2017.

McLeod, Susanna. "RMC's 'Crack Shot' Became Our Top Flying Ace." *Kingston Whig-Standard*, May 28, 2013. Last updated May 28, 2013. thewhig.com/2013/05/28/rmcs-crack-shot-became-our-top-flying-ace/wcm/da78de54-ef6b-b979-8f8e-a0cedc981a7e.

Taylor, Peter Shawn. "Canadians and the Last Great Cavalry Charge, 100 Years Ago." *National Post*, November 16, 2017. Last modified November 16, 2017. nationalpost.com/opinion/canadians-and-the-last-great-cavalry-charge-100-years-ago.

"William Avery 'Billy' Bishop." The Virtual Museum of Canada. Accessed November 2, 2019. virtualmuseum.ca/sgc-cms/expositions-exhibitions/mains-hands/famousnamesquilt/billybishop.html.

27. LONGBOAT'S WIDOW

Arnold, Josée. "Tom Longboat Is Cogwagee Is Everything." Podcast audio. *Discover Library and Archives Canada*. December 23, 2019. bac-lac.gc.ca/eng/news/podcasts/Pages/59-tom-longboat.aspx.

Batten, Jack. *The Man Who Ran Faster Than Everyone: The Story of Tom Longboat*. Toronto: Tundra, 2009.

Cardinal, Will. *Tom Longboat: Running Against the Wind*. Edmonton: Eschia, 2008.

Cronin, Fergus. "The Rise and Fall of Tom Longboat." *Maclean's*, February 4, 1956. Accessed May 7, 2020. archive.macleans.ca/article/1956/2/4/the-rise-and-fall-of-tom-longboat.

Davis, David. *Showdown at Shepherd's Bush: The 1908 Olympic Marathon and the Three Runners Who Launched a Sporting Craze*. New York: Thomas Dunne, 2012.

Hanks, Robert K. "Tom Longboat and the First World War." *Longboat Roadrunners*. Accessed May 7, 2020. longboatroadrunners.com/wp-content/uploads/2013/09/Tom-Longboat-Essay.pdf.

Hill, Amanda. "A Local Love Story." Deseronto Archives, January 16, 2008. Accessed May 17, 2020. deserontoarchives.ca/2008/01/16/a-local-love-story.

Kidd, Bruce. "In Defence of Tom Longboat." *Sport in Society* 16, no. 4 (2013): 515–32.

———. "Tom Longboat." *Canadian Encyclopedia*, July 3, 2013. Last modified July 9, 2018. thecanadianencyclopedia.ca/en/article/tom-longboat.

Maracle, James. "Tom Longboat." *United Empire Loyalists' Association of Canada*, Accessed May 17, 2020. uelac.org/Honours-Recognition/bio/Hall-of-Honour-BofQ-Longboat-2014.pdf.

Miller, J.R. "Residential Schools in Canada." *Canadian Encyclopedia*, October 10, 2012. Last modified January 15, 2020. thecanadianencyclopedia.ca/en/article/residential-schools.

"Residential School Survivors Share Their Story of Healing." *CBC Radio*, February 29, 2016. Last modified February 29, 2016. cbc.ca/radio/unreserved/unreserved-heads-to-six-nations-of-the-grand-river-1.3459885/residential-school-survivors-share-their-story-of-healing-1.3469890.

"Tom Longboat Married: A Quiet Ceremony at St. John's Anglican Church." *Globe*, December 29, 1908.

"Tom Longboat Retrieves His Olympic Defeat." *Globe*, December 16, 1908.

"Tom Longboat Wedded, A $10,000 Marathon Race." *Toronto Daily Star*, December 29, 1908.

Unwin, Peter. "Who Do You Think I Am? A Story of Tom Longboat." *Canada's History*, September 13, 2015. Accessed May 7, 2020. canadashistory.ca/explore/first-nations,-inuit-metis/who-do-you-think-i-am-a-story-of-tom-longboat.

"Wed in a Church Tonight." *Toronto Daily Star*, December 28, 1908.

Wencer, David. "Historicist: A Running Start." *Torontoist*, October
    11, 2014. Accessed September 4, 2019. torontoist.com/2014/10/
    historicist-a-running-start.

28. HEMINGWAY HATES TORONTO

Bayliss, Graeme. "In Our Town: Ernest Hemingway in Toronto."
    Torontoist, March 7, 2012. Accessed December 29, 2019. torontoist
    .com/2012/03/in-our-town-ernest-hemingway-in-toronto.

Boles, Derek. "Toronto's 2nd Union Station — 1873 to 1927." Toronto
    Railway Historical Association. Accessed April 3, 2020. trha
    .ca/2ndunionstation.html.

Burrill, William. *Hemingway: The Toronto Years*. Toronto:
    Doubleday Canada, 1994.

Diliberto, Gioia. "A Marriage Unraveled." *Chicago Tribune*, July 1,
    2011. Accessed December 29, 2019. chicagotribune.com/
    opinion/ct-xpm-2011-07-01-ct-oped-0701-hemingway-
    20110701-story.html.

———. *Paris Without End: The True Story of Hemingway's First Wife*.
    Toronto: Harper Perennial, 2011.

"Ernest Hemimgway Rented His Toronto Apartment for $85/
    Month. Now You Can Buy It for $730K." *CBC News*, April 9,
    2019. Last modified April 9, 2019. cbc.ca/news/canada/toronto/
    ernest-hemingway-toronto-apartment-1.5091106.

Hemingway, Ernest. *Dateline: Toronto*. Edited by William White.
    New York: Scribner, 1985.

———. *Ernest Hemingway: Selected Letters 1917–1961*. Edited by
    Carlos Baker. New York: Simon & Schuster, 2003.

———. *A Moveable Feast*. New York: Scribner, 1964.

"The Hemingway Papers." *Toronto Star*. Accessed April 3, 2020. ehto
    .thestar.com.

Hotchner, A.E. *Hemingway in Love: His Own Story*. New York: St.
    Martin's Press, 2015.

Hume, Christopher. "Hemingway in Toronto: Dislike at First Sight."
    Toronto Star. Accessed April 2, 2020. ehto.thestar.com/marks/
    hemingway-in-toronto-dislike-at-first-sight.

29. THE GREAT STORK DERBY

Bateman, Chris. "Historicist: The Great Stork Derby." *Torontoist*,
    October 29, 2016. Accessed April 16, 2020. torontoist.com
    /2016/10/historicist-the-stork-derby.

Goldenberg, David. "How A Dead Millionaire Convinced Dozens of
    Women to Have As Many Babies As Possible." *FiveThirtyEight*,
    December 11, 2015. Accessed April 16, 2020. fivethirtyeight
    .com/features/how-a-dead-millionaire-convinced-dozens-of-
    women-to-have-as-many-babies-as-possible.

Harrison, Dale. "Millar Stork Derby About to be Spanked." *Evening
    Independent*, October 24, 1936.

Hutton, Eric. "Charlie Millar's Million Dollar Joke." *Maclean's*,
    June 15, 1952. Accessed April 16, 2020. archive.macleans.ca/
    article/1952/6/15/charlie-millars-million-dollar-joke.

"Stork Derby Series Faces Toronto; $10,000 Is To Go To Most
    Prolific." *Montreal Gazette*, March 12, 1946.

"'Stork Race' Is Near Its Finish." *Lawrence Journal-World*, October
    19, 1936.

Valverde, Mariana. "Families, Private Property, and the State: The
    Dionnes and the Toronto Stork Derby." In *Sexing the Maple:
    A Canadian Sourcebook*. Edited by Richard Cavelli and Peter
    Dickinson. Peterborough: Broadview, 2006.

30. THE INCORRIGIBLE VELMA DEMERSON

"Apology For Woman Jailed Over Chinese Boyfriend." *CBC News*,
January 7, 2003. Last modified January 7, 2003. cbc.ca/news
/canada/apology-for-woman-jailed-over-chinese-boyfriend-
1.381428.

Backhouse, Constance. *Carnal Crimes: Sexual Assault Law in
Canada, 1900–1975*. Toronto: The Osgoode Society for
Canadian Legal History, 2008.

Barc, Agatha. "Nostalgia Tripping: The Andrew Mercer Reformatory
for Women." *blogTO*, September 25, 2010. blogto.com/city/2010/
09/nostalgia_tripping_the_andrew_mercer_reformatory_for_
women.

Bhimji, Shabir, and Rose Sheinin. "Dr. Edna Mary Guest: She
Promoted Women's Issues Before It was Fashionable." *Canadian
Medical Association Journal* 141 (November 15, 1989).

Bradburn, Jamie. "Historicist: The KKK Took My Baby Away."
Torontoist, March 13, 2016. Accessed June 8, 2019. torontoist
.com/2016/03/historicist-the-kkk-took-my-baby-away.

Chan, Arlene. "Chinese Immigration Act." *Canadian Encyclopedia*,
March 7, 2017. Last modified March 7, 2017.
thecanadianencyclopedia.ca/en/article/chinese-immigration-act.

Chenier, Elise. "Sex, Intimacy, and Desire Among Men of Chinese
Heritage and Women of Non-Asian Heritage in Toronto, 1910–
1950." *Urban History Review* 42, no. 2 (Spring 2014): 29–43.

———. "Sex Work and the Ward's Bachelor Society." In *The Ward:
The Life and Loss of Toronto's First Immigrant Neighbourhood*.
Edited by John Lorinc, Michael McClelland, Ellen Scheinberg,
and Tatum Taylor. Toronto: Coach House, 2015.

Demerson, Velma. *Incorrigible*. Waterloo: Wilfrid Laurier University
Press, 2004.

————. "The Mercer." Velma Demerson. Accessed May 27, 2020. velmademerson.wordpress.com/the-mercer.

Devereux, Cecily. "Woman Suffrage, Eugenics, and Eugenic Feminism in Canada." *Woman Suffrage and Beyond: Confronting the Democratic Deficit*, October 1, 2013. Accessed May 31, 2020. womensuffrage.org/?p=22106.

Hallett, Mary E. "Nellie McClung." *Canadian Encyclopedia*, April 1, 2008. Last modified October 3, 2018. thecanadianencyclopedia .ca/en/article/nellie-letitia-mcclung.

Filey, Mike. *Toronto Sketches 6: The Way We Were*. Toronto: Dundurn Press, 2000.

Fraser, Jennifer Lorraine. "Awards: Acknowledging Absence and Situating Toronto's Incarcerated Women — 1919–1940." M.A. thesis, OCAD University, 2016.

Freeman, Elizabeth. *The Wedding Complex: Forms of Belonging in Modern American Culture*. Durham: Duke University Press, 2002.

"'It's a Heavy Load': Former Prisoner Babies Demand Apology, Recognition." *CBC News*, May 26, 2019. Last modified May 26, 2019. cbc.ca/news/canada/ottawa/former-prison-baby-reflects-on-notorious-andrew-mercer-reformatory-1.5144705.

Larocque, Sylvain. *Gay Marriage: The Story of a Canadian Social Revolution*. Toronto: James Lorimer, 2006.

Marshall, Tabitha. "Tommy Douglas and Eugenics." *Canadian Encyclopedia*, June 7, 2019. Last modified June 7, 2019. thecanadianencyclopedia.ca/en/article/tommy-douglas-and-eugenics.

Myers, Tamara, and Joan Sangster. "Runaways and Riots: Patterns of Resistance in Canadian Reform Schools for Girls, 1930–60." *Journal of Social History* 34, no. 3 (Spring 2001): 669–97.

Panneton, Daniel. "Incorrigible Women." *Maisonneuve*, April 18,
    2018. Accessed May 30, 2020. maisonneuve.org/
    article/2018/04/18/incorrigible-women.

"Remembering Velma Demerson — The Woman Jailed in Toronto
    for Living with Her Chinese Fiancé." *As It Happens*, May 29,
    2019. Last modified May 30, 2019. cbc.ca/radio/asithappens/as-
    it-happens-wednesday-edition-1.5154357/remembering-
    velma-demerson-the-toronto-woman-jailed-for-living-with-
    her-chinese-fianc%C3%A9-1.5154359.

Sangster, Joan. "Incarcerating 'Bad Girls': The Regulation of Sexuality
    Through the Female Refuges Act in Ontario, 1920–1945. *Journal
    of the History of Sexuality* 7, no. 2 (October 1996): 239–75.

Thomas, Clara. "Incorrigible." *Canadian Woman Studies* 26, no. 1: 110–11.

Valpy, Michael. "A Dark Passage in Ontario's Past." *Globe and Mail*,
    March 22, 2002. Accessed May 27, 2020. theglobeandmail.com/
    news/national/a-dark-passage-in-ontarios-past/article25293699.

Van Dyk, Lindsay. "Canadian Immigration Acts and Legislation."
    Canadian Museum of Immigration at Pier 21. Accessed
    May 31, 2020. pier21.ca/research/immigration-history/
    canadian-immigration-acts-and-legislation.

Wieditz, Thorben. "Liberty Village: The Makeover of Toronto's King
    and Dufferin Area." *Centre for Urban and Community Studies
    Research Bulletin* 32 (January 2007).

Wong-Tam, Kristin. "Remembering Toronto's First Chinatown."
    In *The Ward: The Life and Loss of Toronto's First Immigrant
    Neighbourhood*. Edited by John Lorinc, Michael McClelland, Ellen
    Scheinberg, and Tatum Taylor. Toronto: Coach House, 2015.

31. THE CLAY LADIES

Boyanoski, Christine. *Loring and Wyle: Sculptors' Legacy*. Toronto:
    Art Gallery of Ontario, 1987.

Cameron, Elspeth. *And Beauty Answers: The Life of Frances Loring and Florence Wyle.* Toronto: Cormorant Books, 2007.

McLean, Helen. "Remodelling The Girls." *Globe and Mail*, December 8, 2017. Accessed November 2, 2019. theglobeandmail.com/arts/ remodelling-the-girls/article726558.

Sisler, Rebecca. *The Girls: A Biography of Frances Loring and Florence Wyle.* Toronto: Clarke, Irwin, 1972.

32. HEARTBROKEN SPIES

Bethune, Brian. "They Were 'to Set Europe Ablaze.'" *Maclean's*, October 24, 2008. Accessed July 17, 2019. macleans.ca/culture/ they-were-to-set-europe-ablaze.

MacKinnon, Gordon. "The Story of the University of Toronto Soldiers' Tower." *University of Toronto Alumni.* May 9, 2010. Accessed June 1, 2020.

MacLaren, Roy. *Canadians Behind Enemy Lines, 1939–1945.* Vancouver: UBC Press, 2011.

Phillipson, Donald J.C. "Sir William Stephenson." *Canadian Encyclopedia*, January 23, 2008. Last modified March 4, 2015. thecanadianencyclopedia.ca/en/article/sir-william-stephenson.

Pickersgill, Frank. *The Making of a Secret Agent.* Toronto: McClelland and Stewart, 1978.

Porter, Mckenzie. "The Scholar Buchenwald Couldn't Break." *Maclean's*, December 2, 1961. Accessed July 17, 2019. archive .macleans.ca/article/1961/12/2/the-scholar-buchenwald- couldnt-break.

Scott, Alec. "Behind Enemy Lines." *University of Toronto Magazine*, September 21, 2007. Accessed July 17, 2019. magazine.utoronto .ca/campus/history/u-of-t-world-war-two-stories.

Stafford, David. "Camp X." *Canadian Encyclopedia*, February 7,

2006. Last modified August 1, 2018. thecanadianencyclopedia
.ca/en/article/camp-x.

University of Toronto Alumni. "The Soldiers' Tower." Accessed June 1,
2020. alumni.utoronto.ca/soldierstower.

Vance, Jonathan F. "Understanding the Motivation to Enlist."
*Bearing Witness: Perspectives on War and Peace from the Arts
and Humanities.* Montreal: McGill-Queen's University Press,
2012.

———. *Unlikely Soldiers: How Two Canadians Fought the Secret War
Against Nazi Occupation.* Toronto: HarperCollins, 2008.

33. MIRIAM'S JUDAICA

Arnett, George. "Auschwitz: A Short History of the Largest Mass
Murder Site in Human History." *Guardian*, January 27, 2015.
Accessed April 19, 2019. theguardian.com/world/2015/jan/27/
auschwitz-short-history-liberation-concentration-camp-
holocaust.

Gould, Allan. "Birth Amidst Death: Toronto Woman's Son Born
in Dachau." *The Canadian Jewish News*, June 16, 2010.
Accessed April 19, 2019. cjnews.com/perspectives/opinions/
birth-amidst-death-toronto-womans-son-born-dachau.

Gruberová, Eva, dir. *Born in a Concentration Camp.* Germany:
WDR, 2010.

O'Connor, Joe. "Pregnant in Auschwitz: Toronto Holocaust Survivor
Recalls Split-Second Decision That Saved Her and Unborn
Son." *National Post*, August 25, 2012. Accessed April 19, 2019.
nationalpost.com/news/canada/pregnant-in-auschwitz-toronto-
holocaust-survivor-recalls-split-second-decision-that-saved-her-
and-unborn-son.

"Six Jewish Babies Born in Dachau Reunite 65 Years Later." *Haaretz*,

April 27, 2010. Accessed April 19, 2019. haaretz.com/1.5106982.

Sokol, Al. "Passover: Time to Give Thanks." *Toronto Star*, April 21, 1997.

"SS Concentration Camp System." *The Wiener Holocaust Library*. Accessed April 19, 2019. theholocaustexplained.org/the-camps/ss-concentration-camp-system/journeys.

United States Holocaust Memorial Museum. "Auschwitz." Accessed April 19, 2019. encyclopedia.ushmm.org/content/en/article/auschwitz.

United States Holocaust Memorial Museum. "Kaufering." Accessed April 19, 2019. encyclopedia.ushmm.org/content/en/article/kaufering.

34. THE BLIZZARD

Barc, Agatha. "The Great Toronto Snowstorm of 1944." *blogTO*, December 15, 2010. Accesssed June 1, 2020. blogto.com/city/2010/12/the_great_toronto_snowstorm_of_1944.

Goddard, John, and Richard Crouse. *Rock and Roll Toronto: From Alanis to Zeppelin*. Toronto: Doubleday Canada, 1997.

Taylor, Doug. "A Wartime Christmas in Toronto — 1944." *Historic Toronto*, January 8, 2015. Accessed June 1, 2020. tayloronhistory.com/tag/great-snow-storm-of-1944-toronto.

Wilson, Sharry. *Young Neil: The Sugar Mountain Years*. Toronto: ECW Press, 2014.

Young, Scott. *Neil and Me*. Toronto: McClelland and Stewart, 1997.

35. LITTLE GREEN

Andrews, Valerie. "White Unwed Mother: The Adoption Mandate in Postwar Canada." M.A. thesis, York University, 2017.

Bego, Mark. *Joni Mitchell*. Lanham, MD: Taylor, 2005.

Canadian Public Health Association. "History of Family Planning

in Canada." Accessed July 24, 2020. cpha.ca/history-family
-planning-canada.

Daniel, Reola. "Adoption — Both Sides Now." *Western Report*, April
21, 1997.

Ellwood, Alison, dir. *Laurel Canyon: A Place in Time*. New York:
Epix, 2020.

France, Kim. "Joni Mitchell Gives Peace A Chance." *US*, November
1998.

Henderson, Stuart. "'All Pink and Clean and Full of Wonder?'
Gendering 'Joni Mitchell,' 1966–74." *Left History* 10, no. 2
(2005): 83–109.

———. *Making the Scene: Yorkville and Hip Toronto in the 1960s*.
Toronto: University of Toronto Press, 2011.

Jennings, Nicholas. *Before the Gold Rush: Flashbacks to the Dawn of
the Canadian Sound*. Toronto: Viking, 1997.

Johnson, Brian D., and Danylo Hawaleshka. "Joni's Secret."
Maclean's, April 21, 1997.

Lacy, Susan, dir. *Joni Mitchell: Woman of Heart and Mind*. London:
Eagle Rock Entertainment, 2003.

Marom, Malka. *Joni Mitchell: In Her Own Words*. Toronto: ECW
Press, 2014.

Monk, Katherine. *Joni: The Creative Odyssey of Joni Mitchell*.
Vancouver: Greystone, 2002.

Montgomery, Simon. "A Chronology of Appearances." JoniMitchell.com.
Last modified August 3, 2020. jonimitchell.com/chronology/
byyear.cfm?year=1964.

Posner, Michael. "Little Green a Little Blue." *Globe and Mail*, April
11, 1998.

Stojsic, Leslie. "Among the Canvases: Behind the Scenes at Joni
Mitchell's Home." *CBC News*, June 11, 2013. Last modified June

12, 2013. cbc.ca/news/canada/among-the-canvases-behind-the-scenes-at-joni-mitchell-s-home-1.1358489.

Weller, Sheila. *Girls Like Us: Carole King, Joni Mitchell, Carly Simon — and the Journey of a Generation*. New York: Atria, 2008.

Wirth, Jim. "Song to a Seagull." *Ultimate Music Guide*, May 2017.

Van Rijn, Nicolaas. "How Joni Mitchell's Daughter Found Mom and Became Whole." *Toronto Sun*, April 18, 1997.

Yaffe, David. *Reckless Daughter: A Portrait of Joni Mitchell*. New York: Sarah Crichton, 2017.

36. I WOULDN'T HAVE IT ANY OTHER WAY

Bowman, Rob. "Is Toronto Finally Ready for Jackie Shane?" *NOW*, October 18, 2017. Accessed August 14, 2020. nowtoronto.com/music/features/the-return-of-jackie-shane.

———. "Jackie Shane: Baby, Do What You Want." *Numero Group*, 2019. Accessed August 14, 2020. numerogroup.com/d/jackie-shane-baby-do-what-you-want.

Fensterstock, Alison. "Jackie Shane, a Force of Nature Who Disappeared, Has a Story All Her Own." *The Record: Music News from NPR*, October 25, 2017. Accessed August 14, 2020. npr.org/sections/therecord/2017/10/25/559775225/jackie-shane-a-force-of-nature-who-disappeared-has-a-story-all-her-own.

Gaber-Katz, Elaine. "How Jackie Shane Helped 'Satisfy My Soul.'" In *Any Other Way: How Toronto Got Queer*. Edited by Stephanie Chambers, Jane Farrow, Maureen FitzGerald, Ed Jackson, John Lorinc, Tim McCaskell, Rebecka Sheffield, Tatum Taylor, and Rahim Thawer. Toronto: Coach House, 2017.

Jennings, Nicholas. "Transgender Soul Singer Jackie Shane Thrilled Crowds." *Globe and Mail*, March 2, 2019. Accessed

August 14, 2020. theglobeandmail.com/arts/music/
article-transgender-soul-singer-jackie-shane-thrilled-crowds.

"The Late Jackie Shane in Her Own Words: A Rare Interview with
the Pioneering Musician." *CBC Radio*, February 8, 2019. Last
updated June 21, 2019. cbc.ca/radio/q/friday-feb-8-2019-
david-foster-jackie-shane-and-more-1.5009904/jackie-shane-
in-her-own-words-a-rare-interview-with-a-living-legend-
1.5010217.

Maynard, Stephen. "'A New Way of Lovin'": Queer Toronto Gets
Schooled by Jackie Shane." In *Any Other Way: How Toronto
Got Queer*. Edited by Stephanie Chambers, Jane Farrow,
Maureen FitzGerald, Ed Jackson, John Lorinc, Tim
McCaskell, Rebecka Sheffield, Tatum Taylor, and Rahim
Thawer. Toronto: Coach House, 2017.

McIntosh, Andrew. "Jackie Shane." *Canadian Encyclopedia*,
February 12, 2020. Last modified February 12, 2020.
thecanadianencyclopedia.ca/en/article/jackie-shane.

Myseum. "No Other Way: The Story of Jackie Shane." Accessed
August 14, 2020. myseumoftoronto.com/programming/
jackie-shane.

"Transgender Pioneer Jackie Shane Reflects On Her Re-Emergence
& Grammy-Nominated Album." *Billboard*, January 16, 2019.
Accessed August 14, 2020. billboard.com/articles/news/
grammys/8493849/jackie-shane-album-transgender-pioneer-
any-other-way.

Wilson, Carl. "'I Bet Your Mama Was a Tent-Show Queen.'"
Hazlitt, April 22, 2013. Accessed August 14, 2020. hazlitt.net/
longreads/i-bet-your-mama-was-tent-show-queen.

Wilson, Tom. *I Am Tommy: On Stage and Backstage*. Victoria:
FriesenPress, 2018.

37. ELIZABETH TAYLOR'S LOVE NEST

Brehl, John. "Liz Shivers at Airport — 'It's cold, I'm tired.'" *Toronto Daily Star*, January 29, 1964.

Cobb, David. "Dief Finds that Big Crowd's Not for Him." *Toronto Daily Star*, January 29, 1964.

Duff, Morris. "'Nice to See You Again Luv' — Dick." *Toronto Daily Star*, January 29, 1964.

Eichler, Margrit. "Divorce in Canada." *Canadian Encyclopedia*, September 19, 2016. Last modified September 16, 2016. thecanadianencyclopedia.ca/en/article/divorce-in-canada.

"It's 'Crying Shame' Liz on Pedestal — Minister." *Toronto Daily Star*, January 29, 1964.

Kashner, Sam. *Furious Love: Elizabeth Taylor, Richard Burton, and the Marriage of the Century*. New York: Harper, 2010.

Kirby, Blaik. "2,000 Mad, They Missed Liz." *Toronto Daily Star*, January 29, 1964.

Library and Archives Canada. "Acts of Divorce, 1841–1968." Last modified May 27, 2020. bac-lac.gc.ca/eng/discover/vital-statistics-births-marriages-deaths/divorce-1841-1968/Pages/acts-divorce-1841-1968.aspx.

"Liz Taylor's Toronto Courtship, Montreal Wedding." *CBC News*, March 24, 2011. Accessed March 2, 2020. cbc.ca/news/entertainment/liz-taylor-s-toronto-courtship-montreal-wedding-1.998892.

Mankiewicz, Joseph L., dir. *Cleopatra*. Los Angeles: 20th Century Fox, 1963.

Mudhar, Raju. "Elizabeth Taylor and Richard Burton Caused a Stir in Toronto." *Toronto Star*, March 23, 2011. Accessed March 2, 2020. thestar.com/entertainment/2011/03/23/elizabeth_taylor_and_richard_burton_caused_a_stir_in_toronto.html.

Ward, Peter. "History of Marriage and Divorce." *Canadian Encyclopedia*, February 7, 2006. Last modified April 7, 2016. thecanadianencyclopedia.ca/en/article/ history-of-marriage-and-divorce.

Wells, Jennifer. "The Toronto Romance of Liz Taylor and Richard Burton." *Toronto Star*, July 3, 2010. Accessed March 2, 2020. thestar.com/news/gta/2010/07/03/the_toronto_romance_of_ liz_taylor_and_richard_burton.html.

38. THE NAPALM GIRL

"AP 'Napalm Girl' Photo from Vietnam War Turns 40." *Deseret News*, June 2, 2012. Accessed May 2, 2020. deseret.com/2012/6/2 /20416367/ap-napalm-girl-photo-from-vietnam-war-turns-40.

Chisholm, Patricia. "Vietnam Victim Finds Peace in Canada." *Canadian Encyclopedia*, March 17, 2003. Last modified December 15, 2013. thecanadianencyclopedia.ca/en/article/ vietnam-victim-finds-peace-in-canada.

Chong, Denise. *The Girl in the Picture: The Story of Kim Phuc, the Photograph, and the Vietnam War*. London: Penguin, 2001.

———. "What Happened Next ... The Story of What Became of the Napalmed Girl in the Most Famous Vietnam Picture Is Extraordinary. So Is the Story of How the Picture Was Taken. A New Book Tells Them Both." *Guardian*, September 3, 2000. Accessed May 2, 2020. theguardian.com/theobserver/2000/ sep/03/featuresreview.review.

Cohn, Martin Regg. "The Napalm Victims No One Noticed." *Toronto Star*, April 16, 2000.

Garebian, Keith. "Review: From Infamy to Ajax." *Toronto Star*, October 17, 1999.

Kim Phuc, Phan Thi. *Fire Road: The Napalm Girl's Journey Through the Horrors of War to Faith, Forgiveness, and Peace*. Chicago: Tyndale House, 2017.

"The Long Road to Forgiveness." *NPR*, June 30, 2008. Accessed March 21, 2020. npr.org/templates/story/story.php?storyId=91964687? storyId=91964687.

Lumb, Rebecca. "Reunited with the Vietnamese 'Girl in the Picture.'" *BBC News*. Last modified May 17, 2010. news.bbc.co.uk/1/hi/ world/asia-pacific/8678478.stm.

Scrivener, Leslie. "'I Think About That Picture and I Cry.'" *Toronto Star*, June 9, 2012.

Sheridan, Kathy. "Kim Phuc, the Napalm Girl: 'Love is More Powerful than Any Weapon.'" *Irish Times*, May 28, 2016. Accessed June 1, 2020. irishtimes.com/life-and-style/people/ kim-phuc-the-napalm-girl-love-is-more-powerful-than-any-weapon-1.2661740.

Ut, Nick. "Picture Power: Vietnam Napalm Attack." *BBC News*, May 9, 2005. Accessed March 20, 2020. news.bbc.co.uk/2/hi/4517597.stm.

39. MAGGIE AT THE EL MO

Benson, Denise. "Then & Now: The El Mocambo, 1989–2001." *Then & Now: Toronto's Nightlife History*, October 7, 2014. Accessed March 23, 2020. thenandnowtoronto.com/2014/10/ then-now-the-el-mocambo-1989-2001.

Bidini, Dave. "The Hidden History of How the Rolling Stones Pulled Off Their Legendary Secret El Mocambo Show." *National Post*, May 12, 2015. Accessed March 31, 2020. nationalpost.com/entertainment/music/the-hidden-history-of-how-the-rolling-stones-pulled-of-their-legendary-secret-el-mocambo-show.

Bradburn, Jamie. "A Brief History of the Legendary El Mocambo."
    Torontoist, September 23, 2014. Accessed March 23, 2020.
    torontoist.com/2014/09/a-brief-history-of-the-legendary-
    el-mocambo.

Cobb, David. "Maggie in Wonderland." *Maclean's*, March 21, 1977.
    Accessed May 7, 2020. archive.macleans.ca/article/1977/3/21/
    margaret-in-wonderland.

Eichler, Margrit. "Divorce in Canada." *Canadian Encyclopedia*,
    September 19, 2016. Last modified September 16, 2016.
    thecanadianencyclopedia.ca/en/article/divorce-in-canada.

English, John. *Citizen of the World: The Life of Pierre Elliott Trudeau,
    1919–1968*. Toronto: Knopf Canada, 2006.

———. *Just Watch Me: The Life of Pierre Elliott Trudeau, 1968–2000*.
    Toronto: Vintage Canada, 2010.

Flippo, Chet. "Keith Richards Busted: Stone's Future Cloudy."
    Rolling Stone, April 7, 1977. Accessed March 31, 2020.
    rollingstone.com/music/music-news/keith-richards-busted-
    stones-future-cloudy-249378.

———. "Keith Richards Meets the Mounties and Faces the Music."
    Rolling Stone, May 5, 1977. Accessed March 31, 2020. roll-
    ingstone.com/music/music-news/keith-richards-meets-the-
    mounties-and-faces-the-music-98458.

"Flying Home to Join Trudeau, Margaret Says From Dance Floor."
    Globe and Mail, May 24, 1979.

Geddes, John. "Pierre & Maggie: The Untold Story." *Maclean's*,
    October 26, 2009. Accessed May 7, 2020. macleans.ca/news/
    canada/pierre-maggie-the-untold-story.

"Getting Divorced Becomes Easier in Canada." *CBC Archives*,
    July 2, 1968. Accessed May 7, 2020. cbc.ca/archives/entry/
    getting-divorced-becomes-easier-in-canada.

Goddard, Peter. "Mrs. Trudeau Hears Rolling Stones." *Toronto Star*, March 5, 1977.

Jennings, Nicholas. "Toronto Feature: El Mocambo Tavern." *Canadian Encyclopedia*, February 6, 2013. Last modified July 2, 2015. thecanadianencyclopedia.ca/en/article/toronto-feature-el-mocambo-tavern.

Ricci, Nino. *Pierre Elliott Trudeau*. Toronto: Penguin Canada, 2009.

Trudeau, Margaret. *Changing My Mind: A Memoir*. Toronto: HarperCollins Canada, 2010.

"Trudeau: 'There's No Place for the State in the Bedrooms of the Nation.'" *CBC Archives*, December 21, 1967. Accessed March 31, 2020. cbc.ca/archives/entry/omnibus-bill-theres-no-place-for-the-state-in-the-bedrooms-of-the-nation.

Wright, Robert. *Trudeaumania*. Toronto: HarperCollins Canada, 2016.

40. THE MICHAELS

Abe, Fraser. "A History of the Toronto Pride Parade." *IN Magazine*, May 16, 2019. Accessed June 2, 2020. inmagazine.ca/2019/05/a-history-of-the-toronto-pride-parade.

Bradburn, Jamie. "Historicist: How the St. Charles Tavern went from Chinese-Food Restaurant to Popular Gay Bar." *Torontoist*, June 25, 2016. Accessed June 2, 2020. torontoist.com/2016/06/historicist-the-st-charles-tavern.

———. "The March to Pride." *Torontoist*, June 20, 2014. Accessed May 6, 2020. torontoist.com/2014/06/the-march-to-pride.

———. "Toronto Bathhouse Raids (1981)." *Canadian Encyclopedia*, February 3, 2013. Last modified April 17, 2018. thecanadianen-cyclopedia.ca/en/article/toronto-feature-bathhouse-raids.

Brent, Bob. "Crown Attorney Sues Boss and Wins." *Toronto Star*,
    October 1, 1992.

Brown, Eleanor. "The Odd Couple." *Xtra*, May 30, 2001. Accessed
    May 6, 2020. dailyxtra.com/the-odd-couple-46204.

Carlberg, Amy, Sarah Duong, Erica Lenti, Michael Lyons, and Samira
    Mohyeddin. "An Oral History of Toronto's Pride Parade."
    Torontoist, July 3, 2016. Accessed June 2, 2020. torontoist
    .com/2016/07/the-oral-history-of-pride-toronto.

Chenier, Elise. "A Place Like The Continental." In *Any Other Way:
    How Toronto Got Queer*. Edited by Stephanie Chambers,
    Jane Farrow, Maureen FitzGerald, Ed Jackson, John Lorinc,
    Tim McCaskell, Rebecka Sheffield, Tatum Taylor, and Rahim
    Thawer. Toronto: Coach House, 2017.

DeMara, Bruce. "Police Sensitive to Training on Gay Lifestyles."
    Toronto Star, June 12, 1993.

Duder, Cameron. *Awfully Devoted Women: Lesbian Lives in Canada,
    1900–65*. Vancouver: UBC Press, 2011.

Gollom, Mark. "Toronto Bathhouse Raids: How the Arrests
    Galvanized the Gay Community." *CBC News*, June 22, 2016.
    Accessed June 2, 2020. cbc.ca/news/canada/toronto/
    bathhouse-raids-toronto-police-gay-community-arrests-
    apology-1.3645926.

Gombu, Phinjo. "Court Rules Same-Sex Couples Have Pension
    Rights." *Toronto Star*, December 10, 1998.

Grozelle, Renee S. "The Rise of Gay Liberation in Toronto: From
    Vilification to Vindication." *Inquires Journal* 9, no. 1 (2017).

Hall, Joseph. "Subject of Article Sues Over Charges." *Toronto Star*,
    December 10, 1991.

Hooper, Tom. "Cruising the History of Policing Gay Sex in
    Toronto Parks." *Torontoist*, March 20, 2017. Accessed June 2,

2020. torontoist.com/2017/03/cruising-history-policing-gay-sex-toronto-parks.

Huffman, Tracy. "Court Rules in Favour of Same-Sex Marriage." *Toronto Star*, July 13, 2002.

———. "Gay Couples Seeks Supreme Test." *Toronto Star*, May 28, 2001.

Jackson, Ed. "Making Places for Toronto's Queer history." *Spacing*, June 15, 2017. Accessed May 6, 2020. spacing.ca/toronto/2017/06/15/making-places-torontos-queer-history.

Kopun, Francine. "Same-Sex Law Activist Weds." *Toronto Star*, July 12, 2008. Accessed May 6, 2020. thestar.com/news/gta/2008/07/12/samesex_law_activist_weds.html.

Leshner, Michael. "Attorneys-General Are Not Above the Law." *Toronto Star*, March 10, 1994.

———. "Fight for Rights Can't be Muzzled by Government." *Toronto Star*, July 7, 1995.

———. "Let's End the Hate Against Gay, Lesbian Parents." *Toronto Star*, May 23, 1995.

Leshner, Michael, and Michael Stark. Interview by Adam Bunch. Email. May 18, 2020.

Lorinc, John. "From Banns to DOMA." In *Any Other Way: How Toronto Got Queer*. Edited by Stephanie Chambers, Jane Farrow, Maureen FitzGerald, Ed Jackson, John Lorinc, Tim McCaskell, Rebecka Sheffield, Tatum Taylor, and Rahim Thawer. Toronto: Coach House, 2017.

Mackenzie, Ian. "Who's on First: A Heap of Newlyweds." *Xtra*, July 9, 2003. Accessed May 6, 2020. dailyxtra.com/whos-on-first-43680.

"Marching Brave." *Maclean's*, June 21, 2019. Accessed May 6, 2020. macleans.ca/marching-brave-lgbq-rights-canada.

Maynard, Stephen. "Through a Hole in the Lavatory Wall: Homosexual Subcultures, Police Surveillance, and the Dialectics of Discovery, Toronto, 1890–1930." *Journal of the History of Sexuality* 5, no. 2 (October 1994): 207–42.

McCaskell, Tim. "Pride: A Political History." In *Any Other Way: How Toronto Got Queer*. Edited by Stephanie Chambers, Jane Farrow, Maureen FitzGerald, Ed Jackson, John Lorinc, Tim McCaskell, Rebecka Sheffield, Tatum Taylor, and Rahim Thawer. Toronto: Coach House, 2017.

McClelland, Colin. "Canada's Gay Pride Parade Celebrates New Same-Sex Marriage Ruling." *Napa Valley Register*, June 30, 2003. Accessed June 2, 2020. napavalleyregister.com/news/canada-s-gay-pride-parade-celebrates-new-same-sex-marriage/article_fe4acc3b-ebc7-5d7f-9aea-96989157fd02.html.

Patch, Catherine. "For the Love of Mikes." *Toronto Star*, July 13, 2002.

Picher, Forrest. "Coming Clean About Operation Soap: The 1981 Toronto Bathhouse Raids." *Active History*, June 23, 2015. Accessed June 2, 2020. activehistory.ca/2015/06/coming-clean-about-operation-soap-the-1981-toronto-bathhouse-raids.

Sismondo, Christine. "Halloween Balls: From Letros to the St. Charles." In *Any Other Way: How Toronto Got Queer*. Edited by Stephanie Chambers, Jane Farrow, Maureen FitzGerald, Ed Jackson, John Lorinc, Tim McCaskell, Rebecka Sheffield, Tatum Taylor, and Rahim Thawer. Toronto: Coach House, 2017.

Stanley, John D. "Toronto." *GLBTQ Archives*, 2004. Accessed June 2, 2020. glbtqarchive.com/ssh/toronto_S.pdf.

Steed, Judy. "Gay Lawyer Battling for Job Benefits and Promotion in Ontario Ministry." *Toronto Star*, September 17, 1991.

Tyler, Tracey. "Gay Couple Hope to Get Married Today." *Toronto Star*, June 10, 2003.

Tyler, Tracey, and Tracy Huffman. "Gay Men Get Married After Appeal Court Ruling." *Toronto Star*, June 11, 2003.

EPILOGUE: THE ONGOING HISTORY OF KISSING IN TORONTO

Dempsey, Amy. "Toronto Kiss Map Plots 'Kisstory' of Toronto." *Toronto Star*, July 6, 2011. Accessed August 22, 2020. thestar .com/life/2011/07/06/toronto_kiss_map_plots_kisstory_of_ toronto.html.

Hale, Monica. "The Immigration Story of Monica Hale (English War Bride)." Canadian Museum of Immigration at Pier 21. Accessed August 26, 2020. pier21.ca/content/the-immigration-story-of-monica-hale-english-war-bride.

Fraser, Chris Kay. "The Story of the Toronto Kiss Map." Toronto Kiss Map. Accessed August 18, 2020. torontokissmap.com/ the-story-of-the-toronto-kiss-map.

Li, Anita. "Valentine's Day 2012: Toronto Kiss Map Reveals Best Smooch Spots in the City." *Toronto Star*, February 7, 2012. Accessed August 22, 2020. thestar.com/life/2012/02/07/ valentines_day_2012_toronto_kiss_map_reveals_best_ smooch_spots_in_the_city.html.

McLeod, Donald W. "Smooching in the Streets, Mincing at Queen's Park: Gay Rights Protests of the 1970s." *Toronto Star*, June 27, 2015. Accessed August 25, 2020. thestar.com/news/insight /2015/06/27/smooching-in-the-streets-mincing-at-queens-park-gay-rights-protests-of-the-1970s.html.

"The Smack in Court." *Toronto Daily Star*, December 12, 1905.

Toronto Kiss Map. Accessed August 18, 2020. torontokissmap.com.

Winsa, Patty. "Before Pride, There was a Kiss: Toronto Gay Activists Look Back on 1976 Protest." *Toronto Star*, June 27, 2015. Accessed August 25, 2020. thestar.com/news/insight/ 2015/06/27/before-pride-there-was-a-kiss-toronto-gay-activists-look-back-on-1976-protest.html.

ABOUT THE AUTHOR

Adam Bunch is the author of *The Toronto Book of the Dead*, creator of the Toronto Dreams Project, and host of the *Canadiana* documentary series, which was nominated for a 2020 Canadian Screen Award. He's taught history at George Brown College, and his work popularizing Toronto's past has earned an honourable mention for a Governor General's History Award. Adam is a former history columnist for *Spacing* and has written for *Torontoist* and the *Huffington Post*. He has also spent years as a music journalist. Adam has lived in Toronto since he was two months old, growing up along the Humber River, raised on stories of Hurricane Hazel and of Marilyn Bell, of jazz era swing clubs and war-time romances. He lives on St. Clair West.